Let the Cannon Blaze Away

Let the Cannon Blaze Away

LECTURES ON THE CENTENNIAL OF AMERICAN INDEPENDENCE

Given at

Berlin, Dresden, Florence, Paris and London

in 1876

Joseph P. Thompson

New Introduction by David Dykstra

Solid Ground Christian Books
Birmingham, Alabama

Solid Ground Christian Books
2090 Columbiana Rd, Suite 2000
Birmingham, AL 35216
205-443-0311
sgcb@charter.net
http://solid-ground-books.com

Let the Cannon Blaze Away
LECTURES ON THE CENTENNIAL OF AMERICAN INDEPENDENCE

Joseph Parrish Thompson (1819-1879)

First published 1877 by James Osgood & Co., Boston, MA

American Heritage Classic Reprints
By Solid Ground Christian Books

First printing of new edition May 2005

Cover work by Borgo Design, Tuscaloosa, AL
Contact them at nelbrown@comcast.net

ISBN: 1-932474-77-3

Introduction to the New Edition

A few years ago I was in attendance at a mission's conference when the keynote speaker (from South Africa) said the following: "Whenever you leave America, in whatever direction you go, you take a step down morally." Most of the attendees were American pastors, and to say that we were surprised in hearing that assertion would be an understatement. The speaker however, was a pastor himself, an experienced world traveler, and an astute observer of people and the societies and cultures they produce. His assertion was absolutely correct.

Bill Bennett has echoed that pastor's assertion in these words: "A sober, a sophisticated study of our history demonstrates beyond cavil that we have provided more freedom to more people than any nation in the history of mankind; that we have provided a greater degree of equality to more people than any nation in the history of mankind; that we have created more prosperity and spread it more widely, than any nation in the history of mankind; that we have brought more justice to more people than any nation in the history of mankind; that our open, tolerant, prosperous, peaceful society is the marvel and envy of the ages."[1]

These kinds of positive assessments *can* co-exist with mourning over what is wrong in America. We do well to mourn over all the baser aspects of American culture in the twenty-first century. The Lord gave this command to a scribe who stood in the midst of those assigned to destroy the city of Jerusalem: "Go through the midst of the city, even through the midst of Jerusalem, and put a mark on the foreheads of the men who sigh and groan over all the abominations which are being committed in its midst."[2] To the executioners themselves came this sobering command: "Go through the city after him and strike; do not let your eye have pity and do not spare."[3] The *only* ones to be spared

---

[1] Bill Bennett, *Why We Fight*, p. 150-151, Doubleday.
[2] Ezekiel 9:4.
[3] Ezekiel 9:5.

were the people who mourned over Jerusalem's sins. Indifference to moral evil is itself a moral crime.

No American Christian can be pleased with contemporary American culture. At the same time however, we *can* say with the author of this book: "There are Americans of whom I am ashamed; but I am not ashamed of America. There are things in America for which I blush; but I do not blush to own myself an American."[4]

This reprint of Joseph Thompson's *Lectures On The Centennial of American Independence* comes at a time in our country's history eerily reminiscent of America in 1876. He tells us, for instance, that many Americans traveling abroad "preferred not to be known as Americans, and would gladly exchange their nativity for that of an Englishman, a Frenchman, or a German."[5] It is not much different today. We live in a season of what one writer has called "the moral purism of blaming America first."[6]

Thoughtful Americans in 1876 were ashamed of much that was happening in American society. Although he was never charged with impropriety himself, scandal had plagued the administration of President Ulysses S. Grant. On July 6, 1876 newspapers throughout the country reported the defeat of General Custer and his men at the battle of the Little Big Horn. The Indian warfare that had gone on and on, with atrocities committed by both sides, was the daily fare of the newspapers. Whether it was governmental ineffectiveness in protecting pioneers from Indian atrocities, or atrocities committed against the Indians themselves, the effect was the same, in that America looked bad to the rest of the world. Then, there was the disputed election of 1876, a dispute that made the race between George W. Bush and Al Gore seem like child's play. Rutherford B. Hayes won out over Samuel Tilden, but not before a sweetheart deal was struck that removed Federal troops from the south and exposed southern blacks to the terrorism of white supremacy, a terrorism as real, as evil, and as violent as any we know today.[7]

---

[4] Joseph Thompson, *Let The Cannon Blaze Away*, p. vii.
[5] Ibid, p. vii.
[6] Jean Bethke Elshtain, *Just War Against Terror*, Basic Books, p. 91.
[7] Stephen Ambrose, *To America: Personal Reflections Of An Historian*, p. 58ff. Simon and Schuster, NY, NY.

1876 was not then a very good year, and yet it was the centennial year. On July 4, 1776 final approval was given by the Continental Congress to the *Declaration of Independence.* Only John Hancock signed the document that day, but the die was cast and there was no turning back.

Joseph Thompson's *Lectures on the Centennial of American Independence* is reprinted with a new name, drawn from a statement made by John Hancock. Benedict Arnold and Ethan Allen had captured Fort Ticonderoga and its fifty-nine British cannon. Those heavy guns had been brought through the Berkshires to Boston by Henry Knox and his men. On the morning of June 17, 1775, Captain Thomas Bishop of H.M.S. Lively rushed to the quarterdeck to an amazing sight on the heights above Boston. In but one night, fortifications had appeared that were evidently not the work of amateurs. Now, cannons looked down on Boston and on the British fleet. John Hancock, one of the richest men in America, had received a request from General Washington to open fire on Boston. Hancock rose in Congress to say: "Nearly all I have in the world is in the town of Boston; but if the expulsion of the British troops and the liberty of my country demand that my houses be burned to ashes, issue the order and let the cannon blaze away."[8]

Let The Cannon Blaze Away is apologetic in form. It is a defense of the American Revolution, the *Declaration of Independence*, the *Constitution*, and our entire form of government.

Joseph Parrish Thompson was a pastor in New York City from 1845 to 1871. He was succeeded in the ministry there by the great William M. Taylor of Scotland. Upon his retirement for health concerns in 1871, Thompson's congregation voted to give him a severance gift of $55,000; a huge sum in that period, and one that indicated something of the love and esteem in which he was held. It was Thompson who was asked to preside over and preach at the funeral of the great J.W. Alexander held in Princeton, NJ on August 3, 1859.

One cannot but admire a man who went to England and from British documents themselves, proved the legitimacy of the American Revolution. He gave lectures in Britain, France,

---

[8] Joseph Thompson, *Let the Cannon Blaze Away*, p. 53.

Germany, and Italy, and became a leading apologist in his day of America and its institutions.

In 1848 a great Frenchman spoke of his own country in contrast to America. Here are his words: "In the last sixty years we have changed eight or ten times our government and our constitution; have passed from anarchy to despotism; tried two or three forms of the republic and of monarchy; exhausted proscription, the scaffold, civil and foreign war; and after so many attempts, and attempts made with the fortune and the blood of France, we are hardly more advanced than at the outset. The constitution of 1848 took for its model the constitution of 1791, which had no life; and today we are agitating the same questions that in 1789 we flattered ourselves that we had resolved. How is it that the Americans have organized liberty upon a durable basis, while we, who surely are not inferior to them in civilization—we who have their example before our eyes,—have always miscarried."[9]

In *Let The Cannon Blaze Away* you will learn the answer to Edouard Laboulaye's question. We need this reprint, and we do well to study it. We would also do well in this politically correct time to heed Shelby Steele's advice and "allow the greatness of Western civilization to speak for itself."[10]

On a trip to Europe and the Middle East, Mark Twain described the reaction to seeing an American ship in full sail flying the Stars and Stripes. "She came speeding over the sea like a great bird. Africa and Spain were forgotten. All homage was for the beautiful stranger. While everybody gazed, she swept superbly by and flung the Stars and Stripes to the breeze! Quicker than thought, hats and handkerchiefs flashed in the air, and a cheer went up! She was beautiful before–she was radiant now. Many a one on our decks knew then for the first time how tame a sight his country's flag is at home compared to what it is in a foreign land. To see it is to see a vision of home itself and feel a thrill that would stir a very river of sluggish blood."[11]

America needs this book at this hour. It is not however, only for Americans. Recall that these were lectures given in

---

[9] Ibid, p. 107.
[10] Bill Bennett, *Why We Fight*, p. 100.
[11] Mark Twain, *The Innocents Abroad*, BMC, p. 50-51.

Europe and in Britain. I am often amazed at the ignorance of too many Americans regarding our own history. I am often just as amazed at the ignorance of the rest of the world with regard to America and its institutions. Too many Americans today are ashamed of America. Too many non-Americans display a sense of superiority to America. Joseph Thompson's *Let The Cannon Blaze Away* should go a long way to correct both of these errors.

David Dykstra
Wantage, New Jersey
May, 2005

CONTENTS.

How this Book grew vii
"The Day we celebrate" xiii
The Lincoln Tower xxiii

LECTURE I.
GROUNDS AND MOTIVES OF THE AMERICAN REVOLUTION.

Not revolution in the European sense, but restoration, or reconstruction of political society. Independence not sought by the Colonies, but forced upon them. A nation defined. The Colonies had all the attributes of a nation. Preliminary Congresses. Dignity and influence of the Revolution. Proximate causes. Unjust taxation. Reply to "The Westminster Review." "Stamp Act" but a sign of a principle, like Tetzel's sale of indulgences. The "town-meeting" the equivalent of the Teutonic *Gemeinde*. Franklin's examination before Parliament. Religion in America a training for liberty. John Robinson and his teachings. The pious yeomanry of New England. Dr. Emmons. Local government. Boston "Tea-Party." First stand at Lexington and Concord. Battle of Bunker Hill. Franklin and Frederic on the Hessians. Hancock, Washington. Independence declared. 1

LECTURE II.
DOCTRINES OF THE DECLARATION OF INDEPENDENCE.

Signers of the Declaration. Not doctrinaires. Many men of professional training. Their work has stood. No going back to monarchy. The grand syllogism of the Declaration. Principles to be balanced with each other. The Declaration a testimony against materialism. Equality of men as the spiritual offspring of God. Their right to the free use of their powers, and the full enjoyment of happiness. Government must secure these ends. Suffrage and official place not natural rights. Views of Jefferson. John Stuart Mill. Liberty and government not ends in themselves, but means to a higher end. The right of revolution. The conditions that define and limit it. False notions of French revolutionists. Reasons why the French Revolution failed; mainly the lack of ethical grounds. The indictments of the Declaration against the King of Great Britain. The Declaration valid against new perils. . . 55

CONTENTS.

LECTURE III.
ADOPTION OF THE CONSTITUTION.

Difference between the constitution of a nation and a national constitution. Laboulaye on the Constitution of the United States. The first government extemporized. The second a confederation of States. Why this failed. The plan impossible in America. Anxiety of Washington, Madison, and other patriots. Need of a strong government. Views of Hamilton. The breaking up of the Confederacy imminent. Shays's Rebellion. The Federal Convention of 1787. Ability of its members. Their fidelity in their work. Wisdom in dealing with slavery and confederacy. Grand results in harmonizing local government with supreme national authority, and in equalizing the States under a government by the people. Washington as General and President; the typical man of his age; the embodiment of the American idea; contrasted with Frederic the Great and Napoleon. 106

LECTURE IV.
THE NATION TESTED BY THE VICISSITUDES OF A CENTURY.

Its Constitution the great contribution of modern times to the science of government. It has survived the test of party-spirit, of sectionalism, of foreign war, of financial crises, of territorial expansion, of promiscuous immigration, of threatened disintegration with civil war, and the assassination of the Head of the State. No other government has endured so many and so great vicissitudes with less of evil to itself and to society. 159

LECTURE V.
THE NATION JUDGED BY ITS SELF-DEVELOPMENT AND ITS BENEFITS TO MANKIND.

The life of a nation not estimated by length of years, but by what the years have accomplished. The United States contrasted with Russia, France, and Germany. Physical development not materialistic. Reply to Carlyle and Dickens. Case of California. Progress in education, science, letters, and arts. Church-life. Power of the voluntary principle. Inventions serviceable to mankind, — lightning-rod, cotton-gin, compound blow-pipe, steamboat, telegraph with Atlantic cable, anæsthetics, sewing-machine, writing-machine, reaping and mowing machines, fog-signals, &c. Institutions for diversified and collective humanity. 200

LECTURE VI.
THE PERILS, DUTIES, AND HOPES OF THE OPENING CENTURY.

Luxury and corruption. These not peculiar to a republic. Russia, Turkey, Persia, Austria, Italy, France. Examples from earlier times. Risks of universal suffrage. Race animosities. Political centralization. Ultramontane schemes. Resources in the intelligence, morality, and patriotism of the people; in the fact that the government, while fixed in principles, is flexible and improvable in forms. Need of improved civil service, of the cumulative ballot, of an educational test, and of training for the higher statesmanship. Future of the republic assured in the character of the people. . 248

PUBLISHERS' NOTE 312
INDEX 319

HOW THIS BOOK GREW.

THESE Lectures are published in obedience to the call of the audiences that listened to them in Berlin, Dresden, Florence, Paris, and London.[1] Those audiences comprised many persons of the highest condition and culture in Germany, Italy, France, and England, — statesmen, jurists, diplomatists, professors, authors, divines, — as well as the chief representatives of American society in the great capitals of Europe. An auditory so diversified and so distinguished must have satisfied the ambition of any lecturer: but I am more proud to recognize their attendance as a compliment to my country; and most heartily do I thank my honored hearers for their earnest interest in the unfolding of American national life, and for their flattering request that the facts presented from the platform might again be laid before them in the more leisurely form of the printed page.

When I announced a course of lectures on the "Origin and Development of the United States as a Nation," to be given in the hearing of Europeans, some of my countrymen were of opinion, that, in the painful aspect of public affairs at home, it were better that Americans abroad should say or do nothing that should call attention to their country, already the subject of so much adverse criticism. There were those, even, who went so far as to say that they preferred not to be known as Americans, and would gladly exchange their nativity for that of an Englishman, a Frenchman, or a German.[2] Though I re-

---

[1] See Publishers' Note, p. 312.
[2] When Schopenhauer, the German pessimist, was in Italy, he was accustomed to decry his country in presence of his French and English acquaintances. "The German fatherland," said he, "has reared no patriot in me. I am ashamed to be a German, they are so stupid a people." A Frenchman once replied, "If I thought so of my nation, I should at least hold my tongue about it."

spected the former feeling as much as I despised the latter, I could not entertain it under the peculiar conditions of the Centennial year. "America is under a cloud," said some to whom I was ready to listen with deference; "and the less that is said of her, the better. Till these disgraceful exposures are forgotten, we must hide our heads in silence, and trust to vindicate our country by deeds rather than by words."

My answer was, "I do not seek to give publicity to my country abroad, nor would I in any way obtrude her institutions and history upon the notice of foreigners. But the publicity exists: she herself has given the occasion. The Centennial and the Exposition have drawn the eyes of the world upon her; and, though there may be in some quarters a relish for the political scandal just now so rife, there will be among thoughtful men a readiness to review the history and experience of a nation, that, in its first century, has taken rank with the first powers of the world. My purpose is to deal with my country in the candid spirit of historical criticism; and history, and, above all, the philosophy of history, is what no lover of truth and of man should fear to unfold. Besides, if my country is under a cloud, shall I skulk behind that cloud, and, in the day of her calamity, seek to hide my nativity? There are Americans of whom I am ashamed; but I am not ashamed of America. There are things in America for which I blush; but I do not blush to own myself an American. If my country is dishonored, brave and manly words for her may be heroic deeds. *Pulchrum est benefacere Reipublicæ, etiam bene dicere haud absurdum est.* All that I am I owe to my country. My training was in her schools. My knowledge, faith, principles, whatever I value as a man, whatever makes manhood of value to me, I have learned of her. She shall have from me no wavering allegiance. Where my country is right, I shall stand for her against the world; where she is wrong, I shall stand by her, and labor to correct the wrong, and bring her to the right again. And, above all, if there are wrongs in her that are not of her, it is my sacred duty as a patriot and a Christian to separate the good from the evil, and show the inherent purity, dignity, and strength of the republic against the vices that assail all human institutions."

With such convictions, it seemed to me that the Centennial year was a time for sowing seeds of thought concerning society and government, — seed sifted from that great harvest of experiment and experience that a century had ripened in the New World. It seemed to me, also, that the field was open and inviting; that, at a time when the leading nations of Europe are agitated with questions of political organization and of social reform, — especially with such topics as suffrage, the ballot, popular education, capital and labor, and the relations of Church and State, — an impartial review of the political, moral, industrial, and social development of the United States would be welcomed by thoughtful men in other countries as a contribution, for profit or for warning, toward the solution of their own problems. To say that the interest manifested by European scholars and statesmen in the topics of these Lectures did not disappoint this expectation would be far too little for my gratitude. To repeat what they publicly said upon those topics would be quite too much for my modesty. Suffice it, that to have given occasion for such hearty and generous tributes to my country as were publicly uttered by Prof. Zumpt of Berlin, Prof. Villari of Florence, Prof. Whittmeyer of Paris, Sir Benson Maxwell, Sir James Anderson, Sir George Campbell, M.P., Sir Dudley Campbell, M.P., Mr. Henry Richard, M.P., Mr. M'Lagan, M.P., Mr. M'Arthur, M.P., Prof. Sheldon Amos of London, Prof. Legge of Oxford, Rev. Henry Allon, D.D., and others of like standing, was more than a compensation for the care and cost of preparing and delivering the Lectures. Would that those of my countrymen who fancy that the United States have lost the respect and confidence of men of culture abroad could have listened to such cordial and discriminating testimony to their worth and standing among the nations!

If these Lectures shall have any value for American readers, it will lie in the fact that they were written abroad, and with an eye to the queries of foreigners. Hence back of the objective presentation of facts is the subjective desire of meeting difficulties that are rather felt than stated. Having spent, in all, some seven years of my life in foreign countries, in the study of their peoples and institutions, and in intercourse with their better citizens, I have dispossessed myself of narrow national prejudices, and am able to speak of my own country with more of judicial fairness than might be possible, if I were writing amid the mingled patriotic and partisan excitements of the Centennial year at home. I trust, at least, that I have maintained the sober judgment of history; and I hope, also, that the conviction of the wisdom and stability of American institutions, that has grown upon me as I have studied them from a distant point of view, will impart strength to any who may be wavering amid internal conflicts. The experience of the past shows that the nation may go through many and serious trials without being at all in danger of its life. There is no fear that the Ship of State is going under just because she has shipped a few seas, perhaps has sprung a leak, and we are called to do some hard and dirty work at the pumps.

I would here give emphasis to a point too often overlooked in the comparison of the United States with England and Germany, — that the distinction between society and the government is much more marked in America than in Europe. Though it happens in England and in Germany that men of small calibre, and sometimes of doubtful antecedents, are elected to Parliament, yet in both countries the government combines and centres in itself the best elements of society. Indeed, in Prussia the government is the quintessence of the national morality and culture: hence any serious delinquency of the government would argue a corresponding defect in society itself. Quite otherwise is it in the United States. Indiscriminate suffrage on the one hand, and political indifference on the other, there give opportunity to the worst elements of society to rise to the surface, and incorporate themselves into the government. This may or may not be a condemnation of democratic institutions; but it is not necessarily a condemnation of American society. In the United States, the integrity and culture of the government are not the measure of these qualities in society. Who, for instance, would estimate the moral and intellectual *status* of New York by the City Government as compared with the Chamber of Commerce, the Century Club, or even with a dinner-company at the house of any gentleman of good social standing? But, naturally enough, foreigners take the government to represent the people, and hence form very erroneous notions of American society. Indeed, few foreigners who visit the United States for the purpose of book-making have the opportunity of knowing the best society, for lack of personal introduction; and hence their criticisms upon American culture reflect back upon themselves the circles in which they moved, and expose them to the ridicule of society for such companionship. I venture to hope that these pages may help to correct such misunderstandings, and to establish a criterion of both government and society in the United States.

I have been urged to put the Lectures into the form of a text-book for students, but think it better to preserve the style in which they were given: first, because this has more of directness and freshness; next, because this is the style in which the hearers of the Lectures will expect what they have asked to see in print; and, lastly, because this will show how, in point of fact, the United States have been set before European critics under circumstances of no ordinary delicacy. At the same time, the conscientious care which I have bestowed upon the text of the Lectures in all matters of fact, and the notes and references with which they are supplemented, may commend them to the use of the student, even in the absence of a more scientific form. That the opinions which the Lectures express upon the great variety of topics of which they treat will be acceptable to all readers is not to be expected, nor even to be desired, since an independent thinker most respects in others the quality that he asserts for himself, and puts forth his convictions, not with a primary view to their being accepted, but because he must needs speak what he thinks, and hopes thus to gain for his thoughts and suggestions precisely what they may be worth in the estimate of truth and in the interest of humanity.

In conclusion, I would express my obligation to Prof. Dr. Lepsius, royal librarian, and to Dr. A. Potthast, librarian of the *Reichstag*, at Berlin, for the facilities they have kindly given me for consulting books pertinent to my subject, and to the Government of the United States for public documents placed at my disposal. I am indebted to the Hon. Marshall O. Roberts of New York for files of journals, official reports, and other material made use of in my statistical compilations.

I take occasion, also, to renew my thanks, already orally expressed, to the committees in the several cities where the Lectures were delivered, for their valuable services in preparing and conducting the arrangements for the course.

As germane to the subject, and belonging to the record of the Centennial, I have prefixed to the Lectures two speeches made in London July 4, 1876.

THE DAY WE CELEBRATE.

SPEECH AT THE "CENTENNIAL DINNER" AT THE WESTMINSTER PALACE HOTEL, LONDON, JULY 4, 1876.

MR. PRESIDENT, YOUR EXCELLENCY THE MINISTER OF THE UNITED STATES, MY LORD MAYOR, LADIES AND GENTLEMEN.

THE day *we* celebrate? No, Mr. President and gentlemen, this day gives to every American all of celebrity he has or can hope to attain. We cannot honor, we cannot exalt, this day, save by becoming in personal character, and in public as well as private life, all that the day has made us capable of being as citizens and as men. He who lives ignobly, who abuses liberty to license and corruption, who neglects the spiritual laws of his being, and makes freedom pander to sordid and selfish aims, would desecrate the day by taking this toast upon his lips! For that which marks the day is that it made *us* possible as men born under the largest opportunities of freedom, and the highest incentives to self-development that such opportunities can supply; made possible to every man the highest *manhood* of which he is capable. Great as were its benefits to us as citizens, what it did for us as men is infinitely greater; and therefore it is a day not for Americans alone, but for mankind, to hold memorable and illustrious.

I thank God that this birthday of the United States as a nation does not commemorate a victory of arms. War preceded it, gave occasion to it, followed it; but the figure of Independence shaped on the Fourth of July, 1776, wears no helmet, brandishes no sword, and carries no stain of slaughter and blood. I recognize all that war has done for the emancipation of the race, the progress of society, the assertion and maintenance of liberty itself; I honor the heroes who have braved the fury of battle for country and right; I appreciate the virtues to which war at times has trained nations, as well as leaders and armies: yet I confess myself utterly wearied and sated with these monuments of victory in every capital of Europe, made of captured cannon, and sculptured over with scenes of carnage. I am sick of that type of history that teaches our youth that the Alexanders and Cæsars, the Frederics and Napoleons, are the great men who have made the world; and it is with a sense of relief and refreshment that I turn to a nation whose birthday commemorates a great moral idea, a principle of ethics applied to political society, — that government represents the whole people, for the equal good of all. No tide of battle marks this day; but itself marks the high-water line of heaving, surging humanity.

Neither is the separation of the American colonies from the mother-country the chief thing that this day commemorates. That separation, indeed, marked and defined the principle of the Declaration of Independence, but was not the substance of the Declaration. I can fancy that a mother whose eldest daughter had run away from home, married against her will, and set up for herself, might become so reconciled by time as even to join her daughter in commemorating her self-willed wedding-day. But we could not have the bad taste to invite our English friends to join us in celebrating the runaway match of Britain's eldest daughter with that untitled and untamed fellow called "Independence," over the sea. No, my friends: when we think of England, it is not that we are divided from you, but that we were born of you, and are inseparable in the common heritage of literature and law, of freedom and faith; and therefore the sons of the men who fought against each other a century ago can feast together to-day.

That which marks the Declaration of Independence is that then, for the first time in the political thought of the world, was formulated *human personality* as, by the will of God, the chief factor and concern of civil government. In the past, the State, the Church, the School, had too commonly used man as their subordinate, made to serve their ends, and to count but as a cipher in questions of privilege and power. The American Declaration did not level any of these institutions, — the State, the Church, the School, — but it exalted man, through these and over these, to the point where he could use them all as his instruments for his service and culture. There was no radicalism in the Declaration, no communism, no atheism, but a wondrous humanism glorified by the divine, — " all men are created equal." The Declaration did not seek to overturn the State, but to establish it as ordained for the good of man. It did not make war upon religion, but set forth the right of man to life, liberty, and the pursuit of happiness, as an endowment from his Creator, and therefore having the sanction of true religion. But it so defined the relations of men and things, that every institution of society should be valued and cherished in proportion to its adaptation to the well-being of man. Need I remind you how the principle then formulated and proclaimed is fast becoming the rule of government in all Christian states? Need I remind you how, in this century, the British Parliament has made itself illustrious by lifting the good of the individual above the traditions and customs of the past, and making man himself the argument for reform? how, having swept the curse of slavery from coast, island, and sea, England now tells her officers, that, in every case affecting the life, liberty, and happiness of a fellow-being, the instinct of humanity should guide the decision of justice? Take care of the man first, and look to the quibbles of the law afterwards. What America declared a hundred years ago, that Britain also does. It is because it threw the shield of liberty and law, of government and religion, over human personality, that this day deserves to be marked, not only in the annals of a nation, but in the calendar of time.

I grant you freely, that neither the people of the United States in the aggregate, nor their government on the average, has realized the hope of the founders of the nation, or the ideal of the Declaration of Independence. But as man, however imperfect, and, if you please, fallen, is still the son of God, and that divine original is the grand motive and incentive to his recovery and exaltation; so, however degenerate and unworthy men may be as sons of freedom, that high prerogative remains the argument and hope for their final elevation. And, besides, what right have we as yet, in any land, to look for a perfect society? Indeed, what would a society be worth for our mental and moral discipline that had no more problems to be solved, no more dangers to be met, no more evils to be overcome? The very things that threaten and sometimes shame us give fibre to our manhood, and teach us the nobleness of labor, sacrifice, and suffering for the common good. For one, having given my active life to the great social and moral conflicts of my time, though I can submit to a retirement enforced by physical causes, I could never withdraw into a condition of mental indifference or of moral supineness toward questions affecting the welfare of my country or of man. I need such questions for my own soul's health; to keep me up to the standard of manly virtues; to make me broader, wiser, stronger, while life shall last. A "rest" of stagnation is death. And the country needs the quickening, energizing influence that comes of struggling toward a higher development. It may seem, for the moment, to be against us, that we have such and such evils to encounter; but it is greatly for us that we meet and master them.

The century has been one of such striving and mastery. With all their shortcomings, the United States have not been a failure. It is hard, indeed, to satisfy our friends on this side of the water. For instance, a leading London journal of this morning, that seeks to be kindly even to the verge of condescension, regrets that the United States have done so little for the world beyond increasing the affluence of the means of animal existence. But, while gently chiding this alleged preponderance of "material" growth, our critic rates us roundly for having curtailed our national wealth by not adopting its own notions of free trade: "Their growth (i.e., the United States) would have been still greater, had not false and foolish notions of protective legislation deceived the democracy of America." True, no doubt; but what shall we do? If we grow, we are "material:" if we don't grow material enough, we are "false and foolish."

The same journal would help us to the celebration of

the Centennial by putting into our mouths the theme which it fancies shall find "expression in a thousand shapes throughout this livelong day," — " Our forefathers were a handful of men, and we have become a great people." But I venture to say that no American patriot to-day will find his inspiration in such a theme; for, Mr. President and gentlemen, that which we honor in our fathers is that they disdained the material and the earthly, and were ready to sacrifice life and fortune for truth, freedom, right, — for *ideas* they had thought out for themselves, and would fight out for mankind. And that which we are proud of to-day — so far as we dare be proud at all — is, not that they were few and we are many, that they were small and we are great, but that they put the spiritual before the material, right before might, man before money, freedom and faith before all; in a word, that they were men, and we are the inheritors of their manhood.

The record of the United States is something more than of material growth. They have proved the possibility of free popular government upon a scale to which the Roman Republic of five hundred years was but a province; they have shown that such a government can cope with gigantic evils and wrongs, and is strong to maintain itself against rebellion and war; they have shown that the tendency of such a government is to peace and good-will, that it fosters industry and invention, diffuses knowledge fairly and fearlessly among the people; they have reconciled liberty and law, freedom and order; they have shown how religion, learning, and science flourish under freedom; and though there may be a lack of some forms of culture, as developed by institutions of favoritism, there is a high grade of average culture, as well as comfort, fostered by equality. In view of all the physical and social conditions of their great problem, the American people may well take courage and hope to-day from the experience and results of the century. What we now need is to measure our rights by our *duties*, and our manner of discharging these; to make freedom the guaranty of social order, of public purity, of justice and honor at home, of peace and faith abroad.

And may I not accept the circumstances under which

we meet to-day as an augury that the two English-speaking nations will take a new point of departure for their common welfare in the opening century? First, has not the time fully come when these two nations shall study how to be helpful to each other, and to promote one another's good? It is always well to cherish the habit of seeing the good in our neighbors. Indeed, who would live in a community where perpetual tattling and fault-finding was the rule? Has not the time fully come for public sentiment in both nations to teach journalism and authorship that we don't care to hear ill-natured tattle about our neighbors; don't care to know how the boors in either country use their knives and forks, or pronounce their slang, but do have a hearty, manly interest in learning each what the other is doing for education, for temperance, for virtue, for religion, for trade, for reform; that we are glad to hear good of one another, and not ashamed to learn from each other some good and helpful thing in the great, common problems of our free Christian civilization?

Next, these two nations should stand by one another for the maintenance of civil and religious liberty. I do not mean that we should form an alliance offensive and defensive, or take up a crusade for freedom. But there is a power that is growing stronger than armies, — the public opinion of enlightened peoples. Let the world feel the moral force of our united opinion; know that England and the United States back one another up for that civil and religious liberty which we have wrought out, and which we hold before all other peoples of the earth. And, once more, let us stand together for the peace and moral order of the world, — at peace between ourselves, and commending peace to the nations by all our influence in treaties and conventions, in word and in deed.

The other day I stood at Ilfracombe, and watched the sun as he went down straight into the bosom of the Atlantic; thus certifying me that there was nothing to divide the shore on which I stood from that other shore I hold so dear, save the ocean, that washes both alike with the same ever-recurring waves. Recalling how the names that dot that English coast, from Barnstaple around to Plymouth, are reproduced upon the shore of New England,

I felt how tender and sacred to our fathers were the haunts and homes of the mother-country, and how impossible it should be to separate lands so joined in common baptism. At that moment some smaller waves, more ambitious than the rest, as if they would carry the ocean at their backs, leaped up to overwhelm and sweep away the cliffs of England, but fell back in their own foam and spray, leaving nothing but the slime and weeds of the sea. So let it be, so shall it be, with the restless, fuming agitators, who, thinking to have the people at their backs, would dash either nation against the other. Let them sink back into their own spume, while we listen to the deep, everlasting harmony that rolls between. That ocean fills the awful chasm that else had divided us, and is now the highway of peace and good-will. In the fore-part of the century now closed, that ocean twice carried the fleets of England to desolate our coasts with war: but the last half of the century gave birth to the steamship, quickening the exchange of commerce and travel; and to the Atlantic cable, making the depths of the sea vital with thought and intelligence. May these be the augury of the new century! O England, mother of saints, mother of martyrs, mother of heroes, mother of scholars, poets, statesmen! — England, mother of freedom and faith, of colonies and of nations! — God keep thee ever in thy bright and glorious way! and keep us nobly by thy side, till this brave speech of ours, fast overmastering the languages of the world, shall teach the nations that the English tongue knows only words of truth and freedom, of right and love! Then come again the day we celebrate.

The friendly spirit in which this speech was reproduced in the leading journals of London, of the Provinces, and of Scotland, was a pleasant token of the extent to which old prejudices have given place to an enlightened liberality. But it was curious to notice how, in some quarters, the reviving of the American Declaration seemed to revive the antipathies of a century ago. As an example of this, I give the following editorial from "The Sussex Daily News" of July 6: —

CENTENNIAL OF AMERICAN INDEPENDENCE.

"With braying of trumpets, and booming of guns, the centenary of American independence has been kept. There have been great spectacles in Philadelphia, much dining and speechifying in London. A Dr. Thompson was particularly grandiloquent on this side of the Atlantic, and enlarged upon the Declaration of Independence with great unction. He said, 'The American Declaration did not level any of these institutions, — the State, the Church, the School, — but it exalted man, through these and over these, to the point where he could use them all as his instruments for his service and culture. There was no radicalism in the Declaration, no communism, no atheism, but a wondrous humanism, glorified by the divine, — "all men are created equal."' No communism or atheism, certainly, but a good deal of inaccuracy. How any one who knows any thing of human life can say that all men are created equal passes our comprehension. The one great fact which strikes the most superficial observer, and which overwhelms the most thoughtful, is the enormous inequalities to be found among men born in the same land even, not to say those born in different lands. They are unequal in physical strength, in mental gifts, in the possession of wealth, in the number of friends, in all their surroundings. Even if we take the same class, the differences are enormous. They begin before birth: they continue till the last hour of life. The child of profligate, drunken parents, has not a thousandth part of the chances of a child whose parents are virtuous and sober. If we take different classes, the inequalities are still greater. It makes all the difference to a man in London whether he is born in one postal district or in another. The child who is registered in 'W.' or 'S.W.' has ten times the chances of one registered in 'E.' or 'N.E.' A person of very ordinary capacity may rise to very high office in the state. as we may see at the present time, if only he happen to belong to the ruling families. On the other hand, one could almost weep to think of the number of men, with genius sufficient to have shaken the senate or to have founded our empire, who have died and made no sign. simply because they were born the sons of tradesmen or laboring-men. 'Mute, inglorious Miltons' and 'village Hampdens' have passed from poetry into a proverb; so certain is it that great minds have passed away without making themselves known, simply for lack of opportunity. The waste of mental power is as great as the waste of seeds that are scattered by the winds over the earth, and perish on waste. stony places, or are trampled under foot on the dusty highway. If it be said that real genius will always find an opportunity, and make its way, we reply. that perhaps the most transcendent minds will; but, even then, much harder is the task where the surroundings are unfavorable. But there is no need to dwell upon such extreme cases. We must all know plenty of them in every-day life. We must all have seen, over and over again, men beginning the career of life on fairly equal terms, so far as abilities go: yet, because the external circumstances were propitious in the one case, and unfavorable in the other, the one has attained prosperity; the other has had to lament that all the voyage of his life 'is bound in shallows and in miseries.' If it be said that the statement that 'all men are created equal' means simply that they are born with equal rights, how will that console the child of sin and crime when he sees the child of luxury and virtue? The second has the right to place himself among the rulers of the land: what rights has the first, save to the workhouse and the jail? It is time that such blatant nonsense came to an end. All men are *not* created equal, either in mind, body, or estate. We may be perplexed and overwhelmed by the greatness of the inequalities, and we may try to shut our eyes to them; but they exist none the less because we choose to go blindfold."

Knowing the candor and courtesy of the English press, I sent a brief reply to this criticism, which was kindly published, without comment, in "The Sussex Daily News" of July 29. I reprint that letter here, because its leading query remains unanswered; and the fact that no English statesman or philosopher would dare deny that government should impartially secure the equal birthright of all to "life, liberty, and the pursuit of happiness," shows how the doctrine of the Declaration has permeated English society.

To the Editor of "The Sussex Daily News."

Sir, — In your issue of July 6, you did me the honor to make my speech at the American Centennial dinner in London the text for some just and excellent remarks, showing that "all men are *not* created equal, either in mind, body, or estate." What you say is not only true in itself, but serves to illustrate the wisdom of the Declaration of Independence, and to fortify its position. I speak of the Declaration purely as a contribution to political ethics, and without reference to forms of government or the constitution of society.

The Declaration avoids the "blatant nonsense" that men are equal intellectually, socially, or politically; but it declares that "all men are created equal" in the right to "life, liberty, and the pursuit of happiness." Speaking to those who were familiar with the document, I did not think it necessary to enlarge upon the "self-evident truths" by which the Declaration defines and limits its affirmation of equality. I am persuaded, that, for the truth of history, you will lay before your readers this statement of the real doctrine of the Declaration; and I beg you to inform me whether there is to-day in England a statesman or a philosopher who would deny that all men are created with an equal right to live, with an equal right to the free use of their powers in making the most of themselves and their existence, and an equal right to all the happiness they can lawfully pursue and attain.[1] To-day these are commonplaces concerning man and

---

[1] For the full import of this doctrine, and the exact meaning of equality in the Declaration, the reader is referred to the second Lecture.

government, that England accepts no less than the United States. But, as I said in London, "that which marks the Declaration of Independence is, that then, for the first time in the political thought of the world, was formulated *human personality* as, by the will of God, the chief factor and concern of civil government." This notion of equality is simply a question of fact in political science,

I am, sir, with high respect, yours truly,

JOSEPH P. THOMPSON.

BERLIN, 11 July, 1876.

THE LINCOLN TOWER.

[Attached to Christ Church, in the Westminster-bridge Road, Lambeth, London, is a fine stone tower, which was erected to commemorate Pres. Lincoln and the abolition of slavery in the United States. The cost of this tower was seven thousand pounds, of which one-half was raised in America by the Rev. Newman Hall, pastor of the church, during his visits in 1867 and 1873. On the morning of July 4, 1876, Christ Church, which is a perpetuation of Surrey Chapel, was dedicated with appropriate religious services; and, at the close of these, the Lincoln Tower, which from base to summit was decorated with the flags of England and the United States, was inaugurated by Sir Thomas Fowell Buxton, Bart. After this ceremony, cheers were given for the Centenary of American Independence, and in memory of Washington and Wilberforce, for each of whom a chamber in the tower is named. Adjoining the church, and forming with it an admirable architectural group, is Hawkstone Hall, a well-appointed building, to be used for those auxiliary social, benevolent, and reformatory meetings and works for which Surrey Chapel was famed. The services of dedication and inauguration were followed by a collation in Hawkstone Hall. At the inauguration of the Lincoln Tower, the following speech was made in the name of American citizens interested in this international memorial.]

THE tower outside the building, no less than this inner sanctuary, is consecrated to the glory of God; for, though it bears upon its front an honored human name, its spire points upward to "the Name that is above every name," "of whom the whole family in heaven and earth," of every kindred and tongue and people and nation, is named. The name you have inscribed upon the tower is worthy of this association; for ABRAHAM LINCOLN shall stand in history as a synonyme of the Christian virtues, — truth, fidelity, honor, magnanimity, meekness, gentleness, patience, self-sacrifice, love to man, and faith in God; the man who bore the heaviest burdens and trials of his country and his fellows, who endured years of obloquy and hatred 'such as few have been called to suffer, but lived "with firmness in the right as God gave him to see the right," and died "with malice toward none, with charity for all."

The tower is "a memorial of emancipation." It was fitting, surely, that a house of worship projected at the moment of the emancipation of four million slaves should mark the date of its erection by so grand an epoch for humanity; and it was eminently significant that such an event should be chronicled by a church bearing the name of Him who came "to preach the gospel to the poor, to heal the broken-hearted, to proclaim liberty to the captives, and the opening of the prison to them that are bound." "This day is this scripture fulfilled in your ears." These walls that you have built shall be "stones of memorial" to all generations, witnessing how close Christianity takes Humanity to her heart.

This exemplification of Christianity has always marked the ministry and work of Surrey Chapel, and is henceforth to be perpetuated by most admirable arrangements in your new home. While the church proper shall be kept sacred, as it should be, to the worship of God, the adjoining suite of buildings provides for the practical ministrations of Christianity to Society, especially for the enlightenment and amelioration of the masses. Humanity is housed under the same roof with Christ. That is your answer to the materialism of the age, and to the social and political philosophy that would undertake to reform and elevate the masses, not only without the gospel, but even by decrying it. You say to such reformers, "It was Christianity that first really cared for man; it is Christianity that cares for him still, and so makes possible your philosophy of reform; and Christianity shall continue to care for man when your philosophy shall have exhausted the philanthropy it has borrowed of the gospel without union with its source."

It is because of this practical work for man that Surrey Chapel has always been of special interest to Americans. If there is one thing that marks American society, and makes the American nation worth commemorating to-day, it is that man is there the first object of thought and care, and this through the development of his spiritual nature, — man set free under the guidance of the gospel, man to be kept free by means of his moral and religious culture. It is because Surrey Chapel works practically on this platform and toward this ideal that it finds such favor in the

United States, and has always been sought out by Americans visiting London. But we owe to Mr. Newman Hall the special privilege of sharing directly in your prosperity and your work by contributions to the memorial tower. His personal character and influence secured those contributions: and his hold upon Americans was due, first, to his earnestness and power as a preacher of the gospel; and, next, to his sagacity in discerning, and his courage in maintaining, the right side in our great civil conflict. He foresaw from the first that our real struggle was with slavery, and that slavery was doomed; and having thrown his whole soul into the conflict in which Lincoln was leader and martyr, and done so much to form a right sentiment in England, he is entitled to call the Lincoln Tower " a token of international good-will." As such I am proud to recognize and acknowledge it in the name of my countrymen. If the Atlantic cable shall at once convey to America the report of your doings here to-day, I am sure that above the ringing of bells, the booming of cannon, the jubilations of independence, there will go up to God the voice of Christian thanksgiving for this your fellowship, and the prayer that the peoples so truly one in Christian thought and feeling may be ever one in "international good-will."

But, if I stay much longer in England, that word "international" will cease to be for me a talisman; for I am fast losing my sense of nationality, if not of personal identity. I have just been down to Devonshire; and I was so struck with the familiarity of the names called out at the railway-stations, that I took out my map, and, just in that western bit of England, found some twenty towns with which I am familiar in New England, — Dorchester, Wareham, Portland, Portsmouth, Lyme, Taunton, Dartmouth, Exeter, Barnstaple, Biddeford, Hampstead, Plymouth, Falmouth, Malden, Milford, Reading, Weymouth, Wilton. Your whole map might be laid down on our side of the water; only we have no "Land's End" over there, or at least have not found it yet. At Plymouth, in the fine new Guild Hall, I was shown a splendid memorial window of the Pilgrim Fathers. There, amid the proud memories of Hawkins, Drake, Frobisher, Raleigh, Blake, and other heroes of England's maritime glory, stand on the barbican those heroes of conscience and the gospel, about to step aboard "The Mayflower,"—the richest freight that ever England sent to sea. Fresh from these memories I came back to London, to stand on the Fourth of July within the Lincoln Tower, the token of international good-will, and hear you sing "Coronation" and "America" as heartily as if you were at the Centennial in Philadelphia. Can you wonder that the tears start for very joy as I fancy myself at home?

But let us beware of making "international" a word of cant. The international is born of the Christian, not the Christian of the international. In Hugo Grotius, the law of nations was conceived of Christian light and love. Let us not think to broaden Christianity by calling *that* international. All our names and terms would but narrow the gospel that is for every creature, the church that knows no limit of land or sea, of earth or time. How dare we restrict the Church of Christ to our communion, to our order, to our nation, or even our international alliances? In our social spirit and our political policy, the international sentiment does, indeed, make us broader. Not so as members of the body of Christ. It is his spirit that makes us broad; that lifts us out of all our prejudices and conceits; that teaches us how in him there is neither Greek nor Jew, Barbarian nor Scythian, male nor female, bond nor free. The more we have of that spirit, the more shall we manifest of international, rather of universal, good-will. And is not the spirit of Christ strong enough in England and in the United States, are there not Christian men enough in both countries, to make the governments feel that every difference that may arise between them shall be approached from the Christian point of view, and settled by the principles of Christian morality and equity? Is not our Christianity great enough to keep us in the bonds of peace? The timely assertion of the Christian spirit will preserve international good-will. This tower, upon whose every pinnacle the flags of the two countries lovingly embrace on this Centenary of their separation, is an omen of the new era of international harmony ordered by Christian love. The people who to-day with tearful gratitude shall read the name of Lincoln with that of Washington — how can they ever be estranged from you who have here given both names a sanctuary under the Church of Christ? The Lord bless you, pastor and people, church and congregation, English men and nation, forevermore!

LECTURE I.

GROUNDS AND MOTIVES OF THE AMERICAN REVOLUTION.

ON the Fourth of July, 1776, the then United Colonies of North America awoke to the consciousness of a national life, and declared themselves "*free and independent States*, absolved from all allegiance to the British crown," and " with full power to levy war, conclude peace, contract alliances, establish commerce, and do all other acts and things which independent States may of right do."

This was not a declaration of war with Great Britain, since, for almost fifteen months, the people of the Colonies had been in arms against the British authorities,[1] and for a full year there had been a Continental army, equipped by the Continental Congress, and commanded by Washington.[2] This declaration was not a manifesto of rebellion; for, though the Colonies thus openly threw off their allegiance to the parent-country, the act was justified by success, which transformed it from a rebellion into a revolution. This last term, however, in the political history of Europe, has come to be so identified with sudden and violent upheavals of society, with outbursts of popular passion, and with wild theories of government, that I deprecate the application of it to that moderate, patient, and matured action by which the people of the American Colonies declared that " all political connection between them

---

[1] The battles of Lexington and Concord were fought April 19, 1775; the battle of Bunker Hill, June 17, 1775.

[2] On the 15th June, 1775, the Congress at Philadelphia adopted the army before Cambridge, consisting wholly of New-England troops, as the Continental army, and elected George Washington commander-in-chief. On the 3d July, 1775, Washington took command of the army at Cambridge.

and the State of Great Britain is, and ought to be, totally dissolved."

In the conception of political philosophy, this act of the colonists, formally renouncing the authority of the government under which the Colonies had been planted and administered, and asserting their independence as a nation, was a revolution. But it was not a revolution in the sense of a war upon certain classes, orders, customs in civil society, nor against a form of government as such; not an assault upon an hereditary monarchy in the name of a theoretical democracy; not a struggle for power between different dynasties, factions, or political schools within the State; in one word, not a revolution after the French or Spanish kind.

The colonists renounced their allegiance to George III., not because he was a king, but because they had come to look upon him as "a prince whose character was marked by every act which may define a tyrant," and therefore "unfit to be the ruler of a free people." As Englishmen, and the sons of Englishmen, they were free-born. If the crown had hereditary prerogatives, the subject had hereditary rights; and it was in defence of the rights and liberties of Englishmen against usurped and arbitrary power that they took up arms, and were driven at last to revolution and independence. Call it not "revolution," then, with the smack of European associations in the term: call it rather restoration, recovery, the reconstruction of political society upon that broad and equal basis of rights of person, of property, and of representation, which underlies the institutions of the Anglo-Saxon race.

Nay, it is not so much the act, as the people who did that act, that arrests us in the Declaration of July 4, 1776; a people loyal and true, a people just and brave, generous and forbearing, but a people who are and must be free, — such a people harried by usurpations into that community in danger and in defence which is the first consciousness of national life, lifting itself up before the world, and proclaiming, "We are one; we are free." "*Un grand peuple qui se relève*" was the description by which Comte de Gasparin characterized the uprising of the people of the United States in 1861 to maintain their Constitution and

Government; and, going back to that scene of 1776, we see in the foreground, not the spirit of revolution nor of democracy, but *un grand peuple qui se rel've,* — a people, indeed, far from imposing in numbers or might, but grand in the assertion of right, in the inspiration of justice, in devotion to freedom, and in heroic sacrifice.

To such a people national independence was a foregone conclusion, not, indeed, in their own original purpose, but in the logic of events. It was given in the fact that thirteen Colonies, distinct in origin and institutions, and with diverse and sometimes rival interests, had made common cause in resisting the oppressive measures and demands of the British Government; in the fact, that, nearly two years before, these Colonies had appointed a Congress to consult for their common welfare, and this Congress had put forth a "Declaration of Rights," affirming, among other things, that "the foundation of English liberty and of all free government is a right in the people to participate in their legislative council;" in the fact that a second Continental Congress[1] had now been in session for fourteen months, had taken measures for the common defence, had raised a loan, had organized an army, had passed high resolves; and, above all, in the fact that the battle of Bunker Hill and subsequent engagements had shown that the American militia could stand the fire of British regulars, and could supply the lack of discipline by agility and daring. When Washington heard of that battle, he asked, "Did the militia stand fire?" and when told that they stood under fire until the enemy was within eight rods, and then poured in their own volleys, he said, "The liberties of the country are safe." For more than a year, Washington had been drilling and disciplining the

---

[1] The first Continental Congress, convened at the instance of Massachusetts, met at Philadelphia Sept. 5, 1774. The place of assembly was Carpenters' Hall, at the head of a court running back from Chestnut Street, between Third and Fourth. Many years of my boyhood were spent in a school in that old patriotic hall. The previous Congress at New York, Oct. 7, 1765, was known as the "American Congress."

The Congress of 1774, before adjourning, recommended that a second Congress should be convened in the following May. On the 10th of May, 1775, the second Continental Congress met in Philadelphia. This Congress carried the country through the war of Independence, and, though dwindling in numbers and influence, remained in authority as the central government until the establishment of the Confederation in 1781.

army of which the men of Lexington, Concord, and Bunker Hill, were the nucleus. The "liberties of the country" had been fermenting in the hearts of the people. Men who for more than a year had suffered and counselled and fought together, now that the last overtures of reconciliation were rejected by the British Government, *must* be free and independent, as they were already united and determined; and so the spirit of independence that was in the hearts of the people, in the army, in the air, awoke in Congress the consciousness that the Colonies it represented were a *nation*.

That this consciousness was true, and this declaration not premature, will be evident from a brief analysis of the essential attributes and conditions of a nation. The nation is a people established and settled upon a certain territory as their own, united under a government of their own, and having absolute and exclusive sovereignty within and over said territory and all and each of its inhabitants. These attributes of territorial occupancy, political unity, and independent sovereignty, inhere in the nation or body politic as such, and are quite distinct from forms of government, and modes of administration. These last are but the outward and changeable expression of an inward and permanent fact, — the organs by which the nation, which is the living organism, serves itself, and manifests its life. Sometimes, also, one or more of these essential attributes of the nation — territory, unity, sovereignty — may be in a state of abeyance, or may exist *in posse*, awaiting manifestation *in esse*, without annihilating the national consciousness, or materially impairing the national life. A portion of territory may be held by an invader, and yet the nation live, and live the more vigorously in efforts to recover its lost possessions. Political unity may be disturbed by rebellion, yet the life of the nation, the inherent vitality of the body politic, assert itself the more in maintaining the social organism and its government intact. *Sovereignty* may be brought under by conquest; yet the life of the nation, burning the more intensely that it is pent up, may burst forth with the volcanic *sovereignty* of a revolution. When Marshal Bazaine sought to excuse his irresolution at Metz by saying that he knew not where or what was the government of the country, nor, indeed, whether there was any longer a government to which he owed allegiance, the Duc d'Aumale interposed the passionate exclamation, "*Mais la France, la France!*" That pathetic outburst of patriotism was the cry of the nation, still conscious of its life. Without emperor, king, president, or parliament, without flag, general, army, or battle-cry, without ally abroad, without resource at home, her provinces subjugated, her capital beleaguered, her counsels divided, her inner sanctuary threatened by the torch of the patricide, France still lived, the nation, with a title supreme and absolute to the homage and service of her sons. Germany found a nation to treat with even in the extemporized assembly at Bordeaux; and the world has seen a nation vanquished and dismembered, yet capable of paying an enormous ransom, of re-organizing industry, trade, education, the army, finance, and at length, from the chaos of conflicting elements at Versailles, bringing forth a form of government to represent, at least for a time, the indestructible essence of the body politic. There is still a France, a people occupying a territory of their own, having a substantial unity in a government of their own, with absolute and exclusive sovereignty over its subjects and its soil.

Applying these criteria of a nation to the American Colonies that in 1776 declared their independence, we there find a people numbering two and a half millions, — equal to one-third of the population of England and Wales, and double that of Scotland, at that time; and, of these two and a half millions, the vast majority (say four-fifths) were of the same race, language, and political parentage,[1] — Englishmen and the sons of Englishmen, more truly homogeneous in feeling and speech, in manners and ideas, than were the several parts of Great Britain itself.

We find this people occupying a territory of 820,680

[1] Mr. Burke, in his Speech on Conciliation with America, places the population of the Colonies at 2,500,000, of whom 2,000,000 were English and of English descent. The population of England and Wales was then 7,500,000; that of Scotland, 1,270,000. By the census of 1790, the population of the United States was 3,929,214; that of England, Wales, and Scotland, 10,000,000. Probably in 1776 the Colonies numbered 3,000,000, — a good, healthy nucleus of national life.

square miles, or more than nine times the area of Great Britain;[1] a territory remote from all organized communities, and isolated by the forests, the lakes, and the sea; a territory which they had redeemed from the wilderness to be the abode of civilized man, which they had defended, at cost of their blood and treasure, against Indian tribes and French garrisons, and had covered with townships, cities, villages, and homesteads; a territory whose wooded wastes they had converted into a granary to relieve the scarcity of corn in the mother-country, and whose rocky, ice-bound coasts they had animated with a commerce, which, at that time, almost equalled the foreign trade of England at the beginning of the eighteenth century with the whole world. "No sea," said Mr. Burke, "but what is vexed by their fisheries; no climate that is not witness to their toils. Neither the perseverance of Holland, nor the activity of France, nor the dexterous and firm sagacity of English enterprise, ever carried this most perilous mode of hardy industry [the whale-fishery] to the extent to which it has been pushed by this recent people."[2] Such in their physical condition and achievements were the people who now claimed to be a nation. They had a territory of their own, which they had shown themselves able to occupy and improve, and to hold against all comers.

By force of circumstances, too, they had now attained to political unity under a government which they recognized and upheld as their proper representative. Much as the Colonies differed in their original political settlement, — some being directly provinces of the crown, others proprietary grants, and others chartered companies or settlements,[3] — they all agreed in asserting and cherishing

---

[1] The area of England and Wales is 58,320 square miles; that of Scotland, 31,324: total, 89,644 square miles.

[2] Speech on Conciliation with America.

[3] Massachusetts, Connecticut, and Rhode Island held charters from the crown, by virtue of which the government was largely vested in the freemen of the company or colony. The charters of Connecticut and Rhode Island were so liberal, that, for many years after the Revolution, they served the purpose of State constitutions, — that of Connecticut till 1818, that of Rhode Island till 1842.

Pennsylvania, Maryland, Delaware, and at first, also, New Jersey and the Carolinas, had proprietary governments: i.e., the proprietor who held the grant in person from the crown had also a control in political affairs.

that good old English principle of local self-government, which was fast falling into desuetude in England itself. The Hon. George C. Brodrick, in his valuable essay on "Local Government in England," observes, "It is a curious and instructive fact, that, while the primitive ideal of self-government had become obscured both in English counties and in English boroughs, it not only survived, but acquired a fresh vitality, in the Colonies of New England."[1] By degrees, this local self-government, practised in districts and townships as matter of custom and convenience, expanded in confederate counsel and action in matters of common duty and danger. In those days, before steam-navigation was dreamed of, the mother-country was so distant, and communication was so tardy and irregular, that the colonists were often compelled to act upon their own responsibility, without waiting for the sanction of the crown. As far back as 1643, four of the Colonies of New England — Plymouth, Massachusetts Bay, Connecticut, and New Haven — formed a confederacy for their mutual safety and welfare, especially as against the French and the Indians; and this league, under the name of "The United Colonies of New England," — "a self-governing association of self-governing English commonwealths,"[2] assuming in so far the functions of a distinct sovereignty, — lasted for more than forty years. In 1754, twenty-two years before the Declaration of Independence, a general convention of the Colonies was summoned at Albany to renew a treaty with the "Six Nations" of Indians. Benjamin Franklin proposed a formal union of the Colonies as their only protection against the French. His motto

---

The charter to Lord Baltimore, however, reserved to the colonists a share in legislation; and Penn freely gave the same right to his colonists.

New Hampshire, New York, Virginia, Georgia, and afterwards New Jersey and the Carolinas, were under royal or provincial governments. The governor was appointed by the crown, and also a council, which served as the upper house of the legislature; the lower house being elected by the people. It is sufficient for my purpose to point out the three forms of colonial government, without stating the specific differences under each form.

[1] Cobden-Club Essays for 1875, p. 25.
[2] Palfrey: History of New England, i. 634. As a consequence of the union of New Haven with Connecticut, the confederacy of 1643 was terminated in 1667; but a new league was entered into between Plymouth, Massachusetts, and Connecticut (1672), which was finally dissolved in 1684. Thus the principle of colonial confederation was in action in New England, in the seventeenth century, for a period of forty years.

was, "Unite, or die!"[1] Sometimes such conventions were summoned or sanctioned by the officers of the crown; sometimes they were quite outside the pale of legitimate government as recognized by the crown: but, dictated by necessity, and justified by their beneficial results, they were educating the people to independence of the crown. The union urged by Franklin against the military rival of their parent-country, twenty years later, was formed to protect the rights and liberties of the Colonies against the encroachments of Great Britain herself. Virtually, indeed, the political union of the American Colonies was formed as early as 1765, though few then dreamed of an independent nation as its issue. In June of that year, James Otis of Boston "advised the calling of an American Congress, which should come together without asking the consent of the king, and should consist of committees from each of the thirteen Colonies, to be appointed respectively by the delegates of the people, without regard to the other branches of the legislature."[2] In October of the same year, the representatives of the people of eleven Colonies met in New York " to consult together, and consider of a united representation to implore relief." Petition, re-

---

[1] The proceedings of this convention at Albany, in 1754, are given at length in the Documentary History of New York, vol. ii. pp. 317 seq. They are of exceeding interest in three particulars. (1.) The commissioners to the Congress were appointed by the governors or legislatures of the several Colonies, "in pursuance of letters from the Right Honorable the Lords Commissioners for Trade and the Plantations." Thus the British Government made use of the expedient of a convention of the Colonies for framing articles of union and confederation with the Iroquois as a treaty-making power.

(2.) This Congress, though appointed for the specific purpose of treating with the Indians, took it upon itself to plan a union of the Colonies "for their mutual defence and security, and for extending the British settlements in North America." This plan was referred to the governments of the several Colonies for approval.

(3.) The scheme proposed an act of Parliament, "by virtue of which one general government may be formed in America, including all the Colonies, within and under which government each Colony may retain its present constitution." There was to be a president-general appointed and supported by the crown, and a grand council to be chosen by the representatives of the people of the several Colonies. The acts of the council required to be sanctioned, first by the president, and then by the king. Though this plan never came to maturity, it shows how the colonists cherished local government and union, without aiming at independence.

[2] Bancroft: History of the United States, vol. v. p. 279.

John Adams said of Otis, "He was at the head of the cause of his country.... His oration against *writs of assistance* breathed into the nation the breath of life." — *Works*, vol. x. p. 276.

monstrance, repeal, were in their minds, with no thought as yet of separation and war. But in the very act of thus coming together as directly representing the popular branch in the government, without regard to governors, councils, magistrates, or other parties claiming to represent the crown, they asserted a right of self-government inherent in the people, and a unity of political life above all diversities of form. That union found expression in such sentiments as these: "There ought to be no New-England man, no New-Yorker, known on the continent, but all of us Americans;" the Colonies are "a bundle of sticks, which can neither be bent nor broken." And, while the hands of those delegates draughted a union of the Colonies for their present redress, they unconsciously drew the faint shadowy outlines of the nation, from which the fiery alchemy of war should bring out the resplendent figure of Liberty. The nation was there *in posse;* a people permanently settled upon a territory, which by enterprise, by labor, or by purchase, they had made their own, had redeemed from nature, had enriched by cultivation, had defended from jealous rivals and from savage foes; a people that through forms as yet inchoate, or occasional and flexible, had come to realize their political unity of interest, of spirit, and of action. Nor was the third essential attribute of sovereignty wanting, though as yet there was no formal, coherent organization of sovereign power.

When this Congress of 1765 had adjourned, and so was finally dissolved, the people of the several Colonies ratified its conclusions, and accepted these as their own: and, though nine years elapsed before another Congress was convened, the colonists had the consciousness of a sovereignty latent within themselves; they had before them the precedent of a political assembly emanating directly from the people, criticising and condemning the acts of King and Parliament, issuing remonstrances and appeals to the people and the government of Great Britain, and proposing terms of future concord; in a word, exercising the functions of a distinct political power. With this precedent in view, they felt, that, in any emergency, they could again summon this power of the united people to give such counsel, and take such action, as their common welfare should demand; and when at length, in 1774, a Continental Congress was again invoked, though this body set before it as the chief object of its labors "the union of Great Britain and the Colonies on a constitutional foundation," yet, in the very fact of summoning a body of their own creation to treat with the parent-country of such questions as union, obedience, allegiance, the instinct of the colonists was leading them to the recognition of a power as yet incorporeal and indefinable, — the sovereignty of the nation. When this Congress put forth the resolve, that "the inhabitants of the English Colonies in North America . . . are entitled to life, liberty, and property, and they have never ceded to any sovereign power whatever a right to dispose of either without their consent;" and, further, " that they are entitled to a free and exclusive power of legislation in their several provincial legislatures," — then this nascent sovereignty had already taken on its positive form. The " Declaration of Rights " in 1774 was the herald of the " Declaration of Independence " in 1776: it needed only that this last magic word should be spoken, and a new nation stood unveiled before the world, equipped with territory, with unity, and with sovereignty.

This nation must needs pass through a baptism of fire and blood before she could wear unchallenged on her brow the name *The United States of America*. More than five years of war, and seven years of nominal hostilities, before, in September, 1783, the independence of these United States shall be recognized by Great Britain; nearly thirteen years of political experiment and uncertainty, before, in March, 1789, the republic shall be definitively established under a Constitution, with George Washington as its first president: yet the nation came into being on that fourth day of July, 1776, when the Continental Congress at Philadelphia issued the Declaration of Independence. That Declaration was put forth with the utmost deliberation, dignity, and solemnity. The representatives who signed it, " in the name and by the authority of the good people of the Colonies," pledged to each other " their lives, their fortunes, and their sacred honor;" and for the motives of their action, and the rectitude of their intentions, they appealed to "a candid world" and to "the Supreme Judge of the world." The independence they then declared, and the nation that they brought to consciousness by that Declaration, have stood for a hundred years.

I have dwelt thus minutely upon the essential attributes of a nation, because in the fact that the colonists had grown to be a nation is given a justification of the Revolution, and because, also, in this fact is given a conclusive answer to the pretended "right of secession," under which was organized the rebellion of the Southern States in 1861. That plea was, that the Union was a compact of several independent sovereignties, and that any or all of these could at any time withdraw from the compact, renounce the paramount sovereignty of the Union, and fall back upon its original independence as a power, or enter into new compacts with other powers according to its pleasure. But the original thirteen Colonies became independent States only through their union: it was a Congress representing "the good people of the Colonies" that proclaimed the fact of independence.[1] The nation existed long before the Constitution, which it made for a more perfect realization of its inherent and essential unity and sovereignty; the nation existed years before the Articles of Confederation, which were a crude attempt to give expression to that unity and sovereignty, under the pressure of the Revolutionary war; and the nation existed before the Declaration of Independence, by which it declared its own consciousness, and challenged the recognition of the world.[2] The nation might be rent in twain by civil war, or be robbed of a portion of its territory and people by conquest; and it is even conceivable that the nation, acting of its free-will and in its entirety, — in view of the vastness of its territory or its population, or of certain

[1] The Declaration reads, "We, the representatives, &c., . . . do, in the name and *by the authority of the good people* of these Colonies, solemnly publish and declare, that these *united* Colonies are, and of right ought to be, free and independent States." Many of the members of this Congress had been elected directly by conventions of the people.

[2] By the preamble to the Declaration, it was a "PEOPLE" — not a confederation of governments, but a people — that dissolved the political bonds which had connected them with another, and assumed "a separate and equal station" — that is, as a distinct nation — "among the powers of the earth." The nation lay back of all forms of political organization.

features of its physical geography, — might deem it wise to portion off a section of itself as a separate political community, for greater convenience or efficiency of government. But "right of secession" there is and can be none. To admit such a right would be to put into each and every constituent of the nation the means of the political suicide of the whole body. The nation is not a group of distinct commonwealths held together by a rope of sand: it is a people, a living organism, having in itself the inalienable and indivisible functions and attributes of life. Such a nation is the people of the United States of America. The training which fitted that people to be a nation, and necessitated their independence as soon as their right of local self-government was assailed, is a study in political philosophy which more and more attracts the publicists and statesmen of Europe. Thirty years ago, Alexis de Tocqueville advised his countrymen to look to America, not in order to make a servile copy of the institutions which she has established, but to gain a clearer view of the polity which would be best for France; to look to America less to find examples than instruction; to borrow from her the principles, rather than the details, of her laws, — those principles of order, of the balance of powers, of true liberty, of deep and sincere respect for right, on which the American Constitution rests.[1] Prof. von Holst of the University of Freiburg, having spent five years in the United States in the diligent study of their political history and institutions, is now seeking to promote that study in Germany, where correct and philosophical knowledge of American society is so sadly wanting.[2] And Mr. Gladstone has lately said of the independence of the United States of America,[3] "The circumstances of the war which yielded that result, the principles it illustrates, and the remarkable powers of the principal men who took part, whether as soldiers or citizens, in the struggle, . . . constitute one of the most instructive chapters of modern history; and I have repeatedly recommended them to younger men as subjects of especial study."

[1] Democracy in America, Preface to twelfth edition. 1848.
[2] Verfassung und Demokratie der Vereinigten Staaten von Amerika, von Dr. H. v. Holst: Dusseldorf, 1873.
[3] Reply to invitation to the Lexington centenary.

A leading journal of London, having no partiality for the United States, also says, " The Revolution which gave birth to the United States, in some respects may be regarded, even more than the French Revolution, as the starting-point of modern history. It was the first example of a nation completely breaking loose from its position as part of the old historic world of Christendom, starting for itself on entirely new ground, and trusting to its inherent power of organization. . . . We have lived thenceforth in a larger sphere, physically, socially, and politically."[1]

Now, the American Revolution could never have attained to this dignity and power, nor have so commanded the respect of statesmen and philosophers for its benefits to mankind, had it been only or chiefly a revolt against the payment of a tax. It is true that the Stamp Act and other oppressive impositions were the occasion of rousing in the American Colonies the spirit of resistance to the authority of Great Britain: yet it was not the tax as money, but the mode of levying the tax, that they resisted; it was not the pocket that was touched, but the principle, by whose authority the pocket should be opened.

" The Saturday Review " speaks of the American Revolution as a " wanton and needless rebellion : " " needless,"— that is, without basis or plea of necessity to justify it; " wanton," — that is, reckless, without reason or motive, without regard to right, to methods, or to consequences. I quote this characterization of one of the greatest political and moral events of modern history simply to raise the question, whether there exists in England a class of persons of sufficient intelligence to read " The Saturday Review," and yet of sufficient stupidity to be imposed upon by such flippant phrases.[2] To " The Westminster Review," however, one looks for candor, intelligence, and a fair degree of sound and accurate knowledge of the subjects of which it treats. Yet even " The Westminster " is betrayed into a strange misapprehension of the issue between the Colonies and the mother-country. " It has been well pointed out," says this review, " that the principle involved in the war of independence was scarcely

[1] London Times, May 5, 1875.
[2] Notice of the Life of Alexander Hamilton, May 27, 1876.

whether taxation was only just where representation had been conceded, but whether the two hundred and forty million pounds sterling which had been spent by England in defence of her American Colonies from the French invasions from Canada should not, in some measure, be borne by the Colonies in whose interest the war had been undertaken, and for whose benefit the struggle had been prosecuted to a successful issue." [1]

Had the writer taken pains to consult the journals of the House of Commons, and especially the journal of Franklin's examination before the House, or the speeches of Burke, he could not have fallen into so mischievous an error. Of Franklin's testimony I shall speak by and by. But here is the official record of the House of Commons: On the 28th January, 1756, a message was received from the king, that "His Majesty, being sensible of the zeal and vigor with which his faithful subjects of certain Colonies in North America have exerted themselves in defence of his Majesty's just rights and possessions, recommends it to this House to take the same into their consideration, and to enable his Majesty to give them such assistance as may be a proper reward and encouragement." On the 3d February following, the House voted one hundred and fifteen thousand pounds as a recompense to the Colonies, in almost the words of the royal message. This was in the second year after the outbreak of the so-called "French and Indian" or "Old French" war. This war continued for nine years, and was at last terminated by the Treaty of Paris, Feb. 10, 1763. Now, in each and every year of that war, the journal of the House of Commons bears witness, that, on recommendation of the crown, the House made an appropriation to reimburse the Colonies for their excess of outlay in a war that was not simply in their own defence, but for the rights of the crown in America.[2]

The Colonies did not begin the French war. The question of the boundary of Nova Scotia did not directly concern them; and the forts built by the French in the

---

[1] Our Colonial Empire: Westminster Review, April, 1876.
[2] See Journal, vol. xxvii., 28th January and 3d February, 1756, 16th and 19th May, 1757; vol. xxviii., June 1, 1758, April 26th and 30th, 1759, March 26th and 31st, April 28, 1760, Jan. 9th and 20th, 1761; vol. xxix., Jan. 22d and 26th, 1762, March 14th and 17th, 1763.

GROUNDS AND MOTIVES OF THE REVOLUTION.

valley of the Mississippi, though they might eventually menace the Colonies, did not encroach upon the actual settlements, but upon territory claimed by Great Britain. The king's speech at the opening of Parliament, Nov. 13, 1755, recognizing the state of war, said, "Since your last session, I have taken such measures as might be conducive to the protection of *our possessions* in America, and to the regaining of such posts thereof as had been encroached upon or invaded, in violation of the peace, and contrary to the faith of the most solemn treaties."[1]

In November, 1754, in the debate on the Address on the King's Speech, Mr. W. Beckford, M.P., said, "If we attack the French anywhere by land, let it be in America, where we are sure of the utmost assistance our Colonies can give, without subsidy or reward; for though we have for several years treated them in such a manner that they have some reason to be indifferent whose power they may hereafter fall under, yet I am sure they will all join heartily with us in driving the French as far as possible from their confines."[2] And the senior Horace Walpole, who bore us no sympathy, said, "I was glad to hear that our Colonies were able to support themselves. I therefore hope they will not stand in need of much assistance from us; but, if they should, we must give it. Even for them we must fight as if we were fighting *pro aris et focis;* for it is to them we owe our wealth and our naval strength."[3] Surely, then, the Colonies were under no so great obligation to the mother-country for "protection."

In April, 1759, his Majesty "recommends to the consideration of the House the zeal and vigor with which his faithful subjects of North America had exerted themselves in defence of his just rights and possessions; desiring he might be enabled to give them a proper compensation for the expenses incurred by the respective provinces in levying, clothing, and paying the troops raised in that country, according as the active vigor and strenuous efforts of the several Colonies should appear to merit."[4] And the journal records an appropriation of £200,000 as a "proper compensation to the Provinces for the expenses incurred

---

[1] Hansard, xv. 527.   [2] Ibid., xv. 358.   [3] Ibid., xv. 365.
[4] See in Hansard, vol. xv. p. 929.

in levying and maintaining troops for the service of the public."[1]

On the 28th April, 1759, the House made a special appropriation of £2,977 "for reimbursing to the Colony of New York their expenses in furnishing provisions and stores to the troops raised by them for his Majesty's service for the campaign in 1756."

In 1760, on the 31st March, in the vote of supplies as given by Hansard, is this peculiar form: "Upon account, to enable his Majesty to give proper compensations to the Provinces in North America for the expenses they had incurred in levying, clothing, and paying the troops raised by them, according as the active vigor and strenuous efforts of the respective Provinces shall be thought by his Majesty to merit." The sum granted was £200,000. Thus far under George II. George III. came to the throne Oct. 25, 1760; and the journal bears witness, in the same terms as above quoted, that on Jan. 20, 1761, £200,000, on Jan. 25, 1762, £133,333. 6s. 8d., and on March 17, 1763, a like sum, were voted as a compensation to the Colonies.[2]

Burke called attention to these facts in his famous speech on Conciliation with America, and said with just emphasis, "The Colonies, in general, owe little or nothing to any care of ours." In a speech in the Massachusetts legislature, Sept. 8, 1762, James Otis said, "This Province has, since the year 1754, levied for his Majesty's service, as soldiers and seamen, near thirty thousand men. One year in particular, it was said that every fifth man was engaged in one shape or another. We have raised sums for the support of this war that the last generation could hardly have formed any idea of." Such were the facts. "The Westminster Review" says, "The question was, whether the cost of defending the Colonies from the French should not be borne by the Colonies." The King and Parliament, on the contrary, year by year, recognized the fact that the Colonies had freely borne the cost of levying and paying troops to serve against the French, and had so far exceeded their fair proportion of this expense as to deserve compensation from the royal treasury. "The

---

[1] See in Hansard, vol. xv. p. 937.
[2] Ibid., vol. xv. pp. 1003, 1214, seq.

Westminster Review" says that the war was undertaken for the interest of the Colonies." But the King and Parliament felt that the Colonies were assisting England in *her* war with France; were fighting for "the service of the public," and "in defence of his Majesty's just rights and possessions." Surely money voted in gratitude as a "compensation" and "reward" for zealous and vigorous voluntary services and sacrifices on the part of the Colonies could not afterward be made a ground of taxing the Colonies for expenses incurred in their defence. The fact was, that the resources displayed by the Colonies in their own defence excited the envy and cupidity of a later ministry; and, when the fear of France was removed, it was felt that pressure could safely be applied to the Colonies for extorting a revenue for the crown. Hitherto the Colonies had made grants to the crown through their own legislatures: now they were to be directly taxed by Parliament. This was expressly declared in the preamble to the act levying a duty on tea; and Burke pithily said, "It is the weight of *that preamble*, and not the weight of the duty, that Americans are unable and unwilling to bear." This it was that led Otis to assert it as a right of the British Colonies, that "taxes are not to be laid on the people, but by their consent in person, or by deputation."[1]

I have dwelt thus long upon this point, first, because of the respectable character of the review that has been betrayed into this singular error; and, next, because I see not how it is possible for Englishmen to be correctly informed concerning this important period not only of American history, but of their own, so long as the record of the doings of their own government is kept from view, and quite another version of the facts is given by journals in which they are accustomed, and ordinarily with good reason, to confide.

"What do we mean by the American Revolution?" asks John Adams. "Do we mean the American war? The Revolution was effected before the war commenced. The Revolution was in the minds and hearts of the people,

---

[1] See pamphlet on the Rights of the British Colonies Asserted and Proved; first read by Otis to the Massachusetts legislature, then published by him in 1764.

—a change in their religious sentiments of their duties and obligations. . . . Believing allegiance and protection to be reciprocal, when protection was withdrawn they thought allegiance was dissolved." [1] The American Colonies had no quarrel with the English nation, of which they were proud to be a part. The British ministry had itself to thank for American independence. The English people have America to thank for the conservation of their own popular and local freedom, and for their present colonial policy. Parliament now seeks to force upon the Colonies that self-administration for which we fought.

The colonists had taxed themselves freely, largely; had maintained their government, their schools, their colleges, their churches, at their own cost, without grants from the royal treasury;[2] had taxed themselves to equip a militia; and at their own charges had fought with and for England against Spain, France, and the Indians: but the attempt to tax them directly from England, thus over-riding the local legislatures, and ignoring the settled principle of taxation in the English Constitution, they resisted in the very spirit in which the English Commons had once and again stood out against the usurpations of the crown. They were not mercenary, nor niggard; the necessities of the primitive colonists had left the impress of frugality upon the habits of the people: but when, to cover the deficiencies of his budget, the British king sought to convert their thriftiness into a source of revenue to the crown, their notion of money and its uses showed itself in the saying, "Millions for defence, but not one cent for tribute." The king was encroaching upon the rights and liberties which their fathers had brought from England, and which they themselves had always enjoyed either by charter or by custom: he was subverting the people's prerogative of local government. At some point they must make a stand, and it might as well be at the stamp-tax or the tea-tax as at any other act of usurpation.

"Who steals my purse steals trash." Yes, but he is none the less a thief; and he who steals my purse would

---

[1] Works, vol. x. 282, 283.
[2] With the exception of Georgia, whose civil list was a small party-tax on Parliament.

"filch from me my good name," and might even take my life to steal my purse. This royal robber of rights, if unresisted, would soon have taken all; and the moral of the resistance is not dwarfed by its being made when he laid violent hands upon the purse. Man has a right in his own property, just as he has a right in his life, in his home, in his intelligence, in his conscience; and when either of these rights is arbitrarily seized, or stealthily encroached upon, he must strike for this, or he will lose the whole. And Schiller has taught us that "no one can surrender a hair's-breadth of his own rights, without at the same time betraying the soul of the whole State;" and "chains, whether of steel or silk, are chains."[1]

I grant, indeed, that one watchword of the Revolution — "No taxation without representation" — has a metallic sound, — a sound less noble than the demand of the people in Germany to be represented in the government, because every man may be called, at any time, to give his life for his fatherland. But the philosophical view that Mr. Burke took of the resistance of the colonists to the Stamp Act relieves them of the semblance of rating money above life in a contest for the right of the people to a parliament of their own. "Liberty," said Burke, "inheres in some sensible object; and every nation has formed to itself some favorite point, which, by way of eminence, becomes the criterion of its happiness. It happened that the great contests for freedom in this country were, from the earliest times, chiefly upon the question of taxing. Most of the contests in the ancient commonwealths turned primarily on the right of election of magistrates, or on the balance among the several orders of the State. The question of money was not with them so immediate. But in England it was otherwise. On this point of taxes the ablest pens and most eloquent tongues have been exercised; the greatest spirits have acted and suffered. . . . They took infinite pains to inculcate as a fundamental principle, that, in all monarchies, the people must, in effect, themselves mediately or immediately possess the power of granting their own money, or no shadow of liberty could subsist."[2]

[1] Die Verschwörung des Fiesco zu Genua, iv. 6 and iii. 5.
[2] Speech on Conciliation with America.

It was on this fundamental principle that John Hampden planted himself when he refused to pay the trifling sum in which he was assessed for "ship-money." To one of Hampden's station and fortune a rate of thirty-one shillings and sixpence was ridiculously small: but the rate had been levied by the king without the authority of Parliament, and was enforced by distraint of goods and persons; and so Hampden refused to pay his thirty-one shillings and sixpence, took his appeal to the law against the crown, roused the country to resistance to arbitrary taxation, and finally established the entire and undisputed control of Parliament over the supplies, which his biographer characterizes as " the stoutest buttress of the English Constitution." [1]

The mind of Luther had long been struggling toward the light: his heart, distracted with its own conflicts, had seized the promise, "The just shall live by faith." His visit to Rome had been a fearful shock to his ideal of the glory and sanctity of the Church in her capital; but so long as his experiences were purely subjective, and his meditations speculative, though he might be preparing to follow his beloved Augustine and Tauler as theologian and preacher, he had not felt the impulses of the popular reformer, nor thought of projecting the inner conflict of his soul into the outer sphere of conflict and revolt against the Church of Rome. It was the concrete, tangible fact of the open sale of indulgences, the traffic of the Church in sins and pardons, that roused Luther first to protest and remonstrance, and then to defiance and independence; and it was this attempt of the Italian hierarchy to extort from the Germans money for St. Peter's by hawking their souls that gave Luther power with the people against the Pope. His revival of the doctrine of "justification by faith" might have caused a controversy in the schools; but this mercenary greed of Rome roused a nation to assert its independence of the Papal power. Faith and freedom, stirring in thousands of hearts, and latent in thousands more, found an outlet in resistance to this "Stamp Act" of Leo X., by which that most precious of all things, the redemption of the soul, was to be had by buying a strip

---

[1] Memorials of John Hampden, by Lord Nugent.

of paper bearing a remission stamped with the pontiff's name. The act of George III. required that "all deeds and receipts and other legal documents should be written or printed on stamped paper, and that this paper should be sold by the tax-collectors;" and we have the authority of Erasmus, that "the remission of purgatorial torment was not only sold, but forced upon those who refused it."[1]

We are not, then, to judge a great movement simply by the watchwords of the hour: these catch the ear of the people, and rouse their passions for the conflict; they put in concrete form some vital fact or principle, commonly overstated in the heat of controversy or the intensified language of proverb. But, if the movement is really great and lasting, it will be found that back of it lie a history and a philosophy that reach to the profoundest sources of human action. Hence, as Ranke argues, it was not a fortuitous circumstance that the Reformation was, in the first instance, an attack upon the abuses practised in the matter of indulgences. The conversion into an outward traffic of that which was most essentially a concern of the inward man was of all things the most diametrically opposite to the conceptions drawn from the profoundest German theology. Hence nothing could be more shocking and repulsive than the system of indulgences to a man like Luther, with a deep and lively sense of religion, filled with the notions of sin and justification as they had been expressed in books of German theology before his time, and strengthened in these views by the Scriptures, which he had drunk in with a thirsty heart.[2] As the springs of the German Reformation lay deeper than resistance to the sale of indulgences, so the springs of the American Revolution lay deeper than resistance to arbitrary taxation; and as in Germany there were reformers before the Reformation, so in the American Colonies there were defenders of the right of popular government long before the battle of Lexington had made that a question to be decided at the cannon's mouth.

To find the original sources of the American Revolution,

---

[1] Præf. I., Epist. Corinth., opera vii. 851.
[2] Ranke's History of the Popes: Introduction, chap. ii.

we must go back to English customs, precedents, and institutions hoary with antiquity; must go back beyond the history of Saxons and Angles upon the soil of Britain: and those who are wont to sneer at the American Republic as a thing of accident, an experiment without a history, may be shamed, if not edified, by the teaching of history, that the tap-root of that self-government for which America revolted against Britain was in that primitive local government of the Teutonic race, which for long was lost in Germany through the usurpations of petty princes; which, however, had been transplanted to England, and there thrived under more favoring conditions, but which had well-nigh been lost in Britain also, had not the Colonies, with an offshoot of that principle invigorated by a virgin soil, startled Britain into the consciousness of her own decaying liberty by the vital force of theirs.

The colonists did not resist with violence a taxation which was to them illegal; they did not draw blood to save money: with a steady, united, but peaceable front, they opposed one extortion after another as an encroachment upon their right of local government. But, when a blow was struck at the foundation of that right, they took up arms, not against taxes, but against tyranny. On the first page of the American Revolution it is written, in lines of blood, that the *town-meeting* made the Revolution, — made it in self-defence, for its own right of existence.

Now, what was this "town-meeting," that dared go to war with a kingdom? — this little democracy of New-England yeomen, that on the 19th of April, 1775, drawn up on the village green of Lexington, faced twelve times their number of British regulars, and took and gave back their fire? It was the old Anglo-Saxon "town-*moot*," the open assembly of the freemen of the village or the borough, where questions of local government were mooted, — debated, and decided by vote. Here and there in England is still pointed out a "moot-hill," — the hill of meeting, — where such local assemblies, legislative and judicial, were held in the open air. And what was this Anglo-Saxon "town-moot" but that free assembly of the people for choosing their rulers, and making and executing their laws, which Tacitus describes as the political constitution of the Teutonic race? "The Germans," says Tacitus, "choose their kings on account of their nobility, their leaders on account of their valor. On smaller matters the chiefs debate, on greater matters all men, but so that those things whose final decision rests with the whole people are first handled by the chiefs. ... It is lawful also in the assembly to bring matters for trial, and to bring charges of capital crimes. ... In the same assembly, chiefs are chosen to administer justice through the districts and villages."[1] This principle of governing directly by the whole body of freemen in council assembled, the Teutonic constitution carried out to the farthest practicable subdivision of the body politic; viz., the *Landesgemeinde*. Concerning this seat of local sovereignty, a modern English publicist has observed, that, "in this earliest stage of Teutonic society, we find self-government in its most absolute and most uncompromising form. The Greek ideal of a perfectly free State, of every citizen of which it can be said that he governs and is governed, — $ἄρχειν καὶ ἄρχεσθαι$, — is realized. Society and the State are exactly conterminous with each other: neither overlaps the other. Social rights are exactly balanced by public duties, public duties by social rights. The franchise of the old Teutonic community is the amount of public work done on behalf of the community. In a political society of this kind, it is clear that there is no room for even a rudiment of representative government. Society itself does the work of the State, and does not delegate it to others."[2] Upon this political unit — "the true kernel," as Mr. Freeman calls it, "of all our political life" — was formed in the Teutonic constitution a representative system through a series of delegated assemblies; and the primitive political structure of England was formed in this manner, not by division from above downwards, but by union and growth from beneath upwards. In short, the fundamental conception of the State was society exercising its political functions, or local government, — that which Pres. Lincoln, in his home-bred philosophy, styled "the government of the people, by the people, and

---

[1] Tacitus de Moribus Germaniæ, c. 7-13. See also Freeman's Growth of the English Constitution, chap. i.
[2] R. B. D. Morier: Cobden-Club Essays, third series, p. 365.

for the people."[1] This was town-meeting government; for in the town-meeting every freeman had not only his vote, but his word; and to many a man to have his say, or, as my good mother used to phrase it, to give a piece of his mind, is a far higher privilege than to elect others to office, or even to be elected himself. The New-England town-meeting had retained intact and untarnished the three essential rights of the *Landesgemeinde* of our Teutonic ancestors, — to talk, to vote, and, when meddled with, to fight. But the great glory of the American colonists is, that, while they recovered to political society that primitive institution of local government — the village council — which was the common heritage of the Aryan race in its wide dispersion, they showed how, without sacrificing any of the essentials of liberty, this simple democracy of Nature, the source and the last refuge of true popular liberty, could be made to harmonize with, and even give stability to, that grand creation of modern civilization, — the nation with its oneness of interests and powers, its common consciousness, and its continuity of historical development. This was the rich and weighty contribution of the American Revolution to political science and the welfare of mankind.

The first tendency of civilization is in the direction of an apostasy from liberty. In every union for common ends, each individual must surrender somewhat of the personal to the good of the whole. Now, civilization calls for union, for the combination of interests through the concession of particulars. Civilization calls also for strength, in order to its own development and stability, and, it may be, strength for the protection of liberty itself. But there is danger always that this combination shall result in the absorption of the individual, this strength be perverted to the subverting of liberty. In Germany this process was insidious and gradual: first, the kingship grew from a personal superiority in honor to an official supremacy of power; next, the chief servants of the king grew to be great territorial lords, and, as princes, usurped to themselves local possession and rule; then followed hereditary estates, crystallizing society into castes. Cities

[1] Speech at Gettysburg, Nov. 19, 1863.

and leagues preserved the old principle of self-government and association; and the Hundred Court long survived as the unit of Teutonic freedom. The Thirty-Years' war swept away the ancient landmarks; and from that flood emerged the organized absolutism that stood for government, and the privileged classes that constituted the State. In England, happily, the transition from the old Anglo-Saxon forms, with their local political units, to the consolidated unity of the kingdom after the Norman conquest, was accomplished without the annihilation of local self-government; and this survived in charters and franchises held by boroughs, municipalities, and trade-guilds. Moreover, under the new order of things, by which government became concentrated in and around the throne, the principle of popular government emerged in the House of Commons, which asserted the right of originating all financial measures, and of voting all taxes and supplies.

These two principles, then, — that of distributive self-government, and that of taxation only with consent of the taxed, — were thoroughly English. As far back as the reign of Edward III., in the fourteenth century, the Commons scrupled to tax their constituents without their consent, and refused also to grant supplies without pledges and concessions from the king. The same course was pursued under Henry IV.; and the Commons also appointed treasurers of their own to see that the supplies voted to the king were used in a proper and lawful way. More than once, the Commons made a stand against the arbitrary demands of Henry VIII. with regard to supplies to the crown. The greatly increased revenue of the crown under Elizabeth was due to the free grants of the Commons; and, when Charles I. attempted to revive the levying of new customs and imposts by royal prerogative, the Commons made that memorable stand for the control of the public purse by the people, through their representatives, that cost the wilful king, first his crown, and afterwards his head. This principle, then settled in England by statute forever, — that the branch of government that most directly represents the people shall regulate the taxes, and vote the supplies, — is now incorporated with every constitutional government; and thus English liberty has become a precedent and standard for the civilized world. But parliaments are not always mindful of the principles and precedents from which their own rights and powers have sprung; and a century ago it happened in England that a capricious and wilful king found a ministry and parliament pliant enough to use the right of taxing, which parliament had wrested from the crown, in the unconstitutional way of taxing the American Colonies without their consent, — thus dealing a blow at the right of local government, upon which rested the rights of the people as represented in the House of Commons itself; and *that* was the blow that roused the colonists to the danger of losing all their rights as Englishmen by acquiescing in a tax levied without consulting the legislative bodies chosen by themselves.

During the long period of remonstrance that preceded the appeal of the colonists to arms, FRANKLIN, whose sagacity as a statesman equalled his wisdom as a philosopher, was in England, watching for the interests of the Colonies against the usurpations of the Crown and the Parliament. In a letter to Lord Kames, dated London, April 11, 1767, Franklin says, "All the Colonies acknowledge the king as their sovereign. His governors there represent his person; laws are made by their assemblies, or little parliaments, with the governor's assent, subject still to the king's pleasure to affirm or annul them. Suits arising in the Colonies, and between Colony and Colony, are determined by the king in council. In this view they seem so many separate little States, subject to the same prince. The sovereignty of the king is, therefore, easily understood. But nothing is more common here than to talk of the *sovereignty* of PARLIAMENT, and the sovereignty of this nation over the Colonies, — a kind of sovereignty, the idea of which is not so clear; nor does it clearly appear on what foundation it is established."[1] And in a letter to a person unknown, dated London, Jan. 6, 1766, Franklin protested against taxing the Colonies without their consent, by asking, "If the Parliament has a right thus to take from us a penny in the pound, where is

[1] Bigelow's Life of Franklin, vol. i. p. 518.

the line drawn that bounds that right? and what shall hinder their calling, whenever they please, for the other nineteen shillings and elevenpence? Have we, then, any thing that we can call our own?"[1]

That question went to the root of the whole matter in controversy. The colonists had held their own lands, made their own laws, elected their own magistrates, laid their own taxes, levied their own militia; but, should they acquiesce in these new usurpations of King and Parliament, how long should they have any thing that they could call their own? — how long, indeed, could they call themselves their own? In their original settlement, and forms of government, some of the Colonies had been more their own than were others. As I have already pointed out, some had charters which guaranteed to them the right of framing their own laws; some had proprietors, who held from the king the title to the land, and the right of governing; and others, again, were royal provinces, with a governor and council appointed by the king. It had long been a favorite scheme in England to assimilate all the Colonies to the "royal" type. But, from the very necessity of their position, the colonists were left to care for themselves, and hence were accustomed to act for themselves; and, long before the Revolution, the spirit of self-government had asserted itself in all the Colonies, through legislative assemblies chosen by the people, though the forms of local government were most fully developed in the chartered Colonies of New England. There, within a quarter of a century after the settlement of Plymouth, in a population of about twenty-five thousand, were already upwards of fifty distinct town-organizations, each of which, after the manner of the Saxon town-moot and the Teutonic *Gemeinde*, managed its own affairs by votes of the whole body of citizens in town-meeting. "By force of this institution," — as it exists to this day, — "every man in New England belongs to a small community of neighbors, known to the law as a corporation, with rights and liabilities as such, capable of suing, and subject to be sued, in the courts of justice, in disputes with any parties, individual or corporate. Once a year the corporation chooses

[1] Bigelow's Life of Franklin, vol. i. p. 455.

the administrators of its affairs, and determines the amount of money with which it will intrust them, and how this shall be raised. . . . It belongs to the towns to protect the public health and order by means of a police; to maintain safe and convenient communication about and through their precinct by roads and bridges; to furnish food, clothing, and shelter to their poor; to provide for the education of all their children at their common charge;" in a word, "towns severally are empowered to take care of those interests of theirs which they respectively can best understand, and can most efficiently and most economically provide for." [1]

These little democracies were not only the nurseries of liberty, but training-schools for the citizen in the art of government; and they gave to New England her peculiar strength and fitness for beginning that struggle with arbitrary power which led to the war of independence. Other Colonies that lacked this feature in their original constitution were trained to self-government by the hardy manhood and self-reliance that came of battling with the wilderness and the Indians, and by the necessity of guarding their frontier, and of providing for needs that were neglected or postponed by a government three thousand miles away. Hence the oligarchy which at first existed in some of the Colonies more directly dependent upon the crown was compelled to yield to the demand for a legislative assembly chosen by the people, and directly cognizant of their wants; while the plan for an order of nobility — earls and barons — in the Carolinas never got beyond the paper on which John Locke draughted it for King Charles II. It was too late in history to set up an aristocracy in fever-swamps and log-huts. The men who cleared and tilled the soil must and would own it, and, having something they could call their own, would govern it as well. Even the existence of negro slavery stimulated this demand for colonial freedom, since, by a perversity of human nature, men will often rate their own political liberty above the personal liberty of their fellows. Mr. Burke pointed out this anomaly, that " where slaves are held in any part of the world, those who are free are by far the most proud

[1] Palfrey's History of New England, book ii. chap. 1.

and jealous of their freedom. Freedom is to them not only an enjoyment, but a kind of rank and privilege. . . . In such a case the haughtiness of domination combines with the spirit of freedom, fortifies it, and renders it invincible." And this sagacious observer recognized the fact, and sought to have Parliament recognize it also, that, by one cause and another, it had come to pass, that, " in all the Colonies, the governments were popular in a high degree; some merely popular; in all, the popular representative the most weighty; and this share of the people in their ordinary government never fails to inspire them with lofty sentiments, and with a strong aversion from whatever tends to deprive them of their chief importance."[1]

To these political and social causes which developed in the colonists, and one might almost say necessitated, the habit of self-government, must be added religion, as demanding freedom of conscience, independence of thought, and the recognition of Christian manhood as higher than all forms of society, and orders of government. It is the fashion of liberals in Europe to look upon the Church, and especially the clergy, as antagonistic to political freedom, and an obstacle to the development of modern society in culture; and it is the fashion of conservatives in Europe to look upon popular freedom as hostile to religion, and destructive of the Church as a main bulwark of society. The experience of France before and after her revolution gave color to both these views. But the experience of the United States has been, that freedom had in religion a safe and sure ally; and religion found her security and strength in freedom. In the movements in the Colonies that prepared the way for the Revolution, the religious spirit was a vital and earnest element. Some of the Colonies were the direct offspring of religious persecution in the old country, or of the desire for a larger freedom of faith and worship; and so jealous were they of any interference with the rights of conscience, that their religion was fitly described as "a refinement on the principle of resistance, the dissidence of dissent, and the Protestantism of the Protestant religion."[2] And the Colo-

[1] Speech on Conciliation with America.
[2] Burke: Speech on Conciliation.

nies that were founded in the spirit of commercial adventure, or for extending the realm of Great Britain, became also an asylum for religious refugees from all nations, and, by the prospect of a larger and freer religious life, attracted to themselves the men of different races and beliefs who had learned to do and to suffer for their faith. There were the Hollanders of New Amsterdam (now New York), of that sturdy race that shook off the accursed yoke of Spain, — a people whose boast it was "that common laborers, even the fishermen who dwelt in the huts of Friesland, could read and write, and discuss the interpretation of Scripture;"[1] there were the Germans of Pennsylvania, who brought with them the recent memories of the Thirty-Years' war for the freedom of the faith; there were the Swedes of Delaware, with the proud memory of their great Gustavus, who had saved Protestantism to Germany, and consecrated the Reformation with his blood; there were the Huguenots of New York and the Carolinas, who brought from France the life-blood of its industry and thrift, of its honor and its faith; and even the Catholic settlers of Maryland, by the sagacity of their leader in procuring a chartered freedom for their own faith, had guaranteed an impartial protection to other forms and faiths than theirs. Not only in New England itself, but in the Presbyterian and Reformed systems south of New England, the Calvinistic type of theology largely predominated; and, say what men will of the harshness of Calvinism in some aspects, the almost arbitrary despotism that it imputes to God in his decrees inspires a resolute, almost defiant, freedom in those who deem themselves the subjects of his electing grace: in all things they are "more than conquerors," through the confidence that nothing shall be able to separate them from the love of God. No doctrine of the dignity of human nature, of the rights of man, of natural liberty, of social equality, can create such a resolve for the freedom of the soul as this personal conviction of God's favoring and protecting sovereignty. He who has this faith feels that he is compassed about with everlasting love, girded about with everlasting strength; his will is the tempered steel that no fire can melt, no force can

---

[1] Fisher: History of the Reformation, p. 286.

break. Such faith is freedom; and this spiritual freedom is the source and strength of all other freedom.

Thus it came to pass that the religious wars and persecutions of Europe in the sixteenth and seventeenth centuries were a training-school for the political independence of the United States of America in the eighteenth century. Diverse and seemingly incongruous as were the nationalities represented in the Colonies, — Dutch, French, German, Swedish, Scotch, Irish, English, — they had all imbibed, either by experience or by inheritance, something of the spirit of personal independence, and especially of religious liberty. Gustavus Adolphus designed his colony of Swedes for the benefit of "all oppressed Christendom." Penn the Quaker established Pennsylvania as "a free colony for all mankind," where the settlers "should be governed by laws of their own making." The first charter of the Jerseys — which were largely peopled by Quakers, and Scotch and Irish Presbyterians — declared that "no person shall at any time, in any way, or on any pretence, be called in question, or in the least punished or hurt, for opinion in religion." And Oglethorpe's Colony of Georgia was founded to be a refuge for "the distressed people of Britain, and the persecuted Protestants of Europe:" there the German Moravian settled side by side with the French Huguenot and the Scotch Presbyterian, under the motto, "We toil not for ourselves, but for others."

So in all the Colonies the diverse elements of race, of education, of belief, were fused in the broader elements of religious liberty, and regard for man, even as the diverse modes of political organization, begun in diverse modes and motives of colonial settlement, were fused in the broader spirit of popular representation and local government. In a word, the elements of fusion in the Colonies were more powerful, if less numerous, than the elements of rivalry and discord. But the crystallizing centre around which those elements should gather and cohere was the political organization of New England, the unit of which was the town-meeting, in which society was the state, and right was law.

That organization had its perfect type in the Colony of the Pilgrims at Plymouth, which anticipated by more than a hundred and fifty years the American doctrine of government by the people, through equal laws made by themselves, and officers chosen by themselves, under a *written* covenant or constitution as the supreme and final authority. In that little band on "The Mayflower" were developed the principles of liberty, — spiritual, political, ecclesiastical, — with a breadth of base, a harmony of proportion, a union of justice, order, and authority, with freedom, that no political philosophy has yet transcended, and no political society attained. That covenant which they framed and signed on board the vessel as she lay at anchor at Cape Cod, in which, "for the more orderly carrying-on of their affairs, by mutual consent they entered into a solemn combination, as a body politic, to submit to such government and governors, laws and ordinances, as should by a general consent from time to time be made choice of and assented unto," — that simple covenant of twenty lines, which has served as the model of a free constitutional government, has sometimes been ascribed to the accident of the ship being carried so far to the northward of her intended port, that the patent of settlement under which the voyagers sailed was made void and useless, and they were obliged to take measures to govern and protect themselves. But how came the forty-one men who signed that covenant by a political wisdom so far above that to be found in any average company of colonists or emigrants? How came they, in an unexpected emergency, to frame a civil government so as to combine justice with equality, popular legislation with magisterial authority, personal freedom with the general good of the Colony? They had acquired this wisdom through their experience of self-government in the Church, and from the teaching and training of their pastor. He had taught them spiritual freedom, — that *Freiheit des Geistes* that Germany won by her Thirty-Years' war, yet has to contend for anew in this generation. Winslow, the third governor of the Plymouth Colony, has left on record the parting words of their pastor to the Pilgrims as they set sail from Leyden. "He charged us before God to follow him no farther than he followed Christ; and, if God should reveal any thing to us by any other instrument of his, to be ready to receive it as ever we were to receive any truth by his ministry; for he was very confident the Lord had more truth and light yet to break forth out of his holy word. He took occasion also miserably to bewail the state of the reformed churches, who were come to a period in religion, and would go no farther than the instruments of their reformation. The Lutherans could not go beyond what Luther saw; for, whatever part of God's word he had further revealed to Calvin, they had rather die than embrace it; and so, you see, the Calvinists they stick where he left them. A misery much to be lamented: for though they were precious shining lights in their times, yet God had not revealed his whole will to them; and, were they now alive, they would be as ready to receive further light as that they had received. . . . For it is not possible the Christian world should come so lately out of such anti-Christian darkness, and that full perfection of knowledge should break forth at once."[1]

In these wise, liberal, and noble counsels, spiritual freedom and progress are based upon the broad and enduring principle of allegiance to truth, the duty of the soul to seek for light, to accept light from whatever source, and to obey and follow truth above and beyond all teachers and authorities whatsoever. There is no basis of personal independence so deep and firm as this. Men so trained could never submit to tyranny in Church or in State.

A like lesson in ecclesiastical freedom the Pilgrims had learned from their pastor, who taught that "any competent number of believers in Christ have a right to embody into a church for their mutual edification;" that, "being embodied, they have a right to choose all their officers;" that "no churches or church-officers whatever have any power over any other church or officers, to control or impose upon them, but are all equal in their rights and privileges, and ought to be independent in the exercise and enjoyment of them." . . . "The Papists," said he, "place the ruling power in the pope; the Episcopalians, in the bishop; the Puritan, in the presbytery: we put it in the body of the congregation, the multitude, called the church." But, while he insisted thus strenuously upon the completeness and the independence of the

[1] New England's Memorial, p. 407.

local church, he held also the communion of the churches in counsel and brotherhood, and the unity of all believers in the one body of Christ, the only true, spiritual, holy, universal church.

In such teachings and practice was laid the foundation for local government in matters of immediate and personal concern, and also for co-operation and sympathetic unity in things of the higher general welfare. Men who had been accustomed to choose their own spiritual teachers and guides, to administer the affairs of the church by their direct votes or by officers of their choice, were prepared to take the direction of civil government also, when this was thrust upon them by the necessity of their position. And their wise, far-sighted pastor had provided them for this also. He who had trained them in spiritual independence and ecclesiastical freedom gave them counsel how to combine the exercise of popular sovereignty with that dignity, order, and authority which are the true divine right in the State. In his farewell letter he said, "Whereas you are to become a body politic, using amongst yourselves civil government, and are not furnished with persons of special eminency above the rest to be chosen by you into office of government, let your wisdom and godliness appear not only in choosing such persons as do entirely love and will promote the common good, but also in yielding unto them all due honor and obedience in their lawful administrations; not beholding in them the ordinariness of their persons, but God's ordinance for your good; not being like the foolish multitude, who more honor the gay coat than either the virtuous mind of the man, or the glorious ordinance of God. But you know better things, and that the image of the Lord's power and authority which the magistrate beareth is honorable, in how mean persons soever; and this duty you may the more willingly, and ought the more conscionably, to perform, because you are to have them for your ordinary governors which yourselves shall make choice of for that work."[1]

A government ordered with such wisdom and goodness would more than realize the Republic of Plato. The

---

[1] New England's Memorial, p. 18.

pastor of the Pilgrim Church was also the founder of the Pilgrim Commonwealth, though he remained in Holland, and died an exile from England, and a stranger to America. The birthplace of that freedom, civil and religious, which at length incorporated itself in the United States, was not Lexington, nor Philadelphia, nor Yorktown, but Leyden; and the father of American liberty was not Adams, nor Franklin, nor Henry, nor Jefferson, nor Warren, nor Washington, but *John Robinson*, who found in his New Testament the warrant for freedom of conscience, freedom of the church, and freedom of the commonwealth.

What manner of men such a discipline produced is read in the history of New England for generations. Hume sneers at the Puritan emigrants to New England as men "who had resolved forever to abandon their native country, and fly to the other extremity of the globe, where they might enjoy lectures and discourses of any length or form which pleased them;" yet in the same breath he gives the honest praise, that "they laid the foundations of a government which possessed all the liberty, both civil and religious, of which they found themselves bereaved in their native country."[1]

Now, it was this very determination to hear sermons in the form that pleased them, and to endure sermons of any length, provided they were full of sound doctrine, and strong, clear reasoning, that showed and stamped the intellectual and moral character of the early New-England commonwealths. To the first settlers, sermons were spiritual gymnastics. They had few books, and fewer newspapers; and the sabbath service supplied the social and intellectual excitement of the week. I doubt if the world had ever seen, or can now produce, just such a yeomanry as the yeomanry of New England down to the days of the Revolution, — so thoughtful, so earnest, so devout, so disciplined in manly thinking and heroic faith by the pulpit, at once the freest and the strongest power of that simple age. What that pulpit was we know from the sermons of Cotton, Shepard, Prince, Wise, Davenport, Edwards, Hopkins, Bellamy, and their peers, — preachers

---

[1] Hume: History of Great Britain, chap. lii.

who dealt with their hearers as Christians "of full age," who required the "strong meat" of Christian doctrine.[1] Many of these preachers were pastors of country parishes, their hearers the farmers of the district, the mechanics and small tradespeople of the village, with here and there a man of books and culture; and when we read their long argumentative discourses, with such lofty spiritual doctrine, such keen, strong logic, such nice metaphysical distinctions refined to the twentieth subdivision, such earnest, fervid appeals to conscience, to reason, and to Scripture, and remember that these sermons were preached to men who lived by the sweat of their brow, that the sermon was looked forward to on Sunday, was talked over in the family on Sunday evening, and with the neighbors through the week, we see what stuff the yeomanry of New England were made of, and to what manhood they were trained. There were drawbacks, to be sure, in every such community; tares were mingled with the wheat; there was a decline from the primitive vigor in morals as well as in faith: yet the training that the yeomanry of New England had mainly through her pulpit was a moral force that the historian must know and measure, if he would comprehend the spirit of American liberty, and the motives and forces of the American Revolution.[2]

Take an instance later down, while the old spirit of New England still lingered in the country towns of Massachusetts, after the war of the Revolution had so unsettled the condition of society. Read the sermons of Nathanael Emmons, — like a demonstration of Euclid for clearness of argument and closeness of reasoning, like an essay of Addison for polish of style, — and consider that such sermons were preached for fifty years to a plain country parish, and that Emmons lived among them till past ninety years, revered like an Oriental patriarch, obeyed almost like an Oriental sheik, and you will see

[1] Heb. v. 14.
[2] It is through lack of experimental acquaintance with the type of piety that marked the early Puritans and Presbyterians of America, and also through lack of any recent experience in Germany of the pulpit as a stimulating and renovating force in society, that so many German writers on America, even the most candid and capable among them, have altogether failed to comprehend and describe American life and society. They have missed its most vital element, because there was nothing answering to it in their own consciousness.

where lay the power of independent thought and action in New England.[1] I remember, in my boyhood, two venerable farmers of Connecticut, — the one over sixty, the other over ninety, — who used to stand in their shirt-sleeves in the sultry field, and talk of God's sovereignty and man's freedom, and things invisible and eternal, and quote Paul and Augustine, Calvin and Milton, in a way that could put a young theologue to the blush. Men who could discuss such themes with the scythe or the sickle in hand could take up the sword and the musket as sons of liberty, because sons of God.

I do not exaggerate this influence of the pulpit of New England upon her liberties. Boston was the focus of resistance to the usurpations of the crown. The General Court of Massachusetts originated the measures that resulted in the union of the Colonies: perhaps the most important of these was that of "Committees of Correspondence," who should keep each Colony advised of what was passing in all the others, and should concert plans of action for the friends of freedom. Now, it was a congregational minister who proposed this idea to a leading patriot, and he got it from his experience in church affairs. In 1766, Dr. Jonathan Mayhew, pastor of the West Church in Boston, wrote to James Otis these wise and weighty words. Dating his letter "Lord's Day morning, June 8," he says, "To a good man all time is holy enough; and none is too holy to do good, or to think upon it. Cultivating a good understanding and hearty friendship between these Colonies appears to me so necessary a part of prudence and good policy, that no favorable opportunity for that purpose should be omitted." He then advises that

[1] Rev. Dr. N. W. Taylor told me that Dr. Emmons once preached in his pulpit when he was pastor of the Centre Church, New Haven. After service Dr. Taylor remarked, "The people listened very attentively." Dr. Emmons answered dryly, "People will always listen when you give them something worth listening to." This was not always the case, however, even with his own congregation at Franklin; for, as the story goes, one hot summer's day, the farmers, wearied with a week of haying, grew drowsy under Dr Emmons's close argumentation: whereupon he came to a sudden pause, which, of course, woke them up; when he said, "I see that this sermon cannot keep you awake: I have another in my pocket that I will give you instead." He then deliberately preached the second sermon, and kept them awake. And a pastor could venture to say and do such things who was elected and supported by the people, because he always *did* give them "something worth listening to," and they were trained to hear and value it.

the General Court should issue circulars to the legislative assemblies of the other Colonies upon the repeal of the Stamp Act, and other matters, " expressing a desire to cement and perpetuate union among the Colonies, as perhaps the only means of perpetuating their liberties." He then adds, " You have heard of the *communion of churches :* . . . while I was thinking of this in my bed, the great use and importance of a *communion of colonies* appeared to me in a strong light, which led me immediately to set down these hints to transmit to you." This conception of some formal and active union of the Colonies was afterwards carried out by such Committees of Correspondence proposed by Massachusetts.

This same Dr. Mayhew had made himself famous by his clear and bold enunciation of the doctrine of Paul concerning obedience to the civil power, as laid down in the thirteenth chapter of the Epistle to the Romans. In a discourse that was widely published, Mayhew argued that Paul does not teach implicit and absolute submission to rulers as such, but grounds the duty of obedience upon the end for which rulers are instituted, — the good of society. Hence " the apostle's argument is so far from proving it to be the duty of people to obey and submit to such rulers as act in contradiction to the public good, and so to the design of their office, that it proves the direct contrary. For if the end of all civil government be the good of society, if this be the thing that is aimed at in constituting civil rulers, and if the motive and argument for submission to government be taken from the apparent usefulness of civil authority, it follows, that, when no such good end can be answered by submission, there remains no argument or motive to enforce it; and if, instead of this good end's being brought about by submission, a contrary end is brought about, and the ruin and misery of society effected by it, here is a plain and positive reason against submission in all such cases, should they ever happen. And therefore, in such cases, a regard to the public welfare ought to make us withhold from our rulers that obedience and submission which it would otherwise be our duty to render to them." [1] Here was no appeal to popular

[1] Discourse concerning Unlimited Submission, &c., January, 1750.

passion, no declamation about the right of revolution, but a sober, argumentative statement of the true relation between rulers and subjects. This sermon of Mayhew anticipated by sixteen years the doctrines of the Declaration of Independence; and we cannot wonder that men trained in such political ethics were ripe for revolutionary measures, as their last resort against tyranny. We know also that books of law were in great demand in America, and that the works of Locke, Algernon Sidney, Milton, and like expounders of the rights of man, were in the hands of the yeomanry of New England, as well as of publicists in all the Colonies.[1] It was such a people, with such preaching and such reading, that George III. attempted to deprive of their local government.

The assault was foreshadowed by the proposal of the Board of Trade to raise revenue out of the American Colonies by direct authority of the king, and by restrictions on American trade and manufactures, intended to keep the Colonies in a state of dependence upon Britain. Franklin narrates, that, in 1757, Lord Grenville, then president of the council, said to him, "You Americans have wrong ideas of the nature of your constitution: you contend that the king's instructions to his governors are not laws, and think yourselves at liberty to regard or disregard them at your own discretion. . . . But such instructions, so far as they relate to you, are the law of the land; for the king is the legislator of the Colonies."[2] The House of Commons, still mindful of their own struggles with the royal prerogative, were unwilling to sanction this step toward absolutism; but, says Franklin, "by their conduct towards us in 1765, it seemed that they had refused that point of sovereignty to the king, only that they might reserve it for themselves."[3] And the attempt of Parliament

---

[1] Burke said of America, "In no country, perhaps, in the world, is the law so general a study. The profession itself is numerous and powerful; and in most provinces it takes the lead. The greater number of deputies sent to the Congress were lawyers. But all who read (and most do read) endeavor to obtain some smattering in that science. I have been told by an eminent bookseller, that in no branch of his business, after tracts of popular devotion, were so many books as those on the law exported to the plantations. The colonists have now fallen into the way of printing them for their own use. I hear that they have sold nearly as many of Blackstone's Commentaries in America as in England." — *Speech on Conciliation with America.*

[2] Bigelow's Life of Franklin, i. 366.   [3] Ibid., 368.

to over-ride the colonial legislatures by direct taxation roused the selfsame spirit of resistance that the Commons had put forth against like usurpations of the crown. To make laws for the Colonies, and to levy taxes upon them, without either consulting their own legislatures, or giving to the Colonies a proportionate representation in the national Parliament, was a violation of their charters, an innovation upon their long-conceded privilege of "being governed by laws of their own making," and, above all, an invasion of their fundamental rights as Englishmen, which must lead to their being degraded from English subjects to mere dependants, and finally to political serfs. Energetic remonstrances against this usurpation were put forth either by the colonial legislatures, or by their agents in London: and such was the vigilance of the Colonies, that, for a period of twelve years from 1749, they succeeded in baffling any overt attempt upon their liberties; till in 1761 the acts of trade were enforced by the Court of Admiralty in a way so arbitrary and insulting, that Boston, then the chief port, was roused to resistance, and James Otis made his memorable declaration, that "an act of Parliament against the Constitution is void."[1] At the

---

[1] The Board of Trade figures so largely in the history of this period, that its constitution and powers are deserving of special mention. Burke does not hesitate to characterize it as a political "job, a sort of gently-ripening hot-house, where eight members of Parliament receive salaries of a thousand a year, for a certain given time, in order to mature at a proper season a claim to two thousand" (*Speech on the Economical Reform*). This Board was a device of Charles II., formed by combining in one the Council for Trade and the Council for Plantations. In this form it survived but three or four years (1669-73); but in 1695 King William revived the Board of Trade with amplified powers, to checkmate a move in Parliament for bringing trade and the plantations under the more immediate control of that body. Though the Board was only an advisory council, it originated much of the mischief that was brought upon the Colonies. As Palfrey well remarks (vol. iv. 21), its very name "expressed what was intended to be the spirit of colonial administration. The Colonies were to be made auxiliary to English trade. The Englishman in America was to be employed in making the fortune of the Englishman at home." In 1721 the Board of Trade recommended to the king a scheme for bringing the Colonies "under his Majesty's immediate government;" that they should all be put "under the government of one lord-lieutenant or captain-general, from whom other governors of particular provinces should receive their orders in all cases for the king's service. By this means a general contribution of men or money may be raised upon the several Colonies in proportion to their respective abilities." This scheme for over-riding the charters and legislatures of the Colonies was not then openly attempted; but the spirit of such usurpation was carried out in many ways. Thus in 1733, against the remonstrance of some of the Colonies, duties were levied for the king upon all sugar, rum, molasses, spirits, &c., imported into the

same time, the judges in the Colonies were made dependent upon the good pleasure of the king; that is, were made tools of the crown. Still the people held their ground.

At length there arose a more determined and sagacious enemy of popular freedom than those the Colonies had hitherto baffled, — a minister who combined subtilty of invention with comprehensiveness of purpose, and energy of will, — Charles Townshend, first lord of trade, who scrupled at nothing, that he might abrogate the rights and privileges of the colonial assemblies, and make the authority of Parliament direct and absolute. Charters, laws, precedents, pledges, were to be set aside, and taxes imposed by Parliament, to be enforced, if need be, by a standing army. It was early in 1763 that Townshend broached his audacious scheme; but not till two years later did the ministry and Parliament have the courage, rather the infatuation, to put it into effect, by the act requiring all business and legal documents to be written or printed upon stamped paper, to be had only of the tax-collectors. For five and twenty years this particular measure had been hovering in the air, — now suggested by some colonial governor as a quietus to the troublesome scrutiny of the legislature in voting supplies; now proposed by a lord of trade or of the treasury as a direct and easy way of raising revenue; again urged by the merchants of London, with a view to lessening the taxes of the empire; but at every point watched and warded off by the colonists, until at last it was attempted to be forced upon them as a means of subjugation, a test-measure of prerogative in taxation, or, at least, of *priority* in levying a tax. It came upon them, therefore, with all the aggrava-

Colonies. On Feb. 16, 1749, a bill was laid before Parliament "to regulate and restrain paper bills of credit in the British Colonies and Plantations:" but Hansard reports (vol. xvi. p. 563), " As it contained a clause for subjecting our Colonies and Plantations to such orders and instructions as should from time to time be transmitted to them from the crown, it raised a general opposition from our Colonies and Plantations upon the continent of America;" and the bill was finally dropped. The series of measures that culminated in the Stamp Act of March 6, 1765, proceeded in the line of subjecting the Colonies to the *direct* control of the crown, and of a parliament subservient to the crown; and the resistance of the Colonies was simply a defence of rights established by charter or by usage against such usurpation. The English voter of to-day has reason to thank them for a stand that arrested royal dictation in England.

tion of an evil so long dreaded as to be an object of hate; and it came as the symbol of usurpation and tyranny. The Stamp Act said, in effect, "that the Americans shall have no commerce, make no exchange of property with each other, neither purchase, nor grant, nor recover debts; they shall neither marry, nor make their wills, unless they pay such and such sums in *specie* for the stamps which must give validity to the proceedings."[1] Now, the American people of this generation have freely imposed upon themselves just such taxes to meet the enormous costs of war. But in 1765 they were not asked nor suffered to lay stamp duties on themselves, but at every step of life, from the cradle to the grave, were made to feel this annoying interference of a government in which they had no voice. The Stamp Act, like the late attempt to tax matches in England, set every house on fire. That it roused the mob to violent resistance is not to be wondered at; yet sober friends of liberty deplored, and sought to check, excesses that might prejudice their cause. But these sober people resisted the Stamp Act: first, by agreeing to trust to personal honor in matters of trade and law, so as to dispense with the stamped documents; by agreeing, as a measure of retaliation, to import no British goods for use or wear; by banding together in remonstrances to Parliament and for the defence of colonial rights; and, finally, by making stamp duties so odious, that no one could be found willing to take the office of collector. A stamp-officer was meaner than the publican in Judæa. With a guard at his beck, he slunk from public opinion. Through this unarmed resistance, the Stamp Act was repealed within a year after it was passed. That repeal was largely due to the personal influence of Franklin, who lived constantly in London as agent of the Pennsylvania Colony, and by correspondence and conversation with public men, and contributions to the press, labored to induce Parliament to retrace a step, that, if persisted in, must lead to open hostilities. At last Franklin was summoned before the House of Commons, in committee of the whole, to be examined touching the feelings and wishes of the Colonies. The examination lasted ten days: it was

[1] Bigelow's Life of Franklin, i. 671.

deep and thorough, sometimes keen and hostile: but the wisdom, tact, knowledge, candor, boldness, of the plain philosopher, conquered the prejudices and the pride of Parliament; and the journal of the Commons records, " Feb. 13, 1766, Benjamin Franklin, having passed through his examination, was excepted from further attendance;" and, " Feb. 24, the committee reported that it was their opinion that the House be moved that leave be given to bring in a bill to repeal the Stamp Act;" and, on the 18th of March, the king signed the repeal. Well did the countrymen of Franklin, in striking a medal in his honor, coupling his political triumphs with his triumphs over nature, surround his head with the legend: —

" Eripuit cœlo fulmen, sceptrumque tyrannis," — " He drew the lightning from heaven, and wrested the sceptre from tyrants."

As a specimen of the shrewdness of Franklin, take his last two answers to the House of Commons.

Question. — What used to be the pride of the Americans?

Answer. — To indulge in the fashions and manufactures of Great Britain.

Q. — What is now their pride?

Ans. — To wear their old clothes over again till they can make new ones.

Those were answers that every manufacturer and tradesman in England could understand. Other answers display no less boldness than shrewdness.

Q. — If the Stamp Act is not repealed, what do you think will be the consequences?

Ans. — A total loss of the respect and affection the people of America bear to this country, and of all the commerce that depends on that respect and affection.

Q. — If the Stamp Act should be repealed, would it induce the assemblies of America to acknowledge the right of Parliament to tax them?

Ans. — No, never! . . . No power, how great soever, can force men to change their opinions.

But the great value of Franklin's testimony is, that it caused to be spread upon the journal of the House of Commons a statement of the attitude of the Colonies toward the mother-country, that could not then be contradicted; and that is the standing vindication of the Colonies in afterwards taking up arms in their defence. It had been urged that the stamp tax was a just method of recovering from the Colonies what Britain had spent on their account in wars with the French and Indians. This is the statement which has been revived by "The Westminster Review;" and, though I have answered it conclusively from the parliamentary journals of the time, I would now emphasize the fact, that it was refuted by Franklin before the House of Commons, and the refutation put on record at the time.

Q. — Do you think it right that America should be protected by this country, and pay no part of the expense?

Ans. — That is not the case. The Colonies raised, clothed, and paid, during the last war, near twenty-five thousand men, and spent many millions.

Q. — Were you not reimbursed by Parliament?

Ans. — We were only reimbursed what, in your opinion, we had advanced beyond our proportion, or beyond what might reasonably be expected from us; and it was a very small part of what we spent. Pennsylvania, in particular, disbursed about five hundred thousand pounds; and the reimbursements, in the whole, did not exceed sixty thousand pounds.

Concerning the French and Indian war, Franklin testified, "I know the last war is commonly spoken of here as entered into for the defence, or for the sake, of the people in America. I think it is quite misunderstood. It began about the limits between Canada and Nova Scotia; about territories to which the *crown* indeed laid claim, but which were not claimed by any British *colony*. None of the lands had been granted to any colonist: we had, therefore, no particular concern or interest in that dispute. . . . The Indian trade is a British interest; it is carried on with British manufactures, for the profit of British merchants and manufacturers: therefore the war, as it commenced for the defence of territories of the crown (the property of no American) and for the defence of a trade purely British, was really a British war; and yet the people of America made no scruple of contributing their utmost towards carrying it on, and bringing it to a happy conclusion."

Again he said, "America has been greatly misrepresented and abused here, in papers and pamphlets and speeches, as ungrateful and unreasonable and unjust, in having put this nation to an immense expense for their defence, and refusing to bear any part of that expense. The Colonies raised, paid, and clothed near twenty-five thousand men during the last war, — a number equal to those sent from Britain, and far beyond their proportion: they went deeply into debt in doing this; and all their estates and taxes are mortgaged for many years to come for discharging that debt."

Franklin reminded the House, that, in response to messages from the king, they had annually voted during the war two hundred thousand pounds for compensation to the Colonies.[1] "This is the strongest of all proofs that the Colonies, far from being unwilling to bear a share of the burden, did exceed their proportion; for if they had done less, or had only equalled their proportion, there would have been no room or reason for compensation."[2]

There was no disputing these facts at the time. Here was the open testimony of King and Commons that the Colonies were loyal, brave, generous; were even forward to tax themselves for the defence of the crown: yet King and Commons would now extort money from them by a stamp duty griping every man's purse. The Colonies had never been a farthing's expense to the government of Britain,[3] and, until their liberties were threatened, had never caused anxiety or trouble. As Franklin testified, "They submitted willingly to the government of the crown, and paid in their courts obedience to the acts of Parliament. Numerous as the people are in the several old provinces, they cost you nothing in forts, citadels, garrisons, or armies, to keep them in subjection. They were governed by this country at the expense only of a little pen,

---

[1] This was barely two-fifths of their actual outlay.
[2] Hansard gives Franklin's examination nearly in full; and, in his report of the debate on the repeal of the Stamp Act, says, "The Colonies being repaid part of their debt is convincing proof that Parliament were of opinion they had contributed beyond their abilities" (xvi. 205).
[3] With the single exception of Georgia.

ink, and paper: they were led by a thread. They had not only a respect, but an affection, for Great Britain, — for its laws, its customs and manners, — and even a fondness for its fashions, that greatly increased the commerce." Yet this loyal and willing people had been dealt with like aliens and malcontents, to be subjected by the arm of power.

The Stamp Act was indeed repealed, but only as a matter of expediency, since Parliament made the fatal mistake of confounding a conflict of principle with a distaste for a measure of policy; and, while repealing the Stamp Act, it passed a bill declaring the absolute power of Parliament to bind America, and thus struck a wanton blow at the principle of local government in the Colonies. Against this assumption to govern the Colonies without respect to their own legislatures, Franklin had distinctly warned the Commons, that the Colonies " think it extremely hard and unjust that a body of men in which they have no representatives should make a merit to itself of giving and granting what is not its own, but theirs, and deprive them of a right they esteem of the utmost value and importance, as it is the security of all their other rights." In the parliamentary debate on the repeal of the Stamp Act, Pitt said, " The Commons of America, represented in their several assemblies, have ever been in possession of the exercise of this their constitutional right of giving and granting their own money. They would have been slaves if they had not enjoyed it."[1] Camden took the same ground in the Lords. On this point the Colonies were consistent, united, and steadfast. They never shifted their ground, never invented pretexts for thwarting the British Government, never opposed for the sake of opposing, never schemed for independence, never resisted on the score of money alone; but, having freely and loyally met their dues, they withstood the attempt to extort money by direct levies of Parliament. This identity of the question of taxes with the question of rights was the core of the controversy between the Colonies and Parliament: hence the joy at the repeal of the Stamp Act was short-lived; for it soon became evident that Parliament was aiming, not at taxation as a means of revenue, but at political subjugation, for which enforced taxation was the ready instrument.

[1] Jan. 14, 1766. Hansard, vol. xvi. 100.

GROUNDS AND MOTIVES OF THE REVOLUTION. 47

In March, 1766, the Stamp Act was repealed. In the following June, Townshend, in the House of Commons, openly advocated the annulling of all colonial charters, and the substitution of a uniform government, proceeding from the crown, by which the local assemblies should be restrained, and the royal governors, judges, and attorneys be rendered independent of the people;[1] and, a year later, this reckless and resolute opponent of the freedom of the Colonies was the leader of the British ministry, and persuaded Parliament to test again its power in America by taxes upon sundry imports, and especially tea.[2]

That roused the women of America, whose tea-parliaments were invaded by a tax on their favorite beverage. In every village, in every circle, it was resolved to drink no tea till the tax should be repealed. The good dames culled the herbs of the field, dried these, and brewed from them a tea that could not but make them the more bitter against Parliament every time they tasted it. In many places, a decree of social exclusion was pronounced against any who should drink a cup of tea. The town of Lexington resolved, "If any head of a family in this town, or any person, shall from this time forward, and until the duty be taken off, purchase any tea, or sell and consume any tea in their family, such person shall be looked upon as an enemy to this town and to his country, and shall by this town be treated with neglect and contempt." In a small village community of that day, what sentence could be more galling than this of being outlawed by that supreme court of America, — public opinion?

As no tea could be sold, the merchants ceased to import it. But the British premier said, "The king means to try the question with America;" and the attempt was made to force tea upon the Colonies. Three tea-ships arrived in Boston Harbor; but a guard of citizens refused to let them land their cargo. An immense meeting of the people called upon the governor to order the ships back to England: he refused; and a band of men disguised as Indians went to the ships, and, in the most quiet and orderly manner, dropped their three hundred and forty chests of tea into the water. This was the famous "Boston Tea-Party"

---

[1] See Townshend's Speech in Bancroft, vi. 9.   [2] June, 1767.

of Dec. 16, 1773; and so well did the participants disguise themselves and their secret, that nobody was ever brought to account for it. Yet this mild riot brewed in England a fearful storm. First came the Boston Port Bill, closing the port to all trade; but other seaports refused to profit by the patriotic sacrifices and sufferings of Boston, and then restraining acts were imposed upon the commerce of all the Colonies. Next followed the quartering of an army upon the people; and in 1774 the Regulation Acts, destroying free government and free speech. What was the effect of this last blow has been told by one of the clearest lawyers of the United States in his Centennial Address at Lexington:[1] —

"The Regulation Acts were radical and revolutionary. They went to the foundations of our public system, and sought to reconstruct it from the base on a theory of parliamentary omnipotence and kingly sovereignty. The councillors had been chosen by the people through their representatives. By the new law they were to be appointed by the king, and to hold at his pleasure. The superior judges were to hold at the will of the king, and to be dependent upon his will for the amount and payment of their salaries; and the inferior judges to be removable by the royal governor at his discretion, he himself holding at the king's will. The sheriffs were to be appointed by the royal governor, and to hold at his will. The juries had been selected by the inhabitants of the towns: they were now to be selected by the new sheriffs, — mere creatures of the royal governor. Offenders against the peace, and against the lives and persons of the people, had been tried here by our courts and juries; and in the memorable case of the soldiers' trial for the firing of March, 1770, we had proved ourselves capable of doing justice to our enemies. By the new act, persons charged with capital crimes, and royal officers, civil or military, charged with offences in the execution of the royal laws or warrants, could be transferred for trial to England, or to some other of the Colonies.

"But the deepest-reaching provision of the acts was that aimed at the town-meetings. They were no longer

[1] Richard H. Dana, jun.

to be parliaments of freemen, to discuss matters of public interest, to instruct their representatives, and look to the redress of grievances. They were prohibited, except the two annual meetings of March and May, and were then only to elect officers; and no other meetings could be held, unless by the written permission of the royal governor; and no matters could be considered, unless specially sanctioned in the permission. Am I not right in saying that these acts sought a radical revolution, a fundamental reconstruction of our ancient political system? They sought to change self-government into government by the king; and, for home-rule, to substitute absolute rule at Westminster and St. James's Palace. They gave the royal governor and his council here powers which the king and his council could not exercise in Great Britain, — powers from which the British nobles and commons had fought out their exemption, and to which they would never submit."

Thus far Mr. Dana. I have now established the three points that I laid down at the outset: (1) The American Colonies had no quarrel with the English nation, of which they would have been proud to remain an integral part; (2) The British ministry had itself to thank for American independence; (3) The English people owe to the American Revolution no small share in the conservation of their own local and popular freedom against the encroachments of the crown, and also in that wise and liberal policy that now retains English Colonies within the British Empire.

To enforce the subversion of local government in the Colonies, a British army was quartered upon the people; and the first aim of its commander was to disarm the militia, that, under authority of their legislature, the towns had organized, and which had been always ready to defend the crown of England against foreign foes. That handful of the men of Lexington, who, on the morning of the 19th April, 1775, drew themselves up in military order on their village green to await the British regulars, represented the town in its ancient rights of government and of defence. It was not liberty alone, but law, — the English law of a thousand years, — that was embodied in that little company. The demand to lay down their arms was a demand to surrender the liberty of the people and the sovereignty of law; and they refused. There they stood, — wives, children, neighbors, looking on, — sixty freemen upon their own soil, and that soil the little campus of the town militia; stood to represent the right of the town to exist, and its determination not to yield its immemorial rights; stood facing eight hundred British regulars; refused to surrender their trust; refused to give up their arms, and with these the right of bearing arms; refused to disperse, and thus to abandon the town-right of muster; stood still till they were fired upon, being resolved to put Britain in the wrong, by showing that her government was bent upon destroying the liberties of her subjects, and trampling out local government by arbitrary power. In violation of the chartered rights of Massachusetts, in violation of militia laws that the king himself had taken advantage of for his help against the French, the British troops were sent to seize all military stores in the keeping of the towns, and to disarm the militia. Against this usurpation, Lexington had written to Boston, "We trust in God: we shall be ready to sacrifice our estates, and every thing dear in life, yea, and life itself, in support of the common cause." The men of Lexington kept their vow: —

> "They went where duty seemed to call:
> They scarcely asked the reason why;
> They only knew they could but die;
> And death was not the worst of all.
> Of man for man the sacrifice,
> Unstained by blood save theirs, they gave.
> The flowers that blossomed from their grave
> Have sown themselves beneath all skies." [1]

Those men of Lexington and Concord stood for English liberty and the English constitution against a despotic revolution attempted by a bullying king and a toadying parliament. That I do not use these epithets unadvisedly, or in a hostile spirit,[2] "The London Times" bears witness

---

[1] Whittier.
[2] I am truly sorry to use such terms concerning the powers that were; but I have sought in vain for more euphonious words to express the exact

in its calm and candid leader upon the hundredth anniversary of the battle of Bunker Hill: "While the great majority of the British people, as represented in public opinion and in literature, was on the American side, the government and the majority in both houses of Parliament were absolutely proof against every consideration of humanity, prudence, or common sense. . . . The greater part of the American contention in that war was equally shared by the British people. The principles of popular representation, and no taxation without it, self-government by popular municipal institutions, the independence of the judicial bench, and complete responsibility in the exercise of all power and patronage, were equally at stake on both sides of the Atlantic." . . . But the politicians " were maintaining the principles of utter absolutism;" and the British Government "persisted in the struggle with reckless and inhuman obstinacy."[1]

The battle of Bunker Hill, on the 17th June, 1775, showed the British what stuff the colonists were made of, and what they could do when put upon their mettle. That battle is not to be judged upon the scale of modern warfare; but old soldiers, who had been in European wars, testified that they had never seen so hot a conflict, or so many losses in proportion to the force engaged. On the one side, three thousand British regulars marching with bulldog courage up the hill under cover of the fire of their fleet; on the other, squads of militia, who had worked all night in putting up the breast-works from which they poured forth their deadly musketry. More than a thousand British fell, dead and wounded; five hundred Americans, the Americans quitting their trenches only when their powder gave out, then fighting with the but-ends

---

truth. Also these are not original. Thackeray says of George III., "He bribed; he bullied; he darkly dissembled on occasion; he exercised a slippery perseverance and a vindictive resolution, which one almost admires as one thinks his character over."

As to the subserviency of Parliament, its own journals witness for that. But the people of England were not with Parliament. That it is possible for Parliament to run counter to the spirit and will of the nation, even in these days of a free and enlarged suffrage, was made evident by the almost contemptuous disregard of public feeling in passing the Royal Titles Act of 1876. Americans, who are often so grossly misrepresented by their own Congress, are not disposed to cherish a grudge against the English people for the misdoings of Parliament a century ago.

[1] Times, June 17, 1875.

of their muskets, and retreating with little disorder from an enemy too crippled for pursuit. The British had won the hill; but the moral victory was with the Americans. Hence we date our emancipation from that battle, and the heroes of Bunker Hill are our immortals: —

> " On Fame's eternal camping-ground
> Their silent tents are spread."

The news of Bunker Hill put the British Government in a rage. The Revolution must be put down by overwhelming numbers. Unhappily, Germany was then in a position to serve as the recruiting-ground of British despotism; and while France gave us her Lafayette, and Poland her Kosciusko, Brunswick and Hesse hired out their soldiers by the thousand to suppress our liberties; though Prussia somewhat redeemed the disgrace through the scorn of the great Frederic for such infamy,[1] the services of Baron Steuben in drilling our raw volunteers, and the heroic sacrifice of De Kalb in our cause. With their German mercenaries, the British Government thought the subjugation of the Colonies an easy task. They would make Boston a base of operations and supplies, and overawe the continent. But now there was a Congress at Philadelphia, and Washington was at Cambridge as commander-in-chief of the Continental army. Too weak in

---

[1] Franklin, writing from Paris 1 May, 1777, said of the traffic in Hessians, "The conduct of these princes of Germany, who have sold the blood of their people, has subjected them to the contempt and odium of all Europe. The Prince of Anspach, whose recruits mutinied and refused to march, was obliged to disarm and fetter them, and drive them to the seaside by the help of his guards, himself attending in person. In his return, he was publicly hooted by mobs through every town he passed in Holland, with all sorts of reproachful epithets. The King of Prussia's humor of obliging those princes to pay him the same toll per head for the men they drive through his dominions as used to be paid him for their *cattle*, because they were sold as such, is generally spoken of with approbation, as containing a just reproof of these tyrants." — BIGELOW's *Life of Franklin*, ii. p. 393.

In a valuable note to this passage, Mr. Bigelow has gathered the following important items. In a letter to Voltaire, Frederic says of the Landgrave of Hesse, "S'il était sorti de mon école, il ne se serait point fait Catholique, et il n'aurait pas vendu ses sujets aux Anglais comme on vend le bétail pour l'égorger." — *Œuvres posth. de Frédéric*, tom. i. p. 325.

In a letter to Lord North, dated from Kew Aug. 20, 1775, George III. said, "The only idea these Germans ought to adopt is *the being contractors* for raising recruits, and fixing the price they *will deliver them* at Hamburg, Rotterdam, and any other port they may propose." Can any Englishman or German read that to-day without indignant shame?

powder and artillery to risk an engagement, Washington resolved first to hem the British in Boston, and then to drive them out; but, when he was ready to bombard the city, he hesitated to destroy the property of friends in punishing foes, and so applied to Congress for authority. Its president, John Hancock of Boston, was reputed to be the richest man in America; and his property was largely in houses, which, from their position, must be among the first to fall, should Washington open fire upon the city. Rising in his place, Hancock said, "Nearly all I have in the world is in the town of Boston; but if the expulsion of the British troops, and the liberty of my country, demand that my houses be burned to ashes, issue the order, and let the cannon blaze away." At length the cannon were ready to blaze away; but the British fleet and army made an ignominious retreat.[1]

Up to this time, little had been thought, and less said, by the leaders, touching independence as an issue of the conflict. Even Washington still hoped for a reconciliation that should secure the Colonies in the rights for which alone they had taken up arms. But the flames of war were kindling coastwise all along the Colonies; and, with these, the fire of independence was kindling in the hearts of the people. At length the force of events, and the vehemence of public feeling, compelled Congress to take up the measure of independence. For days the Declaration had been debated; and on the 4th of July the old State House of Philadelphia was besieged by an impatient populace, while the bell-ringer waited hour by hour in the belfry for the signal that he should announce the Declaration ratified. At last the signal came, and at every stroke rang out the legend that years before had been cast upon

[1] During the winter of 1775-76, Washington held Gen. Howe's army in Boston under siege. With an army of only sixteen thousand men he guarded a semicircle of eight or nine miles, his centre being at Cambridge, his right wing at Roxbury, and his left upon the Medford River; thus cutting off from Boston all supplies by land. But Washington lacked ammunition, money, and clothing for his troops; and was hampered by the system of *colonial* enlistment, which made him dependent upon the governors of the several Colonies for recruits. Under these discouragements, he had to build up an army, and hold it together. On the night of March 4, 1776, Washington fortified Dorchester Heights; and, as his position was made stronger and more threatening day by day, Gen. Howe evacuated Boston, and embarked for Halifax on the 17th March. Congress presented Washington with a gold medal in commemoration of this event.

the rim of the bell: "*Proclaim liberty throughout the land unto all the inhabitants thereof.*"[1] As president of the Congress, John Hancock had signed the declaration that "these Colonies are free and independent States." With his own hand he has issued the supreme order for the expulsion, not of the British troops only, but of the British government and name. *Now* "LET THE CANNON BLAZE AWAY."

---

[1] This bell was first hung in 1753. During the Revolutionary war it was taken down and buried, to avoid its being captured by the enemy. It was a favorite pleasure of my boyhood to climb the tower, and sit under the bell at the stroke of twelve. Years ago, on a festive day, it was cracked; and it has ever since been preserved as a national relic.

LECTURE II.

DOCTRINES OF THE DECLARATION OF INDEPENDENCE.

THE men who, as a Congress of the Colonies, adopted the Declaration of Independence, indulged in no idle rhetoric when they said, "For the support of this Declaration, with a firm reliance on the protection of Divine Providence, we mutually pledge to each other our lives, our fortunes, and our sacred honor." Two of them, John Hancock and Samuel Adams, had already been proclaimed rebels and outlaws; and a price was set upon their heads.[1] The famous *mot* of Franklin shows how clearly their colleagues realized what they were doing when they put their names to the Declaration. As the members of the Congress came to the final vote upon the document, Hancock

[1] On the 12th of June, 1775, Gen. Gage, then royal governor of Massachusetts, proclaimed martial law throughout the Province, at the same time making an offer of pardon in the following terms: "I do hereby, in his Majesty's name, offer and promise his most gracious pardon to all persons who shall forthwith lay down their arms, and return to the duties of peaceable subjects; excepting only from the benefit of such pardon SAMUEL ADAMS and JOHN HANCOCK, whose offences are of too flagitious a nature to admit of any other consideration than that of condign punishment" (Journal of the Provincial Congress, p. 331). The Boston Gazette (of June 24, 1775), with better wit than rhyme, thus parodied this exception: —

> "But then I must out of this plan lock
> Both Samuel Adams and John Hancock;
> For those vile traitors (like bedentures)
> Must be tucked up at all adventures,
> As any offer of a pardon
> Would only tend those rogues to harden."
> (Quoted in Wells's Life of Samuel Adams, ii. 310.)

John Adams testifies that "James Otis, Samuel Adams, and John Hancock, were the three most essential characters, the first movers, the most constant, steady, persevering springs, agents, and most disinterested sufferers and firmest pillars, of the whole Revolution." Of these, he rates Otis first; but he describes Samuel Adams as "the wedge of steel to split the knot of *lignumvitæ* which tied North America to Great Britain." — *Works*, x. 268.

said, "We must be unanimous; there must be no pulling different ways; we must all hang together." — "Yes," replied Franklin, "we must all hang together, or we shall all hang separately."[1] That flash of wit reveals the situation, — a group of men, mature in years and in experience, signing away their lives, if need be, for their liberty, yet with a perfect consciousness of the meaning of the act, and, in this moment of solemnity and of peril, displaying a calm and cheerful confidence in their cause.[2] It was one thing for an eager, impatient populace outside the Hall of Independence to demand the Declaration, and to greet its passage with huzzas, with bonfires, and illuminations; and it was another thing for those fifty-six delegates of the Colonies within the hall to issue that Declaration upon the pledge of their honor, their fortunes, and their lives. It was one thing for the mob in various cities, as the news of the Declaration reached them, to burn royal governors in effigy, and throw down the statues of the king[3] and his ministers; and it was another thing for the framers of the Declaration to build a pedestal, — that might be their own mausoleum, — upon which Liberty and Union should stand so firmly, that they could never be thrown down.

These were no fiery revolutionists, intent upon a work of destruction; no enthusiastic *doctrinaires*, thinking to build of the smoke and ashes of society a new political order for mankind. They loved England, — some of them as the land of their birth;[4] most of them as the land of their fathers; all of them as the then foremost land of freedom and culture, whose empire they would gladly share, if this should preserve liberty to the subject equally with loyalty to the crown. They were averse to war; for

---

[1] Bigelow's Life of Franklin, ii. 360. This could hardly have been at the signing, which was simply a matter of form, some time after the treasonable *act* itself.

[2] Every one has heard of the saying of Hancock, as he signed the Declaration in his large, bold hand, "John Bull can read that without spectacles;" and of Charles Carroll, who, when it was suggested that he might escape because there were others of his name, added, "*of Carrollton*," saying, "Now they'll know where to find me."

[3] Washington was in New York when the statue of George III. in the Bowling Green was demolished. He condemned such violent proceedings in a general order, saying, "The general hopes and trusts that every officer and man will endeavor so to live and act as becomes a Christian soldier, defending the sacred rights and liberties of his country."

[4] Eight of the signers were born in Great Britain.

they had had experience of its cost and waste and losses in the defence of their own frontiers. They were averse to a change of government; being satisfied with their local administration, if its freedom could be preserved in harmony with the national Parliament. They were men of experience in affairs, accustomed to act with reason and deliberation, and honored with the confidence of their fellow-citizens in an age when office was yet an honor, and politics not yet a trade. The average age of the signers of the Declaration was somewhat over forty: only two of them were under thirty, one-half of them were forty-five and upwards, seventeen were over fifty, and seven over sixty years. The fervor of youth was controlled by the prudence and firmness of middle life, and guided by the wisdom and dignity of age. Of the whole number of fifty-six, thirty-nine had received a liberal education: of these, twenty-four were in the profession of the law, four were doctors of medicine, one was president of a college.[1] In addition to the eight who were born in the old country were twelve who had visited England and the continent of Europe; and, of these, seven had pursued their studies at Eton, Edinburgh, Cambridge, and the Inner Temple. One of the signers was a nephew of the Dean of St. Paul's;[2] another, the grandson of the Bishop of Worcester;[3] a third had been honored with the freedom of the city of Edinburgh.[4] Not a few of them — John Adams, Thomas Jefferson, Benjamin Franklin, Robert Morris, Benjamin Rush, Roger Sherman, Oliver Wolcott — have left memorials in science, law, finance, statesmanship, diplomacy, of which any nation might be proud; and their collective state papers commanded the admiration of their age.[5] These, then, were not a body to be hurried by impulse into rash innovations. Nor were they. The British Government forced war upon the Colonies, and the war forced independence.

When Franklin retired from his post at London as agent of the Colonies, in March, 1775, the utmost that was thought of was resistance, and resistance as a means

---

[1] John Witherspoon of Princeton. [2] Francis Lewis of New York.
[3] Francis Hopkinson of Philadelphia.
[4] Richard Stockton of New Jersey.
[5] Pitt and Burke were warm in their praise.

toward reconciliation. Separation was but a dream or a dread. When Franklin reached home, he was met with the news of Lexington; and, the day after his arrival, he was chosen a member of the Continental Congress. Then followed Bunker Hill, and the threats of British officers to lay waste the country by foreign mercenaries. At this stage, the American philosopher wrote to a former friend in London,[1] —

MR. STRAHAN, — You are a member of Parliament, and one of that majority who has doomed my country to destruction. You have begun to burn our towns, and murder our people. Look upon your hands! they are stained with the blood of your relations. You and I were long friends: you are now my enemy, and I am
Yours,   B. FRANKLIN.

The tone of this letter shows that public spirit in the Colonies had already grown determined and defiant. A letter to Josiah Quincy from Franklin, in the following April (1776), marks the progress of the spirit of independence: "You ask, When is the Continental Congress by *general consent* to be formed into a supreme legislature, alliances defensive and offensive formed, our ports opened, and a formidable naval force established at the public charge? I can only answer, at present, that nothing seems wanting but that 'general consent.' The novelty of the thing deters some; the doubt of success, others; the vain hope of reconciliation, many. But our enemies take continually every proper measure to remove these obstacles; and their endeavors are attended with success, since every day furnishes us with new causes of increasing enmity, and new reasons for wishing an eternal separation; so that there is a rapid increase of the formerly small party who were for an independent government."[2]

Two months later, this party of independence had grown to embrace almost the entire Congress, and the great body of the people of all the Colonies.[3] But the

---

[1] Bigelow's Life of Franklin, ii. 343.   [2] Ibid., ii. 357.
[3] The Revolution was born of the heroic spirit of America, and represented the life of her people. Mr. Josiah Quincy once narrated to me how in his boyhood he used to go to read to John Adams, then toward his ninetieth year. The delight of the old patriot was to listen to Cicero de Senectute; and he would take up in advance the glowing periods, saying, "O præclarum diem, quum in illud divinum animorum concilium cœtumque

patriots who were charged with the responsibility of affairs felt their way with the caution of men, who, knowing the calamities of war and the risks of revolution, realized their personal accountability to their country, to the world, to history, and to God. On the seventh day of June (1776), a resolution was laid before Congress in these words: —

"*Resolved*, That these United Colonies are, and of right ought to be, free and independent States; that they are absolved from all allegiance to the British crown; and that all political connection between them and the state of Great Britain is, and ought to be, totally dissolved."

After three days' discussion, a committee was appointed to draught a declaration to the effect of the resolution, and the whole subject was postponed to the first day of July: on that day the Declaration of Independence was taken up by the House in committee of the whole, and, after three days of spirited and thorough discussion, was adopted, and authenticated by the signatures of the president and secretary of the Congress. Hence the 4th of July is the proper anniversary of the Declaration.[1] But Con-

proficiscar, quumque ex hac turba et colluvione discedam! Proficiscar enim non ad eos solum viros, de quibus ante dixi, verum etiam ad Catonem meum, quo nemo vir melior natus est, nemo pietate præstantior; cuius a me corpus crematum est — quod contra decuit, ab illo meum — animus vero non me deserens, sed respectans, in ea profecto loca discessit, quo mihi ipsi cernebat esse veniendum."

Grand old hero! thus joining the patriotic fellowships of earth to the company of the spirits of the just. One day young Quincy said to him, "It is disputed whether you, Mr. Adams, or Mr. Jefferson, or Franklin, started the idea of independence: pray tell me how it was." — "Neither Jefferson nor Franklin nor I can claim that honor: independence sprang from the hearts of the people. When I was a student of law, I taught school at Worcester, and boarded round in the families of the farmers; and, as I heard them talk, I got such ideas of the state, of liberty, and of patriotism, as satisfied me we must come to this at last."

[1] On the 2d of July, Congress adopted the resolution of June 7, "That these United Colonies are, and of right ought to be, free and independent States; that they are absolved from all allegiance to the British crown; and that all political connection between them and the state of Great Britain is, and ought to be, totally dissolved." This act of separation filled John Adams with such transport, that he wrote, "The second day of July, 1776, will be the most memorable epoch in the history of America, to be celebrated by succeeding generations as the great anniversary festival." But the issuing of the Declaration two days later, which announced to the world the independence of the States, was seized upon as the fact to be commemorated. (For details as to dates, see Jefferson's Autobiography, and the Letters of John Adams to Mrs. Adams.) The alleged declaration of independence at Mecklenburg, N.C., May 20, 1775, is not sufficiently

gress, sensible of the magnitude of this act, and desiring to proceed with solemnity and deliberation, caused the Declaration to be engrossed on parchment; and, on the second day of August, this copy was signed by each and every member of the Congress. Then "thirteen clocks were made to strike together, — a perfection of mechanism which no artist had ever before effected." [1]

But, while Congress was thus deliberate in the act and the form of the Declaration of Independence, many of the leaders were enthusiastic for the separation from Great Britain, and sanguine of success. Witherspoon described the public spirit as not only ripe for independence, but rotting for want of it. There was in everybody's mouth this apothegm from Paine's trenchant tract styled "Common Sense:" "England is too ignorant of America to govern it wisely, too jealous of America to govern it justly, and too distant from America to govern it at all." Rising to the fervor of a prophet, John Adams said, "Live or die, survive or perish, I am for the Declaration. . . . It is an event to be commemorated, as the day of deliverance, by solemn acts of devotion to God Almighty. It ought to be solemnized with pomp and parade, with shows, games, sports, guns, bells, bonfires, and illuminations, from one end of the continent to the other, from this time forward forevermore." Fifty years after, this untiring patriot, who had served his country as minister plenipotentiary to France, England, and other countries of Europe; who for eight years was Vice-President under Washington, and four years was President after Washington, — John Adams, then nearing his ninety-first birthday, on the night of the 3d of July lay sinking into the sleep of death. The morrow was the jubilee of independence; and at daybreak he was roused from his lethargy by the ringing of bells and the booming of cannon. With a bewildered look, he asked the occasion of this noise of cannon and bells; and, being reminded that it was "Independence Day," he kindled with the memories of half a century, cried "Inde-

authenticated to take its place in history; and, in any case, it is clear, from the correspondence between Jefferson and Adams upon the subject, that neither of them had any knowledge of the resolutions said to have been passed at Charlotte.

[1] John Adams: Works, x. 283.

pendence forever!" and expired. At almost the same hour, on that same fiftieth anniversary of national independence, the Virginian patriot who draughted the Declaration, who was Vice-President under Adams, and President after him, — Thomas Jefferson, — also died. Another fifty years have gone, the hundredth anniversary of the Declaration of Independence has come, and the work they did stands, — stands broader, firmer, more appreciated and honored, than in their day. The words in which Mr. Webster commemorated Adams and Jefferson have gathered force in these past fifty years: "No age will come in which the American Revolution will appear less than it is, — one of the greatest events in human history; no age will come in which it shall cease to be seen and felt on either continent, that a mighty step, a great advance, not only in American affairs, but in human affairs, was made on the 4th of July, 1776." [1]

In the century that has passed since that day, the United States have gone through every experience possible to a nation, save that of being conquered and held by a foreign power; the voluntary abandonment of one form of government — the Confederation of 1777–81 [2] — for another, — the Constitution of 1788; [3] severe financial crises, from the Continental currency of the Revolution down to the "greenbacks" of the civil war; two great foreign wars, — that of 1812 with Great Britain, in which the United States won renown as a naval power, and that of 1845 with Mexico, in which the United States acquired an immense reach of territory from Texas to the Pacific Ocean; the violence of political parties, especially in the strifes over the currency, the tariff, and slavery; the corruption of the civil service, and the degeneracy of public officers; the formidable rebellion of 1861, with the four years of civil war that followed it; the assassination of one President, and the attempt to impeach another; the amendment of the Constitution, so that newly-emancipated slaves were admitted to vote, and made eligible to office on

[1] Oration on Adams and Jefferson: Works, vol. i. 116.
[2] The Articles of Confederation were adopted by Congress 15th November, 1777, but not finally ratified by the Colonies until March, 1781.
[3] The Constitution was reported to Congress Sept. 28, 1787, and in the course of 1788 was so far ratified by States as to go into operation March 4, 1789.

the basis of universal suffrage; an enormous public debt created by the war, and the spirit of speculation and extravagance that the war had fostered; the reconstruction of disordered States, and the reviving of their industry in face of hostile factions and races; and, worst of all, a medley of foreign immigration, with its ignorance and impudence, its priestcraft and pauperism, its radicalism and rationalism, its sensuality and its superstition: all these manifold tests and perils have the United States gone through successfully, triumphantly, in their first century of national life, though at each phase of excitement, each approach of danger, the prophets of evil gave warning of the dissolution of the Union, the subversion of the republic.

Of late, European critics have invented for the United States a new danger, or rather have revived a peril that was thought imminent in the early days of independence. Those political owls of the Old World that cling to the shades of the middle ages, with that air of superlative wisdom which this particular species of owl knows so well to put on, now sing, " To-who with your republic: you'll come to a monarchy at last." But, as I listen to these oracles of night, I ask, " Do you, then, threaten us with a monarchy as a calamity? or do you wish that we should become monarchists in order to re-assure you of your position and principles by the failure of ours?" To all such prophets and counsellors I would say, " Ponder the lessons of the century, and if you yourselves would not,

> ' Like the owl by day,
> If he arise, be mocked and wondered at,'

then learn from Americans to be so well satisfied of the excellence and stability of your own government, that, without either boasting or envy, you can leave other people to be satisfied with theirs. I do not advocate a republic for you, nor recommend it as a panacea for your social evils. The fundamental doctrine of American republicanism is, that every people should have such government as best pleases itself; and, if a monarchy best pleases you, that is no affair of ours." To our Prussian critics especially, I am wont to say, " I can but congratulate you upon having the best reigning house of modern history, and the best sovereign, surrounded with the ablest ministry, of the present stage; and having these, with two constitutions, two parliaments, and universal suffrage to boot, I beg you to be so far content as to look calmly upon a great, free, happy people beyond the sea, and, without prejudices or prophecies, to study their history with a view to ascertain *why* they are *what* they are." Here is an organic, independent republic, a hundred years old, resting upon a foundation of local self-government and provisional union that had stood for a hundred and fifty years before. This national life is to be studied in the moral and social forces that shaped it into being; in the ethical and political truths upon which it established itself as a self-contained and independent power; and in the political forms through which it has developed its freedom, its unity, and its strength. The nascent forces of the nation I have considered in the previous Lecture: in this we are to study its basis of ethical and political truths; and, in the next, the forms of its political development. The remaining Lectures of the series will be given to the fruits of this national life under the several modes of political, social, industrial, educational, and religious activity.

The ethical and political doctrines upon which the government of the United States is founded were put forth in the Declaration of Independence as "self-evident truths," and concern the essential and inalienable rights of men, the source and the functions of government, and the right of revolution. In judging of this document, one should keep in mind that it is a "declaration" of political principles, and not a dissertation on political philosophy defining and defending those principles. The Congress that published independence knew they were doing a great act, and gave the reasons for that act, — not the reasons of the reasons. The rhetoric, indeed, is open to criticism, as somewhat too strained and declamatory for a state paper; but judged by the oratory of the British Parliament of the same period, and by the then prevailing tone of literature, it was less faulty for its purpose than it may seem to our severer taste; and, besides, some extravagance of expression may be pardoned to men who were defying a superior power at the peril of their lives.[1] Yet theirs was no vaporing pronunciamento: the Declaration has the vehemence of truth and strength. It begins by recognizing the comity of nations, and appeals to that high court of international equity by which the claims and doings of each individual people must be judged, — the aggregate opinion of the civilized world. Without waiting for the prestige of success, or seeking the recognition of separate powers, the United States declared themselves a nation, and put themselves before the court of nations upon the merits of their cause, with facts, truths, rights, addressed to the common consciousness of mankind. The existence of a nation being determined by certain natural laws or causes under a superintending Providence, they set forth the evidence that no premature or wilful outbreak, but such inevitable causes, had compelled this act of independence. " When, in the course of human events, it becomes necessary for one people to dissolve the political bands which have connected them with another, and to assume among the powers of the earth the separate and equal station to which the laws of nature and of nature's God entitle them, a decent respect to the opinions of mankind requires that they should declare the causes which impel

---

[1] In some points, Congress improved the draught as prepared by Jefferson. For "*inherent and* inalienable rights" they substituted "*certain* inalienable rights." After the phrase, "Let facts be submitted to a candid world," they struck out the boastful statement, "*for the truth of which we pledge a faith yet unsullied by falsehood.*"

While the document was under criticism, Franklin relieved the sensitiveness of Jefferson by this story: "When I was a journeyman printer, one of my companions, an apprenticed hatter, having served out his time, was about to open shop for himself. His first concern was to have a handsome signboard with a proper inscription. He composed it in these words, '*John Thompson, Hatter, makes and sells Hats for ready Money,*' with a figure of a hat subjoined. But he thought he would submit it to his friends for their amendments. The first he showed it to thought the word 'hatter' tautologous, because followed by the words 'makes hats,' which showed he was a hatter. It was struck out. The next observed that the word 'makes' might as well be omitted, because his customers would not care who made the hats: if good, and to their mind, they would buy, by whomsoever made. He struck it out. A third said he thought the words 'for ready money' were useless, as it was not the custom of the place to sell on credit: every one who purchased expected to pay. They were parted with; and the inscription now stood, '*John Thompson sells hats.*' '*Sells* hats,' says his next friend: 'why, nobody will expect you to give them away. What, then, is the use of that word?' It was stricken out; and *hats* followed, the rather as there was one painted on the board. So his inscription was ultimately reduced to John Thompson, with the figure of a hat subjoined."

After all, it would not make a bad figure if the Declaration were Thomas Jefferson and a liberty-cap!

them to the separation;" and to this end they say, "Let facts be submitted to a candid world." Here was no secret conspiracy, aiming to get control of power by treachery and assassination; no *coup d'état*, trusting to audacity and surprise for its success; no mob of adventurers, threatening slaughter and death to whoever should oppose them, and carrying anarchy and destruction in their path; but a body of men trained in the service of the State, selected by their countrymen for their intelligence, prudence, and experience, addressed themselves with the calmness of truth, the earnestness of conviction, the confidence of right, to the common sense and the common conscience of their age, and to the tribunal of history. With all their lofty notions of popular rights and national independence, the American revolutionists did not feel at liberty to disturb the peace and order of the world, without openly justifying their proceeding before the world. They did not utter a cry for help; for they meant to help themselves. They did not appeal for moral support; for they found support in the justice of their cause. But, deeming themselves and their cause worthy of respect, instead of suing for admission into the family of nations, they at once took their "equal station among the powers of the earth," with a Declaration exhibiting for their pedigree the inalienable rights of man, for their patent the laws of nature and of God, and for their bearings independence supported by justice, and already baptized with fire and blood. With the perfect consciousness of "the rectitude of their intentions," the authors of the Declaration appealed "to the Supreme Judge of the world," and, "with a firm reliance on the protection of Divine Providence," staked life, fortune, honor, upon their cause.

The Declaration, as I have said, is not a dissertation on political science; yet it is grounded in a philosophy of man and of government that shows its authors to have been well trained in the logic of thinking and of expression; and it even opens with a syllogism, the conclusion of which is inevitable, if the premises of the first and middle terms be admitted as self-evident truths. In the first Lecture it was shown that the Revolution originated in a contest for existing and ancestral rights in the exercise of local government. These rights are all assumed in the Declaration; are woven into its whole texture; but they appear under the form of charges and protests against the "usurpations" of the King of Great Britain; while the Declaration goes down to the foundation of popular government in the natural rights of man, and in the source of civil government and its proper functions and duties.

"We hold these truths to be self-evident, that all men are created equal; that they are endowed by their Creator with certain inalienable rights; that among these are life, liberty, and the pursuit of happiness; that, to secure these rights, governments are instituted among men, deriving their just powers from the consent of the governed; that, whenever any form of government becomes destructive of these ends, it is the right of the people to alter or to abolish it, and to institute a new government, laying its foundation on such principles, and organizing its powers in such form, as to them shall seem most likely to effect their safety and happiness." Couched in these successive asseverations is the syllogism: —

(1.) All men are possessed of certain inalienable rights.

(2.) The possessors of these rights form or assent to governments for the protection of the same.

(3.) When government would destroy these rights, their possessors may destroy the government in order to preserve the rights.

Men had read much, thought much, learned much, before they framed these propositions; and their lives were consistent with their logic. We have done justice to their sincerity and heroism: it is their logic that now concerns us; for in that lay the germs of a philosophy that should reconstruct or modify modern society.

In weighing the propositions laid down in the Declaration, one should consider how difficult it is to formulate a principle, and especially to reduce principles of politics and ethics to axioms. In the effort to compress a philosophy into a proverb, or to reduce a science to definitions, the mind is apt to fix itself upon the single truth or truths before it with an intensity of concentration that excludes correlative or qualifying truths. Hence there is a tendency to over-statement, or one-sided statement, in the first announcement of a discovery, whether in physics, politics, or morals. But one should remember, also, that the progress of knowledge (as, for instance, in theology, in psychology, and in geology) has been largely through a series of over-statements and counter-statements, — one principle pushed with vehemence till it met its corrective, and, by the attrition of controversy, each wore the other down to its just proportions; or until the new truth, entering like a wedge, forced its way into the system of truth by compelling a re-adjustment of the relations of things. So of these doctrines of the Declaration; viewed apart, perhaps over-stated, yet containing truths that required emphasis to gain a hearing, and wedging ideas into the social structure that compelled a re-adjustment of the political elements and order of the world. The fine point of that wedge was this tiny sentence of five words, "*All men are created equal:*" once that gains entrance, it makes a huge crack in any society that is constructed of privileged orders in Church and State; and, if well driven home, it must reduce all artificial privileges to the level of natural gifts, opportunities, services, attainments. Radical as this may seem in the bald statement of the doctrine, yet the equality set forth in the Declaration of Independence is not a radicalism that any honest man should be afraid of, since it is grounded in the highest moral reason, is directed to the highest personal and social happiness, and fenced about with justice and good-will.

It would be absurd to charge upon the authors of the Declaration of Independence the absurdity of meaning that all men are, or could be, or ought to be, equal in station, in capacity, in claim to consideration, in adaptation to political service or office, or even in the possibility of rising to the same degrees in honor, power, genius, wealth, renown. No community of human beings could exist with such equality, and perform the functions of life. As in the physical universe, so in the universe of mind: "There are celestial bodies, and bodies terrestrial; but the glory of the celestial is one, and the glory of the terrestrial is another. There is one glory of the sun, and another glory of the moon, and another glory of the stars; for one star differeth from another star in glory."[1] Nowhere are men brought into life under equal conditions, and nowhere do men prove themselves of equal calibre and fibre where their surroundings are proximately the same. In France it does not make men equal to paint out the old royal and imperial names of streets and public buildings, and paint over these, "*Liberté, Égalité, Fraternité;*" and in the United States it does not make men equal to give them universal suffrage, without respect to nativity, color, race, or condition. Yet there is a profound and far-reaching sense in which the doctrine of the Declaration is true, "that all men are created equal;" and the just perception of this truth gives dignity and strength to the national life. This equality is predicated of men as *men*, and as created beings: that is to say, in the contemplation of the Creator, as rational and moral beings they are of equal worth and right in respect of the use of the powers, and the enjoyment of the means and pleasures, of such existence. In this view, all men are alike "endowed by their Creator with certain inalienable rights;" and "among these are life, liberty, and the pursuit of happiness." Who would dare deny this equality of universal humanity? — the right of every man to *live* without hinderance or question from others; the right to *freedom* in the use of his powers of body and mind, — freedom to make as much as lies within him of life and its opportunities, to make the most of himself as a man; and the right to the fair procurement and enjoyment of all the *happiness* within his reach. By what warrant can any man pretend to be above or distinct from his fellows in the right to live, the right to use his powers of living, the right to enjoy all the good he can fairly attain? These rights inhere in the nature of man, and are "inalienable." To living in a community, or a political society, it is essential that these rights of the individual be in some measure qualified or curtailed for the good of the whole; but this is not because, in these particulars, any of the community can claim a right superior to others to which these must yield, but simply that each may enjoy his own natural rights to the

[1] 1 Cor. xv. 40, 41.

fullest extent possible, by securing to every other the like equitable enjoyment of his rights; that is, that each may enjoy the largest freedom and happiness possible without encroaching upon the rights of others, or being encroached upon by others, in the pursuit of their equitable freedom and happiness.

In the hour of shipwreck no man can say to another, "The life-boat shall be kept for me; for I have better right to live than thou." And when the boat is tossing in mid-ocean, without food or water, and the dread moment comes when one must die to save the rest, it is not birth, nor rank, nor wealth, nor genius, nor office, but the lot cast among men as equals, that determines who shall live, and who shall die. On board the ship of state, though some are commanding officers, some the paying passengers, and some the working crew, all are equal in these essential rights, — to live, to be free, and to be happy. If the ship is laboring, and must be lightened, they will throw overboard what seems to them fittest and handiest, — king, lords, commons, army, church, constitution, *plebiscitum ;* and, if she must go down, *sauve qui peut* will be the one law and cry of equalized humanity. The equality of men as taught in the Declaration lies deeper than all forms of government. It teaches, that, in the contemplation of the State, all men should be equal as objects of care and of right; that the State should care for all alike, and be just to all alike. So far as human action falls within the scope of civil government, laws should be equal, justice equal, protection equal, opportunity of development equal, for all.

In the Declaration, this equality was asserted against the tyrannical usurpations of the king and parliament of Great Britain: in our time it requires to be asserted against the more harsh and inexorable tyranny that is set up for the laws of nature. The tyranny of men can be resisted and overthrown; but the tyranny of nature, once established, can neither be resisted nor evaded. The Declaration proclaims "that all men are *created* equal," and "that they are endowed by their *Creator* with certain inalienable rights." Their rights are given by God, and therefore cannot be taken away by men. If, then, the doctrine of materialists is true, if there is no Creator, if man is not the loved and gifted child of God, then one great pillar of American liberty falls. Agonizing and fecundating forces, contesting or polarizing atoms, give us no such doctrine of the equality of men in the right to be, to act, to enjoy. Whatever may be true of other species, with men the "struggle for existence" does not issue in "the survival of the fittest," but oftener of the violent, the cunning, the cruel. By that law there is no basis for human equality as the defiance of tyranny, the defence of liberty. For this, there is need of the moral perception that sees in the weakest and the lowliest the man, created by God for life, for freedom, and for joy. If superstition has been the handmaid of tyranny, materialism is tyranny itself. I grant that weighty arguments for the rights of men, for freedom of political organization and local government, may be derived from science, philosophy, experience, history; but none of these is so significant, so sweeping, so conclusive, nor are all of them together so weighty and enduring, as this single sentence, "All men are created equal." Let Americans ever stand upon that one sublime declaration, and hold fast the liberty that is *there* given them by "the laws of nature and of nature's God."

The second proposition of the Declaration is, "that, to secure these rights, governments are instituted among men, deriving their just powers from the consent of the governed." Here, more especially, must one keep in mind what was before said of one-sidedness of statement in a document intended to justify a particular measure, and to emphasize truths that were the refuge and defence of mankind against despotic power. Thus the Declaration speaks nowhere of duties, but only of rights; for its authors held that the Colonies had discharged their duties as loyal subjects of the crown, until the invasion and threatened annihilation of their rights compelled them to throw off their allegiance. It was rights that were in question, rights that were in jeopardy; and a bold, strong assertion of rights was what the case demanded. In such a document there was no call to qualify the statement of rights by a statement of their correlative duties, which existed in the very reason of things, and would assert themselves in due time.

So of the statement that "governments derive their just powers from the consent of the governed." The men of '76 did not look forward to a time when that same nation, whose independence they proclaimed " in the name and by the authority of the good people of the Colonies," would for years maintain, by force of arms, its government over several of its own States without " the consent of the governed," and this with every ground of reason and of right: they did not even look forward to the close of the war of independence, when, in the very State of Massachusetts, which led on the war against British taxation, a rebellion should break out against paying debts of the United States contracted for the war, and taxes levied by the State without " the consent of the governed; " and Massachusetts should invoke the aid of Federal troops in putting down her own citizens, and, having suppressed the rebellion with a strong hand, should sentence the ringleaders to death, also without "the consent of" these refractory subjects. In a word, the Congress of 1776 did not think it necessary to fortify the doctrines of the Declaration against such abuses and absurdities as would lead to the disintegration of society, and make government the prey of factions, or the sport of individual wills. It was not individual, personal wills that they were thinking of when they spoke of "the consent of the governed." The right of self-government in communities, the right of representation in some form in the government, the right to be recognized in laying taxes and framing laws, as parties having a substantial voice in the same, — this was the right that the British Parliament had attempted to wrest from them by an arbitrary government, a government without consent; and therefore they laid such stress upon governing with " the consent of the governed," without reference to the mode of government, or the manner in which such consent should be ascertained. Interpreted by its own light, this second proposition of the Declaration, like the first, contains a deep, far-reaching truth, — a truth by which to hold governments to their place and duty in the interest of mankind.

Man must live in society. In a solitary, single-handed contest with wild beasts, with untamed nature, and even with his own physical wants, it would fare hard with him as to the enjoyment of life, liberty, or happiness; and, in fact, he is born into and for society, and there he must abide. But, while the existence of society requires some mutual adjustment of the rights of individuals, only by crime against society can one forfeit any of his natural, personal rights. Crime apart, these rights are inalienable; and the independence of civil society, and its development in culture, require that these rights be guaranteed intact; that every man shall have equal security with any other in life, freedom, happiness, and shall be protected and encouraged in making the most of his powers, capacities, and opportunities for good.

The good to be sought in civil society is not, as Beccaria, Priestley, and the Bentham school would have it, an affair of the multiplication-table, "the greatest happiness of the greatest number," but the best possible facilities for happiness placed impartially within the reach of all. In artificial rights, the public good may sometimes claim the sacrifice of individual interests; as, for instance, when a right of way is taken through private lands. But no plea of public good can take away from me one natural right, so long as I am guiltless of crime against the public welfare. For the individual voluntarily to sacrifice life, freedom, happiness, to some public end, is noble, is divine; but for the majority to deprive him of these for the sake of "the greatest happiness of the greatest number" is an outrage upon that which is noble and divine in man. Society must leave to its every member his equal right to life, liberty, happiness. And what society must leave intact, that must the state secure. The state does not exist as an end in itself: it is the creation of society for its own conservation. Government is instituted by society, or rather it emerges from society as a condition necessary to its own existence. With society grow up institutions, customs, laws; and these, in time, take on the organic form of government. In every political society there is a latent sovereignty,—a power not only charged with exhibiting and defending the society against other powers without, but capable of maintaining the society within itself. But this power must be used for the well-being of the society whose attribute it is. Society does not exist for the state, but the state for society; and hence government is bound to secure to the integral members of society those rights upon which, as we have seen, society itself must rest for independence and culture. For the preservation of these rights, there is need of safety and order, the feeling of security, and hence need of government, to give to society security and permanence in and through the inalienable rights of its personal constituents.

The correlative duties of the citizen to the government belong to another category: we are here concerned with the ends and obligations of civil government. And we might almost say, it is the right of every man *to be governed;* i.e., to be under law and authority competent and willing to maintain all just rights, and thus to make him secure in the rights that are justly his. In social anarchy, there is no security for personal rights; and it is of the fundamental philosophy of society, that, "to secure these rights, governments are instituted among men." Take away that conception, and by what pretext under heaven should a government exist? Could men owe allegiance to a government that should avowedly disregard their right to life, liberty, and happiness, and seek to trample out those rights by despotic power? Would society ever purposely establish such a government, or willingly recognize its authority? Do slaves owe allegiance to the force that enslaves them? The second proposition of the Declaration of Independence is fundamental to human society, — that governments exist, not by virtue of force, nor to maintain the power and rule of the governing, but to secure the rights of the governed.

But here observe the admirable wisdom of the Declaration in its specification of rights. On this point, the omissions of the document are almost as important to its true interpretation as are its express declarations. Indeed, in commenting upon certain passages in the paper as he reported it, and which Congress voted to strike out, Jefferson makes the observation, that "the sentiments of men are known not only by what they receive, but what they reject also;"[1] and we may apply this rule of construction

---

[1] Jefferson's Works, vol. i. p. 19.

to his own omissions in the original draught of the Declaration. This, be it remembered, is a political document, and deals with political grievances and political rights. It is a document designed to justify to the world and to posterity the act of a people in declaring themselves a distinct nation; and it rests that action upon the fact that men are endowed with certain inalienable rights which government is bound to secure, but which the British Government had persistently sought to destroy. Now, when the specification of these rights is given, there is no mention, no hint even, of suffrage or of office-holding as a right with which man is endowed by his Creator. Had they conceived of suffrage as a natural right, and of eligibility to office as essential to human equality, and that a just government must secure these rights, then surely, in laying down the "inalienable rights" upon which all righteous government must be based, they would not have omitted these, nor have given them a secondary place under such generalities as life, liberty, and happiness. But in truth they had no thought of classing these political rights, or rather political trusts and privileges, with those natural rights that are in all men equal and inalienable. The distinction between these two classes of rights — rights that are natural to man as a being, and rights that are acquired by certain acts or conditions, or created by society — is of supreme importance for testing certain modern theories of popular government in contrast with the government actually contemplated by the Declaration of Independence. That I may enjoy my natural right to life, liberty, happiness, it is not necessary that I should in any way rule over you, or attempt to control your actions by authority. It may, indeed, be necessary to the just enjoyment of our several rights, both yours and mine, that there be some competent authority above us both to cause us to respect each other's rights, if we will not do this from a sense of justice and honor; but such an authority is not an exercise of the right itself, nor a part of the natural right, but a something brought in from without to secure the enjoyment of said natural right under the conditions and limitations proper to human society. The natural rights enumerated in the Declaration require nothing but opportunity, and, for the most part, to be let alone.

Quite the reverse is it with political suffrage and political office. These, in their very nature, imply the act of governing others, and assume a qualification to govern. By what test, then, or evidence, shall we find in man a created equality in and for governing, answering to equality of right in life, liberty, happiness? Surely it is far from a "self-evident" truth that every man has by birth the right to govern his fellows. To claim this for all men alike is absurd, since a society of equal governors would make actual government void. For each or any to claim this for himself is to assume the prerogative of kingship. Government is a science; and to govern is a faculty, a capacity, an art, with which some men appear to be specially endowed by nature, to which others may attain by study, discipline, experience, but for which most men show a very small measure either of endowment or of aptitude. Since the very act of governing, even to the extent of participation in government by suffrage, affects society in its every interest, and may put its every interest, and its very existence, in jeopardy, no one can claim it as his right to govern, unless he can show his competence to govern, to such extent, at least, as he demands to participate in government.

We have seen, that, in the political society, each man retains his equal natural rights, and that society is bound to conserve these impartially for all its members; but in the state, which is the *governing* function of society, no man can have a right, except upon the basis of duty accomplished toward the state in fitting himself intellectually, morally, practically, to the best of his ability, for its service. Since government emerges from society, and is for the behoof of society, it is for society to determine in what form, and by what persons, it shall be governed; and each political society must determine this for itself, in its own way. Hence there is no natural right to rule, nor to vote; but each and every form of participation in the state-function or governing-power of society is a trust, a privilege, conferred or conceded by society itself, subject to such conditions as society may impose. Here the principle of "the greatest happiness of the greatest number," which cannot be maintained in the sphere of purely natural rights, may have its legitimate application.

As a physical or sentient being, man is entitled to life; as a being of intelligence and will, he is entitled to liberty; as a being of moral affections, hopes, desires, sympathies, he is entitled to happiness: these are natural rights with which he is endowed by his Creator, and for which he is in no way obliged to his fellows. But man is also a political being, adapted to live in society and under government; and it is impossible to conceive of him in that relation except as owing duties to his fellows, and deriving benefits from his fellows; so that every right that he acquires as a member of political society is of the nature of an obligation to the members in common of the same society. Hence such rights are distinct in their ground and tenure from natural rights, and can never be brought within the same category.

No political philosopher of recent times has gone farther than John Stuart Mill in maintaining natural liberty, or "the sovereignty of the individual over himself." Yet Mill has also shown, with his accustomed clearness, that there is a "rightful limit" to that sovereignty, at which "the authority of society" begins. "Every one," says Mill, "who receives the protection of society, owes a return for the benefit; and the fact of living in society renders it indispensable that each should be bound to observe a certain line of conduct towards the rest. This conduct consists, first, in not injuring the interests of one another, or rather certain interests, which, either by express legal provision or by tacit understanding, ought to be considered as rights; and, secondly, in each person bearing his share (to be fixed on some equitable principle) of the labors and sacrifices incurred for defending the society or its members from injury and molestation. These conditions society is justified in enforcing, at all cost, to those who endeavor to withhold fulfilment." Nor is this all that society may do. "If one has infringed the rules necessary for the protection of his fellow-creatures, individually or collectively, the evil consequences of his acts do not then fall on himself, but on others; and society, as the protector of all its members, must retaliate on him, must inflict pain on him for the express purpose of punishment, and must take care that it be sufficiently severe."

Mill goes on to argue " that misapplied notions of liberty are a real obstacle to the fulfilment by the State of its duties." He asks, " Is it not almost a self-evident axiom, that the State should require and compel the education, up to a certain standard, of every human being who is born its citizen?" And he does not scruple to say that " the laws which, in many countries on the Continent, forbid marriage, unless the parties can show that they have the means of supporting a family, do not exceed the legitimate powers of the State; and, whether such laws be expedient or not, they are not objectionable as violations of liberty."[1]

Without following Mr. Mill in all his specific applications, we must agree that this large concession to the rights and powers of the State by so sturdy a champion of individualism and so acute a philosopher, and especially his insisting that the State should not be impeded in its duties by misapplied notions of the liberty of the citizen, points to a radical distinction in fact and kind between natural rights, and rights originating in, or conferred by, society. That Mr. Jefferson perceived this distinction, and therefore purposely omitted all mention, in the Declaration of Independence, of voting or ruling from his enumeration of the rights with which all men are endowed by their Creator, is plain from his correspondence. Thus, in his letter to Mr. Coray, dated Oct. 31, 1823, after forty-seven years' experience of the doctrines of the Declaration, in recommending a government for Greece, Mr. Jefferson says, " The equal rights of man, and the happiness of every individual, are now acknowledged to be the only legitimate objects of government. Modern times have the signal advantage, too, of having discovered the only device by which these rights can be secured ; to wit, government by the people, acting not in person, but by representatives chosen by themselves; that is to say, by every man of ripe years and sane mind who either contributes by his purse or person to the support of his country." Could any thing be clearer or wiser than this statement? Immediate participation in the government by each and every man as a man is not at all necessary to the idea of popu-

[1] On Liberty, by John Stuart Mill, pp. 134, 142, 189, 194.

lar government. The people govern by representatives; and this government by the people is not itself one of the equal rights of man, but is a "*device* by which these rights can be secured." Nor has every man an equal right to choose representatives in this government by the people: for, according to Mr. Jefferson, he must be of mature age, and capable of forming a sound judgment; and he must serve his country with his purse or his person; or, as he puts it in another letter, "among the men who either pay or fight for their country, no line of right can be drawn."[1] This political right of sharing in the government requires evidence of capacity, and proof of service rendered, or duty done. It is not, therefore, a natural right, but a right or trust fixed by society upon its own terms. Mr. Jefferson argues truly, that it is safe to commit this trust largely to the people; but he never loses sight of the fact, that it is a trust to which are appended certain qualifications and conditions. Speaking of juries, he says, "The people, especially when moderately instructed, are the only safe, because the only honest, depositaries of the public rights, and should, therefore, be introduced into the administration of them *in every function to which they are sufficient.*" The words that I have emphasized qualify the right or trust by the capacity or sufficiency; and Jefferson shows his meaning by urging Mr. Coray to prepare his countrymen for independence "by improving their minds, and qualifying them for self-government."

In a letter of May 8, 1825, to Henry Lee, Jefferson states this to have been the object of the Declaration of Independence: "Not to find out new principles or new arguments never before thought of, not merely to say things which had never been said before, but to place before mankind the common sense of the subject, in terms so plain and firm as to command their assent, and to justify ourselves in the independent stand we are compelled to take." He admits that the leaders of the Revolution were novices in the science of government, by which he intends that they had not, in advance, framed a system of independent government; and it is evident, that, at the date of the Declaration, they had not decided what form

---

[1] To John Hampden Pleasants, April 19, 1824: Works, vol. vii. 345.

of government they should adopt. Those who now regard suffrage as one of the natural, inalienable rights of man, can find no warrant for this doctrine in the Declaration of Independence, nor in the writings of the apostle of American democracy, Thomas Jefferson. In his view, suffrage was a prerogative of society, to be intrusted to individuals competent and worthy to exercise it. Does any ask, How comes society by this prerogative? The answer is, By the right and necessity of caring for its own existence. History, philosophy, experience, teach but one lesson; and no amount of theorizing can ever make it otherwise than that, in point of fact, in every political society, they who can rule will and must rule, though bound to rule with equal justice toward all. This is nature, equity, common sense, and leads to true republicanism.

Mr. Jefferson's theory of the best government was, that the actual governing power should be in the hands of the few who by nature and by training have both character and capacity for administering affairs; and these he designates the "natural aristocracy." In an elaborate letter to John Adams,[1] — more an essay than a letter, — written after both had filled the office of President, Jefferson says, "I agree with you, that there is a natural aristocracy among men. The grounds of this are virtue and talents. . . . This natural aristocracy I consider as the most precious gift of nature for the instruction, the trusts, and government of society." Observe here how far Jefferson was from accounting all men equal to the function of governing, or endowed for this by the Creator, and entitled to it as a personal and inalienable right. "An artificial aristocracy, founded on wealth and birth, without either virtue or talents," he said, "is a mischievous ingredient in government; and provision should be made to prevent its ascendency." But an aristocracy of nature, born to rule, Jefferson believed in, as he had reason to; "and indeed," as he says, "it would have been inconsistent in creation to have formed man for the social state, and not to have provided virtue and wisdom enough to manage the concerns of the society. May we not even

---

[1] Oct. 28, 1813: Works, vi. 223.

say, that that form of government is the best which provides the most effectually for a pure selection of these natural *aristoi* into the offices of government?"

This selection for office of the persons qualified and designated by nature to rule he would leave to the body of the people, as being entitled to a voice in the composition of their government, and as likely, in their own interest, to select good and true men for this trust. He would "leave to the citizens the free election and separation of the *aristoi* from the *pseudo-aristoi*, of the wheat from the chaff. In general, they will elect the really good and wise. In some instances, wealth may corrupt, and birth blind them, but not in sufficient degree to endanger the society." It is clear, then, that the Declaration of Independence does not confound political powers with natural rights, the right of living and enjoying life with the right of ruling.[1]

To point the distinction between the rights with which man is endowed by his Creator, and rights that are intrusted or conceded to him by the political society of which he is a member, we may refer conclusively to the trial by jury. This is regarded as the very kernel of the *Magna Charta* of King John, which makes that instrument the palladium of every Englishman in respect of life, liberty, and property, — the possession of which last is, to most men, a synonyme for happiness. The Charter declares, "No freeman shall be taken or imprisoned, or be disseized of his freedom or liberties or free customs, or be outlawed or exiled, or any otherwise damaged, nor will we pass upon

---

[1] Some years ago, in an address to the Phi Beta Kappa Society at New Haven, on How to build a Nation, I argued for a "guild of the cultivated" to crown a republican society, and give order and beauty to its affairs. The objection, that this would be to create an aristocracy, I met by pointing out that the Church of Christ is the most presumptuous aristocracy under heaven, claiming to be composed of "the saints," "the holy," "the sons of God," and to constitute upon earth a "kingdom of heaven," above all other kingdoms. But, at the same time, the Church is the one example on earth of a pure and ennobling democracy; for this hierarchy of God is open to every man to enter it, simply by purifying and ennobling his own character; and, once within its pale, all are brethren. So should it be with the governing hierarchy in the republic, — open to all men through conditions of intelligence, character, worth, that would make them personally nobler, and at the same time lift them to the noblest sphere of equality. Such a "guild of the cultivated" would, I think, stand higher than Jefferson's "natural aristocracy," and yet open a wider or more democratic range of selection of the instruments of power.

him, nor send upon him, but by lawful judgment of his peers, or by the law of the land;" and this promise Mr. Hallam styles "the keystone of English liberty." [1]

In the Declaration of Rights put forth by the first Continental Congress in 1774, it was resolved, "That the respective Colonies are entitled to the common law of England, and more especially to the great and inestimable privilege of being tried by their peers of the vicinage according to the course of that law." The Declaration of Independence charged it as a crime upon the King of England, that, in many cases, he "had deprived the colonists of the benefits of trial by jury." And the Constitution of the United States provides, that, "in all criminal prosecutions, the accused shall enjoy the right to a speedy and public trial by an impartial jury of the state and district wherein the crime shall have been committed;" and also, that in suits at common law, where the value in controversy shall exceed twenty dollars, the right of trial by jury shall be preserved." But this much-vaunted right, the chosen defence of life and liberty against tyranny and injustice, has none of the qualities that mark life and liberty as natural and inalienable rights. The keystone of liberty it well may be; yet trial by jury is no part of man's natural liberty,—the palladium of natural rights, but not itself one of those rights. What is there, for instance, in nature, to impart the sanctity of justice to the deliberation of *twelve* men and the unanimity of their verdict, rather than to a majority of fifteen jurors, as in Scotland? Moreover, experience has shown that juries may be biassed, bribed, intimidated, and may do the grossest injustice to the accused, or the highest injury to society and the laws. What is wanted for the safety of the innocent, and the punishment of the guilty, is knowledge, wisdom, experience, and the spirit of justice, in the administrators of the law; and hence, in the United States as well as in Great Britain, there is a growing disposition, in many cases, to dispense with a jury, and trust to arbitration, or to the decision of a judge, subject to appeal. But that is no natural right that can thus change its basis through experience or expediency: it is a contrivance for

[1] Middle Ages, b. ii. cviii.

the protection of individual rights through the machinery of social organization; and, since all men possess certain inalienable rights, they have also a right to the best institutions for securing those rights. As to the jury, Jefferson found in this contrivance almost a democratic participation in the judicial function of government, — a sort of revival of the Teutonic Gemeinde, in which every freeman might be a judge.[1] Yet how gladly would the average citizen escape being summoned from his business or his pleasures to fulfil his inalienable duty of hearing causes, and sitting in judgment upon the actions of his fellows! But men do not thus lightly throw away their natural rights. In truth, provisions for ruling and judging are of society, and must be ordained by each political society in its own way. In some societies, the rule will be that of superior intelligence or endowment; in some, of power; in some, of conceded privilege or custom; and, in others, the rule of the majority. Mr. Jefferson placed it in the last. "Where," he asks, "shall we find the origin of *just* powers, if not in the majority of the society? Will it be in the minority? or in an individual of that minority?" This is the key to the statement of the Declaration, that governments "derive their just powers from the consent of the governed." He was not thinking of a poll of equal rights, that each individual as an "inalienable" voter might "consent" to be governed thus or so, but of the community, the political society, in some method of its own, framing, commissioning, or consenting to, the government under which it should live; and, in this view of its meaning, this statement of the Declaration, like those that precede it, is also true, and of deep and far-reaching significance for governments and for mankind.

It was by a vote of both houses of Parliament in 1688, setting a precedent for the Philadelphia Congress of 1776, that the throne of Great Britain was declared vacant; for-

[1] Yet, curiously enough, Jefferson's own doctrine of human rights in the Declaration of Independence did away with the fundamental argument upon which the jury had stood as a defence of persons and rights. So long as privileged classes exist in society, there is a savor of democratic freedom in the rule that every man shall be tried by his *peers*. But, in the republic, class distinctions are done away, and, as before the law, every man is the peer of every other. Hence a democracy deprives the jury of its old-time distinction as "the palladium of liberty."

asmuch as King James II. "had endeavored to subvert the constitution of the kingdom by breaking the original contract between the king and the people, and had violated the fundamental laws," and moreover, "by withdrawing himself out of the kingdom, had abdicated the government." But it was only a very small majority of the same Parliament that voted to offer the crown to William, Prince of Orange; yet, to this day, Great Britain has consented to be governed by the settlement made at the close of the Revolution. An assembly hurriedly chosen and irregularly convened at Bordeaux, representing at best but a part of France, and deputed for the one business of making a peace, and ridding the capital and country of an enemy, — this extemporized assembly raised an army, fought against and seized Paris, transferred the capital to Versailles, made a treaty of peace, raised a loan, paid an enormous debt, emancipated the nation, exercised sovereignty in every form, and though composed of legitimists, Orléanists, imperialists, and republicans of every grade, at last compromised upon a government compounded of a person, a name, and a constitution; and this government exercises its just powers of law and order with the acquiescence of France, — "the consent of the governed." Sometimes too, where a government originates in usurpation, or where its measures at first seem arbitrary, the acquiescence of the people after the fact, their condoning the irregularity by partaking of its fruits, gives to the government a color of just power and of popular sanction. In short, every government is bound to keep constantly in view the best good of the totality of its subjects, to identify itself with the welfare of the society over which it presides, to be mindful of the wants and wishes of the political community whose organ it is, to set the people in its common-weal before and above the State in its *personnel*, to guard the rights of all with an impartial hand; and only so far as a government is animated by this spirit, and acts for these ends, are its powers just, or can it, in political ethics, claim the right to be.

The attachment of a people to their government may be variable; their sentiment toward officers and policy may change with men and measures; their loyalty may be that of enthusiastic devotion, of calm acquiescence, or of patient endurance: but there inheres in every body politic a latent right of revolution; and, so long as the people do not revive this right, the government *de facto* is presumed to hold its powers with "the consent of the governed."

This right of revolution is the third point made by the Declaration of Independence; or, rather, it is the conclusion of its famous syllogism. The fact of revolution, or of repudiating an existing government, and setting up another in its stead, was that which the Declaration was framed to justify. The first proposition being that all men are created equal, and endowed by their Creator with certain inalienable rights, among which are life, liberty, and the pursuit of happiness; and the second proposition being, that, to secure these rights, governments are instituted among men, deriving their just powers from the consent of the governed, — the conclusion is reached, that, "whenever any form of government becomes destructive of these ends, it is the right of the people to alter or to abolish it, and to institute a new government, laying its foundation on such principles, and organizing its powers in such form, as to them shall seem most likely to effect their safety and happiness." Observe the unimpassioned dignity of this statement. It has been alleged that the style of the Declaration betrays the impetuosity of youth; but though, at the date of its composition, Jefferson was only thirty-two years of age, and had not quite toned down his rhetoric, yet in this passage of the document he exhibits that philosophic caution and precision which won for him in after-life the title, "the sage of Monticello." Precisely at the point where the European revolutionist of recent type would have exploded in fiery declamation, Jefferson is as calm, clear, and precise as if he were writing his scientific essay on a standard of uniform length, or that on the method of obtaining fresh water from salt. The radical change of government is to be sought only in the last resort, when government has become destructive of the fundamental rights of society, for the security of which it was established; and then it may be altered or removed only for the purpose of erecting some better structure for the safety and happiness of the people. And, as if this cautious statement of the right of revolution were not enough, further cautions are given as to the application of a right, which is somewhat analogous to the right of exploding gunpowder to arrest a conflagration: "Prudence, indeed, will dictate that governments long established should not be changed for light and transient causes; and accordingly all experience hath shown that mankind are more disposed to suffer while evils are sufferable than to right themselves by abolishing the forms to which they are accustomed. But when a long train of abuses and usurpations, pursuing invariably the same object, evinces a design to reduce them under absolute despotism, it is their right, it is their duty, to throw off such government, and to provide new guards for their future security. Such has been the patient sufferance of these Colonies; and such is now the necessity which constrains them to alter their former systems of government."

The abstract right of revolution I do not require to argue. This is to society what the right of self-defence is to the individual. Since government is a function of society, if, through injustice and usurpation, the government becomes an unbearable oppression, destructive of the ends for which society exists, there must rest in society, which gives being and form to the state, an ultimate right to redress itself by displacing, or otherwise changing, the falsified government in the interest of a true and righteous ordering of the state. But this right, more, perhaps, than any other, needs to be qualified and restricted in the interest of society itself. So great are the calamities of civil war, so frightful the horrors of anarchy, that the overturning of government by violence may be rightfully attempted only for the ends of justice, for the higher good. There must be in it that which appeals to the moral sense as just and right to warrant a movement that may deluge the land with blood, and send mourning into every house. This point, as we have seen, is guarded in the Declaration of Independence, which makes the right of revolution hinge upon the safety and happiness of the people when these are in peril of destruction from the existing government.

But even with right motive upon its side, and a high and worthy end in view, a revolution should not be ventured upon merely to get rid of annoyances or grievances that reach not to the core of society, and that time might relieve or allay, but to redress accumulated and unbearable wrongs for which there seems no other remedy. This rule, likewise, is fully recognized in the Declaration: no established government should be violently changed " for light and transient causes ; " but the people should rather " suffer while evils are sufferable." Abuses and usurpations protracted and undisguised, tending always to destroy the rights of the subject, and bring him hopelessly under despotic power, — these justify and demand a revolution as their remedy. Yet even at this point, when there is every legal and moral justification for recourse to arms, it may be well to pause, and see if there be a fair prospect of success to warrant the fearful responsibility of attempting it. As Lord Brougham has pithily said, " The evils must have become intolerable before the resistance is to be attempted: the parties whose rights are invaded must first exhaust every peaceful and orderly and lawful means of obtaining redress. An insurrection is only to be justified by the necessity which leaves no alternative ; and the probability of success is to be weighed, in order that a hopeless attempt may not involve the community in distress and confusion." Every one of these qualifying conditions was fully met in the state of the American Colonies when they put forth their Declaration of Independence. They were not revolutionists in theory, but defenders of society, and restorers of humanity, in fundamental rights. Indeed, what is commonly conceived of as a political right of revolution, I prefer to characterize as the moral *duty of resistance* to tyranny and wrong, even to the extent of breaking up the whole established order of things, — a duty which, when the case arises, men must be ready to perform, or, for example's sake, to perish in the attempt; and this moral distinction also is not wanting in the Declaration of Independence, which affirms, that, when it is the obvious design of a government to reduce a people under absolute despotism, " it is their right, it is their *duty*, to throw off such government."

I come back, then, to the wisdom and moderation of this Declaration as one of the marvels of political history, — that men in the very act of revolution, while proclaiming their independence, were so careful to measure their rights and define their duties, and to guard the future peace and order of society against the perversion of the precedent they were compelled to set. They clothed their Revolution with the sanctity of duty by throwing around it the three conditions required to vindicate a war of society upon government: (1) The movement must be founded in justice, and have in view the deliverance of society from evil, and its re-establishment upon the sound basis of the public good; (2) The evils against which it protests must be grievous and unbearable wrongs; (3) Revolution should appear to be the only, and at the same time a feasible, mode of redress. Bad government, at the worst, may be better than anarchy; and such are the horrors of civil war, that no people should dare attempt a revolution save in the last resort against desperate wrongs, and with a reasonable hope of success in the attempt to win justice by the sword. The French Constitution of June 24, 1793, declared that "every order against a person, in cases and forms not specified by law, is arbitrary and tyrannical," — a proposition the truth of which is now generally admitted, except during a state of siege; but the article added, "The person against whom such an order should be executed by force has the right to resist it by force,"[1] — a declaration that goes far beyond the naked right of self-defence, and would authorize every citizen, and much more any body of citizens, when aggrieved by an unjust act of government, to resist by violence in the first instance, and hence would keep alive in the body politic a latent fever of rebellion, liable to break out upon the slightest provocation. Such a "right of revolution" would arm the citizens *en permanence* as a police against the government, and subject the authority of the State to the caprice and anarchy of individual wills. It might overthrow a bad government, but could never establish good and stable society.

Mr. Jefferson, during his residence in Paris, seems to

[1] Article 11.

have had his head turned for a moment by the political philosophy that prepared the French Revolution. Writing from Paris in 1789, he said, " The earth belongs always to the living generation: they may manage it, then, and what proceeds from it, as they please, during their usufruct. They are masters, too, of their own persons; and, consequently, may govern them as they please. But persons and property make the sum of the objects of government. The constitution and the laws of their predecessors are extinguished, then, in their natural course, with those whose will gave them being. This could preserve that being till it ceased to be itself, and no longer. Every constitution, then, and every law, naturally expires at the end of thirty-four years. If it be enforced longer, it is an act of force, and not of right."[1] Again he wrote from Paris, "The late rebellion in Massachusetts has given more alarm than I think it should have done. Calculate that one rebellion in thirteen States, in the course of eleven years, is but one for each State in a century and a half. No country should be so long without a revolution."[2]

This theory of revolution would make of government a pendulum, but without even a fixed centre of oscillation: it would build the State upon the slope of a volcano or the bank of a mountain-torrent on a deliberate calculation of an eruption or an inundation once in a generation. It ignores the fact that men of at least three several generations are always mingled together, and profit contemporaneously by each other's labors; for, though vital statistics have averaged a generation at thirty-three years, the curtain does not fall upon the stage of life three times in a century that the earth may be cleared of one generation, and another may appear. Generations do not march on and off the stage in platoons. Men are born and grow, and society and the state are things of growth; for there enter into the constitution of society and of government certain *ethical* principles that have a permanent life. When one generation with toil and blood has won freedom of thought and freedom of conscience, and has caused these to be incorporated with the political organism of society, no after-generation is at liberty to vacate the

[1] Letter to Madison: Works, iii. 106.   [2] Ibid., ii. 331.

charter of these rights. Human society is organic, and exists in continuity, having certain uniform, transmissible, and indefeasible interests, that each generation, in turn, receives as a heritage from the past in trust for the future.[1] The extravagances of Mr. Jefferson, just quoted, reflect the French philosophy of the eighteenth century concerning man, liberty, the social compact, and kindred themes of Diderot, Rousseau, Voltaire: they illustrate the vicious maxim of Diderot, that "the first step towards philosophy is incredulity;" and would make the first step towards society a mutual distrust, the first step towards the state a chronic insecurity. The American doctrine of revolution, on the contrary, was clearly and consistently maintained by John Adams. "The means and measures of ours," he wrote, "may teach mankind that revolutions are no trifles; that they ought never to be undertaken rashly; nor without deliberate consideration and sober reflection; nor without a solid, immutable, eternal foundation of justice and humanity; nor without a people possessed of intelligence, fortitude, and integrity sufficient to carry them, with steadiness, patience, and perseverance, through all the vicissitudes of fortune, the fiery trials and melancholy disasters they may have to encounter."[2] All these conditions were fulfilled in the men who led the American Revolution; and, when Adams thus characterized it, he had before him its results of more than forty years. It is due to Jefferson to say that he emerged from the visionary philosophy of the French revolutionary era, and returned to the sober discrimination that marks the declaration of the American Revolution;[3] but his momentary aberration serves to point more sharply the distinction between the notions of man, liberty, society, and the state, that mark the two greatest events of the last century, — the American Revolution and the French. The American Revolution based itself upon a declaration of the equal rights of men, and issued in a republic under a constitution approved by the people: the French Revolution also

[1] I have expanded this argument in an address to the Union League Club, entitled Revolution against Free Government not a Right, but a Crime.
[2] Written in 1818: Works, x. 283.
[3] Letter to Lafayette, Feb. 14, 1815: Works, vol. vi. 421.

put forth a declaration of the rights of man, and resolved the nation into a republic with a constitution. But at this point the analogy ceases; and the two movements, starting from the same idea, and aiming at the same end, diverge as widely in their methods and their philosophy as in their practical results to the nations and to mankind. The American Colonies revolted against the usurpation of a government that distance and alienation had rendered almost foreign, and threw off forms that had dwindled to shadows. The French nation revolted not only against a government and its oppressions, but against the whole constitution of society upon its own soil: the monarchy, the nobility, the clergy, the body of landholders, the administration of education, of justice, of police, the civil and criminal codes, the entire fabric and material of what for ages had been the social structure of France, were tumbled into the abyss; and from that chaos of terror and blood it was sought to create a new world of order, freedom, light. But the masterful philosophy that shaped and guided the American Revolution was not there. Mirabeau possessed this; but it perished with that "head" which was his only "party." Lafayette essayed it; but France had no Washington: and so the nation, stripped of king and priest, of state and church, of loyalty and reverence, of form and precedent, put its faith in a philosophy of freedom and of man, that began in the negation of that spiritual life which alone makes man worthy of freedom, or freedom a boon to man.

It is but just to the French Revolution to say, that, if its excesses were monstrous, its provocations were also monstrous. If it filled Europe with the stench of its abominations, this was because society was already rotten to the core. One cannot fairly compare the French Revolution with the American without allowing for the difference between the two nations in geographical position, in historical and social antecedents, and also in race-training and temperament. France was not left, has never since till now been left, to work out her problems alone. She has never been free from the necessity of maintaining a great army; and, with a nation under arms, freedom is always in duress. But, after all these concessions, there remains a vital divergence in the philosophy of the two movements.

The French theorists mistook the source of power for the foundation of freedom. Perceiving that power in the State should emanate directly or indirectly from the people, they fancied that universal suffrage was the equivalent and the guaranty of personal and national freedom. Borrowing a phrase from the American Declaration of Independence, they, too, declared that "government is instituted to insure to man the free use of his natural and inalienable rights:" but they defined these rights as "equality, liberty, security, property," and asserted that "every citizen has the right of taking part in the legislation;" thus practically merging all human rights in the right of suffrage, as they had merged all political power in the sovereignty of the people. To them political liberty was not a means of securing men in their proper freedom, but was itself the end, the supreme good, of man and of society. "The French Republic," said they, "places the constitution under the guaranty of all virtues."[1] Thus they traced freedom to a political foundation, and vested it in a political form. Regarding this as the ultimate good, they declared, "When government violates the rights of the people, insurrection of the people, and of every single part of it, is the most sacred of its rights, and the highest of its duties."[2] This constitution was ordered to be engraved on tablets, and set up in the hall of legislation and in public places; but, having been accepted by the people in their primary assemblies, it came back to be strangled in the convention that gave it birth. To-day again one reads in Paris, on the palaces, the churches, the museums, the libraries, the parks, the abattoirs, the very cemeteries, *Propriété Nationale, Liberté, Égalité, Fraternité*, — to be wiped out, perhaps, by the mop of the next *régime*.

The American Declaration of Independence, on the contrary, makes the essence of freedom not political, but *ethical*, — the attribute of man as a spiritual person: and the State, which by forms of political liberty is to guard this freedom, which is older and higher than itself, derives

---

[1] Constitution, Art. 123.   [2] Declaration, Art. 35.

from it something of its spiritual dignity; so that the body politic is possessed also of a moral personality. Hence the Declaration does not couch natural rights in political forms, but makes the whole nature of man — physical, intellectual, and moral — the basis of rights for which political society is bound to care, and before which governments must fall when they attempt to destroy the rights, inherent in personality, with which man is endowed by his Creator. As a sentient being, man has the right of life; but why is his life a right girt about with law, when he takes at will the life of other animals, and feeds upon theirs to sustain his own? As a creature of intelligence and will, man is capable of freedom, and has the right to liberty of thought, speech, movement, action. But why is liberty a right to him, when at his pleasure he puts restraint upon other animals, and makes them his servants? As a being of a moral nature, with national affections, imagination, taste, the power of choosing good, capacity of virtue, man is capable of *happiness*, — a term that is never degraded to the animal passions and pleasures, — a term descriptive only of an intelligent, free, moral person. The good of such a person is higher than all laws of nature, higher than all material things and all conventional forms. The pursuit of happiness is an inalienable right, with which he is endowed by his Creator. As a social being, he retains all these original qualities and endowments: they cannot be alienated by social contract; they cannot be merged in political forms. Society is but an instrument for the more perfect development of this transcendent person in the best use and enjoyment of life, through liberty and the pursuit of happiness; and society compounded of such personalities is itself a spiritual organism, with the right to freedom and to the most consummate good for the whole body and for all its parts. Before this spiritual dignity of manhood, government must bow as to a nature higher than its own. Government cannot use man as a mere numerical factor in the social machine. Because of this original, spiritual dignity of his nature, government must make his life, his liberty, his happiness, its care, and see that these have their fullest play. Before this inherent, inalienable dignity, government must go down, if it shall dare infringe upon the natural rights of man. And yet, because the well-being of man is above all other considerations, even that which threatens him with evil should not be rashly overthrown, lest the violence should do him greater harm. There is the American doctrine of man, of freedom, of government, of revolution, — that man, who is first in order of being, should have a political and social state suited to his endowments; that the true life of society is to be sought, not by perpetual revolution, but by progressive evolution; not by overturning, but by uplifting.

The French philosophy of the eighteenth century failed to construct a free and stable society, because it failed of that spiritual conception of society and man that underlies the American Declaration. The philosophy of Mill, Comte, Buckle, fails for the same reason. Neither materialism nor positivism can provide a basis for freedom in the individual or in the community. You cannot have the play of "Hamlet" without the Prince of Denmark; and, in the great drama of freedom, you cannot move forward without that grand impersonation of freedom, — man, as endowed by his Creator with the gift and capacity of liberty and happiness. Society can give no man freedom: all men are created equal.

> "What constitutes a State?
> Not high-raised battlements or labored mound,
>   Thick wall or moated gate;
> Not cities proud, with spires and turrets crowned.
>   No: men, high-minded men, —
>   Men who their duties know,
> But know their rights, and, knowing, dare maintain, —
>   These constitute a State."

Upon the principles thus laid down, the Declaration of Independence proceeds to justify the rejection of British rule by an enumeration of specific grievances. The king is charged with attempting to subvert the legislative power in the Colonies, by suspending legislatures, by dissolving them, by refusing to sanction their acts; by denying new elections; by forcing upon the Colonies the direct legislation of the British Parliament, without permitting them to be represented in the Parliament, or even to be heard there by petition. The king is charged with attempting to control or to corrupt the judiciary by making the judges dependent on his will alone; by exempting his officers, civil and military, from trial within the Colonies for offences there committed; by abolishing in many cases the right of trial by jury; by arresting, without warrant of law, colonists for alleged offences against the government, and transporting them to England, to be there punished by arbitrary power. The king is charged with setting up a military jurisdiction over the Colonies, making the military independent of and superior to the civil power by quartering armed troops upon the Colonies, sending foreign mercenaries to subdue them, and by inciting negroes and Indians to insurrection. The king is charged with attempting to destroy the prosperity of the Colonies by restricting immigration, refusing grants of lands, cutting off trade, and imposing taxes without consent. And, as the crowning grievance, the king is charged with taking away the charters of the Colonies, and attempting to subvert their fundamental right of local government. For years, these growing usurpations had been opposed by petition and remonstrance, but in vain. It was evident that the object of the king was the establishment of an absolute tyranny over the Colonies. He was trying to subjugate them by force, — ravaging their coasts, and burning their towns; and there was nothing left for them but to fall back upon their inalienable rights, and make a stand. The proofs of these several charges they had already laid before the world. History has ratified their action; and mankind confess their obligation to the framers of that great charter of freedom, which was the first to formulate the functions of government in harmony with the natural rights of man, and to cement government and people, law and liberty, power and right, in a way that should endure the strain of war and the severer strain of success.

Two other grievances, not named in the Declaration, had strong influence in provoking the Revolution, — the slave-trade, which had been forced upon the Colonies in the interest of British commerce; and the attempt to force upon all the Colonies the English Church Establishment, which had always existed in some. In the first draught of the Declaration, preserved by Mr. Jefferson, there was a protest against the slave-trade, which in vigor, and pungency of rhetoric, surpassed any thing else in the document, and which, from the pen of a slaveholder, is a faithful testimony to reason and conscience struggling for the right. Let it speak for itself: —

"He has waged cruel war against human nature itself, violating its most sacred rights of life and liberty in the persons of a distant people who never offended him, captivating and carrying them into slavery in another hemisphere, or to incur miserable death in their transportation thither. This piratical warfare, the opprobrium of infidel powers, is the warfare of the Christian king of Great Britain. Determined to keep open a market where men should be bought and sold, he has prostituted his negative for suppressing every legislative attempt to prohibit or to restrain this execrable commerce; and, that this assemblage of horrors might want no fact of distinguished die, he is now exciting these very people to rise in arms among us, and to purchase that liberty of which he has deprived them, by murdering the people on whom he also obtruded them, thus paying off former crimes committed against the liberties of one people with crimes which he urges them to commit against the lives of another."

The fact that Jefferson wrote these words in a Declaration that he expected the entire Congress would adopt and send forth to the world, and that John Adams, Benjamin Franklin, Robert R. Livingston, and Roger Sherman, his colleagues on the committee, agreed to report his draught to the Congress for adoption, shows that the authors of that paper were not vaporing about universal liberty to cover their own struggle for independence, but were honestly devoted to the rights of man, and ready to rest the argument for liberty upon manhood, without thought of race, color, or condition. But the conditions were new and strange. They were attempting a great revolution upon most unequal terms: without unanimity, they must fail; and, to secure that unanimity, the moral and logical conviction of the many yielded to the supposed interests and feelings of the few. Jefferson writes in his autobiography, "The clause reprobating the enslaving the inhabitants of Africa was struck out in complaisance to South Carolina and Georgia, who had never attempted to restrain the importation of slaves, and who, on the contrary, still wished to continue it. Our Northern brethren also, I believe, felt a little tender under these censures; for though their people had very few slaves themselves, yet they had been pretty considerable carriers of them to others." [1]

It is easy now to say, that, in slurring over the fact of slavery, they made a fearful mistake; that they fastened upon the front of liberty a stigma that only the blood of the nation could wash out. It is easy to say, that with a higher faith in right and duty, a nobler courage and sacrifice for man, a loftier vision of the future, they would have set freedom and humanity a century forward. Can we be so sure of this? Let us not bedaub their sturdy work with our cheap rhetoric. They were honest, and did what they could. Their call was to make a nation; and, spite of all defects, they did make a nation, in whose fibre freedom and manhood were so ingrained, that, when recalled to the consciousness of its first principles, the nation was capable of restoring the rights of man at cost of three thousand million dollars and three hundred thousand lives. "Cursed be he that setteth light by his fathers; and let all the people say, Amen." [2]

That the rumor of erecting the Colonies into an episcopate of the Established Church fired the zeal for revolution, we have the explicit testimony of John Adams, who says that "this contributed as much as any other cause to arouse the attention, not only of the inquiring mind, but of the common people, and urge them to close thinking on the constitutional authority of Parliament over the Colonies;" [3] and in 1768 the Assembly of the Province of Mas-

[1] Works, vol. i. 19.   [2] Deut. xxvii. 16.
[3] Works, x. 185.
"If Parliament could tax us, they could establish the Church of England, with all its creeds, articles, tests, ceremonies, and titles, and prohibit all other churches as conventicles and schism-shops" (John Adams: Works, x. 287). This pretence was, in fact, set up by Dr. Sherlock, Bishop of London, in a letter to the king in council, February, 1759: "The Church of England *being established* in America, the Independents, and other dissenters who went to settle in New England, could only have *a toleration*" (Colonial Documents of New York, vii. 360). The bishop seems to have argued in this wise: The name "Virginia" was at first vaguely given to the whole coast of North America between the thirty-fourth and the forty-fifth degrees of north latitude; that is, from Cape Fear to Halifax. In the charter of the actual Colony of Virginia, it was stipulated that religion should be established according to the doctrine and rites of the Church of England; and now, a hundred and fifty years later,

sachusetts instructed their agent in London strenuously to oppose such an episcopate, as a peril to liberty, civil and religious.[1] Though this grievance was not named in the Declaration, the founders of the government provided against such a peril by abolishing all religious tests for political office, and enacting that "Congress shall make no law respecting an establishment of religion, or prohibiting the free exercise thereof."

But as their excessive caution in regard to slavery entailed upon the nation the conflict of a century, so this unbounded confidence in liberty threatens the opening century with conflict with a spiritual despotism that seeks to use the forms of freedom for controlling the votes, the schools, the laws, the moneys, of the republic, in the interest of a foreign potentate the most absolute and unyielding. Yet the principles of the Declaration are equal to this emergency. A new danger will rouse Americans once more to the consciousness of their history and of their trust; and the nation that first emancipated itself from political despotism, and next from domestic

---

when the boundaries of Virginia were definitely fixed, and other Colonies had their limits and other rights defined by charters, the bishop put forth the preposterous claim, that, by virtue of the first charter of Virginia, the Church of England should be held to be established in New England also. How the people of Boston relished this doctrine is shown by a caricature in the Political Register of 1769, entitled An Attempt to land a Bishop in America. A ship is at the wharf: the lord-bishop is in full canonicals, his carriage, crosier, and mitre on deck. The people appear with a banner inscribed with "Liberty and Freedom of Conscience," and are shouting, "No lords, spiritual or temporal, in New England!" "Shall they be obliged to maintain bishops that cannot maintain themselves?" They pelt the bishop with Locke, Sidney on Government, Barclay's Apology, Calvin's Works; and the unhappy prelate is glad to take refuge in the shrouds, crying, "Lord, now lettest thou thy servant depart in peace." This protest was not against a church, but against an enforced Establishment; and the books show in what strong reading the colonists were nourished. (See the picture in Thornton's Pulpit of the American Revolution.)

The Society for the Propagation of the Gospel in Foreign Parts was active in this scheme for establishing the Church through an American episcopate, to be supported, of course, by tithes. In October, 1776, Dr. Charles Inglis, Rector of Trinity Church, New York, wrote to the society, "The present rebellion is certainly one of the most causeless, unprovoked, and unnatural that ever disgraced any country. . . . Although civil liberty was the ostensible object, yet it is now past all doubt that an abolition of the Church of England was one of the principal springs of the dissenting leaders' conduct." He testifies that "all the society's missionaries in New Jersey, New York, Connecticut, have proved themselves faithful, loyal subjects," shutting up their churches rather than cease praying for the king; and he urges the episcopate as an encouragement to such fidelity (Doc. Hist. of New York, iii. 637 *seq.*).

[1] Life of Sam. Adams, i. 157.

slavery, will vindicate the independence of society and the state against the worse tyranny of ecclesiastical interference and control. Just because, in the immortal concept of the Declaration, man is a spiritual creation, endowed with the right to life, liberty, and the pursuit of good, so much the more must society keep intact its spiritual organism, its moral personality, the independence of which is life, liberty, happiness.

NOTE.

Since the foregoing Lecture was prepared for the press, I have had the pleasure of reading the more prominent orations which the celebration of the Centenary of Independence called forth in the United States, — that of the Hon. William M. Evarts at Philadelphia, that of the Rev. R. S. Storrs, D.D., at New York, that of the Hon. Charles Francis Adams at Taunton, and that of the Hon. Robert C. Winthrop at Boston. It is a fine testimony to the Declaration as a document of political ethics, that it could furnish to minds of such high and varied powers the theme of thoughtful and admiring discourse from so many different points of view. Neither orator crossed the track of the others, nor did the orations run in parallel lines of thought; yet each found in the Declaration — its antecedents, its incidents, its principles, its results — matter for a discourse of more than ordinary fulness and power; and it is only when one has read the whole four of these masterful productions, and gathered into one their total impressions, that he begins to realize how great an event, in history, in philosophy, and in the political and social ordering of the world, was the utterance that went forth from Independence Hall in Philadelphia on the Fourth of July, 1776. All these orators have passed the period of youthful enthusiasm, and neither of them was ever addicted to extravagance of speech. They have had large training and experience in law, divinity, statesmanship, letters, history; yet with every one of them the theme tasked the powers of the orator, as it before had tasked Choate, Everett, Webster. Nothing that was said about the Declaration could approach the silent eloquence of the instrument itself, as the original parchment, with the autographs of John Hancock, Samuel Adams, John Adams, Roger Sherman, Oliver Wolcott, Benjamin Franklin, Charles Carroll *of Carrollton*, Thomas Jefferson, and the sixfold row of worthies, was held up to the gaze of thousands on the spot where it was first read to the people. It could have been said of this parchment, as Webster said of the Bunker-hill Monument, "It is itself the orator of this occasion. . . . It looks, it speaks, it acts, to the full comprehension of every American mind, and the awakening of glowing enthusiasm in every American heart, surpassing all that the study of the closet, or even the inspiration of genius, can produce. . . . Its speech is of patriotism and courage, of civil and religious liberty, of free government, of the moral improvement and elevation of mankind, and of the immortal memory of those who, with heroic devotion, have sacrificed their lives for their country."[1] The Declaration was one of those epoch-making events whose influence can be measured only with

> "The golden compasses, prepared
> In God's eternal store to circumscribe
> This universe and all created things."

Having finished the preceding analysis of the Declaration before I was favored with the light which these several orators have thrown upon it, I prefer to let that stand as it was, and to put into the form of a supplementary note such further reflections as the orations have awakened. It is with diffidence that I set forth, or rather emphasize, another interpretation of the instrument than any made prominent by my scholarly colleagues; and it is with deference that I diverge at any point from their historical perspective of the event and its results. These orators agree in separating the philosophical substance of the Declaration from the political reasons given for declaring the Colonies "free and independent States." The whole virtue of the instrument lies in the first sentence of the second paragraph, beginning, "We hold these truths to be self-evident." Of this Mr. Adams says, "I have considered these significant words as vested with a virtue so subtle as certain ultimately to penetrate the abodes of mankind all over the world; but I separate them altogether from the solemn array of charges against King George which immediately follow in the Declaration." Now, to maintain for the Declaration its just place in political philosophy and among the few great historic charters of human freedom, we must be careful, on the one hand, not to claim for it too much, whether in intent or in result, and, on the other hand, not to obscure the essential truths of the instrument by forms or acts that were but incidental or consequential. In particular, we should not look to the Declaration for too much of novelty in political theory, nor too absolute a transformation in political forms. Mr. Evarts, for instance, quotes with approval the saying of Burke, "A great revolution has happened, — a revolution made, not by chopping and changing of power in any of the existing States, but by the appearance of a new State, of a new species, in a new part of the globe. It has made as great a change in all the relations and balances and gravitations of power as the appearance of a new planet would in the system of the solar world." Applied to the *Constitution* of the United States, which went into effect in 1789, this simile would be as accurate as it is beautiful: that did indeed mark "a new species" of political organization. But democracy was not new, a republic was not new, at the time of the Revolution. Burke was not ignorant of the precedents in Greek and Roman history, in the Italian republics, in the Federation of the Swiss, in the Dutch Republic; all which exempli-

[1] Works of Daniel Webster, i. 86.

fied more or less the doctrine of popular government. The American Revolution did not, like its successor in France, begin with a proclamation of the republic as thenceforth to mark a new era in the calendar, and give date to all decrees. Concerning forms of government, the Declaration is absolutely silent. It utters the voice of "*a free people*" resolved to disown a "tyrant" who is "unfit to be their ruler;" but it does not propose any change of government more specific than the quiet and orderly transformation of the "United Colonies" into "free and independent States." The act dissolving "all political connection between them and the State of Great Britain," though it constituted "a new State," did not create "a new species" of State.

Neither is it quite correct to speak of the Declaration as having abolished from American society all castes, ranks, orders, and all hereditary titles, privileges, and distinctions, whether of State or Church. In truth, excepting the occasional attempt of some royal governor or council to ape an aristocracy, none of these things existed in the Colonies, nor had been there from their first foundation. "The arts, sciences, and literature of England, came over with the settlers. That great portion of the common law which regulates the social and personal relations and conduct of men came also. The jury came; the *habeas corpus* came; the testamentary power came; and the law of inheritance and descent came also, except that part of it which recognizes the rights of primogeniture, which either did not come at all, or soon gave way to the rule of equal partition of estates among children. But the monarchy did not come, nor the aristocracy, nor the church, as an estate of the realm. Political institutions were to be framed anew, such as should be adapted to the state of things. But it could not be doubtful what should be the nature and character of these institutions. A general social equality prevailed among the settlers; and an equality of political rights seemed the natural, if not the necessary, consequence."[1] Thus the whole history and training of the colonists had established the fact that Burke read with such philosophic clearness, — "that the disposition of the people of America is wholly averse to any other than a free government."[2] Hence it was no novelty to them, no creation of "a new species" of State in severing the one tie that held them in nominal allegiance to the throne, to cut loose from an established church, an hereditary peerage, and every artificial caste and privileged order in the State. Living without these, they had naturally developed and strengthened that liberty, which, as Englishmen, they had inherited and enjoyed, without, perhaps, looking farther back than to *Magna Charta* for its origin and justification. Indeed, at the outset, what Mr. Burke said of the English Revolution was quite as true of the American, — "The Revolution was made to preserve our *ancient* indisputable laws and liberties, and that *ancient* constitution of government which is our only security for law and liberty."[3] Indeed, Mr. Burke himself said he

---

[1] Daniel Webster, Oration on the Completion of the Bunker-hill Monument: Works, i. 101.
[2] Letter to the Sheriffs of Bristol, 1777.
[3] Reflections on the Revolution in France.

considered "the Americans as standing at that time, and in that controversy, in the same relation to England as England did to King James II. in 1688."[1] In their earlier struggles with king and parliament, the colonists contended for their "rights as *Englishmen*" against the encroachments of arbitrary power. In his examination by the House of Commons, Franklin testified that they resisted the Stamp Act by virtue of "the common rights of Englishmen;" and the "Declaration of Rights" made by the first Continental Congress in 1774 was based mainly upon the English Constitution, and asserted, that, by derivation from their ancestors, the colonists were "entitled to all the rights, liberties, and immunities of free and natural-born subjects within the realm of England."

But the Declaration of Independence advanced beyond all charters, customs, grants, laws, heritages, to the natural and inalienable *rights of man* as the foundation of liberty and the sacred trust of government. As a purely philosophical conception, this was not original with Jefferson. In 1764 James Otis had said, "The first principle and great end of government is to provide for the best good of all the people." "Nothing but life and liberty are actually heritable." "The colonists are men: the colonists are therefore free-born; for, by the law of nature, all men are free-born, white or black." "A time may come when Parliament shall declare every American charter void; but the natural, inherent, and inseparable rights of the colonists as men and as citizens would remain, and, whatever became of charters, can never be abolished till the general conflagration."[2] It is highly probable that Jefferson had read the tract of Otis that made so great a stir on both sides of the Atlantic. But these sentiments were not new with Otis: a century before, Algernon Sidney had gone to the scaffold for the right of the people to govern themselves; and Jefferson owns to having read Sidney on Government. In the letter that Sidney prepared as his dying testament, he re-affirmed the principles of his "Discourses of Government," — "that God hath left nations to the liberty of setting up such governments as best please themselves;" and "that magistrates are set up for the good of nations, not nations for the honor or glory of magistrates."

The same doctrine was taught from the Scriptures by the early divines of New England. These devout students of the Bible learned from that book, more than any other, the first principles of civil and religious liberty. In May, 1637, Thomas Hooker, first pastor of Hartford, preached a sermon on the foundations of civil government, in which he laid down these positions: —

"I. That the choice of public magistrates belongs unto the people by God's own allowance.

"II. The privilege of election, which belongs to the people, therefore, must not be exercised according to their humors, but according to the blessed will and law of God.

"III. They who have power to appoint officers and magistrates, it is in their power also to set the bounds and limitations of the power and place unto which they call them."

[1] Appeal from the New to the Old Whigs.
[2] See in Bancroft, v. 203, 204.

But these had been the scattered utterances of individuals,—food for reflection in the closet, but not yet the basis of action in affairs. Now, that which the Declaration did was to put the doctrine of the natural equality of men in their essential rights, and the duty of government to secure these rights, into the form of axioms as the basis of political society, and to enforce these self-evident truths by the will of a whole people. The people came to the consciousness of holding their rights, not as Englishmen, but as men. In defence of liberties which the crown and parliament were seeking to revoke or suppress as mere chartered privileges of British subjects, they had been driven back upon those natural and inalienable rights which were antecedent to all charters, and which made them as men superior to governments, which could have lawful existence only as the servants and guardians of these personal rights in the collective interest of society; and the consciousness of these rights they declared not as a thesis in political philosophy, nor a theory of government, but by embodying the personality of the nation in these self-evident truths. This, too, in words so few, so clear, so exact, so just, so strong, so glowing, that nothing can be added to or taken from their original statement: "We hold these truths to be self-evident, that all men are created equal; that they are endowed by their Creator with certain inalienable rights; that among these are life, liberty, and the pursuit of happiness; that, to secure these rights, governments are instituted among men, deriving their just powers from the consent of the governed; that, whenever any form of government becomes destructive of these ends, it is the right of the people to alter or to abolish it, and to institute a new government, laying its foundation on such principles, and organizing its powers in such form, as to them shall seem most likely to effect their safety and happiness." Here stands forth a people clothed with rights in its proper personality, and therefore entitled to clothe itself with a form of government according to its own nature and will. There is no going behind this statement, and there is no going beyond it. I must repeat with emphasis, that the equality and rights asserted in the Declaration are personal and natural endowments, and not political claims nor concessions. All men, as individuals, are equal in the right to life, to liberty of personal action, and to the pursuit of good. The function of the State is defined by this normal equality of rights; but these rights are not in their origin or nature *political*. Bluntschli[1] has shown, that, strictly speaking, *political* equality can come into existence only within the organized community of the State; and also, that if, in the strict meaning of political equality, all individuals were simply and exactly equal, the State could not possibly exist, since the conception of political inequality is necessarily involved in the fundamental distinction of the governing and the governed. Equality by nature, equality before the law, and equality of treatment by government, are not *political* equality; and political equality is *not* affirmed by the Declaration. The most ignorant and imbruted man in the United States has the same right that I have to live, to choose his place and mode of living,

---

[1] Allgemeinen Statsrechts, b. i., c. 9, § iv.

to make his way in the world, and to share the good things of life to the fullest measure that he can attain by the free use of his powers. The government is bound to see that he has these rights to the largest degree compatible with the same rights in others. If the government tramples upon his rights, it tramples also upon mine; and I am bound to make common cause with him against any encroachment upon rights that by nature are "equal" to us both. But whether these rights can be best secured to the community and to himself by making this ignorant, imbruted creature *the government*, or a partaker in the government, is a question that the Declaration leaves to political philosophy and the experience of society.

No doubt, as Mr. Evarts has clearly shown, " as to the Constitution of the new State, its species is disclosed by its existence. The condition of the people is equal: they have the habits of freemen, and possess the institutions of liberty. When the political connection with the parent State is dissolved, they will be self-governing and self-governed of necessity." But, at the same time, we must be careful not to confound the declarative act of 1776 with the creative and formative act of 1789. The Constitution was the product of consummate wisdom as to the form of a free government, — " a new State of a new species;" but the Declaration stands supreme as a declaration of political ethics. The Constitution has been, and may yet be, amended; the Declaration never. The Constitution, and the government established under it, may even be subverted, and pass away; but the truths of the Declaration must remain " self-evident " so long as civil society shall exist on the earth. The forms in which truth is embodied may change or perish; but truth as *thought* is immortal. The Constitution is a form: the Declaration is a thought. It is the felicity of American liberty that it combines the highest philosophical thought of liberty with the best structural forms of liberty as yet devised. The strength of English liberty is, that it is a thing of growth, and possesses at once the vitality drawn from the soil, and the veneration inspired by transmission from ancestors. It lives on from generation to generation through inherited institutions, without the guaranties of a written constitution. French liberty, on the other hand, began with the revolutionary proclamation of natural rights, and has always attached a special virtue to the formula of a constitution. Now, American liberty combines the advantages of both, and thus counterbalances the defects of either. All that was valid and vital in English liberty was carried by the earlier emigrants across the sea. The common heritage was theirs; and they took with them the institutions of law and custom by which this was guarded and transmitted. They built society upon that foundation. When, at length, this hereditary freedom was assailed, they at first shored it up with charters and precedents, then laid underneath it the broader, surer foundation of the rights that God had given to all men alike, and afterward built about the whole structure of liberty, natural and institutional, the strong buttresses of the Constitution. No principle of liberty has yet been thought out that is not already in the Declaration; no ordinance of freedom has yet been devised that is not already in the common law and the Constitution.

I trust that this analysis has redeemed for the Declaration its true glory, showing how, as a philosophic thought, it stands above the Constitution, which is a political form. The Constitution did indeed create "a new State of a new species:" the Declaration proclaims how every State, of whatever species, must be ordered, if it would justify its claim to be. It *formulated human personality*, as by the will of God, the chief factor and concern of civil government.[1] But, while we assert for the Declaration the foremost place in the political thought of mankind, we should be careful not to claim too much for it in the line of direct, visible results. Mr. Adams thus sums up "the results arrived at by the enunciation of the great law of liberty in 1776:—

"1. It opened the way to the present condition of France.

"2. It brought about perfect security for liberty on the high and narrow seas.

"3. It led the way in abolishing the slave-trade, which, in its turn, prompted the abolition of slavery itself by Great Britain, France, Russia, and, last of all, by our own country too." [2]

This statement is marked by the judicial clearness and fairness so characteristic of Mr. Adams; and it is, in the main, borne out by the history of the century. Yet, in tracing a connection between the movements of freedom in the first century of our national life and the Declaration with which that century opened, we should be upon our guard against the logical fallacy, *post hoc propter hoc*. In the closer contact of nations induced by modern civilization, influences are so ramified, and there is so much simultaneousness as well as consentaneousness of movement, that it is not easy to trace single events to a specific antecedent. At the first, the successful achievement of independence by the United States, and the inauguration of a republican government, stimulated in other lands the fever of popular government. For a time, a declaration of rights and a constitution were regarded as the panacea for the woes of political society. By and by experience showed there were cases in which the remedy might be worse than the disease: still, for long, the example of a thriving, peaceful nation without royalty, aristocracy, establishment, or army, and almost without taxes, was the envy of foreign peoples, and the standing argument for government by the people. Then, by degrees, the blot of slavery grew so large and dense, that it overshadowed the lustre of free institutions. Next came internal commotions and a civil war, that at first revealed weakness, and the possibility of disruption. The old charm of peace and union was gone. The magnificent uprising of the nation, the development of military resources and capacity, and the final success of the war for the Union, together with the overthrow of slavery, not only revived confidence in the republic, but lifted it into admiration. Then followed the era of taxes, extravagance, paper-money, official corruption, and of universal depression in finance and trade, which has suddenly turned popular government into a political scandal. Through all these phases of

---

[1] See Speech at the Centennial Dinner in London.
[2] Speech at Taunton.

American influence upon foreign affairs, it is difficult to trace with calmness and certainty the results for good of the Declaration of Independence upon the destiny of mankind. Still those results are even now greater than we can measure. On the one hand, we must free the Declaration from all failures and delinquencies of the American people under it; and, on the other hand, we should remember that it is too soon to look for its results in corporate forms in human society. It required seventeen centuries for Christ's doctrine of the divine birthright and brotherhood of man to work itself up to the point of public proclamation as the foundation of the State. Other toiling, groaning ages may yet attend the realization of that Declaration in emancipated, self-governing peoples. But the day of redemption is sure. Science has taught us the conservation of energy through the transformation of work into heat, and of heat into work. The blows the men of '76 struck upon the anvil of liberty did not cease with the sparks that then set the Colonies aflame: they generated a heat that has passed into the atmosphere of the globe, that has kindled in millions the hope of liberty, and that, taking on the form of work, has given energy and potency to movements of popular reform, and shall yet start the mighty enginery that shall regulate all social and political institutions in harmony with the good of the people.

It has been proposed that Americans shall henceforth discontinue the reading of the Declaration of Independence on the Fourth of July. So far as the indictment of George III. is concerned, the suggestion has some practical value; since it is hardly worth while to keep in remembrance the petty tyrannies of a very petty sort of tyrant, whose chief title, indeed, to a place in history, is, that his will was stubborn enough to cost him an empire. But the Declaration stands high above the grounds of separation; and, while other nations are proclaiming by monuments and festivals the triumphs of military force, it were an injustice to posterity, and a shame to history, if that nation should be silent that first proclaimed the dignity and worth of man. Never, never let the American people cease to magnify the day which declared that "all men are created equal; that they are endowed by their Creator with certain inalienable rights; and that, to secure these rights, governments are instituted among men, deriving their just powers from the consent of the governed."

LECTURE III.

ADOPTION OF THE CONSTITUTION.

THE constitution of a nation may be quite another thing from a national constitution. The latter may be written on parchment, and attested by seals, signatures, and oaths, and yet have within it no particle of the life of the nation, nor give to this a durable form. The former, as in England, may be unwritten and conventional, the growth of ages; the life of the nation shaping to itself form and features appropriate to its condition. An able expounder of the English Constitution says, " The received doctrine as to the relations of the two houses of parliament to one another, the whole theory of the position of the body known as the cabinet, and of its chief, the prime-minister, every detail, in short, of the practical working of government among us, is a matter belonging wholly to the unwritten constitution, and not at all to the written law. . . . We now have a whole system of political morality, a whole code of precepts for the guidance of public men, which will not be found in any page of either the statute or the common law, but which are in practice held hardly less sacred than any principle embodied in the Great Charter or in the Petition of Right."[1] It is greatly to the honor of the English people that they are able to govern themselves with so much evenness and stability, while dispensing with a formal constitution.

And, on the other hand, one of the foremost patriots and publicists of France, Édouard Laboulaye, just after

---

[1] Growth of the English Constitution, by E. A. Freeman, M.A., pp. 109, 113.

the revolution of 1848, said,[1] "In the last sixty years we have changed eight or ten times our government and our constitution; have passed from anarchy to despotism; tried two or three forms of the republic and of monarchy; exhausted proscription, the scaffold, civil and foreign war; and after so many attempts, and attempts paid with the fortune and the blood of France, we are hardly more advanced than at the outset. The constitution of 1848 took for its model the constitution of 1791, which had no life; and to-day we are agitating the same questions that in 1789 we flattered ourselves we had resolved. How is it that the Americans have organized liberty upon a durable basis, while we, who surely are not inferior to them in civilization, — we who have their example before our eyes, — have always miscarried?"

The answer to this question I have anticipated, in part, in the last Lecture, by a comparison of the two peoples in their antecedents, their institutions, their surroundings, and, above all, in their ethical beliefs and motives. But, in this point of constitution-making, it will also be seen that the Americans, with a rare felicity, succeeded in incorporating the constitution of the nation, which is its life-principle, with the national constitution, which gives to the national life its definitive form and expression. They not only achieved independence, but, in the happy phrase of the French critic, they "*organized* liberty." This success was due to training, to methods, and to men, or rather to that mysterious conjunction of men and events that makes the genius of an epoch akin to inspiration.

None has divined this more clearly than Laboulaye, nor pictured it with more strength and grace of outline, or beauty of coloring. "It was amid obstacles without number that the founders of American liberty organized a government. One cannot forget the sad spectacle that America presented at the moment when the peace obtained by our efforts promised her happy days. The newly-born republic just missed dying in its cradle. Ten years of war had impoverished the country; paper-money had led fatally to bankruptcy; no credit, no money, no finance; the weakness of the central power encouraged the inde-

[1] Études morales et politiques, par Édouard Laboulaye, p. 285.

pendence of the particular States; disunion was everywhere; anarchy and sedition threatened with approaching ruin that new government, the impotence of which England proclaimed with a secret joy; and already in America itself, on that soil where no king had yet been, there was talk of a monarchy as the only *régime* that could found and maintain the unity of a great country.

"Then it was, when all seemed lost, when Washington himself began to despair of the future, — then it was that there were found men clear-sighted enough to see the remedy for so many evils, bold enough to propose it, and devoted enough to undertake a work apparently impossible, — to reclaim biassed opinion, to direct minds toward one common end, and, spite of all prejudices and all particular interests, to found the Union. With no other means than speech and the pen, these plain citizens proclaimed the necessity of a constitution that should unite so many scattered members, caused Congress to adopt their project of a revisory convention, determined the country in the choice of its institutions, defended these institutions against the attacks of passion or of error, and, by dint of patience and courage, finally endowed America with that democratic organization which constitutes its strength and greatness.

"Such was the work of Franklin, Randolph, Madison, Jay, and of those two men united by a constant friendship, and whom history will never separate, — the one, Washington, the grandest character of modern times in his disinterestedness and his perseverance; the hero who under a stern front concealed the passion that ruled his whole life, — the love of country and of liberty: the other, that loving soul, that generous heart, that ready mind, which fortune found always at its level; that soldier, orator, writer, legislator, financier, who was by turns the arm, the pen, and sometimes the thought, of Washington, — the brave, the chivalrous, the unfortunate Hamilton. The separation of powers, the independence of the President and the administration, guaranties against usurpation by the assembly, the *rôle* of the judicial power, the distribution of the right of suffrage, communal and provincial liberty, individual liberty, right of association, liberty of the press, — there is not one of these delicate questions,

ADOPTION OF THE CONSTITUTION.

which, after protracted examination by the legislators of the United States, was not settled with admirable wisdom and reason. Upon the merit of their solution, time, that irrefragable judge, has pronounced without appeal."[1]

We have seen that the Colonies went to war with the mother-country without organizing a distinctive government, and without even contemplating a change in the form of government under which they had hitherto lived. The Continental Congress that met in Philadelphia in May, 1775, was an extemporized assembly for counsel and conciliation. Recognizing the war that had begun at Lexington and Concord as the common cause of the Colonies, it adopted the army of New England as the Continental army, and appointed Washington to the chief command, but at the same time declared, "We have not raised armies with designs of separating from Great Britain, and establishing independent States. Necessity has not yet driven us into that desperate measure." And this was after the battle of Bunker Hill would seem to have made separation both a necessity and a duty.[2] As Washington passed through New York on his way to his command, the legislature of that province presented him with an address, in which they spoke of "an accommodation with the mother-country" as "the fondest wish of every American soul." And in his reply Washington said, "Be assured that every exertion of my worthy colleagues and myself will be extended to the re-establishment of peace and harmony between the mother-country and these Colonies. As to the fatal but necessary operations of war, when we assumed the soldier, we did not lay aside the citizen; and we shall most sincerely rejoice with you in that happy hour, when the establishment of American liberty on the most firm and solid foundations shall enable us to return to our private stations n the bosom of a free, peaceful, and happy country."[3]

Within a year, we find the Congress at Philadelphia forced to declare that very separation from Great Britain

[1] Études morales et politiques, pp. 279-281.
[2] The battle of Bunker Hill was June 17; this declaration of Congress on the 6th of July following (1775).
[3] Pennsylvania Journal, July 5, 1775; see in Moore's Diary of the American Revolution.

which it had disavowed as "a desperate measure." Thus sprang into being the union of "free and independent States," at war with the greatest naval power of the world, yet having no executive head, and no government but a Congress of less than sixty members, originally chosen while the Colonies were yet subject to the mother-country, and for the main purpose of securing the liberties of the Colonies in harmony with their allegiance to the crown. In organizing the Continental army, and in declaring independence, Congress knew that it was backed by the will of the people: it found the state of war existing, and made provision for it. The war necessitated independence, and Congress proclaimed the fact. It must needs stand by its own proclamation, and go on to govern the nation it had ushered into being. To change front in face of an enemy is always a difficult and dangerous manœuvre; and Mr. Lincoln's homely adage, "Don't swap horses in the middle of the stream," justifies the Congress in not attempting to create a radically *new* government at the very moment of defying and irritating the enemy by the declaration of independence. Though Congress exceeded its original powers, its government was not a usurpation, but a necessity. Quickened by the flames of war, the nation was struggling through a political chaos toward its own organic life.

With the exception of Washington himself, who never underrated the gravity of the situation, the leaders of the Revolution seem to have fancied that the war would be soon over; that a single campaign would satisfy Britain of the impossibility of subjugating America, and bring her to conditions of peace. But when Britain continued to send fleets and armies swollen by mercenaries, and Washington reported, that having little ammunition, and no regulars, he could only act on the defensive, Congress was obliged to rouse itself for a conflict of indefinite duration, and perhaps doubtful issue, and in this emergency found itself without authority, without money, without supplies, except in the spontaneity of popular enthusiasm. Now, popular enthusiasm is apt to subside under disappointment, disaster, or delay; and a legislative body chosen to represent the popular will is sure to wane in authority and influence, unless often refreshed by new elections from the people. So was it with the Long Parliament in England; so was it with the French Assembly of Bordeaux that prolonged itself to weariness at Versailles; and so too, a century ago, as the war of the American Revolution began to drag, and the original force of cohesion under pressure was somewhat relaxed, the people showed an increasing reluctance to allow a Congress that was chosen for an occasional emergency of counsel to transform itself into a permanent government of power; and the Congress itself, conscious of its inability to provide the sinews of war, or to enforce its own acts, early took measures for a government suited to the new condition of the country. In these steps it followed, not theory, but experience, as its guide.

Franklin, whose practical sense was almost an equivalent for prophetic sagacity, was the first to propose "Articles of Confederation and Perpetual Union," which he did as early as July 21, 1775,—almost a year before the Declaration of Independence: and, a month before that act, Congress had appointed a committee to devise a plan of confederation; the notion of some being, that the formation of a government ought to precede the assumption of a station among sovereigns. So complicated, however, was the question of a united central government, that it was not until Nov. 15, 1777, that Congress adopted such a plan, and not till March, 1781, that this went into operation as a government ratified by all the States. A few years sufficed to demonstrate the utter failure of this scheme; but the experiment was necessary to show the futility of a confederacy of independent States upon the broad and diversified theatre of the American continent, and to prepare the way for that National Constitution which is the highest product of political wisdom yet wrought out for combining liberty with order, equality with unity, co-ordinate self-government with supreme central sovereignty. The framers of the Confederacy failed through following precedents not suited to their condition, and by fearing to clothe free institutions with the power needful for their security, lest this should be turned to their destruction: the framers of the Constitution succeeded by providing in government itself a method and a motive for preserving free institutions from that disintegration to which they tend alike through their inertia in times of security, and their centrifugal force in times of danger. The study of the failure will enable us the better to appreciate the success.

The Congress of 1776 had before them these precedents in American history to guide them in framing a government: *first*, the practice of local self-government, under various forms, in all the Colonies; and, *secondly*, the occasional union of the Colonies, upon equal terms, for counsel or action for preserving their several liberties, or guarding against some impending danger. They had been called into existence by local assemblies, regularly or irregularly convened, which represented the right and interest of the people in governing themselves; and their union — first as a Congress of all the Colonies, and now of the independent States — was for the very purpose of maintaining the liberties of the people under their forms of local independence. Hence it was natural, that, in framing a government to perpetuate union, they should make it their first care to secure the independence of the States, and keep intact their sovereignty. They took up arms for the independence of the Colonies of a control outside of themselves. The usurpations of king and parliament upon their prerogative of local government had made them jealous of any central head, executive or legislative; and the States would not consent that Congress should directly enroll an army, but retained the control of their several quotas, lest, in the pride of victory, some ambitious general might use the army to overawe the liberties of the people.[1]

Outside of their colonial experience, the Congress of 1776 had no recent examples to guide them but the republics of Switzerland and of the Netherlands, and these both were confederacies; and, in point of fact, the confederation that Congress finally commended to the

---

[1] Washington frequently complained of this dependence of the army upon so many local, scattered, and sometimes jealous and discordant heads, as impairing its unity and efficiency, preventing the formation of veteran and disciplined troops, and often crippling his resources on the eve of important movements. There can be no doubt that it greatly prolonged the war of independence, and, at times, made its issue dubious.

States was modelled as nearly as possible upon the union of Utrecht of 1579. The five provinces of the Netherlands that entered into the compact of Utrecht agreed that "each province should retain its particular privileges, liberties, laudable and traditional customs, and other laws; that the provinces should defend each other against all foreign or domestic potentates, provinces, or cities, provided such defence were controlled by the generality of the union; that no truce or peace was to be concluded, no war commenced, no import established, affecting the generality, but by unanimous advice and consent of the provinces; and none of the united provinces, or of their cities or corporations, were to make treaties with other potentates or states without consent of their confederates."[1]

Each of these features is found in the "Articles of Confederation and Perpetual Union" under which the United States of America were organized in 1781. The Confederacy was a "league of friendship" between independent States, "for their common defence, the security of their liberties, and their mutual and general welfare." Its fundamental article declared, "Each State retains its sovereignty, freedom, and independence, and every power, jurisdiction, and right which is not by this Confederation expressly delegated to the United States in Congress assembled." This Congress consisted of a single house: its members were appointed annually by authority of the legislatures of the States; and each State could recall its delegates during the year, and send others in their stead. Each State maintained its delegates at its own cost. The voting in Congress was by States: each State had but one vote. No act could be passed without the consent of a majority of the States; and, in many cases, the consent of nine of the thirteen States was required. Though Congress had the right and power of determining on peace and war, of sending and receiving ambassadors, and entering into treaties and alliances, yet, in case of invasion or of imminent danger, a single State could go to war, and equip an army and navy of its own; and also, with the sanction of Congress, two or more States could enter into

---

[1] Motley: Dutch Republic, vol. iii. 411, 412.

a special treaty or confederation between themselves, and single States could make a commercial or other alliance with foreign powers. The charges of war, and other expenses incurred by Congress for the common defence and general welfare, were assessed upon the several States in proportion to the value of all land granted or surveyed within each State; but the quota of a State could be raised only by the authority and direction of its own legislature. The Confederacy had no judiciary to enforce its acts, and no executive head to represent and administer its authority: from first to last, it was a compact between States whose independent sovereignty was jealously guarded at every point. Such a compact must fall to pieces as soon as the necessity was over that called it into being, and, indeed, because of that very necessity.

It is true that in Switzerland we have an example of a confederacy of independent cantons without a personal head; the executive and administrative authority being vested in a federal council of seven. But this is possible, because, first, the area of Switzerland,[1] being only one two hundred and twenty-fifth part of the area of the United States, is so small as to admit of direct democratic government, as in the cantonal assemblies of Appenzell, Ausser, Rhoden, Uri, and Unterwalden, and in subdivisions of other cantons; and, next, because the constant pressure of external danger gives to the Swiss Bund an internal force of cohesion greater than the divisive tendencies of mountains and lakes, of language and religion. Should the Swiss push their local independence to the extreme of separatism, they would fall a prey to their powerful neighbors.[2] Their union may lack the massive strength and the sunny warmth of their Alps; but there is also a coherence in the glacier as it lies locked in the arms of the mountains.

How different the geographical and political position of

---

[1] The superficial area of Switzerland is 752 geographical square miles; that of the United States, 169,589.

[2] This came near being the case thirty years ago, when the Sonderbund, or separate league of the Catholic cantons, furnished to France and Austria a pretext for meddling in the internal affairs of Switzerland. Nothing but the patriotic uprising of the people at the call of the Diet, like the enthusiastic rally for the Union in the United States, saved Switzerland from being virtually appropriated and governed by the greater powers.

the United States under the Confederation of 1781! The thirteen Colonies, when they entered upon the war with Great Britain, occupied, in all, an area of 420,892 square miles, stretching along a sea-coast of 1,300 miles. By the peace of 1783, the title of the United States was secured to all the territory claimed by Great Britain east of the Mississippi, south of Canada, north of Florida and of the thirty-first parallel, — a total area of 827,844 square miles; being fifty-four times greater than the whole area of the Swiss Confederation. The independence of the United States having been acknowledged by Great Britain and the leading powers of Continental Europe, the American Confederacy, separated from them all by an ocean not yet traversed by steam, had few dangers or fears from without. Hence, as I have hinted, the very emergency that compelled the States to co-operation for war would intensify their individuality on the return of peace. That emergency was the preservation of local self-government; and the doctrine of the Declaration of Independence, touching the right of the people to have a government satisfactory to themselves, if pressed to an extreme, might encourage a State in maintaining its own sovereignty apart, and contending for its own interests against the claims of the Confederacy.

This would indeed have been a perversion of the Declaration, as well in letter as in spirit. That was "a declaration by the representatives of the *United* States of America:" it spoke "in the name and by the authority of the good *people* of the Colonies," in their totality as one political commonwealth, and declared "that these *United Colonies* are, and of right ought to be, free and independent States." The Colonies, as united through their Congress, constituted a new body politic, which declared itself a separate and independent power among the nations. But an independence which was based upon union could not logically imply that any State could declare itself independent of the rest. Nevertheless, there was a lurking danger in this direction. Just as to usurpation from without was opposed the union of "free and independent States," so to the danger of a central control from within would be opposed the centrifugal force of local independence. And so indeed it was. Congress had assessed the several States in due proportion for the debt of the war of independence; but some of the States took no measures for providing their quota, and one positively refused to do any thing toward the liquidation of that sacred charge.[1] Peace was proclaimed Sept. 3, 1783. On the 25th February, 1787, Mr. Madison wrote to Edmund Randolph, "No money comes into the Federal treasury; no respect is paid to the Federal authority; and people of reflection unanimously agree that the existing Confederacy is tottering to its foundation. Many individuals of weight, particularly in the Eastern District, are suspected of leaning toward monarchy. Other individuals predict a partition of the States into two or more confederacies."[2] Pennsylvania and New Jersey on the one hand, Virginia and Maryland on the other, had entered into special compacts without the consent of Congress; and the legislature of Virginia not only refused to apply for the sanction of Congress, but actually voted against the communication of the compact to Congress.[3] Georgia and Massachusetts had raised troops without consent of Congress; Connecticut had taxed imports from Massachusetts; some of the seaboard States had taxed adjoining States that must trade through them; some, by their navigation laws, "treated the citizens of other States as aliens."[4] Thus the principle of local self-government was pushing itself to the destruction of co-operation even for the public order and safety; the centrifugal force of separatism was rending the Confederacy asunder.

With great clearness Mr. Madison pointed out that "the radical infirmity of the Articles of Confederation was the dependence of Congress on the voluntary and simultaneous compliance with its requisitions by so many independent communities, each consulting more or less its particular interests and convenience, and distrusting the compliance of the others."[5] And Mr. Wilson of Pennsyl-

[1] New Jersey in 1786: see Journals of Congress, vol. iv. p. 622. According to Mr. Madison, Connecticut likewise refused to pass a law for complying with the requisitions of Congress (Rives's Life of Madison, ii. p. 108).
[2] Papers of James Madison (ed. 1820), vol. ii. 620. [3] Ibid., p. 712.
[4] Ibid., ii. 711, 712. [5] Ibid., ii. 692.

vania[1] thus sharply satirized the change that had come over public sentiment since the pressure of a common danger was withdrawn: "Among the first sentiments expressed in the first Congress, one was, that Virginia is no more, that Massachusetts is no more, that Pennsylvania is no more: we are now one nation of brethren; we must bury all local interests and distinctions. This language continued for some time. The tables at length began to turn. No sooner were the State governments formed than their jealousy and ambition began to display themselves: each endeavored to cut a slice from the common loaf to add to its own morsel, till at length the Confederation became frittered down to the impotent condition in which it now stands."

The perils of the Confederacy brought Washington from his retirement to save by his counsels the liberty he had won by his sword. "No morn," said he, "ever dawned more favorably than ours did, and no day was ever more clouded than the present. . . . We are fast verging to anarchy and confusion. Thirteen sovereignties pulling against each other, and all tugging at the Federal head, will soon bring ruin on the whole."[2] "What a triumph for our enemies to verify their predictions! What a triumph for the advocates of despotism to find that we are incapable of governing ourselves, and that systems founded on the basis of equal liberty are merely ideal and fallacious!"[3] In a word, the centrifugal tendency of local self-government had well-nigh separated the Confederacy into its primitive atoms.

This process of disintegration was favored by that inertia which seems to paralyze free institutions in times of outward security. In hereditary forms of government, monarchical or aristocratic, there is always a class to whom government is an occupation, and the exercise or conservation of power is the business of life. Like the royal house of Prussia, they are trained to government as a profession; like the House of Lords in England, they must care for government as a necessity of their own existence. They cannot let government alone, lest it slip

[1] Papers of Madison, ii. 825.
[2] Letter to Madison, Nov. 5, 1786: see in Sparks and in Madison.
[3] Letter to Jay, 1st August, 1786.

altogether from their hands. But Freedom asks for nothing so much as to be let alone. She wishes neither to govern nor to be governed; and though fierce as a lioness for her cubs when her retreat is threatened, yet she loves to rest unconscious of danger, and, unless pressed for life, will molest none who do not molest her. But as with the human constitution, so with the constitution of civil society, inertia is fatal to life. Unless something be done to excite its powers to activity, these will presently sink into decay, or succumb to the first disorder. Hence, for the preservation of free institutions, there must be some device for investing government with dignity, responsibility, and authority, so that it shall be an object to wise and good men to devote their lives to public affairs, to make statemanship their science, and politics their profession. True, this would also make government a prize for the ambitious and designing; but, under any system, we must take the risks of human nature as it is, and compound with it on the best terms possible. Left to their own inertia, free institutions will die of inanition, or fall a prey to faction, conspiracy, or invasion. But a strong government set to watch over liberty will provoke the vigilance that must be the safeguard against its own abuse. Happily for the life of the American Republic, there were at that day men who had the perspicacity to see this, and the courage to avow it; chief among them Alexander Hamilton and George Washington. Hamilton viewed the crisis from the lower plane of human passions and political experiences; Washington, with the comprehensive wisdom and supreme moral judgment that marked the slow but certain processes of his mind. Hamilton argued that " the great and essential principles for the support of government are, (1) An active and constant interest in supporting it; (2) The love of power; (3) An habitual attachment of the people, its sovereignty being immediately before their eyes, its protection immediately enjoyed by them; (4) Force, by which may be understood a coercion of laws, or coercion of arms; (5) Influence, or a dispensation of those regular honors and emoluments which produce an attachment to the government." But, by the confederate system, "all the passions of avarice, ambition, interest, which govern most individuals and all public bodies, fall into the current of the States, and do not flow into the stream of the General Government. The former, therefore, will generally be an overmatch for the General Government, and render any confederacy in its very nature precarious."[1] Hence Hamilton contended for a *national* government, in distinction from " an association of independent communities into a *federal* government." After a fair trial of confederation, Washington wrote, " I confess that my opinion of public virtue is so far changed, that I have my doubts whether any system, without the means of coercion in the sovereign, will enforce due obedience to the ordinances of a general government, without which every thing else fails." And again: " We have probably had too good an opinion of human nature in forming our confederation. Experience has taught us that men will not adopt and carry into execution measures the best calculated for their own good, without the intervention of a coercive power. I do not conceive we can long exist as a nation, without having lodged somewhere a power which will pervade the whole Union in as energetic a manner as the authority of the State governments extends over the several States."[2] Yet Washington was thoroughly opposed to the idea of a monarchy as the solution of the problem, and had spurned with indignation the suggestion of the army that he should make himself king or dictator.

It was for Madison to point out how that control of the whole, that Washington and Hamilton insisted on, could be secured with safety to the parts. " Congress," he said, " have kept the vessel from sinking; but it has been by standing constantly at the pump, not by stopping the leaks which have endangered her."[3] He pointed out that " the great desideratum in government is such a modification of the sovereignty as will render it sufficiently neutral between the different interests and factions to control one part of the society from invading the rights of another, and, at the same time, sufficiently controlled itself from setting up an

[1] For an abstract of Hamilton's great speech in the Federal Convention, see Madison Papers, ii. 878-893.
[2] Letter to Jay, Aug. 1, 1786.
[3] Letter to Jefferson, Oct. 3, 1785; Rives, ii. 41.

interest adverse to that of the whole society."[1] How completely the Confederacy had failed of this is shown by an analysis of the system put forth by a statesman of that period: "By this political compact, the United States in Congress have exclusive power for the following purposes, without being able to execute one of them: —

"1. They may make and conclude treaties, but can only *recommend* the observance of them.

"2. They may appoint ambassadors, but cannot defray even the expenses of their tables.

"3. They may borrow money in their own name, on the faith of the Union, but cannot pay a dollar.

"4. They may coin money; but they cannot purchase an ounce of bullion.

"5. They may make war, and determine what number of troops are necessary, but cannot raise a single soldier.

"6. In short, they may declare every thing, *but do nothing.*"

From the fatal collapse of free government that the wisest statesmen of the Confederacy feared, there were but two ways of escape, — the one by the division of the Confederacy into smaller republics, that should be related to each other, as to foreign powers, by treaties of commerce and alliance; the other by the erection of a strong central national government. The first of these was already talked of, especially by some extreme advocates of practical democracy and state sovereignty in Massachusetts. A letter of Mr. Monroe to Patrick Henry, dated New York, 12th August, 1786, contains this apparently authentic statement: "Committees are held in this town, of Eastern men, and others of this State, upon the subject of a dismemberment of the States east of the Hudson from the Union, and the erection of them into a separate government. To what length they have gone I know not, but have assurances as to the truth of the above position, with this addition to it, that the measure is talked of in Massachusetts familiarly, and is supposed to have originated there. The plan of the government in all its modifications has even been contemplated by them."[2]

---

[1] Paper on the Vices of the Political System of the United States, April, 1787; Rives, ii. 216.
[2] Rives's Life of Madison, ii. 122.

ADOPTION OF THE CONSTITUTION.

On the other hand, Washington, in his circular letter to the governors of the several States just before he retired from the army, had strongly urged that the States should yield to the General Government the powers necessary to provide against anarchy and confusion. "It is indispensable," he said, "to the happiness of the individual States, that there should be lodged somewhere a supreme power to regulate and govern the general concerns of the confederated republic. . . . Whatever measures have a tendency to dissolve the Union, or contribute to violate or lessen its sovereign authority, ought to be considered hostile to the liberty and independence of America, and the authors of them treated accordingly."[1]

Happily for the preservation of that liberty and independence, the outbreak of rebellion put an end to the scheme of independent State sovereignties, even in Massachusetts, where, perhaps, the feeling against a strong national government was most jealous and active. The armed resistance of Shays and his followers, in 1786, to the collection of taxes, and the enforcement of private claims, found much sympathy among the people; and, in some cases, town-officers went so far as to order their militia to co-operate with the rebels.[2] The civil courts were declared to be "engines of destruction," and were broken up by an armed mob; the State Senate was denounced as a "needless and aristocratic branch of the government;"[3] the tax-gatherers were forcibly resisted; the Federal arsenal at Springfield was attacked by a force of two thousand men: in a word, there was an attempt to resolve society into its original elements, and to clothe the local democracy with absolute and final sovereignty.[4] The government of Massachusetts succeeded in suppressing the rebellion by its own arm, but not until it had invoked the aid of the Federal Congress, and Congress had raised a body of troops for that purpose.[5] A skirmish at Springfield, and the capture of the main body of the rebels at Petersham, brought the affair to an end, with no great loss of life;

[1] Letter of 8th June, 1784: Sparks's Collection.
[2] Wells's Life of Samuel Adams, iii. 229.   [3] Ibid., 223.
[4] See Washington to Madison of Nov. 5, 1786, in Sparks, vol. ix., and Rives's Madison, ii. 175.
[5] Secret Journals of Congress, i. 267-270.

but the horror of anarchy and civil war produced a strong re-action from the scheme of confederated democracies, and strengthened the movement for a vigorous national government. Washington wrote to Madison, "How melancholy is the reflection, that, in so short a time, we should have made such large strides towards fulfilling the predictions of our transatlantic foes! — 'Leave them to themselves, and their government will soon dissolve.' Will not the wise and good strive hard to avert this evil? or will their supineness suffer ignorance, and the arts of self-interested, designing, disaffected, and desperate characters, to involve this great country in wretchedness and contempt? What stronger evidence can be given of the want of energy in our government than these disorders? If there is not power in it to check them, what security has a man for life, liberty, or property?"[1]

That was in November, 1786. The twenty-fifth day of May, 1787, witnessed the dawn of hope. On that day a convention of the States for revising the Federal Government was organized[2] in Philadelphia, with Washington as its president. The convention sat till the 17th September, when it signed, and sent forth for the approval of the nation, that Constitution under which the people of the United States have lived to this day. At the opening of the convention, when a diversity of views had provoked some warmth of feeling, Dr. Franklin said, "We are sent here to *consult*, not to *contend*, with each other; and declarations of a fixed opinion, and of determined resolution never to change it, neither enlighten nor convince us." At the close, when the deputies had signed the new Constitution, Franklin pointed to the president's chair, at the back of which a rising sun happened to be painted, and said that "painters had found it difficult to distinguish in their art a rising from a setting sun. Often and often in the course of the session, and the vicissitudes of my hopes and fears as to its issue, I have looked at that behind the president, without being able to tell whether it was rising or setting; but now at length I have the happiness

---

[1] Nov. 5, 1786: see in Sparks, ix. 207.
[2] The convention met on Monday, May 14, but, for lack of a quorum, did not organize till the 25th.

to know that it is a rising and not a setting sun." Let us hope the sun that rose that day shall never set!

Never man did better service for his country than James Madison in keeping a record of the sayings and doings of that remarkable convention, that embraced such men as George Washington, Benjamin Franklin, Alexander Hamilton, Roger Sherman, the two Pinckneys, Robert Morris, Gouverneur Morris, Rufus King, and James Madison himself. The convention sat with closed doors, and no report of its debates was allowed to be published; but Madison, who was a ready penman, and perfectly conversant with the topics handled in the convention, took copious notes of the speeches, and, in the more important cases, submitted these to the revision of the speakers. On the death of Mr. Madison, these invaluable reports were purchased for the department of state; and in 1840 they were published under authority of Congress, as a legacy to the nation. The testimony of Madison to his colleagues in the convention is now the recognized voice of history: "Whatever may be the judgment pronounced on the competency of the architects of the Constitution, or whatever may be the destiny of the edifice prepared by them, I feel it a duty to express my profound and solemn conviction, derived from my intimate opportunity of observing and appreciating the views of the convention collectively and individually, that there never was an assembly of men charged with a great and arduous trust, who were more pure in their motives, or more exclusively or anxiously devoted to the object committed to them, than were the members of the Federal Convention of 1787 to the object of devising and proposing a constitutional system which should best supply the defects of that which it was to replace, and best secure the permanent liberty and happiness of their country." [1]

From Friday the 25th of May, when it was duly organized, till Monday the 17th of September, when the deputies of twelve States signed the completed Constitution, through all the summer heats, the convention sat continuously, with no interruption except for the Sunday rest, and an occasional day for committees to finish their work.

[1] Introduction to Debates in the Convention: Madison Papers, ii. 718.

No committee was allowed to sit when the convention was in session, nor was any member suffered to be absent from his place so as to interrupt the representation of his State. The convention felt that it had to do with questions of equal and momentous concern to each and every State, and therefore all the States must be present in their deputies during the whole discussion. Not even the work of committees should be an excuse for absence. Those men knew their duty, and did it.

One rule of the convention affords a glimpse at the manners of the times, and shows how far the fathers were from the levelling practice of democracy: it reads, " When the house shall adjourn, every member shall stand in his place until the president pass him," — a practice that existed in the chapel of Yale College in my student days. Washington himself was a master of etiquette, and stood upon it, not only in his famous rejection of Lord Howe's letter to " George Washington, Esq.," but in official intercourse with his own countrymen. Senator Hillhouse used to give a picture of the change of manners from Washington to Jefferson by showing two dinner invitations: the first, " The President of the United States requests the company of the senator of Connecticut;" the second, " Mr. Jefferson requests the company of Mr. Hillhouse." The senator could never reconcile himself to that change of dispensation.

A radical German of Berlin wondered that I halted, and lifted my hat to the late queen-dowager as she drove by on the Linden. I answered, " A republican should be first among gentlemen." It may suit " Young America " to drop the handles of names, and push and elbow where the fathers used to stand and wait; but from my deepest soul do I respect an assembly in which Benjamin Franklin, Oliver Ellsworth, Roger Sherman, Alexander Hamilton, James Madison, stood silent with uncovered heads till George Washington passed by.

Precious as was the work of the convention " for the liberty and happiness of the country," it can be best appreciated by contrast with the measures that they canvassed and rejected. In those four months of daily debate, every theory of government was ventilated, every form of constitution tested in the light of history, philosophy, and experience. As many an inventor might save himself years of toil and trouble by visiting the Patent Office, and seeing how often his machine has come to grief, so many a "rising statesman" might spare himself and the country his patent schemes of government if he should study the debates in the Federal Convention of 1787. Only I suppose that while the world stands, both in mechanics and in government, there will be ever-recurring devices for perpetual motion. Every presidential election starts up some crotchet for a better way of getting presidents, or a way of getting better presidents. Horace Greeley, for instance, was prolific of such crotchets; the latest being to run himself as the candidate of two parties that disliked him almost as much as they distrusted one another. It is an infelicity of the "selfmade" man that he imagines every thing to be as crude as the material of which he fashioned himself, and, having "made himself," feels equal to making or remaking every thing else, not excepting the universe and its Maker.

There are schemes for extending the term of the presidency, for limiting the office to a single term, for electing the President directly by the people, &c. All these projects, and others also, were fully discussed, and finally set aside, by the wisdom and weight of the convention. At one time, the formal draught of the Constitution provided that the President "shall be elected by ballot by the legislature. He shall hold his office during the term of seven years, but shall not be elected a second time." Amendments were proposed, on the one hand, to the extreme of a direct popular choice, like Louis Napoleon's *plébiscite;* on the other, to the extreme of an appointment, by the national legislature, "during good behavior," — a quality that we should be glad to predicate of the legislature itself. After days of discussion, and much elaboration in committees, the convention settled upon the plan, which, with some slight amendments to prevent confusion and rivalry between the offices of President and Vice-President, has worked so long and so well, — a President chosen by popular electors for the term of four years, the question of re-election being left to the circumstances of the hour and the good sense of the people. Mr. Lincoln said to me, after his nomination for a second term, "I do not pretend to be without ambition; yet I have no mean ambition for a re-election: but having carried this burden of war for four years, and been often compelled to act alone, I should like to feel that my countrymen approve my course."

I replied, "Mr. President, you may count upon an indorsement now in quarters where you had least expected it. I have just returned from the service of the Christian and Sanitary Commissions in Gen. Sherman's army in Tennessee and Georgia. One day I said to a knot of soldiers who were off duty, 'Boys, what are you fighting for?' Their answers were a touching and beautiful testimony to their patriotism, and loyalty to the Union. One of them was an Irishman; and his answer is worth repeating in detail. 'What I'm fighting for, shure? It wasn't meeself that made Misther Lincoln President. De'el the bit of it! I'm a Dimmycrat, shure, an' I voted for Douglas. But, you see, Misther Lincoln was elected, an' so was the President by the laws. With that they sez down here in the South, "Be jabers! he sha'n't be the President: we'll break up the Union first." Sez I, "Is it that yer afther, me boys! It's meeself'll be tayching ye better manners." So I shouldered mee musket; an', by jabers! I'll stay here till every man of them sez Misther Lincoln's the President.'

"'Well, Pat,' I said, 'you'll soon have an opportunity of voting for President again. I shall go to Washington soon, and see the President: what shall I say to him?'

"'Would you be afther giving him mee compliments, an' say that it wasn't I that made him President, but it's meeself'll do it this time; for it's jest mee opinion that *the jontlemon that begon this job is the one to go through with it?*'"[1]

---

[1] I notice it is made a merit in Gov. Hayes's letter of acceptance that he pledges himself not to be a candidate for a second term; but I confess this seems to detract from the average manly dignity of the letter. It is like saying, "I fear to trust myself, and fear you would not trust me, to the temptations of a second candidacy." But, if Mr. Hayes is going to reform and reconstruct the civil service, he will have more than a four-years' job on his hands, and may be just the gentleman to go through with it. He should rather have said, "I have not sought this nomination; but I

Mr. Lincoln laughed heartily at the story; then his great tender eyes filled with emotion as he said, "I am glad I have such friends among the plain people, and glad the country can trust in such friends and defenders." Yes, he was "the gentleman to go through with the job" he had begun. His countrymen testified that they had as much need of him as he of them; yet the greatness of the Constitution was shown in that it could do without him, and meet his death without a shock.

The Constitution of the national legislature was discussed by the convention in all its aspects; many being in favor of a single house, such as the Continental Congress and the Congress of the Confederacy: but the result was that admirable composition of two houses, which has made the United States a model for all other peoples attempting republican institutions. Years after, Jefferson, while taking tea with Washington, contended for the advantages of a single house. "Mr. Jefferson," said Washington, "you have just furnished the best argument for two houses: your tea being too hot, you poured it from the cup into the saucer."[1] It has been attempted to prove that Washington was linked to our common humanity by having once got angry, and so angry as to utter an oath. That link is not quite made out; but here we have a surer link with our human nature, in that Washington did once utter a joke, — a bit of philosophical wit worthy of Franklin.

---

accept it at the call of my countrymen. If elected, I shall reward no partisan, and shall dismiss no faithful and competent officer for political opinions. My administration shall be directed to the restoration of specie payments, the reduction of the tariff, the reform of the civil service, the protection of liberty, the establishing of confidence and peace. Should the people ask me to serve them again, I must reserve till then the right of deciding whether I can give any more of my time and strength to the public service." Once fix the civil service so that it cannot be a political machine, and the bugbear of terms vanishes. What the people *need* in candidates is men who cannot be ennobled by office; but having such men in Mr. Adams, Mr. Evarts, and a hundred more, the people do not yet feel the *want* of them, and so amuse themselves with pledges and other conceits about terms of office (October, 1876).

[1] I had this anecdote from the late Judge Daggett of New Haven.

The Constitution of the German Empire, it is true, provides for only one house of parliament. But the *Bundesrath*, which is composed of councillors who represent directly the several governments of the empire, is a check upon the parliament; and the ministry do not, as in England, feel called upon to resign in case of an adverse vote of the house. As yet, this mixed system is an experiment.

Without going further into detail, let me fix your attention upon two points in which the wisdom of the framers of the Constitution was conspicuous in that which they rejected. First, at a time when slavery, or serfdom, was still a common usage of Christian nations, they rejected every proposal to introduce the term "slave" or "slavery" into the Constitution; and it is a curious anomaly that these words were first brought into the Constitution through amendments proposed by abolitionists after slavery had ceased to exist. The Thirteenth Amendment declares that "neither slavery nor involuntary servitude, except as a punishment for crime whereof the party shall have been duly convicted, shall exist within the United States, or any place subject to their jurisdiction;" the Fourteenth Amendment provides that "neither the United States nor any State shall assume or pay any claim for the loss or emancipation of any slave;" and the Fifteenth Amendment declares that "the right of citizens of the United States to vote shall not be denied or abridged by the United States on account of race, color, or previous condition of servitude." Here we have "slave," "slavery," "servitude," in the Constitution, words that never before were there, but were purposely kept out of the instrument by the men that framed it. Pending the conflict on slavery, the extreme wing of the abolitionists denounced the Constitution as "an agreement with hell," and called for a dissolution of the compact and of the Union under it; that is, they would have had the North do, for getting rid of slavery, the very thing that it finally fought the South for attempting to do to preserve slavery. On the other hand, the extreme wing of the conservatives held that "the compromises of the Constitution" recognized slavery, guaranteed it against invasion, and by consequence warranted all measures necessary to the protection and preservation of the system. Neither party read the Constitution in the spirit or the letter of its framers. Entering into public affairs just when this controversy was at the hottest, in starting "The Independent" I took ground with my colleagues that the Constitution was throughout an instrument of liberty; that its framers designed it to protect and perpetuate liberty alone, but its meaning had been overlaid by traditions and interpretations that had become more current and potent than the organic law.[1] That this was the true view was proved by the fact, that after slavery was abolished, though amendments were added to the Constitution to fortify it against the re-establishment of the system, not one word required to be expunged, nor has been expunged, from the Constitution as it had stood from the beginning.

This view is sustained, also, by the debates and doings of the Federal Convention. The convention found itself in face of slavery as a domestic institution in most of the States, and of the slave-trade participated in by some States, though prohibited by the majority.[2] Again and again it was declared by the delegates of North Carolina, South Carolina, and Georgia, that those States would never assent to a constitution that should prohibit either slavery or the slave-trade. Here, then, was a dilemma, the gravity of which it is not easy for us at this day to estimate; or, I may rather say, would be hard to overestimate. Together the Colonies had fought the war of the Revolution, and won their independence as United States. Together these States had framed the existing Confederation; and, now that the Confederation was dissolving for very weakness, they had come together to devise some method of preserving the liberty and union of the country under an appeal that declared "the situation of the United States so delicate and critical as to call for an exertion of the united virtue and wisdom of all the members of the Confederacy."[3] They were met in the capacity of equal and sovereign States: they saw clearly

[1] This was the view of that stanch abolitionist and consistent patriot, Dr. Joshua Leavitt, with whom I had the honor to be associated for so many years in the conduct of the Independent. His philosophic mind saw how to use the Church and the Constitution as instruments for the overthrow of slavery. He gave of his wisdom to pastors and to legislators, and was far more deserving of an honorary testimonial as the leader of emancipation than they who in fact received it.

[2] Massachusetts and Pennsylvania adopted measures of emancipation in 1780, Connecticut and Rhode Island in 1784. New Hampshire followed in 1792, New York in 1799, and New Jersey in 1804. But the household slavery in the Northern States had little in common with the plantation slavery of the South. The former treated the slave as a person, the latter as property. At the period of the Constitution, North Carolina, South Carolina, and Georgia were the only States that had not already prohibited the importation of slaves from foreign countries.

[3] Report of Col. Hamilton: Madison Papers, ii. 702.

that their strength and perpetuity as a Union would require the surrendry by each State of some portion of the sovereignty it so clearly prized, and this surrendry must be acquiesced in by the people of each State in accepting the proposed Constitution. Had a bare majority of States in that convention insisted upon terms of union that must have excluded one-fourth of the whole, this would, indeed, have dealt a final blow to the Confederacy as it then was, but have also defeated the possibility of a stable and united nation. If South Carolina, North Carolina, and Georgia had been excluded from the just nascent Union because of slavery, it was highly probable that Virginia and Maryland would have made common cause with them, though these two States had already prohibited the slave-trade, and many leading statesmen of Virginia favored the abolition of slavery. In that event there would have been two rival confederacies, both weak, and both likely to be distracted with the strife of democratic and monarchic tendencies. Moreover, the three most southerly States had not yet ceded their surplus lands to the public domain; and Virginia might have reclaimed her territory ceded in 1784, if the partnership of the States had been dissolved. These two rival confederacies of States, already exhausted by war, and utterly bankrupt in finances, would have sought to outbid one another in alliances with European powers; and can any man believe, that, after twenty years, there would have existed on the soil of North America a union of free and independent States? Our fathers saw this peril to their own work and the hopes of humanity; and with a wisdom true to the higher instinct of universal freedom, dwarfing an incongruity of the actual with the ideal, they made sure of the possible, and so secured a continent to Liberty and Man. And this they did by making the Constitution an instrument of liberty, and refusing to tarnish it with the name of slavery.

The convention did not do evil that good might come; hardly did they make a choice of evils: their aim was simply and honestly good. Had they driven off the Southern States, so far from helping freedom and humanity through the curtailment of slavery, they would have provoked the zeal of a rival confederacy for the extension of slavery as its peculiar interest and pride. But they refused to adopt slavery, or even to name it; and though the Constitution, in three several phrases, betrays a subjective consciousness of this abnormal thing as existing in society, yet these very phrases were framed with the expectation that slavery would die, and the determination, that, so far as that instrument was concerned, liberty alone should have vital sustenance and active care. The first of these oblique phrases occurs in the third paragraph of the second section of the first article of the Constitution: "Representatives and direct taxes shall be apportioned among the several States which may be included within this Union, according to their respective numbers, which shall be determined by adding to the whole number of free persons, including those bound to service for a term of years, and excluding Indians not taxed, three-fifths of all other persons."

Once and again in the course of debate it was proposed to designate these "other persons" as "blacks," or "slaves;" and in the draught of the Constitution submitted so late as the 12th of September, only five days before its final adoption, was the phrase, "those bound to *servitude* for a term of years," which would mean slaves; but this was altered to "those bound to *service*," which might mean apprentices, so averse was the convention to stamping servitude upon the Constitution.

The second phrase is in the first paragraph of the ninth section of the first article: "The migration or importation of such persons as the several States now existing shall think proper to admit shall not be prohibited by the Congress prior to the year one thousand eight hundred and eight." Why did they not say, "The slave-trade shall not be prohibited"? Gouverneur Morris proposed, "The importation of slaves into North Carolina, South Carolina, and Georgia, shall not be prohibited," &c.; but, on strong objection, he withdrew his amendment. Mr. Dickinson moved, "The importation of slaves into such of the States as shall permit the same shall not be prohibited," &c.; but this was disagreed to *nem. con.* The convention would not suffer slavery to intrench itself within the Constitution by so much as admitting its name. Mr. Madison "thought it wrong to admit in the Constitution the idea that there could be property in men," and that the liberty to import slaves for twenty years would be " dishonorable to the American character."[1]

The third and last of these oblique phrases was one, the forced construction of which, in later years, was the beginning of that sectional strife that could only be quenched in war. It reads, " No person held to service or labor in one State under the laws thereof, escaping into another, shall, in consequence of any law or regulation therein, be discharged from such service or labor, but shall be delivered up on claim of the party to whom such service or labor may be due " (Art. IV. 2, 3). Every word of this clause might stand for runaway apprentices, and every verbal obligation be fulfilled by returning such fugitives, under the system of apprenticeship as it then existed in many States. No doubt runaway slaves were in the contemplation of this clause: but the framers of the Constitution regarded slavery as purely a local institution, existing only by force of the customs and laws of particular States, and not proper to be incorporated with the national Constitution; and, moreover, looking forward to its speedy demise, while providing for the mutual recognition among the States of their several local laws, so far as to avoid legal and judicial collisions, they refused to specify slavery as a thing to be guarded by the national code. I say, *refused* to do this; for, when the matter was under discussion in the convention, Gen. Pinckney expressed the wish " that some provision should be included in favor of property in slaves;" and Mr. Butler moved to require " fugitive slaves and servants to be delivered up like criminals."[2] But the convention, set in its purpose not to affix the seal of slavery to an instrument of liberty, voted down every such proposal; and, instead of ordering that fugitive slaves should be delivered up by force of United-States laws and officers, simply provided against a collision between State authorities through the opposition of local laws and usages. Mr. Madison says, that in the final adoption of the clause as it now stands, " on motion of

[1] Madison Papers, iii. 1627–1629.   [2] Ibid., iii. 1447.

Mr. Randolph of Virginia, the word 'servitude' was struck out, and 'service' unanimously inserted; the former being thought to express the condition of slaves, and the latter the obligation of free persons." No, not even the existence of servitude should have place in this charter of liberty.

The term "person" was studiously adhered to in order to exclude from the Constitution the idea of property in man. This comes out forcibly in the history of the Fifth Amendment proposed by the first Congress under the Constitution, and ratified by the legislatures of three-fourths of the States. This amendment declares that "no *person* shall be deprived of life, liberty, or property, without due process of law." Mr. Sumner brought out the fact, that, "as originally recommended by North Carolina and Virginia, this clause was restrained to the freeman. Its language was, 'No *freeman* ought to be deprived of his life, liberty, or property, but by the law of the land.'" This limitation was rejected, and "person" substituted for "freeman." "The word 'person' in the Constitution embraces every human being within its sphere, whether Caucasian, Indian, or African, from the President to the slave."[1]

In this view, the Supreme Court long ago decided that "slavery is a municipal regulation; is local, and cannot exist without authority of law;"[2] and, when a slave escapes into a State where slavery does not exist, "there is no principle in the common law, in the law of nations or of nature, which authorizes his recapture."[3] The prevailing construction of the Constitution was, that the return of fugitives should be negotiated through State courts and officers, the United States simply holding itself in reserve in the event of a conflict of laws and of jurisdiction. The attempt to transform this regulative princi-

[1] Sumner's Speech on Freedom National, Slavery Sectional.
[2] Miller *v.* McQuarry, 5 McLean, 469; Gilbna *v.* Gorham, 4 McLean, 412. Quoted by Towle, Analysis of the Constitution, 207, 208.
[3] This view was pronounced also by the supreme courts of slave States. Thus, in Mississippi, "Slavery is condemned by reason and the laws of nature: it exists, and can exist, only through municipal regulations" (Harry *v.* Decker, Walker, R. 42).
And again, in Kentucky: "We view this as a right existing by positive law of a municipal character, without foundation in the law of nature or the unwritten and common law" (Rankin *v.* Lydia, 2 Marshall, 470). Quoted by Sumner, Speech in Senate 26th August, 1852.

ple into an active obligation, to be enforced by the laws, the officers, and the people of the United States, making the Constitution an instrument for the protection, and even the propagation, of slavery, was a wide departure from the spirit and intent of the convention of 1787. In that body the strongest protests against the slave-trade and slavery were from statesmen of Virginia. That bold and eloquent orator, Col. George Mason, said of the slave-trade, "This infernal traffic originated in the avarice of British merchants." And of slavery he said, "It discourages arts and manufactures. The poor despise labor when performed by slaves. They prevent the immigration of whites, who really enrich and strengthen a country. They produce the most pernicious effect on manners. Every master of slaves is born a petty tyrant. They bring the judgment of Heaven on a country. As nations cannot be rewarded or punished in the next world, they must be in this. By an inevitable chain of causes and effects, Providence punishes national sins by national calamities. He lamented that some of our Eastern brethren had, from a lust of gain, embarked in this nefarious traffic. As to the States being in possession of the right to import slaves, this was the case with many other rights now to be properly given up. He held it essential, in every point of view, that the General Government should have power to prevent the increase of slavery."[1] This was on the 22d August; and then, if ever, the advocates of slavery might have taken alarm, since, on the 13th July preceding, the Congress of the Confederacy had passed the famous ordinance for the government of the territory north-west of the River Ohio, which declared (Art. VI.), "There shall be neither slavery nor involuntary servitude in the said territory, otherwise than in the punishment of crimes whereof the party shall have been duly convicted." With this pronounced purpose of Congress to exclude slavery from the national domain, and to provide against its establishment in new States, the defenders of slavery might well have been sensitive to the slight put upon the system by the omission to name it in the new Constitution. But a "proslavery man," an advocate of

[1] Reported by Madison, iii. 1400.

the system upon ethical and political grounds, was in those days rarely to be found. Ten of the thirteen States had already prohibited the slave-trade, which Great Britain did not prohibit till twenty years later. The three States whose commercial, domestic, and industrial interests were most nearly identified with slavery, obtained from the convention only a circuitous pledge that this traffic should not be prohibited by Congress before the year 1808. Without that concession, the Union could not have been formed: but in March, 1794, the Congress of the United States prohibited the slave-trade *to* foreign countries[1] (though this traffic was still lively in British merchantmen); and on the second day of March, 1807, twenty-three days before the British Parliament abolished the slave-trade, Congress prohibited the importation of slaves, the act to take effect on the first day of January, 1808, the very instant that the tacit, reluctant permission of the Constitution should expire. Then, as to the rendition of fugitives, the circular of the British Admiralty in September, 1875, — like the Fugitive-slave Law of Congress in 1850, — shows how utterly the government of the hour may misrepresent the moral sentiment of a nation, though justifying its action by technicalities of law; and this whole review may well rebuke the Pharisaism of any in England who would taunt America with a system whose dying struggle their ministry, a strong party in Parliament, and their leading press, did so much to prolong.[2]

[1] Sir William Grant, in his famous decision in the case of the Amédée, in 1807, distinctly concedes to America this priority in denouncing the slave-trade. "In all the former cases of this kind which have come before this court, the slave-trade was liable to considerations very different from those which belong to it now. It had at that time been prohibited, so far as respected carrying slaves to the colonies of foreign nations, by America; but by our own laws it was still allowed. . . . The slave-trade has since been totally abolished by this country, and our legislature has pronounced it to be contrary to the principles of justice and humanity. Whatever we might think, as individuals, before, we could not, sitting as judges in a British court of justice, regard the trade in that light while our own laws permitted it." — 1 ACTON's *Admiralty Reports*, p. 240.

[2] At the delivery of the Lecture, a few among my English hearers took umbrage at this passage; though the great majority, and these the better versed in history and affairs, frankly admitted its truth and justice. Gladly would I avoid reminiscences that could give pain to any; but, in giving an historical retrospect, I dare not suppress important facts to gratify my own feelings or the feelings of friends. I think the passage as it stands in the text states the facts as they were in well-considered words,

At a time when slavery was yet universally recognized, the framers of the Constitution saw they must make some concession to its existence, or forego the constitution of a national republic. Unable to decree the abolition of slavery, but anticipating its speedy extinction, they did secure the exclusion of slavery by name or express sanction from the charter of a free people. How their hopes failed, I shall show in the next chapter; but it is not for us to doubt their wisdom, or impeach their integrity. In making a new chemical compound, it may be important to eliminate it from some deleterious substance: but, in experimenting for this, it is not worth while to begin with blowing up the laboratory and its operators; better wait till retorts, walls, and bomb-proofs are strong enough to risk the explosion. Had Luther separated Church from State, and taken sides with the peasants in their war, how different might have been the fate of Germany and the Reformation! Yes; but did not Luther do enough? Did not our fathers do enough? Or are we so ignoble as to

and none too strongly. Our grievance against Great Britain during the war of 1861-65 was not a financial one. The payment of damages caused by allowing the Alabama to put out from an English port was indeed a question to be settled between the two governments; but, in common with all high-minded Americans abroad, I felt humiliated when the government of the United States brought before the Geneva tribunal the preposterous demand for "indirect claims." This was absurd enough as a bit of exaggerated rhetoric from the lips of Mr. Sumner,—what Mr. Benton would have called "a stump-speech in the belly of the bill:" but from the government as a formal demand, if seriously meant, it was childish; if meant for effect, it was a bit of chicanery grotesque and mortifying to the last degree. We have not yet recovered in Europe from this official proclamation of our "mercenary" character. No! money was not our grievance against Great Britain: it was that she went back on her own traditions of freedom and amity. She was allied to us by treaty; yet, while our accredited ambassador was known to be on his way, she made haste to give the Rebellion a belligerent *status* by the proclamation of "neutrality." England had in many ways admonished us of the evil of slavery; yet when known antislavery men assured her that the Rebellion was in the interest of slavery, and must prove its doom, their voices were not heard. We had in Britain many true and noble friends, whose fidelity to freedom and to international comity deserves all praise. But the visible currents of English feeling set strongly toward secession, and there was no prompt national uprising of Christian England in sympathy for our cause. Perhaps it was better for us that we went through the struggle without that sympathy; but it was not so well for England in the estimate of thoughtful and Christian Americans. Her moral failure in this great emergency of Freedom was to us a wonder and a grief. Thus much the simple truth demands of one whose whole life attests that he has never spoken ill of England. The record must speak for itself. A just recognition of past mistakes may be the surest preparation for good understanding and cordial comity in the future.

complain that they did not leave us a perfect society, in which we might sit at our ease, with nothing to test our patriotism, or discipline our manhood? Over the grave of slavery, — a grave so vast that it swallowed up five hundred thousand sons of America who should have been brothers, — a grave in which, O brethren of the South! my body and blood are buried with yours, — let us be just to the memory of the fathers, and strike hands in perpetual fealty to their Constitution of freedom!

The other point in which the wisdom of the convention of 1787 shone supreme in that which it rejected was its steadfast refusal to admit into the new Constitution the principle of a confederation of States. There was already such a confederation, which members of this convention had assisted to frame. The Congress of that confederation was then in session: the members of the convention sat as the delegates of States, and voted by States, the majority of each delegation casting the single vote of their State; and yet this council of States, in providing a Constitution for the future, repudiated the very basis upon which itself was formed. One has but to read, side by side, the preambles to the Confederation and the Constitution, to mark this significant change. The first opens as follows: "Articles of Confederation and Perpetual Union between the States of New Hampshire, Massachusetts Bay, Rhode Island and Providence Plantations, Connecticut, New York, New Jersey, Pennsylvania, Delaware, Maryland, Virginia, North Carolina, South Carolina, and Georgia." Art. III. — " The said States hereby severally enter into a firm league of friendship with each other, for their common defence, the security of their liberties, and their mutual and general welfare, binding themselves to assist each other against all force offered to or attacks made upon them, or any of them, on account of religion, sovereignty, trade, or any other pretence whatever." Here is no constitution, no body knit together as one being, its every part held and swayed by an inward law of life and growth, but a mere pact, — a pasteboard body without brain or heart, the limbs articulated with strings, which, though capable of pulling all together, have a propensity to individual jerks, at all times hang loosely, and may at any moment snap asunder. It can be safely predicated of such a body, that it won't work just when you most want it to. This confederate body, pieced together by "Articles," never had an executive head, but in the recess of Congress was represented by " a committee of the States."

Turn from this to the grand announcement that heralds the government under which the United States have lived since the 4th of March, 1789: "We, the people of the United States, in order to form a more perfect union, establish justice, insure domestic tranquillity, provide for the common defence, promote the general welfare, and secure the blessings of liberty to ourselves and our posterity, do ordain and establish this Constitution for the United States of America." Ah! we feel here the heart of the nation, beating with the consciousness of unity and of imperishable life; beating with the strong instinct of right, and the calm spirit of peace; beating with even pulse for the good of all; beating with high hope for us and our children, for liberty and man.

This change from a treaty of States to a national Constitution was made with the utmost deliberation, and was contested at every step by the adherents of the old notion of a confederacy. After some preliminary skirmishing in the committee of the whole, this fundamental question between the federal plan and the national plan was the subject of debate for five consecutive days, — a debate in which most of the leading minds of the convention took part, and Randolph, Hamilton, and Madison made those great and now historic speeches that settled the government upon the basis of national unity. The debate ranged about two conflicting propositions. The first, moved by Mr. Patterson in the interest of the smaller States, "*Resolved*, That the Articles of Confederation ought to be so revised, corrected, and enlarged, as to render the Federal Constitution adequate to the exigencies of government and the preservation of the Union:" the second, moved by Mr. Randolph, and recommended by the committee of the whole, "*Resolved*, That a national government ought to be established, consisting of a supreme legislative, executive, and judiciary." There was no attempt to blink the issue raised by these rival propositions. It was seen from the first that there could be no compromise between the two plans. Mr. Lansing said, "That of Mr. Patterson sustains the sovereignty of the respective States; that of Mr. Randolph destroys it." And Mr. Randolph himself said, "The true question is, whether we shall adhere to the federal plan, or introduce the national plan." Each plan was searched and sifted by an exhaustive debate, at the close of which the convention resolved "that the government of the United States ought to consist of a *supreme* legislative, executive, and judiciary,"[1] and so gave the *coup de grace* to the expiring confederacy. That the convention so interpreted its own act is clear from the letter of Washington, its president, to the president of Congress, in submitting the Constitution to that body: "It is obviously impracticable, in the federal government of these States, to secure all rights of independent sovereignty to each, and yet provide for the interest and safety of all. Individuals entering into society must give up a share of liberty to preserve the rest. . . . In all our deliberations on this subject, we kept steadily in our view that which appears to us the greatest interest of every true American, — the consolidation of our Union, in which is involved our prosperity, felicity, safety, perhaps our national existence." On the 17th September, 1787, the convention finished its work: on the 28th September, Congress transmitted the new Constitution to the legislatures of the several States, "in order to be submitted to a convention of delegates chosen in each State by the people thereof." And now this new plan of government, as it was universally regarded, had to undergo the ordeal of these popular tribunals. The battle that had been fought out in the Federal convention was renewed in each State convention, and raged with peculiar violence in the State of New York, where Hamilton, Madison, and Jay did such sturdy service to the cause of national government by their essays under the title of "The Federalist," which soon took rank with the higher statesmanship of the day. At length, by the close of July, 1788, ten months after its adoption in convention, the new Constitution was ratified by eleven States, — Delaware, Pennsyl-

[1] Madison Papers, ii. 858-909.

vania, New Jersey, Georgia, Connecticut, Massachusetts, Maryland, South Carolina, New Hampshire, Virginia, New York. North Carolina held aloof till Nov. 21, 1789; and on May 20, 1790, spunky little Rhody entered into the family, not seeing how she could longer maintain her sovereignty alone. Thus the league resting upon sovereign States was repudiated for the Union emerging out of the sovereignty of the people. The issue raised by war in 1861 was settled by wisdom more than seventy years before; and as we think upon the dignity, the consistency, the vigor, and the glory of the nation as manifested through its Constitution, let us not forget how much we owe to the prudence, the patience, the patriotism, of the convention of 1787, and, above all, of Alexander Hamilton of New York, and James Madison and Edmund Randolph of Virginia.[1]

Of the positive virtues of the Constitution it is less necessary that I should speak in detail; yet I must point out how each of its leading provisions for the actual government is, at the same time, a protection against a peril that might have destroyed the republic. To have admitted in the Constitution a right of secession would have brought on board a case of dynamite with a clockwork adjusted to explode it, and blow up the ship of state within a given number of days. But so vigilant were the framers of the Constitution against inflammable and explosive material, that nothing could be smuggled on board under an evasive manifest, but every article was subjected to a thorough search.[2] Popular government was to be maintained, but the risks of popular excitement and vacillation, and of mobocracy, to be guarded against: so the people are left in possession of local government

---

[1] Though at the last Mr. Randolph declined to sign the Constitution as a whole, it was he that first introduced and advocated in the convention the plan of a *national* government.

[2] In Switzerland there exists among the cantons a federal pact, without the national unity that characterizes the government of the United States. In 1846 a separate league was formed between the Catholic cantons, known as the *Sonderbund*, and based upon the doctrine that the federal pact was "a mere alliance of independent and sovereign states, each of them at liberty to put their own construction upon it, and break it whenever they chose." This pretence was resisted with the whole strength of the Diet; and Mr. Grote, in his Letters on the Politics of Switzerland, has shown that it would lead to the annihilation of all government.

under the laws of the several States, and enabled to participate directly in the general government by choosing their representatives in Congress, and also the electors of a President, in such way as their State legislatures may direct. They can change their representatives every two years; but a gust of popular passion that might sweep away the whole government with one blast, and toss its policy like a shuttlecock, is checked by a presidential term of four years, and by the Senate as a constant factor in the government, whose composition can be changed only gradually during a period of six years. The integrity of the State organizations was to be preserved, and their dignity respected: yet provision must be made against aristocratic cabals of State powers against the liberties of the people, and rebellious cabals against the national authority; and so each State — without regard to age, area, or population — has two senators chosen by its legislature: but in the Senate, instead of voting as in the Confederate Congress by States, each senator may at any time vote against his colleague, and ally himself with another party and policy, or act with entire independence; so that State dictation or cabal is hardly possible, even in the Senate appointed by the States. Nor can the Senate erect itself into an aristocracy, since there is the House of Representatives, fresh every two years from the people, to hold in check any aristocratic usurpation, especially by a vital grip upon the purse-strings.

By this happy balancing of powers, the State — which should properly be an outward formal expression of society itself — is made to rest, not upon any class of persons or of interests, but upon that combination of classes and interests that represents human nature in its totality. The dual system adjusts the two elements in society that answer to the *quantitative* and the *qualitative* in nature.[1] These elements are the democratic and the aristocratic, here combined in the representative and constitutional

---

[1] "In allen Völkern von höherer Art ist ein innerer Gegensatz zwischen dem *Demos* und der *Aristokratie* vorhanden, welcher mit dem Gegensatze der *Quantität* und *Qualität* in der Natur zusammenhängt" (Bluntschli: Allgemeines Statsrecht, b. ii. c. iv.). Bluntschli computes, that, in Europe, the system of two Chambers is adopted by a hundred and seventy-three millions; that of one Chamber, by only nine millions.

republic. While demagogism, mobocracy, and aristocracy are thus guarded against, there is also provision against absolutism. The nation must have an executive head; but this must not admit of the "one-man power." The electors of the President are chosen either directly by the people, or mediately by the legislatures of the States. The electors in each State vote apart, and send a list of their ballots, certified and sealed, to the president of the Senate at Washington; so that popular sovereignty and State organization are both respected in the provisions for electing the head of the nation, though in practice one or both may be reduced to a fiction. The President can make no laws, and assume no powers; and for attempt at usurpation, or other malfeasance in office, he may be impeached by the House, and tried by the Senate. But though he is thus hedged in from all personal aggrandizement and dictatorial power, yet, in his official character, he can, upon occasion, wield an authority more than imperial; for he is the executive of the collective will and might of the people, and "he shall take care that the laws be faithfully executed."

The three great departments of government — legislative, executive, and judicial — are by this Constitution clearly distinguished, and set in stable equipoise. Though the President cannot make laws, nor even originate them, his signature is required to give validity to an act of Congress; and he can withhold this, or can veto any act that he does not approve. But, in either case, the act may still become a law: in the first, by the lapse of ten days (if Congress is still in session); in the second, by the concurrence of two-thirds of both houses in repassing it. Hence, if Congress is rash, the President can check it; if the President is stubborn, Congress can override him: and it may sometimes happen that the House, the Senate, and the President are each a check upon the other; as, for instance, in this year 1876, the House is Democratic, the Senate Republican, while the President seems to have resolved "to fight it out on his own line." Again: should both President and Congress be rash or partisan, there remains the judiciary, whose officers hold during good behavior, and sit aloof from the political excitements of the hour; and the Supreme Court of the United States may set aside acts of Congress approved by the President, as unconstitutional and invalid. That court can maintain the right of the humblest citizen against a wrong committed by the whole power of the United States, legislative and executive. But, when a law is constitutional, there can be no pretence of authority in any quarter against it, nor of right in any body to resist it; for "this Constitution, and the laws of the United States which shall be made in pursuance thereof, shall be the supreme law of the land; and the judges in every State shall be bound thereby, any thing in the Constitution or laws of any State to the contrary notwithstanding:" for the United States are a nation; and the people, not the states, have ordained and established the Constitution. Such was the government which went into practical operation on the fourth day of March, 1789.[1]

[1] The successful framing of such a government was due, in no small measure, to the political spirit in which the people had been trained. Self-government, unity or co-operation, representative authority, and reverence for law, were principles or habits to which the colonists, and especially those of New England, had been accustomed. Their political institutions were based upon these principles; their political spirit was governed by them. The contrast in these particulars between the English and the French settlements in North America is thus pithily stated by Mr. Parkman in his New France: —

"The New-England colonists were far less fugitives from oppression than voluntary exiles seeking the realization of an idea. They were neither peasants nor soldiers, but a substantial Puritan yeomanry, led by Puritan gentlemen and divines in thorough sympathy with them. They were neither sent out by the king, governed by him, nor helped by him. They grew up in utter neglect; and continued neglect was the only boon they asked. Till their increasing strength roused the jealousy of the crown, they were virtually independent; a republic, but by no means a democracy. They chose their own governor and all their rulers from among themselves, made their own government and paid for it, supported their own clergy, defended themselves, and educated themselves. Under the hard and repellent surface of New-England society lay the true foundations of a stable freedom, — conscience, reflection, faith, patience, and public spirit. The cement of common interests, hopes, and duties, compacted the whole people like a rock of conglomerate; while the people of New France remained in a state of political segregation, like a basket of pebbles held together by the enclosure that surrounds them."

This was owing to the fact that the French colonies had no "people," in the political sense of that term. And indeed, to this day, France has hardly recovered from the long historical dependence of the people as subjects upon the State as sovereign. M. Simon, in his eulogy of Rémusat, said, —

"We are a people who only know how to display excessive resignation, or to rush into revolutions. De Rémusat jocosely said, 'There are a crowd of people in France who have only two tastes, — receiving commands, and firing muskets. When tired of one exercise, they pass to the other.' Our history only too much confirms him. Few peoples have passed so often as we from servitude to liberty, and from liberty to servi-

In all the stages of the organization of the American people as a nation, — the war of the Revolution, the Declaration of Independence,[1] the Confederacy, and finally, the Constitution, — it is a pregnant fact, that no measure nor movement was started in the interest of any person, system, or party; but every step was taken for principle and for the common good of the country. Indeed, there was a remarkable jealousy of personal influence and power. The war began without a commander-in-chief; and, at its close, the general, who had shared alike its trials and its triumphs, retired to private life. He desired no office, and there was no office for him to fill, since the government of the Confederacy, which came into existence during the war, avoided any provision for an executive head. When the deficiency of that government became manifest, there was no attempt in any quarter to put forth a new organization under a specific leader, nor to use the name of any leader as an argument for the organization. The movement for a revision of the government arose spontaneously in many quarters, with no concerted plan. The notion of a national government, with one supreme

tude; and, to make matters worse, when we establish liberty, we leave in our midst, through want of time and foresight, all the instruments of depotism."

Lest this should pass for the brilliant antithesis that French oratory delights in, I subjoin the sober, philosophical statement of Laboulaye: —

"The French system reposes upon the Roman idea of the sovereignty of the State. The government is not alone the arm of the nation: it is the soul of it. No doubt the State seeks to inform itself: it surrounds itself with chambers, with advisers, with men versed in affairs; but politically it is the State alone that wills and does. Republic or monarchy, France is always an army that lives by the thought of its chiefs. This fashion of conceiving the rôle of government is not new; it was that of Richelieu and of Louis XIV.; since 1789, it has been that of all parties."

This was said in 1859 in an essay on Alexis de Tocqueville; and it is yet too soon to change materially the statement as a contrast of the French with the American system. In his essay on "L'État et ses Limites,"[*] Laboulaye struck the philosophy of this contrast: —

"It is a fine thing to exhibit to the world a country rich and industrious, an heroic army, a powerful navy, embellished cities, splendid monuments: but there is something more admirable and more grand than all these wonders; that is, the force which produces them. This force, which cannot be too much economized (therein lies the whole secret of politics), — this force, which too many governments slight and neglect, — is the individual; and if there is one truth that science demonstrates, and that history cries out to us, it is, that in religion, in morals, in politics, in industry, in the sciences, in letters, in the arts, the individual is nothing but through liberty."

[*] P. 102.

[1] Congress met in New York on that day: but, for lack of a quorum, the votes for President were not counted until April 6; and, on the 30th of April, Washington took the oath of office as President.

head, came in gradually, and, after the most thorough canvassing by conventions, was accepted as necessary to the safety and welfare of the nation, and not at all through popular enthusiasm for any man as the predestined leader. Yet the man was there, the typical man, the embodiment of the national idea, the predestined leader of the people, first to independence, and next to organized and perpetual liberty; and so, when on the 7th of January, 1789, the several States chose their electors for the first President, but one name was in their minds and hearts; and when on the 4th of February, in each State apart, those electors met, but one name was cast into every urn; and when again, on the 6th of April, in presence of both houses of Congress, those sealed ballots were all opened and declared, there was but one name to be pronounced, — GEORGE WASHINGTON, unanimously elected first President of the United States of America.

The period from 1730 to 1815, so fruitful of great events in the political condition of the world, makes an epoch in the history of modern civilization. Within that period Prussia rose to the rank of a first-class military power, and laid the foundation of that inward strength and that outward respect which make her to-day a leader in the affairs of Germany and of Europe. The American Revolution established a new nation and a new order of political society upon the continent where England, France, and Spain had struggled for supremacy. The French Revolution, upheaving and overturning every institution of France itself, poured its fiery tide over the Alps and the Rhine. The French Empire made and unmade kings and peoples, and swept Europe with its armies from Portugal to Russia. The fall of that empire brought in the reconstruction of Europe with the balance of powers. In this world-making era, marking its beginning, its middle, and its end, stand three figures, each inapproachable by others of his time, and imperishable in personal grandeur and historic moment. History has no other example of three men, their lives overlapping each other, all severally so great in war, in statesmanship, and in executive administration, at eventful crises of their respective nations, which they shaped and guided by their own powers. In their relations to the great problems of political society and of human welfare, it may be said of the first, that he was the *only* man of his country in his time; of the second, it must be said he was the *best* man of his country in his time and for all time; of the third, that he was the *foremost* man of his country in his time, but, in seeking to make himself her only man, fell sadly short of the wisest and the best. For him, at least, the verdict of history is not yet settled, even in his own nation. The generation dazzled with glory was too soon followed by a generation darkened with detraction. Lights and shadows still flit across the Arc de Triomphe. There was enough of glory for France in what he had done to make it an object to piece together the broken Colonne Vendôme, but nothing of personal veneration or enthusiasm in placing him again at its head. But the people of the United States have never passed but one verdict upon their hero; and to that verdict History has put her seal with the approval of all good and noble men. His presence is yet so real and so loved, that Americans seem to shrink from transforming into stone and bronze the Father who still lives in the hearts of his countrymen. The fame of Washington is of a quality so distinct and incontestable, there is no need to depreciate the greatness of others with a view to exaggerate his: rather, the more we exalt others for the separate qualities in which they were brilliant or eminent, the more does he stand apart from and above them all in that combination of excellences that is peculiarly his own; even as, in approaching Mount Washington or Mont Blanc, the heights that awed you from below you must mount over on your way toward him, and find these but parts of the vast foundation on which he towers, or gateways to his temple. The versatile genius of Frederic the Great, his sagacity, brilliancy, epigrammatic wit, his soldierly dash, fertility, inventiveness, his determined selfhood as general, sovereign, author, man, are qualities we can hardly ascribe to Washington, certainly in no comparable degree; but neither had Washington the vanity of Frederic, his self-assertion, his arbitrary will, his fitful unscrupulousness. He could never have written, for he could never have felt, what Frederic has recorded of his motives for invading Silesia: "Ambition, interest, and the desire of making people talk about me, carried the day; and I decided for war." [1] That is frank, but hardly fine.

The world-wide grasp of Napoleon, his power of combination and concentration alike in battles and in laws, his quick origination and bold execution, his magnificent and terrible audacity, are qualities of heroism that we cannot ascribe to Washington; but neither had Washington the intense ambition, the inordinate selfishness, the reckless, despotic egotism, of Napoleon. In seeking his own fame, Frederic never lost sight of the aggrandizement of Prussia; and his personality was a magnified and intensified patriotism, which shone undimmed to the moment of his death. His country owes him lasting gratitude and honor.[2] Napoleon was never lost to the glory of France and of *la grande armée;* but he would make that glory tributary to his own, and feed the people with flattery that they might swell his fame. Frederic was the man for his kingdom; France was a nation for Napoleon; Washington was the man of his country and for his country, who freed and led his nation for liberty and mankind. The passion that ruled the soul of Washington showed scarce a spark in Frederic or Napoleon, — devotion to liberty and to man, without one thought of self.[3] It is with an admiration bordering upon awe, and a sense of humiliation for all pettinesses of our own, that we read the reply of Washington to the overture of his finally victorious army to erect a military government with himself at its head: "Be assured, sir, no occurrence in the course of the war has given me more painful sensations than your information of there being such ideas existing in the army as you have expressed, and I must view with abhorrence, and reprehend with severity. I am much at a loss to conceive what part of my conduct could have given encouragement to an address which to me seems big with the greatest mischiefs that can befall my country. If I am not deceived in the knowledge of myself, you could not have found a person

---

[1] Carlyle attempts to tone this down; but it must stand as a self-revelation of character.
[2] See note at the close of the Lecture.   [3] Ibid.

to whom your schemes are more disagreeable. . . . Let me conjure you, if you have any regard for your country, concern for yourself or posterity, or respect for me, to banish these thoughts from your mind, and never communicate, as from yourself or any one else, a sentiment of the like nature."[1]

No sooner was peace concluded than this immaculate general, who for eight years had served his country without ambition and without pay, appeared before Congress to return the commission he had received at their hands. "The great events on which my resignation depended having at length taken place, I now have the honor of offering my sincere congratulations to Congress, and of presenting myself before them to surrender into their hands the trust committed to me, and to claim the indulgence of retiring from the service of my country. . . . I consider it an indispensable duty to close this last solemn act of my official life by commending the interests of our dearest country to the protection of Almighty God, and those who have the superintendence of them to his holy keeping. . . . Having now finished the work assigned me, I retire from the great theatre of action; and bidding an affectionate farewell to this august body, under whose orders I have long acted, I here offer my commission, and take my leave of all the employments of public life."

A few days after, he wrote to a friend, "I hope to spend the remainder of my days in cultivating the affections of good men, and in the practice of the domestic virtues."

Frederic the Great died; and, twenty years after, the Prussia that he had created lay dismantled, dismembered, disgraced, at the dictation of Napoleon. Napoleon abdicated; and France has wandered between revolution and despotism, through all forms of government, seeking rest, and finding none. Washington twice voluntarily retired from the highest posts of influence and power, — the head of the army, the head of the state; but the freedom he had won by the sword, the institutions he had organized as president of the Federal Convention, the government he had administered as President of the Union, remained unchanged, and have grown in strength and majesty through all the growing years.

[1] Irving's Life of Washington, **iv.**

This significant contrast is, no doubt, to be explained largely by the characters and conditions of the peoples of Prussia, France, and the United States; yet the characters of the leaders had also no mean influence upon the consequence to their peoples of their own departure from the scene of action. Each has left a voluminous transcript of his life in his correspondence and other papers. In the memoirs of Frederic, often the peevish and perverse, sometimes the petty mars the brilliancy of his mind and the honesty of his heart. And what men he chose to have around, or rather under him! As Napoleon is unveiled in letters and memoirs, how is his glory tarnished by the mean, the selfish, the wicked! how unscrupulous in the use of unscrupulous tools for unscrupulous ends! But in reading the correspondence of Washington, — letters covering a long series of years and a vast variety of circumstances, written often under conditions of doubt, of danger, of discouragement and detraction, — though one may find a uniformity of goodness that is sometimes tame, and to some temperaments even tiresome, yet he finds no word nor thought that is little or selfish or vain.[1]

Those who estimate greatness only by illustrious achievements may wonder how a general who fought so few battles, and was so habitually on the line of defence or of retreat, should be acknowledged among the foremost generals of the world: but the crossing of the Delaware, the battles of Trenton, Princeton, Monmouth, his whole handling of the British in New York and New Jersey, and the victorious siege of Yorktown, showed in Washington a combination of all the qualities that achieve military fame; while his patient courage in overcoming every obstacle that jealousy, faction, delay, want of

---

[1] A correspondent of the London Chronicle of July 22, 1780, thus described Washington: "There is a remarkable air of dignity about him, with a striking degree of gracefulness: he has an excellent understanding, without much quickness; is strictly just, vigilant, and generous; an affectionate husband, a faithful friend, a father to the deserving soldier; gentle in his manners; in temper rather reserved; a total stranger to religious prejudices.... No man ever united in his own character a more perfect alliance of the virtues of the philosopher with the talents of a general. Candor, sincerity, affability, and simplicity seem to be the striking features of his character, until an occasion offers of displaying the most determined bravery and independence of spirit." — MOORE's *Diary of the Revolution*, ii. 301.

money, men, arms, ammunition, could throw in his way, justifies the saying, that "misfortunes are the element in which he shines,"[1] and shows us how, like William of Orange, he "was slowly compassing a country's emancipation through a series of defeats."[2]

Those who estimate greatness by memorable sayings of wit or wisdom, or novel and striking utterances of thought, may marvel how one whose average official papers contained so many political and moral commonplaces, expressed with a stately formality of style,[3] should be acknowledged among the foremost statesmen of the world; but Washington's Farewell Address to the People of the United States is a disquisition upon government, that in depth of political wisdom, breadth of practical statesmanship, loftiness of moral principle, historical insight into tendencies, and prophetic foresight of consequences, is unsurpassed by any document that any statesman has yet given to the world.[4]

But we come back once more to his correspondence; and, as we turn over page after page of the volumes of Sparks, how the conviction grows upon us, that, in the author of these letters, we see not only the noblest manhood, but the highest wisdom also, in that rare and masterly good sense which has understanding of men and of times!

The greatness of Washington centred in his moral equipoise. Never did he seek occasion for himself; but from the young surveyor and adjutant of Virginia to the commander of the American army, and from the diffident member of the legislature and of Congress to the Presi-

---

[1] William Hooper of North Carolina.

[2] Motley: Rise of the Dutch Republic, iii. 145.

[3] As one example of commonplace sentiments in a stilted style, take the following passage from Washington's reply to the congratulations of the General Assembly of the Presbyterian Church upon his election to the presidency:—

"While I reiterate the professions of my dependence upon Heaven as the source of all public and private blessings, I will observe, that the general prevalence of piety, philanthropy, honesty, industry, and economy, seems, in the ordinary course of human affairs, particularly necessary for advancing and confirming the happiness of our country. While all men within our territories are protected in worshipping the Deity according to the dictates of their consciences, it is rationally to be expected from them, in return, that they will all be emulous of evincing the sanctity of their professions by the innocence of their lives and the beneficence of their actions; for no man who is profligate in his morals, or a bad member of the civil community, can possibly be a true Christian, or a credit to his own religious society."

[4] See note on Hamilton's agency at end of Lecture.

dent of the United States, whatever occasion came to Washington he was ready to meet it, and did what was laid upon him with balanced judgment, unfaltering serenity, unselfish integrity, and that perfect command of himself that gave him command of men and of powers. The great men of his time who were nearest him most honored him; the people loved and revered him; humanity has adopted him. The hearts of all peoples, sated with the fame of captains and heroes, look up to Washington as the man. Humanity finds its highest hope in the realization in him of its own ideal. And it is a high hope for humanity that it accepts him as its type of greatness; for, in the words of Brougham, " until time shall be no more will a test of the progress which our race has made in wisdom and virtue be derived from the veneration paid to the immortal name of Washington." America, at least, can have no higher: for her he shall stand " first in war, first in peace, and first in the hearts of his countrymen."

NOTE ON FREDERIC AND NAPOLEON.

At the close of this Lecture in Berlin, one German lady said to another, " How can you endure to hear Frederic the Great spoken of so slightingly? This may all be true: but he was every thing to us; and it seems like exposing the faults of one's father."

"But," answered the other, " this picture of Frederic *is* true. My grandfather was in his service for many years, first as page, then as officer; and in our family we always knew of these unhappy traits of Frederic's character. It is all too true; and why shouldn't it be said?"

When the conversation was reported to me, I contented myself with saying, " If the judgment is not correct, it can't hurt Frederic's reputation with you; and, if it is true, his reputation ought still to be great enough to bear it."

I would not be wanting in respect for the devotion that clings to a national hero in spite of his defects, and even refuses to see any dimness in the halo of his fame. Indeed, I may as well confess to a cosmopolitan weakness for everybody's heroes. An advocate of peace, I have, however, no sympathy with the spirit that denounces all military heroes as scourges of mankind, and that will not allow that war can ever be a school of true greatness. But there is a standard of heroic judgment higher than military achievement, even among the heroes of battle; and when we are weighing men in the scale of history, with a view to selecting models for after-ages, we must do justice, though the heavens fall. And surely, if justice is done, some stars must either fall from heaven, or be greatly changed as to position and magnitude.

> "Only on the sad
> Cold earth there are who say
> It seemeth better to be *great* than *glad*."

It is not easy for an American to enter into the enthusiasm for military glory that still possesses the more intellectual portion of society on the continent of Europe. Under the conditions of modern warfare that have so nearly reduced war to an exact science, and armies to calculating machines, there is far less opportunity for strokes of military genius than in the days of Frederic and of Napoleon. But the glorification of the military spirit survives in the homage paid in so many countries to the army as the foremost representative of the national life and power; hence, in estimating historical characters, and ranging heroes in the Walhalla, the European is apt to have another standard from the American, who is trained to look for greatness rather in high moral qualities, and in devotion to mankind. A striking and really a touching instance of the military estimate of life lies before me at this moment. The venerable Field-Marshal Count Wrangel has just completed the eightieth year of his military service, having entered the army at the age of thirteen. At the celebration of this so unusual anniversary, his Majesty the Emperor sent him the following letter: —

MY DEAR GENERAL FIELD-MARSHAL, — The festive remembrancers of your most active life more and more take on the character of a specially favoring Providence. The jubilee of your fifty-years' service, most commonly the close of a military life, lies to-day thirty years behind you; and in these thirty years lie such great services and such eminent deeds, that with you the fiftieth-year jubilee has marked only the beginning of the second division of your famous career. To-day it is full eighty years that you have worn with such distinction the honorable dress of the soldier; and above all things must you to-day be filled with deep emotion at the grace of Almighty God, who has honored you above so many others, in that you are able to look back over so long a time of most praiseworthy activity. To him, the gracious God, before all, be the honor of this day's festival. But I speak not for myself alone, but as the heir of three kings, as deeply moved I to-day thank you in the name of those kings, to whom you have kept the oath of fidelity in such an exemplary manner, and whom you have served with such signality and devotion, that your name for all time will hold an honored place in the history of the Prussian army. That with my whole heart I number you with the prominent men whom the Prussian army has produced, I wish to-day to prove by apprising you that I have concluded at a future day to erect a statue of you, that thereby the latest posterity may retain the knowledge of your services, and my appreciation of them.

As a remembrancer of this day I send you the accompanying sword, the weapon that you have worn for eighty years, with which at Etoges, with your regiment, you cut through the enemy, and which has everywhere shown the troops that you have led the way to victory. As the statue to the world, so may the sword to your remote posterity bear witness of the gratitude and special esteem of

Your grateful, devoted king,
WILHELM.

This beautiful example of life-long loyalty and of royal friendship will be its own monument in history, — honorable alike to the subject and the king. Its influence upon all younger officers will be most stimulating. Said one of these to me the other day, "You republicans cannot know the sentiment of personal loyalty to the king. This devotion is the life of an officer; and there is something in it so very noble and fine." Here was a spirit that would never stop to inquire whether a king was right or wrong; whether the cause is noble or base, just or cruel. This is the true spirit of the soldier. We find it admirably expressed by Gen. Sherman in his answers to the congressional committee upon the employment of troops in the South.

The Chairman. — The object of my inquiry was to ascertain whether troops could be spared from the South to re-enforce the army in the Indian country.

Gen. Sherman. — I am compelled to answer that they cannot be spared, because those who are intrusted with power judge their presence there necessary. That decision to me is sacred and final, and governs me.

Mr. Terry. — You do not, however, say that it is your judgment.

Gen. Sherman. — It is hardly right to ask a soldier for his opinion. Behind his duty he ought not to form an opinion.

This is the only doctrine for a soldier. One can respect it, and honor the man who is true to it. Without this, there could be no military discipline; and, so long as an army is needed for police or for defence, it is vital to the public safety and order that this unquestioning loyalty should be maintained. The saying of Kossuth, "Bayonets think," marks the subversion of all military order and authority.

But, while heartily conceding this, I rejoice yet more heartily that American youth are not trained to look upon the dress of a soldier as honorable, irrespective of the master or the cause he serves, — much less to look upon the mere trade of soldiering as honorable at all; that to them a retrospect of battles and victories, a name in the army, and a memorial sword, are not held up as objects of ambition, the motive of life, and the solace of age. Thank God, they breathe another atmosphere, and have before them another standard of heroism, honor, and greatness. It is by such a standard — that of devotion to freedom, to justice, and to man — that I have attempted to measure Frederic, Napoleon, and Washington. What did they severally attempt? and with what motive? What did they achieve? and to what end? Much as we may concede to the soldier in loyalty to his calling, we may not forget that Frederic and Napoleon had often the game of war in their own hands, could make war or peace at their own will; and hence their ruling motives and aims must be taken into account in judging even of their military achievements. These last must not be suffered to overbalance those obligations of humanity that attend the possession of great genius and power.

Much must be excused in Frederic because of the unhappy experiences of his youth, and the complications of his political inheritance. It is a marvel these had not suppressed all the tenderness and magnanimity that were in his nature. His official utterances on coming to the throne were, no doubt, sincere intentions, formed before the actual experience of power: "Our grand care will be to further the country's well-being, and to make every one of our subjects contented and happy. . . . My will henceforth is, if it ever chance that my particular interest and the general good of my countries should seem to go against each other, in that case my will is that the latter always be preferred." This was honest and noble. But, as he went on in life, Frederic avoided any such collision by the simple expedient of making the good of his country identical with his own will, himself being supreme actor and judge. I have said that his personality was an intensified patriotism; but, *mutatis mutandis*, his patriotism could also be an exaggerated selfhood. Frederic performed prodigies for Prussia; yet some of her own historians — and perhaps his Royal Highness the Crown Prince inclines to their view — are of opinion, that, under the peculiar difficulties of his position, the Great Elector showed even more of military genius and administrative capacity. Frederic put his own stirring impulses into every thing he touched, — into laws, trade, letters, arts, as well as arms. He was indeed the soul of the nation that he filled with a life so grand, so potent, and so lustrous.

His famous secret instructions of Jan. 10, 1757, to Count Finck, bring into fine relief Frederic's self-sacrifice for his country, and may offset a good deal of personal vanity: "If I should have the fatality to be taken prisoner by the enemy, I prohibit all of you from paying the least regard to my person, or taking the least heed of what I might write from my place of detention. Should such misfortune happen me, I wish to sacrifice myself for the State; and you must obey my brother, who, as well as all my ministers and generals, shall answer to me with their heads not to offer any province or any ransom for me, but to continue the war, pushing their advantages, as if I never had existed in the world." This, again, is both frank and fine. But, when we apply to Frederic the touchstone of an unselfish devotion to freedom and to man, he fails where Washington stands; and, without depreciating Frederic, I have simply shown that Washington attained to a higher standard in nobleness of character, and greatness of achievement. Those who prefer the rose-colored view of Frederic will find this at its best in Mr. Bancroft's tenth volume,[1] and at high-flown intensity in Carlyle's "History of Frederic the Second." In corroboration of the view taken in the Lecture, and indeed going quite beyond it, I here quote a few lines from a critic, who in keenness of insight, and calmness of judgment, is unsurpassed, — Mr. James Russell Lowell: —

"Friedrich was doubtless a remarkable man, but surely very far below any lofty standard of heroic greatness. He was the last of the European kings who could look upon his kingdom as his private patrimony; and it was this estate of his, this piece of property, which he so obstinately and successfully defended. He had no idea of country as it was understood by an ancient Greek or Roman, as it

[1] Chap. iii. p. 97 *seq.*

is understood by a modern Englishman or American. . . . We doubt if Friedrich would have been liked as a private person, or even as an unsuccessful king. He apparently attached very few people to himself,—fewer even than his brutal old Squire Western of a father. . . . In spite of Mr. Carlyle's adroit statement of the case, we feel that his hero was essentially hard, narrow, and selfish. . . . The kingship that was in him, and which won Mr. Carlyle to be his biographer, is that of will merely, of rapid and relentless command." Without indorsing this to the full, let me earnestly recommend all who have waded through Carlyle's "Frederic" to read Lowell's critique in his "Study Windows."

Napoleon, like Frederic, had in his youth some noble sentiments of freedom, progress, and universal good-will; but like Frederic, too, he was not principled enough in his higher nature to withstand the lust of domination. In his moody complaints to his brother Joseph, when his mind had been poisoned with suspicions of Josephine, Napoleon touched bottom in his own soul. "I am tired of human nature. I want solitude and isolation. Greatness fatigues me: feeling is dried up. At twenty-nine, glory has become flat. I have exhausted every thing. I have no refuge but pure selfishness."[1] This "refuge" of despondency becomes his tower of strength in supremacy. Seven years later he could write, "*My* people will always be of one opinion when it knows that *I* am pleased, because that proves that its interests have been protected."[2] "I take the greatest interest in your prosperity, and particularly in your *glory*. In your position, it is the first of wants: *without it, life can have no charm*."[3] "If you do not begin [as King of Italy] by making yourself *feared*, you will suffer for it."[4] "There is nothing sacred after a conquest."[5] "I hope, that, by setting to work earnestly to form a good army and fleet, you will assist me to become master of the Mediterranean, which is the chief and perpetual aim of my policy. . . . I would rather have ten years of war than allow your kingdom to remain incomplete, and Sicily in dispute."[6] "To die is not your business, but to live and to conquer. I shall find in Spain the pillars of Hercules, but not the limits of my power."[7]

Just now, Europe is filled with indignation at the outrages committed in Bulgaria by the Turkish army. Seventy years ago, Napoleon, as the conqueror of Italy, had forced upon the people of Naples his brother Joseph as king, much as Louis Napoleon attempted to force Maximilian upon the Mexicans. Neapolitans who resisted this foreign king, upheld by a foreign army, were denounced by Napoleon as rebels; and here are the measures he urged upon his mild and humane brother: "I am glad to see that a village of the insurgents has been burnt. Severe examples are necessary. I presume that the soldiers have been allowed to plunder this village. This is the way to treat villages which revolt."[8] "I am impatient to hear that you have occupied Cassano. Besides this, you should order two or three

[1] Letters to Joseph, July 25, 1798.   [2] Ibid., Dec. 15, 1805.
[3] Ibid., Feb. 7, 1806.   [4] Ibid., March 3, 1806.
[5] Ibid., March 31, 1806.   [6] Ibid., July 21, 1806.   [7] Ibid., July 31, 1808.
[8] Ibid., April 21, 1806.

of the large villages that have behaved the worst to be pillaged: it will be an example, and will restore the gayety, and the desire for action, of your soldiers."[1] "Let the houses of thirty of the principal heads of villages be burnt, and distribute their property among the troops. Disarm all the inhabitants, and pillage five or six of the large villages which have behaved worst."[2] "I am waiting to hear how many estates you have confiscated in Calabria, and how many rebels you have executed. You should shoot in every village three of the ringleaders. Do not spare the priests more than others."[3] "I should like very much to hear of a revolt of the Neapolitan populace. You will never be their master till you have made an example of them."[4] To Joseph as King of Spain: "You must hang at Madrid a score of the worst characters. To-morrow I intend to have hanged here [Valladolid] seven notorious for their excesses. . . . I have arrested here fifteen of the worst characters, and have ordered them to be shot."[5] "When a general has occasion to speak of his strength, he ought to render it formidable by exaggeration, doubling or trebling his numbers."[6]

It would not be fair, indeed, to judge Napoleon at the beginning of the century by the mitigated rules of warfare that prevail toward its close. But neither should we forget that he issued these relentless orders against peoples whose countries he had overrun and subjugated, and upon whom he had imposed rulers and laws alien to their soil and institutions; that he, more than any man of his time, had it in his power to mitigate the cruelties of war, yet he urgently *ordered* the burning and pillaging of villages, which the Turks are condemned for not repressing. Nowhere is the marvellous military and administrative capacity of Napoleon seen to such advantage as in his confidential correspondence with his brother Joseph; yet in these intimate communications one reads also his moral weakness and the secret of his failure. That gentle, humane, wise, and loving brother read him truly, and counselled him aright. As the signs of re-action appeared, Joseph wrote, "I weep over the gradual diminution of an immense glory, which would have been better preserved by generosity and heroism than by any extension of power."[7] And, as the fatal hour drew near, Joseph pointed out how Napoleon could yet re-assure France: "If you will make a lasting peace with Europe, and if, returning to your natural kindness, and renouncing your assumed character and your perpetual efforts, you will at last consent to relinquish the part of the wonderful man for that of the great sovereign."[8] Then comes the proud answer: "As long as I live, I will be master everywhere in France. Your character is opposed to mine. You like to flatter people, and to yield to *their* wishes: I like them to try to please me, and to obey *my* wishes. I am as much a sovereign now as I was at Austerlitz. . . . There is some difference between the time of Lafayette, when the people ruled, and the present time, when I rule."[9] A month later he had signed his abdication.[10]

[1] Letters to Joseph, July 30, 1806.   [2] Ibid., July 13, 1806.
[3] Ibid., Aug 6., 1806.   [4] Ibid., Aug. 17, 1806.
[5] Ibid., Jan. 10 and 12, 1809.   [6] Ibid., Oct. 10, 1809.
[7] Aug. 8, 1810.   [8] March 9, 1814.   [9] March 14, 1814.   [10] April 18

Mons. Thiers has given us the term by which to characterize Napoleon, — "*moral intemperance.*" The French use this term for any excess, or want of regulation; as, for instance, intemperance of study, learning, &c.; just as Festus said to Paul, "Much learning hath made thee mad." "Politics," says Thiers, "is *character* much more than mind; and it was just there that Napoleon failed. Intemperance is the essential trait of his career." "Prodige de génie et de passion, jeté dans le chaos d'une révolution, il s'y déploie, s'y développe, la domine, se substitue à elle et en prend l'énergie, l'audace, l'incontinence."[1] Napoleon lacked the regulative power of deep moral convictions: the elements of his nature, that, in due restraint, would have made him unexceptionably great, drove him to intemperance of ambition, of self-will, of egoism.

Where Napoleon failed, Washington stands pre-eminent. His strength was in self-regulation, in moral equipoise. I confess I was long in searching after the secret of his greatness; and it was not till I went through the patient task of reading his voluminous correspondence that I found it, and found it here, — in his equilibrium of mind and of character; political wisdom, the result of profound reflection, expressed in terms of plain common sense; moral rectitude, undeviating in thought, motive, or action; devotion to country and mankind, in which the consideration of personal interests never appears, except in the form of a personal sacrifice for the common good. In the darkest hour of the Revolution he said, "I see my duty, — that of standing up for the liberties of my country; and, whatever difficulties and discouragements lie in my way, I dare not shrink from it; and I rely on that Being who has not left to us the choice of duties, that, whilst I shall conscientiously discharge mine, I shall not finally lose my reward."[2]

The honor of the "Farewell Address" has been claimed for Hamilton; but the draught in Washington's handwriting, in the Lenox Library, New York, shows that, however Hamilton may have assisted in the work by suggestion and revision, the conception and execution of the address are Washington's own. Nearly every great mind has some supreme moment in which it surpasses itself. Jefferson never wrote another paragraph that would compare with the opening of the Declaration of Independence. The solemn intensity of feeling at his retirement compressed the whole nature of Washing-

[1] Histoire du Consulat et l'Empire, tome xx. p. 718.
[2] A striking and trustworthy testimony to Washington as a general is given by Gen. De Kalb in his letters to the Comte de Broglie. At first he mistook Washington's modesty for timidity, his reserve for vanity, his reticence in councils for lack of independent judgment. Hence De Kalb criticised his new commander as "too indolent, too slow, far too weak," and "too easily led." By and by he recognized in Washington "the best intentions and a sound judgment." Later on he saw that Washington "did more every day than could be expected from any general in the world in the same circumstances." He then wrote to De Broglie, "I think him [Washington] the only proper person, . . . by his natural and acquired capacity, his bravery, good sense, uprightness, and honesty, to keep up the spirits of the army and people."—*See* KAPP's *Life of Kalb*, and GREENE's *Notice in Atlantic Monthly* for October, 1875.

ton into this supreme moment, and showed him to the world a philosopher and statesman of the highest wisdom and virtue.

There is a popular tradition that Frederic the Great sent a sword, or his own portrait, to Washington, with the message, "From the oldest general to the greatest." The story, however, seems to have no evidential authority; and Mr. Bancroft, who had access to the unpublished correspondence of Frederic, says, "I sought for some expression, on the part of Frederic, of a personal interest in Washington; but I found none."[1] But in Washington we see the nobility of manhood that could not be ennobled by the gifts of kings.

[1] One cannot attach any great importance to the Correspondance secrète et inédite sur Louis XVI., Marie Antoinette, &c.; but I give here the passages cited by Mr. Bigelow in his Life of Franklin (ii. 394): "In a letter which the King of Prussia has written to one of his literary correspondents in Paris, this passage occurs: 'I send you my secret against hydrophobia. It should be administered to the British Parliament, which acts like an infuriated fool in the American business. I have the abiding hope that you will don your cuirass against this *God dem;* that you will aid the Colonies to become free, and retake Canada, which they so wrongfully took from you. It is the wish of my heart, and it should be also the dictate of policy' (Nov. 3, 1777). Again: Nov. 17, the king to D'Alembert, 'I like these brave fellows, and cannot help secretly hoping for their success.'"

LECTURE IV.

THE NATION TESTED BY THE VICISSITUDES OF A CENTURY.

THE government of the United States is no longer an experiment; nor is the nation on probation. That the government shall fall, or give place to other forms; that the nation shall decline, and linger on in slow decay, or give place to some fresher stock and another type of civilization, — all this may be written in the Book of Fate. But this would only repeat the lesson of history, — that the permanence of no civilization and of no people is guaranteed, either by political forms, by social institutions, or by conditions of race and territory. Unless there be in the people a spiritual and moral life, working in and through their economic forms toward ever higher and nobler ends, and making the strength of justice and peace their safeguard against outward invasion, then nothing can keep a nation hale with the growth of centuries.

Who can read without a touch of melancholy the closing paragraph of Mommsen's " History of Rome" ? — " We have reached the end of the Roman Republic. We have seen it rule for five hundred years in Italy and in the countries on the Mediterranean. We have seen it brought to ruin in politics and morals, religion and literature, not through outward violence, but through inward decay, and thereby making room for the new monarchy of Cæsar. There was in the world as Cæsar found it much of the noble heritage of past centuries, and an infinite abundance of pomp and glory, but little spirit, still less taste, and, least of all, true delight in life. It was indeed an old world; and even the richly-gifted patriotism of Cæsar could not make it young again. The dawn does not return till after the night has fully set in and run its course." Such was the fate of Rome and of Italy. To other nations the night has never been broken since first it set in; while some are even now struggling doubtfully between day and night. Still the beautiful analogy of Mommsen must not be received as the universal law of history. Sometimes, at least, that which is taken for the setting-in of night is only the coming-on of an eclipse, from whose chill, ghastly, ominous shadow the sun at length emerges, to mount undimmed toward the zenith. An increase of his spots may indicate, not impending obscuration or destruction, but the burning-up of grosser matter by which he intensifies his light and heat.

If the principle of decay is lodged in the very life of nations, then the American people must decline, in their turn; but, so far as any prognostics can be detected in their organic constitution or national life, they need feel no alarm till they shall have advices that Macaulay's New-Zealander has "taken his stand on a broken arch of London Bridge to sketch the ruins of St. Paul's." The nation is not likely to die young: its Constitution has gone through the seasoning process, and come out with new vigor from every attack. Always a power of life, it has shown itself, in time of need, a living power. On retiring from the presidency, Washington said to his countrymen, " This government, the offspring of our own choice, uninfluenced and unawed, adopted upon full investigation and mature deliberation, completely free in its principles, in the distribution of its powers uniting security with energy, and containing within itself a provision for its own amendment, has a just claim to your confidence and your support." To-day a leading organ of opinion in England pronounces the Constitution of the United States "the most sacred political document in the whole world." [1]

The government that Washington commended as "well worth a fair and full experiment" has taken its place in the halls of political science as an authoritative example, has taken its seat in the high court of nations as a co-ordinate power. It no longer asks philosophers to stand by

---

[1] See leading editorial of the London Times, Dec. 9, 1875.

and see how it shall work; it no longer asks the governments of the Old World to be considerate of its youth, and grant it a probationary place in their councils. In its Constitution it has given to philosophers the most important contribution of modern times to the science of government: by that Constitution it tests all other governments, however ancient and revered, and, in virtue of this organized nationality, sits among the nations an arbiter and a judge by the same right that they claim for themselves.[1] The United States are not making an experiment in government for mankind to judge of: they are not on trial, and need no plea. They have accomplished a fact in government that now belongs to the science and history of the world. Though the Constitution of the United States is only eighty-five years old, its spirit is as old as the settlement of the country more than two hundred and sixty years ago. It was the consummate flower of a political society, that, drawing the sap of liberty from the best stock of Europe, had grown with the vigor of a new soil for nearly two centuries. Therefore it is impossible to separate the Constitution from the life of the nation, or this from the nations and ages that had gone before. The framers of the Constitution, indeed, did not consider their work perfect, since they incorporated with the instrument a provision for amending it; and the people of the United States have shown that they do not worship a bit of parchment, since they have amended their Constitution more than once, and are likely to amend it again. This Constitution might not be exactly fitted to any other nation, nor any other nation exactly fitted for such a government; for the government of a people must grow out of their conditions of race, territory, temperament, education, society, development. But, after all these qualifications and abatements, it remains true, that in reconciling liberty with order, individual well-being with the public good, local independence with collective power, the separate responsibility of the parts of government with the joint efficiency of the whole, the Constitution of the United States providing a government by the people, of the people, for the people, *is* the great contribution of modern

---

[1] See note at the end of the Lecture.

times to the science of government, and "the most sacred political document in the whole world."

Theoretically the Constitution speaks for itself, and is for the discussions of schools of political ethics; but it is not too soon to speak of the Constitution practically in these terms of confidence. Trial is no less a test of stability than time. The government of the United States has been tested by every form of mischief and peril that could threaten its existence. Measured by events, it has gone through a vast cycle of national experiences. It is my purpose, in this Lecture, to set in array these vicissitudes of the republic, and leave the facts to answer the predictions of its enemies, and allay the fears of its friends.

We are told that party-spirit will prove our ruin; that the strife of factions, which wrought such mischief in Greece and Rome, in the Italian republics of the middle ages, in the French republic, is intensified in the United States by the license of the press, by the personalities of political campaigns, and by the spoils of office held up as a prize to the winning party; and that this strife must lead at length to blows, to usurpation, or the despotism of a mob. Washington warned his countrymen "in the most solemn manner against the baneful effects of the spirit of party," as the "worst enemy" of popular governments. "A fire not to be quenched, it demands a uniform vigilance to prevent its bursting into a flame, lest, instead of warming, it should consume."[1]

Were we wholly without experience, the occasional violence of party-spirit and the indecencies of the political press might alarm us for the peace of the country and the preservation of public morals. Whatever our party affinities, or our personal feelings towards a particular President, who can read without a feeling of humiliation and disgust such language as this spoken of any incumbent of that high office? — "In all this affair the language of the President has been that of a heartless despot, solely occupied with the preservation of his own authority. Ambition is his crime, and it will be his punishment too. Intrigue is his native element; and intrigue will confound his tricks, and deprive him of his power. He governs by

[1] Farewell Address.

means of corruption; and his immoral practices will redound to his shame and confusion. His conduct in the political arena has been that of a shameless and lawless gamester. He succeeded at the time: but the hour of retribution approaches, and he will be obliged to disgorge his winnings, to throw aside his false dice, and to end his days in some retirement, where he may curse his madness at his leisure; for repentance is a virtue with which his heart is likely to remain forever unacquainted." [1] Now, do not mistake this for a philippic against "Cæsarism," under spasms of *angina pectoris*. It was delivered against Andrew Jackson. De Tocqueville quotes it as the first specimen of the American press that met his eyes on landing in New York in 1831: so the nation has survived that outburst for nearly half a century.

Did ever party-spirit run higher than at the first election of Jackson, and during his controversy with the Bank of the United States? Yet what does the present generation know or care about it all? And what shall we say of an open proposal to go to the seat of government, and drag the President from his chair? Did not such violence of party-zeal threaten the overthrow of the Constitution and the Union? But this was not a conspiracy to kidnap Mr. Lincoln in time of war: it was the talk of "solid men of Boston" against John Adams; and the nation has survived it seventy-five years.

In December, 1875, the House of Representatives passed a vote against a third term of the presidential office, — a topic that has been discussed in the newspapers in no measured words. One or two specimens of the language which the notion of a third candidacy has called forth are worth quoting here. "The President is totally destitute of merit, either as a soldier or a statesman: he has violated the Constitution, and perverted his office to his private use." "The remaining of no man in office is necessary to the success of the government. The people would be in a calamitous situation if one man were essential to the existence of the government. May the President be happy in his retirement! but let him retire." But this was said of *George Washington* when he insisted on

---

[1] Democracy in America, i. 233, Bowen's edition.

retiring, and Congress proposed resolutions of regret at his withdrawal from public life, and of thanks and admiration for his eminent services.[1]

John Adams has left it on record, that in 1793, when Genet sought to coerce the government into a league with France, "thousands of people in the streets of Philadelphia, day after day, threatened to drag Washington out of his house, and effect a revolution in the government, or compel it to declare war in favor of the French Revolution, and against England."[2] And of a like incident to himself he says, "Ten thousand people, and perhaps many more, were parading the streets of Philadelphia on the evening of my *Fast Day*, when even Gov. Mifflin thought it his duty to order a patrol of horse and foot to preserve the peace; when Market Street was as full of men as could stand by one another, and even before my door; when some of my domestics, in frenzy, determined to sacrifice their lives in my defence; when all were ready to make a desperate sally among the multitude, and some were with difficulty and danger dragged back by the others; when I myself judged it prudent and necessary to order chests of arms from the War Office to be brought through by lanes and back-doors, determined to defend my house at the expense of my life, and the lives of the few, very few domestics and friends within it."[3] All that was nearly eighty years ago; and who fears to-day that the National Government will be dethroned by a mob? The Constitution has long lived down that sort of party frenzy.

Never did the spirit of party rage more furiously than in the contest for the presidency between Adams and Jefferson. The latter as the leader of the Democracy, and supposed to be in sympathy with French ideas, was looked upon by Federalists as the incarnation of evil. One New-England minister refused to baptize a child Thomas Jefferson, saying he would rather call it Beelzebub. Another lifted up his dying head to say, "I die loving the Lord Jesus Christ, and hating the Devil and Tom Jefferson." The contest sowed enmity between those two

---

[1] Irving's Life of Washington, v. 241, 260.
[2] Letter to Jefferson: Jefferson's Works, vol. vi. 155.   [3] Ibid.

noble patriots. But years after we find them solacing each other in old age with a correspondence of tender friendship. In one of these letters, Jefferson alludes to that day of strife in these words: " Here you and I separated for the first time. . . . We suffered ourselves to be passive subjects of public discussion; and those discussions, whether relating to men, measures, or opinions, were conducted by the parties with an animosity, a bitterness, and an indecency, which had never been exceeded. All the resources of reason and of wrath were exhausted by each party in support of its own, and to prostrate the adversary opinions. . . . I have no stomach to revive the memory of that day. . . . No circumstances have suspended for one moment my sincere esteem for you, and I now salute you with unchanged affection and respect."[1] There is no lasting peril in parties whose leaders end in cuddling one another for the tomb. The nation has survived all the turmoils of Adams and Jefferson, and can do honor to each without jealousy of the other. No, no! it is not in party-spirit that the doom or disruption of the country lies. Parties are so nearly balanced as to be always a mutual check: they are so parcelled out among districts, counties, states, and so restrained by the elective apparatus for the senate and the presidency, that their majorities in one quarter may be neutralized in another. They cannot centralize; and, there being no army to be bought or used, they cannot terrorize. No mob can rush in upon the government with shouts of "*Le déchéance!*" No Monk can bring his hired soldiery to overawe or disperse the Parliament.

On the matter of party-spirit the anxious American may re-assure himself from the experience of countries other than his own. The German *Reichstag* is a creation of yesterday. Its members are hardly out of leading-strings. But what scenes of turbulence have already been witnessed there under the combined assault of Ultramontranes and the Fortschritts party upon Prince Bismarck's policy! What a spectacle is a party-bout in the French Chamber of Deputies! As to party-spirit in England, we have a telling witness in Lord Macaulay.

[1] Jefferson's Works, vol. vi. 37, 144.

On the 13th September, 1831, Macaulay wrote to his sister, "The aspect of public affairs is very menacing; fearful, I think, beyond what people in general imagine. Three weeks, however, will probably settle the whole, and bring to an issue the question, — reform, or revolution. One or the other I am certain that we must and shall have. I assure you that the violence of the people, the bigotry of the lords, and the stupidity and weakness of the ministers, alarm me so much, that even my rest is disturbed by vexation and uneasy forebodings, not for myself, — for I may gain, and cannot lose, — but for this noble country, which seems likely to be ruined without the miserable consolation of being ruined by great men. . . . I know the danger from information more accurate and certain than, I believe, anybody not in power possesses; and I perceive, what our men in power do not perceive, how terrible the danger is."[1]

In 1833 Macaulay had another scare about the Irish Church Bill, the stubbornness of the peers, and the vacillations of the king. On the 27th of June he wrote again to his sister, "I see nothing before us but a frantic conflict between extreme opinions; a short period of oppression, then a convulsive re-action, and then a tremendous crash of the funds, the church, the peerage, and the throne. It is enough to make the most strenuous royalist lean a little to republicanism to think that the whole question between safety and general destruction may probably, at this most fearful conjuncture, depend on a single man whom the accident of his birth has placed in a situation to which certainly his own virtues or abilities would never have raised him."[2]

Everybody says that Macaulay must have had "a bee in his bonnet" when he wrote such stuff as this. But its publication just now is timely as a warning to other prophets of evil. Macaulay was a student of history, a statesman of experience, a man of candid judgment, and a good knowledge of society and of human nature; yet, in the heat of controversy, every passing political excitement assumed the proportions of a revolution, convulsing society, and overturning the fundamental order of the state. Just

---

[1] Life and Letters, chap. iv.   [2] Ibid., chap. v.

this mistake is constantly made by English critics of American politics. It is well to remember that many an alarming telegraphic report and ominous leader in the morning journal is written, as were these letters of Macaulay, in the small hours, after an exciting debate and exhausting session, when the tired brain sees spectres while the rest of the world is quietly and safely asleep.

What little there was of reason in Macaulay's apprehensions goes to show that party-violence is not a special product nor peril of republican institutions, and that its remedy does not lie in relapsing to a monarchy and a House of Lords. Macaulay, even, sighed for relief from both, and boldly predicted the exchange of the House of Peers for an "Upper Chamber on an elective basis."[1] Mr. Trevelyan testifies, that, in 1839, "public animosity and personal violence had risen to a higher, or, at any rate, to a more sustained temperature than had ever been reached since the period when, amidst threats of impeachment, and accusations of treason, perfidy, and corruption, Sir Robert Walpole was tottering to his fall."

How hot the temperature of that partisan conflict really was, we know from Macaulay's journal: "Thursday, June 11, 1840. I went from the office to the House, which was engaged upon Stanley's Irish Registration Bill. The night was very stormy. I have never seen such unseemly demeanor, or heard such scurrilous language, in Parliament. Lord Norreys was whistling, and making all sorts of noises. Lord Maidstone was so ill-mannered, that I hope he was drunk. At last, after much grossly indecent conduct, at which Lord Eliot expressed his disgust to me, a furious outbreak took place. O'Connell was so rudely interrupted, that he used the expression, 'beastly bellowings.' Then rose such an uproar as no O. P. mob at Covent-Garden Theatre, no crowd of Chartists in front of a hustings, ever equalled. Men on both sides stood up, shook their fists, and bawled at the top of their voices. Freshfield, who was in the chair, was strangely out of his element. Indeed, he knew his business so little, that, when first he had to put a question, he fancied himself at Exeter Hall, or the Crown and Anchor, and said, 'As

---

[1] Life and Letters, chap. viii.

many as are of that opinion, please to signify the same by holding up their hands.' He was quite unable to keep the smallest order when the storm came. O'Connell raged like a mad bull; and our people, I for one, while regretting and condemning his violence, thought it much extenuated by the provocation. . . . At last the tumult ended from absolute physical weariness. It was past one; and the steady bellowers of the opposition had been howling from six o'clock with little interruption."[1] Never was there a more disgraceful scene in the American Congress than this "bear-garden" performance of British aristocracy and conservatism. Yet the British Constitution survived it; and he would be a sorry critic who should judge the institutions and the people of Great Britain by such an outbreak of party-violence. At that day, "The London Times" was as vituperative and personal as was "The New-York Herald" of the same period. Macaulay was then the foremost of English essayists, the most brilliant of parliamentary orators; yet "The Times," in its leading articles, styled him "Mr. Babble-tongue Macaulay," an epithet, which, like Thackeray's "Right Honorable T. B. Maconkey," marks an average level of English journalistic humor. And, when Macaulay and Sheil were sworn of the privy council, "The Times" exclaimed, "These men privy councillors! These men petted at Windsor Castle! Faugh! Why, they are hardly fit to fill up the vacancies that have occurred by the lamented death of her Majesty's two favorite monkeys."[2]

This was no exceptional instance. Such political amenities were too much the manner of that time. On the 1st of October, 1832, Mr. Disraeli issued an address to the electors of Wycombe, in which he characterized the ministry in the following terms: —

"And now I call upon every man who values the independence of our borough, upon every man who desires the good government of this once great and happy country, to support me in this struggle against that rapacious, tyrannical, and incapable faction, who, having knavishly obtained power by false pretences, sillily suppose that they will be permitted to retain it by half-measures, and who, in the course of their brief but disastrous career, have contrived to shake every great interest of the empire to its centre."

[1] Life and Letters of Macaulay, chap. viii.   [2] Ibid.

THE NATION TESTED. 169

If this might be pardoned to the ambitious rhetoric of a young politician, what shall be said of the following extract from a letter of Mr. Disraeli in reply to "The Globe," published in "The Times" of the 9th of January, 1836 ? —

"Like the man who left off fighting because he could not keep his wife from supper, the editor of 'The Globe' has been pleased to say that he is disinclined to continue this controversy because it gratifies my 'passion for notoriety.' The editor of 'The Globe' must have a more contracted mind and a paltrier spirit than even I imagined, if he can suppose for a moment that an ignoble controversy with an obscure animal like himself can gratify the passion for notoriety of one whose works at least have been translated into the languages of polished Europe, and circulate by thousands in the New World. It is not, then, my passion for notoriety that has induced me to tweak the editor of 'The Globe' by the nose, and to inflict sundry kicks upon the baser part of his base body; to make him eat dirt, and his own words, fouler than any filth; but because I wished to show to the world what a miserable poltroon, what a craven dullard, what a literary scarecrow, what a mere thing stuffed with straw and rubbish, is the *soi-disant* director of public opinion, and official organ of Whig politics."[1]

If a man addicted to such language could rise to the highest honors of statesmanship that the British Empire has to offer, there may be hope yet for Dr. Kenealy. It does not matter that all this was forty years ago. I grant that English manners have improved; but my point is, that political blackguardism is not a peculiarity of democracy, and that the remedy for this scandal of free society does not lie in creating peers. Party-spirit, with even violent indecencies of parliament and press, is not a special product nor a special peril of republican institutions. Liberty, indeed, may give exceptional facilities to the spirit of party; but we do well to keep in mind the words spoken by John Adams on the eve of the Declaration of Independence: "I do not expect that our new government will be so quiet as I could wish, nor that happy harmony, confidence, and affection between the Colonies, that every good American ought to study, labor, and pray for, for a long time. But freedom is a counterbalance for poverty, discord, and war, and more."[2]

[1] For more in this style, see Gentleman's Magazine for December, 1876, on Lord Beaconsfield.
[2] See note at close of Lecture.

This spectre of party being laid, we are threatened with the ghost of sectionalism, which already, in the time of Washington, began to stalk abroad as another guise of party-spirit. He regarded it "as matter of serious concern that any ground should have been furnished for characterizing parties by *geographical* discriminations, — *Northern* and *Southern*, *Atlantic* and *Western;*" and the "Farewell Address" contains an elaborate argument upon the community of interest of all sections of the country, their commercial and political interdependence, and the value of the Union to all alike.

In forming the Union, there were jealousies between New England and the South, which, however, yielded to the common necessity. At the moment when Washington entered upon his presidency, emissaries of Great Britain and of Spain were intriguing with political leaders at the West to detach the Western territory from the Union, and establish a separate government in the valley of the Mississippi. This project caused no little uneasiness until the treaties with Great Britain and with Spain satisfied the people of the West that the General Government and the Atlantic States were in no wise unfriendly to their interests, and had secured to them all the rights of navigation they could desire. At the beginning of the century, Aaron Burr was accused of the treasonable design of forming a distinct empire, to be composed of Western States and a portion of Mexico: but the scheme, whatever it was, failed ignominiously; and the purchase of Louisiana soon after bound the East, the West, and the South in a common destiny. From that day, the West has had her own outlet for her granaries to the markets of the world; yet canals and railways have made Boston, New York, Philadelphia, Baltimore, more necessary and valuable to her as marts for her produce than the Mississippi and New Orleans that she once coveted for her exclusive possession. The Hartford Convention, in opposition to the war of 1812,[1] cannot fairly be called a sectional movement: it was a combined peace-and-party demonstration, that soon died of inanition, and in its death involved the political hopes of most of its members and supporters. Historians

---

[1] The convention met in December, 1814.

will agree that the convention was a mistake as a mode of political agitation, and that the time of holding it was inopportune. In the midst of a war which had never been popular, and was still of doubtful issue, the convention put forth a statement of the grievances of a portion of the country because of the war, and proposed certain changes in the Constitution. But the convention never approached the idea of separating New England from the Union. Mr. Webster, who knew well the motives and aims of the old Federalist party, and had studied this question with his usual care, in his speech in the Senate, in reply to Mr. Hayne of South Carolina,[1] said, "There never was a time, under any degree of excitement, in which the Hartford Convention, or any other convention, could have maintained itself one moment in New England, if assembled for any such purpose as breaking up the Union because they thought unconstitutional laws had been passed, or to consult on that subject, or *to calculate the value of the Union.*"

Just after the Hartford Convention, Jefferson wrote to Lafayette, " They have not been able to make themselves even a subject of conversation, either of public or private societies. . . . The yeomanry of the United States are not the *canaille* of Paris. . . . The cement of this Union is in the heart-blood of every American. I do not believe there is on earth a government established on so immovable a basis. Let them in any State, even in Massachusetts itself, raise the standard of separation, and its citizens will rise in mass, and do justice themselves on their own incendiaries."[2]

Nothing in the geographical position nor in the historical antecedents of any portion of the United States, nor any occasional grievance or injustice inflicted on a part by the whole, could provoke sectionalism to a degree that might threaten the disruption of the Union. As a rule, party-lines would overrun and divide all sectional barriers, and specific grievances would be met by political agitation and party combination and change. Sectionalism could become a power only when a section should have some cher-

---

[1] Jan. 26, 1830. Works, vol. iii. p. 315.
[2] Jefferson's Works, vol vi. pp. 425, 426.

ished interest of its own, apart from, and perhaps alien to, the interest of the nation, and should set this local concern above all distinctions of party and all benefits of organic union. For a long period, the peril of sectionalism from such a cause was serious, and at times alarming, — a sectionalism not defined by physical geography, nor degrees of latitude, but by the surveyor's line of Mason and Dixon, and social institutions contrasted by that artificial boundary. This peril, which had aroused the country in 1820, and was then seemingly averted by the Missouri Compromise,[1] took on the positive and formidable aspect of nullification in 1832, when a convention of South Carolina resolved to resist the collection of duties by the United-States Government, and, should their collection be enforced, to withdraw from the Union, and organize a separate government. The champion of nullification was one of the most sincere, upright, and able statesmen the country has produced, — a man who, given his premises, would hold you as in a vice by the relentless screw of his logic. No American can fail to accord to John C. Calhoun the respect due to the highest order of intellect and to perfect sincerity of character; but when he assumed the false premise, that the Constitution was not the fundamental and inalienable law of the nation, but a voidable compact of sovereign States, then the very strength of his logic, and the downright earnestness and sincerity of his character, drove him on to destroy the Union for what he believed to be the right of his State. The first stand was made at the tariff; but this point was too weak to be tenable; and the strong reasoning and burning eloquence of Webster in the Senate, the soldierly decision of Jackson in the presidency, and the spontaneous uprising of the people, put down nullification with the watchword, "*The Union, it must, it shall, be preserved.*" In truth, with the ever-changing phases of agriculture, manufactures, and commerce, and the mobility of political parties upon economical questions, a tariff act of a single Congress could hardly form the nucleus of a sectional contest against the General

---

[1] By this compromise, Missouri was admitted into the Union as a slave State, on the pledge that slavery should be thereafter prohibited in new States north of 36° 30′ north latitude.

Government. Calhoun had the honesty to avow that the prime importance of his doctrine of State-rights and secession lay in the preservation of slavery: and that *was* an interest which the South had in common, to the exclusion of the rest of the Union, — an interest that entered into the whole constitution of society, domestic, industrial, political; into the personal habits of the people, their local laws, their ties of property, marriage, and inheritance. To the protection of this system Mr. Calhoun brought his doctrines of State-rights and secession, and devoted the strength and energy of his remarkable powers through the long period of his public career. I respect Mr. Calhoun none the less, that, in the circumstances of his training, he was a slaveholder; and none the less that he maintained with such manful persistency that state of society with which his own life was involved. He had the courage to say in the Senate, that the doctrine of human equality and liberty proclaimed by the Declaration of Independence was a grave political error;[1] and that "the laws of the slaveholding States for the protection of their domestic institutions are paramount to the laws of the General Government in regulation of commerce and the mail; that the latter must yield to the former in the event of conflict; and that, if the government should refuse to yield, the States have a right to interpose."[2] This determination to renounce the Union, rather than suffer slavery to be restricted, meddled with, or even discussed, was largely the burden of Calhoun's speeches for twenty years. He was honest, and I respect him for that; he was consistent, and I respect him for that; he was courageous, and I respect him for that; just as I respect Pius IX. for saying "Non possumus" to every proposal that he "should reconcile himself to progress, liberalism, and civilization, as lately introduced." I find in Mr. Calhoun no tokens of political envy, of disappointed ambition, or of mean demagogism; but his system made him sectional, dwarfed his vision from the grand scope of nationality, freedom, humanity, for which such powers as his were given, and

---

[1] Speech on the Oregon Bill, June 27, 1848: Works, iv. 506.
[2] Speech on Suppressing Incendiary Publications, April 12, 1836, vol. ii. 532, 533.

concentrated it upon one interest of his one State, — "There is my family and connections; there I drew my first breath; there are all my hopes." [1]

The South was never sectional upon geographical or political grounds. Slavery, an heirloom of the civilization that preceded the era of independence, fostered by her climate and intwined with her growth, made economically valuable through the invention of the cotton-gin, made politically important through the three-fifths rule of apportionment and the expansion of territory, — *this* gave to the South a community of interest in and for herself separate from the general interests of the country, and made her a unit whenever that interest was endangered. It is but just to the patriotism of the South to say that slavery alone made her sectional, intensified her faith in State-rights, and drove her into the fallacy of secession. The war of sectionalism was fought out grandly in the arena of argument, was fought out bravely on the field of battle; and slavery, the cause of sectionalism, fell. What now remains? Hostile sections, imbittered by war, biding their time for a new struggle for ascendency? Let the reception given to the soldiers of Virginia and South Carolina at the celebration of Bunker Hill in June, 1875, answer. Let the late Vice-President of the Southern Confederacy answer. In his speech at Atlanta, July 4, 1875, Mr. Alexander H. Stephens said, "The grand demonstrations in honor of the hundredth anniversary of the destruction of tea at Boston and Baltimore, of the battles of Concord, Lexington, and Bunker Hill, and of the Mecklenburg Declaration, which have brought the different sections into more harmonious accord, are but a prelude to the celebration of the anniversary of the Declaration which is to come off next year in Philadelphia. . . . *The great cause of strife being now removed forever*, why cannot all true friends of constitutional liberty cordially unite in the future for the perpetuation of the principles set forth in the common Declaration of Independence? I insist that we of the South shall never, from any cause, lose our full share of the glories of the ever-memorable 4th of July, 1776." And once more: let Gov. Kemper

---

[1] Speech of Feb. 19, 1847: Works, iv. 347.

of Virginia answer, whose message of Dec. 1, 1875, advocates the Centennial Exhibition at Philadelphia in these patriotic and eloquent words: " The people of Virginia yielded as brave men to the verdict of war; and, giving their parole of honor to be thenceforward faithful citizens of a re-united common country, they at once and cheerfully accepted the results of emancipation, as well as the arbitrament *which ended the question of peaceable secession forever, and made the Union constitutionally indissoluble.* . . . The United States is our country; and it is destined to be the only country for ourselves and our children forever. . . . It were suicidal in us to hold back from any effort which can conduce to the common welfare. . . . Let not Virginia stand aloof from this gathering of her sister States on the spot which gave birth to free government, and where her illustrious sons, a hundred years ago, took so grand a part in rearing the pillars of American liberty. Let her stand there, hand in hand with her sister States, around the hallowed spot, and, uniting with them, give her potent aid in laying deep and strong the foundations of a reconstructed Union, made perpetual by good-will, equal laws, equal rights, and equal liberties for all."

Since sectionalism as between the North and the South was abnormal, and the cause of that old unnatural strife is forever removed, where shall one find on the map of the United States, geographical or political, a basis or suggestion of sectional division? Nature has provided no line of territorial division from east to west. No Alps there lift their everlasting barriers; no Mississippi rolls eastward from the Rocky Mountains to the Alantic coast. The basin of the Mississippi, notwithstanding its enormous dimensions, is marked by Nature for the home of a people having community of interests, and identity of aims. From the westward watershed of Pennsylvania to the eastward watershed of Colorado, the central river drains into itself the entire circulation of the basin; and the farmers and miners of Ohio, Indiana, Illinois, Iowa, Wisconsin, Minnesota, Dakota, Montana, Wyoming, Nebraska, Colorado, Kansas, have a property in the free outlet of the Mississippi as vital as the planters and graziers of Arkansas and the merchants of St. Louis and New Orleans. As to the East and the West, nowhere does the Appalachian range rise to such a height, nor in a line so bold, as to form a sharply-defined barrier; and its own streams and passes have long been utilized for canals and railways binding the Mississippi basin to the Atlantic slope.

The Rocky Mountains might indeed serve for a physical boundary between separate nations; but the material products and wants of the regions upon either side require that these should supplement each other, and this natural interdependence of the parts argues the predestined unity of the whole. Though California and Oregon possess magnificent harbors of their own, lying open to the commerce of Japan, China, and the Indies, the railway has subsidized the Atlantic and Pacific Oceans to combine the traffic of New York and San Francisco for the enrichment of both. How much of the bullion of the Pacific coast finds its way into the exchange of the world through the commerce of the Atlantic coast! The streams of New England turn the seven million spindles that weave the cotton of the South and the wool of the West; and even the granite and ice of her inhospitable climate provide for the wants and comforts of New Orleans and Mobile. The cotton and sugar crops of the South, in turn, find vent largely through the markets and ports of the North; while the vast grain, pork, and beef supplies of the basin of the Mississippi, which would impoverish the country through an *embarras de richesses* were not the glut relieved by eastern outlets, find a ready exchange for the fish and manufactures of the Atlantic slope, and for the imports of its world-wide commerce. Thus the varieties of soil, climate, and production, in ceaseless exchange, the more than three million tonnage employed yearly in the coasting trade, the fifty thousand miles of railway and sixty thousand of telegraph-wires traversing the continent, show how close and constant, how universal and minute, is the industrial circulation of the national life; the vast trains of freight-wagons on the Pacific Railway, marked "New York, Chicago, San Francisco," denote the unity of interests in the Atlantic and Pacific slopes and the

Mississippi basin; the trend of the two great coasts points to the unity of a nation that should possess the northern continent; and, while the physical conformation of the country protests against disruption, the principle of local self-government is the efficient counterpoise to centralization: *Unitas in libertate et libertas in unitate.*

This last sentence anticipates and refutes another prophecy of danger to the American Union. It is pronounced impossible that a republican government should maintain its unity over so vast a territory and such a multitudinous population as will occupy that territory in the next hundred years. History warns us of the perils of territorial expansion to the organic unity of the State. Of the attempt of Rome to rule the Romano-Hellenic world, stretching from the Tagus and the Bagradas to the Nile and the Euphrates, Mommsen observes, " The government of the world, difficult in the attainment, was still more difficult in the preservation: the Roman Senate had mastered the former task; but it broke down under the latter."[1] And it was true also of the Roman Empire, that the weight of the branches broke the tree. Other empires of conquest have followed the same fate, and we are witnesses to-day of the impending dissolution of the Turkish Empire. During the Mexican war, Mr. Webster, in the Senate, said, " I am against all accessions of territory to form new States;"[2] and pointed out the dangers of annexation to the Constitution and the Union. But the dangers he apprehended are over. Westward we have reached the Pacific: we have no hankering for Canada, and she no yearning toward us: in the death of slavery expired the desire of annexing Mexico and Cuba: the suggestion of an interference by the United-States Government in the affairs of either excites no popular enthusiasm; and no party could ride into power to-day by a war-cry of annexation or "manifest destiny."

If there is danger to the Union from extent of territory, and increase of population, this is a danger that the government of the United States shares with most of the great nations of the future, — Russia with her almost

---

[1] History of Rome, book iv. chap. 1.
[2] Speech of 2d February, 1848: Works, vol. v. 280.

yearly accessions of territory in Asia; Germany with her union of kingdoms and duchies, and her annexation of Posen, Schleswig-Holstein, and Elsass-Lothringen; England with her vast colonies and dependencies, and yet possible conquests and protectorates; Austria with her mixed empire, and the tempting provinces of the Danube. In a word, the modern doctrine of nationality favors the assimilation of all the elements of a people — race, language, territory — under common political institutions. Hence, when European critics prophesy danger to the Union from extent of territory, and growth of numbers, we answer, Look at home for the solution of this common problem, and, if you please, common peril, of nationality. The United States have in this problem fewer elements of danger than has any other great and growing people. Their accessions of territory have not brought with them a population alien in race, language, manners, religion, to be held as a subject people, or transformed by the slow processes of time. The acquisition of Mexico or Cuba, to be sure, admitting to political equality whole communities, provinces, people, so utterly foreign to the spirit and ideas of the nation, would be fraught with dangers both to liberty and union. Such wholesale annexation would be quite another test of vitality than the gradual absorption of immigrants, though these, in the end, might count by the million. But our acquisitions, even by conquest, have been of wild lands, or of territory sparsely occupied, never of provinces teeming with a foreign and hostile people; and I have shown already that the common sense and the moral sense of the American people are set against buying or bullying the Mexican and the Cuban into American citizenship. We have not enough of philanthropy for our distracted neighbors, nor enough of ambition for the spread of liberty, to peril the whole future of free institutions by such conquests, whether of policy or of arms; and since the old spring of filibustering is broken, and its motive gone, we are not selfish nor unscrupulous enough to spoil our neighbor because he is weak and his weakness makes him troublesome. The American Republic has little to fear from that sort of expansion that brought ruin to Rome.

Hence, also, the United States is freed from the perilous necessity of governing annexed provinces by the sword. Needful as a standing army may be for protection and defence, needful at times even for the nursing of liberty itself, all history shows that it may become a menace to the freedom of the people, or, what is worse, accustom them to a rule of iron. Vast as is our territory, and multitudinous our population, we are free from the perplexity of conquered provinces of unsympathetic races, and from the necessity of military government.

The secret of the stability of the Union under the strain of territorial expansion was discerned by Washington, and set forth in his Farewell Address: "Is there a doubt whether a common government can embrace so large a sphere? Let experience solve it. To listen to mere speculation in such a case were criminal. We are authorized to hope that a proper organization of the whole, with the auxiliary agency of governments for the respective subdivisions, will afford a happy issue to the experiment. 'Tis well worth a fair and full experiment." At that time the sixteen States of the Union possessed a territory of 827,844 square miles, being nearly seven times as large as Prussia then was (in 1797); but, since the retirement of Washington, the territory of the United States has been quadrupled. The purchase of Louisiana added 1,171,931 square miles; Texas and the Mexican cessions, 968,481 square miles; Alaska, 577,390 square miles; and these, with Oregon and Florida, have enlarged the area of the Union to 3,603,884 square miles, — more than four times that of 1797, and seventeen times the area of the present German Empire. The fair and full experiment of a common government over so large a sphere has come to an issue happy beyond the sanguine yet serious hope of Washington. The reason is, that, in the United States, we do not establish government from above, but build it from beneath. With each advance of population go the institutions of local government. In all their local concerns, the people care for themselves; and then they adhere by instinct to that great national organism that gives them in their very infancy the strength and protection of the full-grown nation. The border-line of the march of occupation may, for a time, be possessed by the lowest elements of society, and marked by lawlessness and ruffianism; but how soon does civilization overtake and efface it all! I have been in a border settlement where I feared to sleep amid the horde of villains around me: ten years later I have found on that spot a town, with schools, churches, houses, looking as peaceful as if they had stood a century; while bar-room ruffianism skulked out of sight. That is American civilization, that follows every footstep of adventure or of gain with the teacher and the preacher, and makes the Indian wild and the pioneer's clearing blossom as the rose. No page of history presents a record of more silent, patient heroism, or more self-sacrificing patriotism, than the all unwritten, unpublished lives of the teachers and missionaries of the West. Yes, it is and shall forever be possible for the Union to hold together, based everywhere upon the same institutions of liberty and light, of order and love.[1]

Quite germane to the question of territory is that of immigration as affecting the unity and permanence of the people of the United States. I count it the social and political marvel of the century that the native-American stock has absorbed such vast promiscuous hordes of foreigners, with so little detriment to itself and its institutions. History gives examples of the migration of tribes and peoples for the occupation of new territories by settlement or conquest; but there is no precedent for a nation receiving into its bosom millions of foreigners as equal sharers in its political rights and powers. With a magnanimity almost reckless, the United States have done this, and have survived. Immigration first assumed proportions worthy of note in the decade from 1830 to 1840, when it reached the figure of 599,000. In the decade from 1840 to 1850, it increased to 1,713,000; and the report of the Bureau of Statistics for 1874 gives for the ten calendar years from Jan. 1, 1864, to Dec. 31, 1873, inclusive, a net immigration of 3,287,994. Compare these figures with the fact that the purchase of Louisiana, over a million square miles, brought with it scarcely twenty thousand white inhabitants, and the nearly a million

[1] See note at end of Lecture.

square miles acquired through Texas and the Mexican cessions brought only some fifty thousand, and it will be seen how much more formidable has been the problem of immigration than that of territory. The good and the evil of this wholesale influx of foreign elements into the body politic of the United States are so nearly balanced, that it is hard to say which preponderates. While it has added vastly to the productive industry and material wealth of the country, it has detracted from the dignity of labor in the eyes of the native American, and has driven out the good old times when the American boy did not scorn to be apprenticed to a trade or a farm, and the American girl to go out to service, or work in a factory. In this respect, the foreign element has somewhat damaged the manly tone and hardy spirit of our people. The common folk do not like to work beside the Irish greenhorn or the German boor: they don't like what smacks of "the pauper labor of Europe."

If, in some quarters, foreign influence has stimulated the culture of music and other arts and amenities of life, on the other hand it has set itself against that wholesome observance of Sunday and of temperance laws which had been the safeguard of the native population against any excess of the physical and sensuous over the rational and spiritual. If, in some aspects, it has liberalized thought and customs, on the other hand it has spread the mischiefs of rationalism and materialism, and has also furnished a constituency for the Romish hierarchy, which, after England had supplanted France and Spain, had well-nigh lost hope of that portion of the American continent. If the foreign elements of the population, being played off against each other, have at times done a good service to a political party, if they have given us now and then a statesman or a scholar, on the other hand they have furnished the chief constituency of the rings that have corrupted our polls and disgraced our civic administration. If they have multiplied population as an element of national wealth, they have multiplied pauperism in a still greater ratio, and have brought with them the feudalistic and communistic notion that government owes a living to the poor. If they have swollen our census tables, they have fearfully swollen our tables of crime.

The last report of the police of New York shows for the year a total of arrests, 84,514.

Of these there were born in the United States . 30,916
" " " in Ireland 38,009
" " " in England and dependencies . 4,385
" " " in Germany 9,597
" " " in all other countries . . . 1,607

Now the census of 1870 gives us the total population of New York, 942,292.

Of these were born in the United States . . . 523,198
" " " in foreign countries . . . 419,094

Hence, in the first place, of the whole number of criminals in New York in that year, notwithstanding the fact that the worst creatures from the country find their way to this metropolis, the native Americans furnished but thirty-five and five-tenths per cent against sixty-three and five-tenths of foreign birth. But this is not the fairest ratio. The population of New York, by the census of 1870, consisted of 523,198 native-born Americans and 419,094 foreigners; and, of these last, 234,557 were Irish, and 151,203 Germans. Hence the native criminality was barely six per cent of the native population, while the foreign criminals were twelve and seven-tenths per cent of the foreign population; and of these the Germans were six and three-tenths of the German immigrants, and the Irish eighteen per cent of the Irish. Again: the police report of New-York City for twelve years, from 1860 to 1872, shows as the total of arrests, 899,544. Of these, 284,591 were native-born (only thirty-one and six-tenths per cent) against 614,953 foreign-born (or sixty-eight and four-tenths per cent). Once more: the census for 1870 gives the total population of the United States at 38,558,371. Leaving out of view the colored people, whose vices and crimes are largely due to a previous state of slavery and the sudden change to a state of freedom, there were in prison on the 1st of June of that year 16,117 native whites and 8,728 foreigners. Here, at first view, the average is against the native population. But, when we divide the population according to nativity, we have 28,111,133 whites of native birth, of whom 1 in 1,744 was in prison, and 5,567,229 of foreign birth, of whom 1 in 638 was in prison. That is the relative ratio for the whole country. If we take the two States of New York and Massachusetts, which, with their large cities and manufacturing towns, attract a great percentage of native vice and crime, and in their seaports retain a large percentage of foreign immigration, we have an astounding result. In 1870 New York had 3,244,406 native inhabitants, of whom 2,323 were in prison on the 1st of June, and 1,138,353 foreigners, of whom 2,046 were in prison; that is, a foreign population of barely one-fourth furnished nearly one-half the occupants of the prisons. Massachusetts had a native population of 1,104,032, of whom 1,291 were in prison, and a foreign population of 353,319, of whom 1,235 were in prison; that is, with less than one-fourth of the population, foreigners furnished full one-half the criminals. Europeans who would judge intelligently American society must weigh honestly such statistics. Surely the sixty-four per cent of imported criminals are not the product of "American civilization." The fact, that, with such tides of crime and pauperism rolling in annually from Europe, the native elements of order and virtue have not only held their own, but have gained upon the population with schools, churches, and law-abiding communities, shows the moral stamina of American society, and the conservative strength of American institutions.

The reason of this lies in the vigor of the native stock, and the vitality of the native morality and religion. The latter topic belongs to a subsequent chapter. But a word is needed here touching the potency of the native-American stock. On this point the most preposterous notions prevail in Europe, and especially in Germany, where one ought to find accuracy in works used as text-books in schools, and in the essays of publicists and statisticians. It is said that the native white population is growing sterile and would run out if not constantly recruited from Europe; that in the United States a mixed race is forming, with as yet no fixed character; that already foreign elements are gaining the preponderance; that ten millions of the population are German.[1] These absurd statements I have publicly exposed in a paper read before the Geographical Society of Berlin. Summarily, the facts are, that,

[1] See Daniel's Geography, and Louis Schade.

by the census of 1870, the total population of the United States was 38,558,371; and the sum total of those who were born in foreign lands was but 5,567,229, and of these the Germans could count only 1,690,410. In addition to the above 5,567,229 foreigners residing in the United States, the census gives 5,324,786 persons, one or both of whose parents were of foreign birth. Hence the entire foreign element in the United States, composed of all living immigrants, and all children even one of whose parents was an immigrant, is represented by 10,892,015. Immigration has reached its maximum, and is likely to decline with the improved condition of Ireland and Germany, and the increased dearness of living in the United States.

Vital statistics show a heavier rate of mortality among the foreign than among the native-born population. In the fifty years from 1820 to 1870, about two millions of the registered immigrants have disappeared by death or return. Dr. Edward Jarvis[1] has proved from official returns, that there are now living in the United States, as descendants from the population of 1790 (when the first census was taken) sixty-two per cent of the present population: twenty-four per cent of the population are native-born of foreign parents (one or both), leaving but fourteen per cent to the actual immigration against sixty-two of the good old colonial stock. Of 1,500,000 men raised by the North during the civil war, over eighty per cent were native-born Americans; and in the Southern army the percentage was still higher. A surgeon who examined thousands of recruits, each man stripped to the buff, told me, that, in all conditions of manly vigor for service as soldiers, the native-born were superior to the foreign-born; and that this held true not only of men from the country, but of men born and reared under the vitiating influence of city life. Life-insurance tables show that the average duration of life in the United States is larger than in England. The native stock of American society has not lost its vigor: on the contrary, it has grappled with this before-unheard-of mass of immigration, and has so far mastered it. It remains only to leave immigration to its normal conditions, without those artificial stimulants

[1] Atlantic Monthly, April, 1872.

that have heretofore been applied in the belief that we had an unbounded extent of land and great scarcity of labor. The "hard times" of the past few years have demonstrated that the country was overstocked with labor, and farmed in excess of market facilities, and that we were drawing upon ourselves prematurely the mischiefs of older countries.

To avert these dangers, the government should altogether refrain from that artificial stimulus to wages, under the fiction of "protection to American industry," which allures foreign labor to come over and compete with American workmen, and underbid them at their side; and should also refrain from any mediation between foreign governments and their subjects with a view to making emigration easy and tempting to the latter. If Ireland was sometime oppressed and impoverished, if ever Germans felt their home-burdens grievous to be borne, it was kind and noble in America to offer freedom and a home to immigrants and refugees. But now that Ireland is freed from her state-church and many of her land-burdens, and is constantly improving, America has no call of philanthropy toward her; and as for Germans, if they imagine they have grievances, they have precisely the same remedy with ourselves, — a constitutional government, and a parliament elected by universal suffrage. Why, then, should we seek to attract them from their fatherland? Why make treaties to ease them of their military obligations in case of emigration? Let them look to their own parliament for such redress as shall seem wise and good for the nation as a whole. Those who run away from their just obligations in one country are not likely to make good citizens in another. If the government of the United States will repeal all treaties of favoritism, and let alone all meddling in the domestic relations of foreign countries, immigration will adjust itself to the law of supply and demand, and prove a blessing to both parties.

"Not long since, I was compelled to take a night's lodging at a private house. For a bed, supper, and grog for myself, my three companions, and three servants, I was charged, on going off without a breakfast next day, the sum of eight hundred and fifty dollars. The lady of the house politely added, that she had charged nothing for the rooms, and would leave the compensation for them to my discretion, although three or four hundred dollars would not be too much for the inconvenience to which she had been put by myself and my followers." This is not the complaint of an American at Vienna during the International Exposition, nor of an Englishman afflicted with Confederate or Turkish bonds. It was the experience of Gen. Baron von Kalb on his way through Virginia, to re-enforce the Southern army, in the spring of 1780. In Philadelphia he paid four hundred dollars for a hat, the same for a pair of boots; and for a good horse "was asked a price equivalent to ten years of his pay."[1] A Tory wit of the time of the Revolution announced that there would be a new issue of paper dollars by Congress as soon as the rags of Washington's army could be spared for that purpose.[2] Another Tory advertised for Continental money at the rate of a guinea per thousand, to be used for papering rooms. Yet this money was an enforced legal tender; and I have read upon the face of a sixpenny note the awful warning, "To counterfeit is death." Jefferson computed that the two hundred millions of dollars emitted by Congress from 1775 to 1779 inclusive were worth, to those who received them, but about thirty-six millions of silver dollars.[3] But the nation survived this degradation of its credit, this bankruptcy of its treasury, and a few years later, under the genius of Alexander Hamilton, produced a financial system that at once gave stability at home, and confidence abroad. In the strong but just words of Webster, "Hamilton touched the dead corpse of the public credit, and it sprang upon its feet."[4]

Again: during the war of 1812 all the banks south of New England suspended specie payments; and their paper "fell so low, that a bill on Boston could not be purchased at Washington under an advance of from twenty to twenty-five per cent." Yet the nation emerged with safety and honor from the financial complications of that day. The war of Gen. Jackson upon the Bank of the United States, and his famous Specie Circular, brought on another finan-

---

[1] G. W. Greene, in Atlantic Monthly, October, 1875.
[2] Moore's Diary of the Revolution, ii. 10.
[3] Works, vol. ix. 259, 260.   [4] Works, vol. i. 200.

cial flurry; yet in 1836 the United States presented the unwonted spectacle of a government having a surplus revenue without levying one direct tax upon the people. The country has passed through commercial revulsions, in which a class of merchants, bankers, and institutions, have proved dishonest; now and then a State has taken upon itself the dishonesty and disgrace of repudiation: but such acts do not represent the tone of commercial or national honor. With a debt of enormous proportions, the United States are in no danger of following the precedent of Turkey; with a depreciated currency and a disordered commerce, they are not going to dishonor their bonds. If Congress will but take the warning of Walsingham in 1780, that "money is on a footing with commerce and religion, they all three refuse to be the subjects of law," the nation will come out of its present depression more sober, more stable, more solid, than ever; and no financial storm shall ever shake its centre, or jeopard its life.

War, always a severe strain upon any nation, brings special risks to a republic. Besides the tax upon industry, finances, loyalty, and life, a state of war in a republic may facilitate encroachments upon popular liberty, and open the way to military usurpation or the rivalries of military factions. One needs but to recall the later history of the Roman Republic, and the Italian Republics of the middle ages, to realize how imminent and fatal such dangers may be. But the people of the United States have three times met these perils, and surmounted them. Not to speak of the wars with Tripoli and Algiers, which gave a mortal blow to piracy in the Mediterranean; the Indian war, in which Gen. Harrison broke Tecumseh's league; the Florida war, that prepared the cession of the territory by Spain; and the later war with the Seminoles, that led to their extermination, — the century has tested the American people by two foreign wars of significance and a civil war of colossal proportions. The war with England in 1812 was entered into with little enthusiasm, and much open opposition; and it dragged along, with no decisive results and some humiliating disasters, till both parties were ready for peace in 1815. But it proved the United States able to cope in arms with the power from which they had won their independence, and especially capable of defying the mistress of the sea. The war was begun to resist the right of search and the impressment of seamen from American vessels: it made the names of Bainbridge, Biddle, Decatur, Hull, Jones, Lawrence, Perry, Porter, Stewart, illustrious in naval warfare; and when Perry quit his sinking flag-ship in an open boat, under fire of the enemy, and, mounting his second ship, captured the entire squadron of Lake Erie, the hitherto unchallenged refrain, "Rule, Britannia, rule the waves," was broken by his laconic report, "We have met the enemy, and they are ours." The closing battles of Lundy's Lane and New Orleans left America mistress of herself, at least from the St. Lawrence to the Gulf of Mexico.

The war with Mexico in 1846, though costing relatively little in treasure and blood, was a severe strain upon the *morale* of the nation. It was not only against the judgment, but against the conscience, of a large body of the people, who looked upon it as an unwarrantable invasion of a neighbor country in order to extend the area of slavery. Though it gave occasion for brilliant feats of arms under Gens. Scott, Taylor, and Wool, and secured to the United States possession of Texas, New Mexico, and California, this acquisition proved a Pandora's box of plagues and woes.

We have seen in the Third Lecture how sedulously the term "slavery" and any formal sanction of the system were kept out of the Constitution, and how general, at that time, was the expectation that slavery would come to an end, as incongruous with the new order of things, and wasteful in the view of political economy. As the sentiment and practice of Christendom then were, slavery having been at first forced upon the Colonies, its existence at the formation of the Union was a thing for which "nobody was to blame;" and it was left, without recrimination, to those who were implicated in it to ease themselves of it in their own way. But, as time went on, the invention of the cotton-gin, by giving new facility to slave-hands, increased the value of slave-labor; and the fact that slaves, though not citizens, were reckoned as three-fifths in the basis of representation, proved to the South a valuable element of political power. Nevertheless, the North and West, inviting immigration, and favoring enterprise and expansion, began to give a political preponderance to free labor: and, inasmuch as the Ordinance of 1787 and the Missouri Compromise had set a barrier to the extension of slavery northward, the system demanded new territory for its own productiveness, and new States for retaining its balance in the Senate; and so the old-fashioned toleration to slavery, doomed to a natural death, gave place to the propagation of slavery by use of the Constitution as its vital force, and to a counter-movement for its abolition as a political danger and a moral evil. If, in the period from 1820 to 1850, the South had resolutely planned the gradual but certain extinction of slavery, I am persuaded that the North would have freely shared with her the financial loss, and left her to transform her domestic institutions in her own way. But when the policy of maintaining and propagating the system was pushed not only over the territory of the continent, but within the territory of the Constitution, the North took alarm; and when, finally, the restrictive compromises of former days were repealed, and the Fugitive-slave Law made the United-States Government active, and the people of the United States personally responsible, in the support and extension of slavery, then that old troublesome, stubborn, sometimes wilful Puritan thing called *conscience* was roused; and this soon entered into and controlled political action. Under the old state of things, the existence of slavery as a purely local institution of the Southern States touched no man's conscience at the North, since the resident of a non-slaveholding State had no more responsibility for it there than in Cuba. He might regret it; but he could not reach it to remove it. But when the repeal of the Missouri Compromise (1854) threw open to slavery territory once consecrated to freedom, and the decision of the Supreme Court in the Dred Scott case held slaves to be property in every part of the national territory, the conscientious men of the North felt, that, through their representatives at the seat of government, they were made personally responsible for a system which they disapproved politically, and condemned morally. Therefore they organized a party against the extension of slavery, and the support of it by the National Government. This organization was not directed against the South as a section, nor against the laws and institutions of the Southern States, but against certain political demagogues of the North, — the worst friends the South ever had, — who courted the support of the South by volunteering to be propagandists of slavery. These were the mischief-makers who arrayed party against party, and section against section. New compromises were essayed; but blood was up. The armed resistance to the slave occupation of Kansas, and the raid of John Brown into Virginia, had opened the gates of war; and the election of Mr. Lincoln, in face of the threat of secession, determined the Southern leaders to put that threat in execution. Mr. Lincoln declared in his inaugural address, " I have no purpose, directly or indirectly, to interfere with the institution of slavery in the States where it exists. I believe I have no lawful right to do so; and I have no inclination to do so." None can doubt the honesty of that statement: for though Mr. Lincoln was opposed to slavery upon moral grounds, and had opposed its extension into free territory upon grounds both political and moral, he was sworn to uphold the Constitution; and he knew that the Constitution gave him no power or pretext of interfering with slavery in the States. Later on, the state of war gave him that power as a measure for suppressing rebellion. But the die was cast. The fact of his inauguration showed that the political rule of slavery was over; and, on the part of the South, secession was a foregone conclusion. As the conscience of the free States was roused by the acts of 1850-54, so now the loyal enthusiasm of the people was roused by the firing on the flag of the nation at Fort Sumter. Then came four years of weary, bloody war, — on the one side for the disruption of the Union, on the other for the maintenance of the Union in its entirety and supremacy. As the executive head of the nation, Mr. Lincoln said, " In the contemplation of universal law and of the Constitution, the union of these States is perpetual. It is safe to say that no government proper ever had a provision in its organic law for its own termination."[1] " The

[1] Inaugural, 1861.

THE NATION TESTED. 191

States have their *status* in the Union, and they have no other legal *status*."[1] " Our popular government has often been called an experiment. Two points in it our people have settled, — the successful establishing and the successful administering of it. One still remains, — its successful maintenance against a formidable attempt to overthrow it."[2] And in that brief address at the dedication of the cemetery at Gettysburg, with a simple pathos that places this among the masterpieces of eloquence, Mr. Lincoln said, " Fourscore and seven years ago, our fathers brought forth upon this continent a new nation, conceived in liberty, and dedicated to the proposition that all men are created equal. Now we are engaged in a great civil war, testing whether that nation, or any nation so conceived and so dedicated, can long endure. We are met on a great battle-field of that war. We are met to dedicate a portion of it as the final resting-place of those who here gave their lives that that nation might live. It is altogether fitting and proper that we should do this.

" But, in a larger sense, we cannot dedicate, we cannot consecrate, we cannot hallow, this ground. The brave men, living and dead, who struggled here, have consecrated it far above our power to add or detract. The world will little note, nor long remember, what we say here; but it can never forget what they did here. It is for us, the living, rather to be dedicated here to the unfinished work that they have thus far so nobly carried on; it is rather for us to be here dedicated to the great task remaining before us, — that from these honored dead we take increased devotion to the cause for which they here gave the last full measure of devotion; that we here highly resolve that the dead shall not have died in vain; that the nation shall, under God, have a new birth of freedom; and that the government of the people, by the people, and for the people, shall not perish from the earth."[3] That prophetic hope was realized when slavery and secession were extinguished together.[4]

But the vindication of the Union against separatism was not the only triumph of the war. The prolonged and

[1] First message, July 4, 1861. [2] Ibid. [3] Nov. 19, 1863.
[4] See note at close of Lecture.

terrible strain to which the nation was subjected in spirit, men, and resources, showed the energy, the endurance, the voluntary sacrifice, the patriotic devotion, of a people self-developed under the institutions of liberty. The rapid equipment of a nation surprised by an attempt upon its organic life demonstrated that a free people can adapt themselves to any emergency, and learn from disaster new lessons of courage, patience, and success. The generalship brought out in Lee and Jackson on the one side, and in Grant, Sherman, Thomas, and others, on the other, and the bravery of the men on both sides, showed that the noblest qualities of heroism and chivalry can be brought out by occasion, where the government is not military, and the people are not compelled to learn the art of war. And the sublime moral spectacle of the disbanding of vast armies, and their quiet return with their leaders to the occupations of peace, has taught the world how a great free nation can accept war as a stern necessity, without courting it as an excitement, or toying with it as a game. And, above all, the war that fought out a political quarrel to the end fought the contestants into that mutual prowess and respect that shall cement a manly and enduring friendship. The nation having passed this fiery ordeal, there was but one more test to which it could be put, — an assault upon its head, with a view to paralyze the government, and throw the country into anarchy. The assassination of Cæsar paved the way for the empire. The assassination of the Prince of Orange was followed by the disastrous dissensions between Maurice and Barneveld. The assassination of Mr. Lincoln was absolutely without effect upon the normal functions of the government. It rekindled for a while the smouldering animosities of the war, and gave greater stringency to the terms of settlement; it elevated to the presidency a man whom the people had not soberly thought of for that contingency, and whose violent eccentricities provoked a somewhat demagogic movement for his impeachment. He was a man of strong, untrained powers, and stronger untamed will, and, in an arbitrary government, might have made an uncomfortable despot. But at heart Andrew Johnson had an honest, even fiery, devotion to the Union; and his gross infirmities of habit, of ignorance, of vanity, and of temper, may be gently buried with his dying request, "Wrap me in the flag of my country."

Of Abraham Lincoln it could be said, as of William of Orange, "He went through life bearing the load of a people's sorrows upon his shoulders with a smiling face. . . . As long as he lived, he was the guiding star of a whole brave nation; and, when he died, the little children cried in the streets." But, though the nation felt the shudder of his death in all its veins, it gathered from his death the whole vigor and virtue of his patient, heroic life. After the lapse of ten years, I can find no fitter words to describe its effect than those with which I sought to re-assure my countrymen on the very day of his assassination: " A chief lesson impressed upon us to-day is the imperishable vitality of government, and the grandeur of our Constitution under all emergencies. We have seen it tested in conflict with foreign powers; we have seen it tested by the fearful strain of civil war, and by the scarce less anxious trial of a presidential election in the midst of war; and it has stood. And now, under this severest shock, — a shock that might shatter a kingdom or an empire into chaos, — it still stands. That mysterious, invisible, impalpable entity we call the State, that intangible something that we call Government, stands forth to-day in awful reality. The sovereignty of the people lifts its next representative into the just vacant chair. The State moves on without pause at the nation's grief, without concussion from the blow that struck down the nation's head. The bullet of the assassin did not touch its vitality. The life of the Constitution was not endangered. The State moves calmly, steadily onward, with no jar in any of its functions. It seems to me that the statue of Liberty which crowns the dome of the Capitol, — that worthy and typical memorial of Abraham Lincoln's administration, — looking calmly down upon the august presence of death, beckoned to the State beyond, saying, 'Let the dead bury their dead: follow thou me.' And the State moved on, and will move on, in the line of freedom and justice, unshaken forever."[1]

[1] Speech at the Union League Club, New York, April 15, 1865.

NOTE ON FOREIGN PREDICTIONS CONCERNING THE UNITED STATES.

There is a curious tendency in foreign critics of American society to resolve every social and political problem within the republic into the question of the continuance of the republic itself. This is done even by critics who bear no ill-will toward America, and are not averse to popular government. A striking example of such political pessimism occurs in the address of Prof. Huxley at the opening of the Johns Hopkins University in Baltimore. Huxley had spoken generously enough of America as a whole, and his own reception in particular; but he closed his address with these words: —

"I cannot say that I am in the slightest degree impressed by your bigness, or your material resources as such. Size is not grandeur, and territory does not make a nation. The great issue about which hangs a true sublimity and the terror of overhanging fate is, What are you going to do with all these things? What is to be the end to which these are to be the means? You are making a novel experiment in politics on the greatest scale which the world has yet seen. Forty millions at your first centenary, it is reasonably to be expected, that, at the second, these States will be occupied by two hundred millions of English-speaking people spread over an area as large as that of Europe, and with climates and interests as diverse as those of Spain and Scandinavia, England and Russia. You and your descendants have to ascertain whether this great mass will hold together under the forms of a republic and the despotic reality of universal suffrage; whether State-rights will hold out against centralization without separation; whether centralization will get the better without actual or disguised monarchy; whether shifting corruption is better than a permanent bureaucracy; and as population thickens in your great cities, and the pressure of want is felt, the gaunt spectre of pauperism will stalk among you, and communism and socialism will claim to be heard.

"Truly, America has a great future before her, — great in toil, in care, and in responsibility; great in true glory, if she be guided in wisdom and righteousness; great in shame, if she fail. I cannot understand why other nations should envy you, or fail to see that it is for the highest interests of mankind that you should succeed; but the one condition of success, your sole safeguard, is the moral worth and intellectual clearness of the individual citizen. Education cannot give these; but it can cherish them, and bring them to the front, in whatever station of society they are to be found; and the universities ought to be and may be the fortresses of the higher life of the nation."

All this is meant for friendly counsel, and it should be received in the same spirit; though the ill-concealed tone of patronage reminds one of "a certain condescension in foreigners," with which the English critic is especially apt to divert us. But no well-informed American can read without a smile the assumption of Prof. Huxley, that every problem that he fancies to arise in the future of American society must involve the existence of the republic; that our "novel experiment" is oscillating between "separation" and "monarchy," and that all our energies must be strained to the one purpose of making the mass "hold together." A scientific study of American institutions might have acquainted him with the protoplasm of our national life, — that local self-government whose vital force is not impaired by extent of territory, or mass of population. This is the "yeast" that leavens the whole lump, and whose fermentation renders the mass porous without destroying its cohesion.

Or, had Prof. Huxley studied scientifically the Machinery Hall at the Philadelphia Exposition, it might have occurred to him that the great Corliss Engine was the analogue of the National Constitution; each separate machine being connected with this by its own band, sharing the central impulse and control, yet doing its own work in its own way; and the vast aggregate of machines, wheels within wheels, performing their diversified functions with a sublime harmony of movement, and conservation of energy, without either concentration, collision, or divergence.

There are certain scolds in England, from Matthew Arnold down to Mrs. Partington, who fancy that the British Constitution is threatened by every new agitation in the politics or the economics of society. An estimable lady said to me in England the other day, "Do you see any hope for England? I fear it is all over with us. We have provoked the Lord by our doings in China and India, and by our worldliness and luxury at home; and now it would seem that the plagues of Darwinism and Ritualism are let loose upon us to devour us. Don't you think we are living under the *Sixth Vial?*"

I was so irreverent as to doubt whether the writer of the Apocalypse looked much beyond the plagues and vials of his own time, and had so much as a speck of England in his prophetic eye; and I felt confident, that, however Darwin and Huxley might disturb the foundations of the universe, they would never lay sacrilegious hands upon the British Constitution; while, as to Ritualism, I was sure the average Englishman had too much common sense in his head to be lured to destruction by the gyrations of some weaker Englishman's heels. No doubt England has to do with problems of very grave import. No doubt exigencies will continue to arise that shall task all the wisdom of her statesmen, and all the patriotism and endurance of her people. The question of dis-establishing the National Church; the labor question, — agricultural, mining, manufacturing; the education question, hitherto but glozed over; the Irish question, that will not down; the Indian question, with the glowing heat of native intelligence, and the Russian glacier crowding on; the woman question, that in England means something more than the airy nothings and puffings of American platforms; the coal question, now that the exhaustion of English mines is matter of mathematical calculation; the industrial question, now that American manufactures begin to compete with English in foreign markets; the navy question, now that other nations are creating fleets to dispute the dominion of the sea; the army question, now that the Continent is transformed into a camp of nations in arms, — these, and many others, are grave and perilous questions for England to grapple with: but he would be a neophyte in political philosophy who should confound such questions with the existence of the British Constitution. The monarchy might not be able to survive another *George* upon the throne; but, aside from this, the advent of a democracy in England is hardly more likely than the return of a Stuart or a Tudor.

Often as I am called upon to speak in England upon public questions, I have never deemed it courteous nor wise for me as a foreigner to meddle in domestic controversies, nor to hint at these as affecting the life or death of the nation, destined to make her " great in glory," or " great in shame." We, too, have our problems, grave, earnest, imminent. But these are questions of party, of policy, of reform, of adaptation, not at all questions of the form of government, of the life of the State. These last do not enter into the thought of the American citizen, do not come within the horizon of political action. They are settled in the very organism of society; and this is part of the life of the individual. Our race-stock is as old and as vital as the English, from which it sprang; our political force and sagacity have not lost by transplanting; our area for the ventilation of necessary social problems is wider, freer, and therefore safer, than that of England. Every question affecting *government* has been tried and determined. The problems hinted at by Prof. Huxley are simply problems of administration and adjustment, and do not come within a thousand leagues of the form and essence of government. Let English critics once master this distinction, and their counsels will be respected where now their croakings are laughed at. Mr. Mill perceived this when he indorsed the opinion of M. de Tocqueville, that "if a community is so situated or so ordered that it can support the transitory action of bad laws, and can await without destruction the result of the *general tendency* of the laws, that country will prosper more under a democratic government than under any other."

NOTE ON PRESIDENTIAL ELECTIONS AND CIVIL WAR.

THE closeness of the presidential vote in 1876, and the charges of fraud, and threats of violence, that the uncertainty of the count gave rise to, called forth in Europe fresh prophecies of civil war and the failure of republican government. The silly suggestion of somebody in New Orleans, that the United States should be transformed into an empire under Gen. Grant, was paraded in German newspapers with an air of triumph, and in delicious obliviousness of the fact, that though an American editor could make such a suggestion, and simply be laughed at, should a German editor propose the abolition of the empire for a republic, and the disbanding of the standing army, he might be treated to a change of air and diet in the nearest jail or fortress. Some English critics have assumed that civil war was imminent, because, as they conceive, the Rebellion broke out with as little warning, through dissatisfaction with the election of a president. It is not surprising that foreigners should have imagined the crisis to be so serious, since so few even of the best-informed European writers have fairly mastered the Constitution and Government of the United States or the characteristics of the American people, and since so much of European experience has pointed to revolution or war as the normal solution of political difficulties. But people should not pronounce upon what they do not understand, nor prophesy without valid tokens of inspiration.[1] Grave and perplexing as was this phase of a presidential contest, the thoughtful American could see in it nothing perilous, nor even threatening. Riots there might be, and heated dispute ; but there was no analogy in the case to the Rebellion of 1861. First, there was not now, as in the Rebellion, any great social, financial, and sectional interest binding one portion or party against the other, and forming at once the motive and the nucleus for resistance and revolt. Though the election of Mr. Lincoln was made a pretext for the Rebellion, the preservation of the system of slavery was its real and only motive. The speech of Mr. Stephens, then Vice-President of the Confederacy, at Savannah, in March 1861, put that point squarely and conclusively. After characterizing Jefferson's doctrine of the rights of nature and the equality of races as an error, and the government founded upon such ideas as resting on the sand, Mr. Stephens said, " Our new government is based upon quite the contrary ideas. Its foundations are laid, its corner-stone rests, upon the great truth, that the negro is not equal to the white man ; that slavery, subordination to the superior race, is his natural and normal condition. Our government is the first in the history of the world that rests upon this great physical, philosophical, and moral truth. . . . The stone which the builders rejected has become the corner-stone of our new edifice."

When we consider in how many States contiguous to one another slavery was the one vital interest of society, the basis of labor, the source of wealth, the drudge of the household and the plantation ; how it had existed from the foundation of the Colonies, and had grown with the Commonwealth, until every life, fortune, and estate was bound up with it, — we see in this interest, concentrated within a circumscribed territory, a motive to violent defence to which there is nothing analogous in the political differences of parties scattered over the whole country, changing their relations and proportions year by year, and, except in the matter of voting, accustomed to act together as neighbors and friends. There is not enough to kindle civil war in the breezes of a popular contest that may change about at the next election. Next : the election of 1876 involved no question of separation, or of change in the form of government. Both parties were alike interested in maintaining the Union and the Constitution : the only dispute was, which party, by legal methods, should gain control of the administration for a term of years. Again : there was no organization on either side for deciding the issue by force. So far as there was any show of force, this was on the part of the actual government, by way of police, as a precaution for maintaining pub-

[1] In a literary circle where false quantity in a Latin quotation was the subject of criticism, Macaulay said, "No one is under obligation to quote: hence, when one does quote, he is bound to quote correctly." No foreigner is under obligation to utter oracles concerning the United States: hence, when a foreigner volunteers to pronounce or prophesy, he is bound to understand what he is talking about, under penalty of being laughed at for a pretentious ignorance. Even the Latter-day Prophecies fall under this rule.

lic order. Even this was deprecated by the political leaders upon both sides, who desired that the election should be decided fairly, without violence or fraud. In point of fact, the political crisis of 1876 brought out in fine relief the merits of the Constitution of the United States and the better qualities of the American people. It showed how marvellously the Constitution has provided for every emergency; that even should the popular election be thwarted by fraud, or declared void through irregularity, no function of the government would be suspended even for a moment. There being neither President nor Vice-President, the President of the Senate — itself a permanent body — would at once become the executive head of the nation; and the Supreme Court is at hand to settle any issues of fact. The crisis exhibited the law-abiding character of the American people. There were days of excitement; there was, of course, more or less loose and wild talk: but public opinion and the press were united in demanding that all legal forms should be observed, and the legal result accepted and obeyed. The practical good sense of the people was also brought out by this peculiar conjuncture of affairs. It was felt that there would be a way out of all complications, as there had been in like complications before. At the opening of the twenty-sixth Congress, in December, 1839, two delegations appeared, contesting the seats of New Jersey. "Now, on first assembling, the House has no officers; and the clerk of the preceding Congress acts, by usage, as chairman of the body till a speaker is chosen. On this occasion, after reaching the State of New Jersey, the acting clerk declined to proceed in calling the roll, and refused to entertain any of the motions which were made for the purpose of extricating the House from its embarrassment." This went on for four days. Then John Quincy Adams rose, and "submitted a motion requiring the acting clerk to proceed in calling the roll. Mr. Adams was immediately interrupted by a burst of voices demanding, 'How shall the question be put? Who will put the question?' The voice of Mr. Adams was heard above the tumult, 'I intend to put the question myself.'"[1] That stroke of common sense solved the whole difficulty. And such confidence has the American in the average common sense of his fellow-citizens, that, during the whole presidential crisis of 1876, gold remained quietly and steadily at the lowest figure.

Notorious and scandalous cases of political corruption had led European critics to look upon American politics as hopelessly given over to venality. Now, here was a case in which only one vote was needed to secure the triumph of a great and powerful party; yet, in all the weeks of uncertainty, no one suggested nor imagined that this one vote could be bought. Peculation in secret, fraud by contrivance, there has been: but, in this case, whoever should betray his trust would certainly be known; and no elector could have the hardihood to face the scorn and obloquy which the whole American people would visit upon such venal treachery. He must flee the country, or, like Judas, go out and hang himself. Upon the whole, the Ameri-

---

[1] Eulogy on John Quincy Adams, by Edward Everett.

can Constitution and the American people have nothing to fear from the judgment of history upon the peculiar tests of 1876.

At the same time, this momentous contest has given emphasis to three measures of reform:—

(1.) The establishment of the civil service upon the permanent basis of character and competence, by providing, on the one hand, that a civil officer shall have no vote, and take no part, in elections, during his tenure of office; and, on the other, that all staff-officers of the government be placed beyond the reach of party favoritism in appointment or removal. What a large, persistent, and irritating element of excitement would be withdrawn from the presidential contest, if there were no hungry thousands struggling over offices either in possession or in expectation!

(2.) The creation of permanent boards of election, whose members shall have no vote, and shall not be eligible to any office, shall be well paid, and be liable to fine and imprisonment for any malfeasance. The ridiculous blunders of nominating electors who were ineligible, and of omitting specific legal conditions, and the suspicions of fraudulent counting, would be obviated, if the registration of voters and the counting of votes were the duty of permanent non-partisan officials — like the town-clerks of Scotland — who had the fear of the states-prison before them if guilty of corruption or fraud.

(3.) The withdrawal of the National Government from political contests in the South. In the treatment of the South, three capital blunders have been made, from the mischief of which the whole land is still suffering. The first blunder was that of treating with the rebels as States, instead of remanding them to a territorial condition, from which new commonwealths should have emerged one by one when thoroughly purified. The alternative of "*in* the Union, or *under* it" — in it as loyal and legalized States, or under it as territories forfeited to the National Government — was originally set forth in my address in New York, of July 4, 1861; and I have reason to believe that Mr. Lincoln regretted not having adopted this as the solution of the problems of slavery and of reconstruction. Of course, it is too late now to retrieve Mr. Seward's cardinal misconception of the situation. The next blunder was that of admitting to suffrage the emancipated blacks, with no conditions of time, character, or education. That mischief, also, seems beyond intervention.

But the worst blunder of all has been the attempt of the General Government to do in the *States* of the South what it might properly have done in *Territories* of the United States. The mischiefs of this policy of intervention are now so apparent, that the good sense of the country demands that it shall be abandoned. The cure of the South must be left to time, and to the workings of self-interest and political ambition under the normal laws of human nature. If, in some districts, whites and blacks will fight, there is no way but to let them fight till they tire of anarchy and bloodshed. But, in most districts, it will be found that politicians, left to themselves, will court the negro vote upon opposite sides; and the bugbear of a "solid South" will vanish before the election of 1880.

LECTURE V.

THE NATION JUDGED BY ITS SELF-DEVELOPMENT AND ITS BENEFITS TO MANKIND.

ON the 18th June, 1875, the Crown Prince of Prussia, by command of his Majesty the Emperor, announced his purpose to erect upon the heights near Hakenberg, in East Havelland, a monument to commemorate the victory of the Great Elector Frederic William at Fehrbellin on the same day of June, 1675. The order ran, "For our house, for our land and people, for the German fatherland, this great and memorable day of victory marks the beginning of the deliverance of German soil from foreign rule; of the revival of Germany's renown in arms, and her peaceful military preparation for defensive and offensive war; of the fulfilment of those rising duties in which the name Brandenburg found and approved its German call. To coming generations of our house, our Prussian people, and the German nation, this monument will serve through all time as a remembrancer of the hard beginnings, the long struggles, the sterling virtues, with which that was grounded and acquired, which it will be their duty and their honor before God and men to hold, to guard, and to strengthen."

These heroic recollections can well stir the pride of every Prussian, and move to admiration, also, every one who honors patriotism in rulers and people, and can respect noble achievement and substantial progress in nations other than his own.

Notwithstanding many re-actions, reverses, failures, — such as led Von Schön to write in 1808, "Fate seems to think necessary the still greater humiliation of Prussia,"[1] — the State that the Great Elector redeemed from Sweden, that Frederic I. raised to the rank of a kingdom, and Frederic the Great to a power on the Continent strong in peace and formidable in war, and which the present reign has advanced to be almost a synonyme of military supremacy, imperial dominion, scientific culture, and the Protestant faith, — this Prussia of two centuries has given the world the most perfect example of that form of political society in which man exists for the State, and the State cares for all his interests in return for the control of all his powers. Though she has been slow in attaining to constitutional freedom and popular representation in government, and in regaining or restoring the remnants of local government that had survived the Thirty-years' war, yet Prussia has produced a civil service remarkable for intelligence, accuracy, fidelity, and honor; an educational system unexampled in universality, and thoroughness as to the rudiments of knowledge, and in facilities for the higher attainments; a church system of as much fairness as could exist without the separation of Church and State; a judiciary, which, at least since Frederic the Great took in hand the miller Arnold's lawsuit, has been noted for exact and impartial justice; an economical system, which, if it bears hard upon some, bears equally upon all, and affords small chance to rogues; and a military system, which, if war must be, and peace a chronic preparation for war, is the most complete and efficient organization for the defence of the nation. Now, all this has been accomplished by one small State, upon an indifferent soil, which dates its self-consciousness as a political power from the victory of Fehrbellin in 1675. A people, then, is to be estimated, not by the years of its political life, but by what it has done in those years for the improvement of society and the behoof of mankind. Russia has seen her thousand years, and in that millennium has been slowly shaping out of chaos and barbarism a civilized State that yet may civilize the barbarian hordes and decaying empires of Middle and Eastern Asia. But, in all these ages, what contribution has Russia made to the true forces of modern civilization, or the science of political

[1] Papers and letters of Theodore von Schön, Berlin, Franz Duncker.

society? Shall I speak of Spain in the splendor of her Moorish civilization, in the glory of her Christian art, commerce, colonization? How little of lasting good has she given to mankind! France has survived her more than thousand years, and was for long the foremost race of Christendom. The whole world is her debtor in literature, science, and art. Her revolution gave to Europe the secularization of political society, the prerogative and potency of peoples, and the example of a peasant proprietorship in the soil. But, unhappily, the political fermentations of France are too much like her champagne, — made for foreign export, and not for use at home; and she has hitherto failed to give the world an assuring example of the combination of liberty with order, of private right with public duty, of individual independence with united sovereignty. Now, it is the proud pre-eminence of the United States that they have given the world that example; and if a nation is to be estimated, not by its years, but by its services to mankind, and if the service is to be estimated by its value to the higher sphere of political science and the nobler sphere of human welfare, may not America, while owning her obligations to the past, feel that she has rendered a just equivalent in the theory and example of a government administered by the will of the people, without hereditary or military power, by the national and spiritual influence of a constitution without physical force, by reverence for law without appeal to terror? In combining freedom with authority, in making religion absolutely free, in relying upon reason and conscience — "the sober second thought" of the people — for support, in balancing all the powers of government, and making the State but a function and an instrument of man, the United States have made a contribution to the ethics of political society that cannot be measured by length of years. The formulating of these principles dates from July 4, 1776; but the principles themselves, in the stuff and training of the American people, are older than Fehrbellin. "By their fruits ye shall know them."

First and most patent of the fruits of American life is the transformation of a vast, unexplored wilderness into the abode of civilized man. How extensive this conquest of Nature has been, I have shown in the Fourth Lecture; but let me here summarize, that, on the Atlantic, the United States coast stretches from 25° to 47° north latitude, about 1,500 miles; on the Gulf of Mexico, from 81° to 97° west longitude, about 1,100 miles; on the Pacific, from 33° to 49° north latitude, 1100 miles; to which is to be added Alaska, on the Arctic Ocean, and that its area in round numbers is 3,000 miles by 1,200, being a total of 3,603,886 square miles. "Its great divisions are (1) The eastern seaboard, and the Appalachian ranges which press so closely upon it: this is the commercial and manufacturing region. (2) The Great Central Valley, pre-eminently the agricultural region. (3) The pastoral, or the region of the plains. (4) The mining region, or the Cordilleras."[1] This vast and diversified territory American enterprise has wrested from the wildness of Nature, and made available to mankind, and the greater part of it within the present century. To the superficial observer, this, indeed, may indicate nothing more than a material civilization; and Carlyle, of all men, was once betrayed into this superficiality. Twenty years ago he wrote, "Brag not yet of our American cousins. Their quantity of cotton, dollars, industry, and resources, I believe to be almost unspeakable; but I can by no means worship the like of these. What great human soul, what great thought, what great noble thing that one could worship or loyally admire, has yet been produced there? None: the American cousins have yet done none of these things. What have they done? They have doubled their population every twenty years."[2] Had Carlyle then never read a page of that greater than

[1] Gen. F. A. Walker.
[2] Latter-Day Pamphlets: the Present Time. It is amusing, by the side of this, to read Macaulay's lament over the lack of "great human souls" and "great noble things" in England: "What a nerveless, milk-and-water set the young fellows of the present day are! —— declares that there is not in the whole House of Commons any stuff, under five and thirty, of which a junior lord of the treasury can be made. It is the same in literature, and, I imagine, at the bar. It is odd that the last twenty-five years, which have witnessed the greatest progress ever made in physical science, the greatest victories ever achieved by man over matter, should have produced hardly a volume that will be remembered in 1900, and should have seen the breed of great advocates and parliamentary orators become extinct among us." Macaulay made this entry in his diary March 9, 1850. Yet Dickens and Carlyle were then at the height of their fame. But we know that Macaulay had no great opinion of Dickens; and he seems not to have taken the trouble to read Carlyle.

"human soul," Jonathan Edwards? nor heard the story of the apostolic Eliot? Had the names of Otis, Hancock, Sam Adams, George Washington, quite faded from the canvas of great souls? Had that "noble thing," — of the delicate and cultured Dr. Kane giving his fortune and his life to the search for Sir John Franklin, in answer to the cry of the wife who refused to be a widow, — had this, and the many like examples of self-sacrifice for science and humanity, never met the eye of the worshipper of heroes? Was there no greatness in the thought of Mills to compass the globe with Christian missions, nor heroism in the men and women who set out to do it? Was there nothing that one could "loyally admire" in the little bands of cultivated men who assumed the hardships of frontier life, that they might make the whole land Christian, and who *did* it? Or was there not enough of fight in such heroism to satisfy the worshipper of power? Carlyle, indeed, predicted that America's battle was "yet to fight." "America, too, will have to strain its energies in quite other fashion than this; to crack its sinews, and all but break its heart, as the rest of us have had to do, in thousand-fold wrestle with the pythons and mud-demons, before it can become a habitation for the gods." But when that day of agony did come, and the nation strained the thews of war, but would not "break its heart" so long as it had a dollar or a life to give to the "great thought," the "noble thing" of holding a continent for law, order, government, constitutional freedom, then where was Mr. Carlyle? Because of his failure to discern the really potent forces in a civilization of which the axe, plough, and hammer were but passing signs, he failed to fulfil his own promise to "wish America strength for her battle," and victory through her agony. But, having got on without help or hinderance from these "latter-day" prophecies, America gently covers their nakedness as she brings to the prophet her octogenarian crown, regretting only that he has not suffered her to twine with it those two most bright and lasting laurels, — love of liberty, and faith in man.

Nowhere is there more need of Carlyle's own protest against shams than in dealing with that sham philosophy that would estimate the civilization of a people by its acres of industry and its millions of workers, and insist that this is simply material. Is there, then, nothing intellectual, nothing moral, nothing scientific, nothing heroic, in all this stir and push in our day, — this rivalry of English, Germans, Americans, for the exploration of Africa, and the introduction of civilization into the heart of that continent? Is the mastery of the wilds of Nature, and the taming of her wilder races, the opening the resources of a continent to the commerce of the world, the improving of rivers, the building of canals, railways, telegraphs, post-roads, — is all this to be rated as but material and mercenary? May there not be thought in it all, may there not even be heart in it all, for the highest good of man? What story of African exploration exhibits more of enduring heroism than was shown by Lewis and Clark, and by Frémont, as they forced their trackless way across the American continent to the Pacific? And where has science won worthier trophies than in the surveying expeditions of that vast interior?

It were most unjust to Germany, a most superficial estimate of her worth in history, to charge her with lack of enterprise or of humanitary zeal, because, shattered as she was by the Thirty-years' war, and surrounded by hostile fires, she concentrated her energies upon her internal development, — the construction of society, — with little thought of a world-mission. She did the work that was given her to do; and by the self-development in literature, science, and art, to which she was so much the more constrained by lack of opportunity for political and commercial expansion, she *has* fulfilled a mission to mankind, and fitted herself for one yet higher. To America was given the mission of redeeming a waste continent, — this to be accomplished first of all; but what she has done in subduing the elementary forces of Nature has been done at every step for the benefit of mankind. From first to last, hers was the march of a civilized people, of a Christian people, who planted as they went the institutions of constitutional freedom, and carried with them, or brought soon after in their train, the Bible, the school, the church, and the home. All that they conquered for themselves they offered with open heart and hand to the whole world. It was hardly mercenary to provide a home for the world's poor; it was hardly materialistic to offer secure and regulated liberty to the world's oppressed. One marvels that Carlyle had not discerned in this some token of that "new and brighter spiritual era that is slowly evolving itself for all men."[1]

Take the strongest possible example of the materialistic and mercenary in our civilization, and we shall see how fast the spiritual and moral have overtaken and are overmastering it. In 1848 the news that gold had been found in California spread like wildfire through the Eastern States, and kindled such a rage for emigration as even America had not before witnessed. Everywhere there was a movement toward the land of promise, — many by the slow toilsome journey in wagons, on horseback, and afoot, across the continent; more by the long and doubtful voyage in sailing-vessels around Cape Horn. Naturally the enterprising and hardy were the first to go; many of the shiftless also. Some went for naked love of gold, counting on sudden fortune; some from love of adventure, or restless love of change; many to better their condition, hoping, by a few years of toil, to lay the foundation of a lasting prosperity. A large percentage of the bad elements of society was in the first emigration to California. Many went who were no longer wanted at the East, or were too much wanted by the police; and many also went only to learn and show how bad they could become when freed from the restraints of settled communities. It was a dreadful medley at the first; and gambling, cheating, thieving, murder, drunkenness, lawlessness, and every vice, ran riot, so that a man held his purchase of life by the bowie-knife and the revolver. It was a sad world-spectacle of the nineteenth century; but it was a *world*-spectacle of human depravity, not a special exhibition of American life.

Already, in 1850, California showed a population of 22,000 foreigners, or nearly one-fourth in a total of 92,000; in 1860, 146,000 foreigners in a population of 378,000; and in 1870, a foreign population of 210,000 against 350,000 native born. To-day, in the city of San Francisco, one-half the population, i.e. 73,719, are of for-

[1] Signs of the Times.

eign birth, of whom 12,000 are Chinese, 14,000 Germans, and 33,000 English and Irish. California should be estimated in the light of these facts. In her origin she was an anomaly. Strugglers for fortune, adventurers, desperadoes from both hemispheres, thrown suddenly and promiscuously together, nearly three thousand miles distant from the seat of government, with the desert and the Sierras between, with no time as yet for an efficient civil organization, and no adequate military force at hand, — this was indeed a condition of things in which human nature could show its common depravity, but for which no people nor institutions could fairly be held responsible. But what happened? and what has come of it? From this anarchy and chaos we presently see society emerging, and demanding safety, order, law. Serious, earnest men, shrewd, practical men, staid, good men, will make California their home, and have it fit for homes for their wives and children. There is no home, no civilization, without woman; and, in the first rush for gold, she had been left behind. But, now that woman is looked for in California, the ruffian and the rowdy, the loafer and the blackleg, must get out of the way. Order comes to the front as a Vigilance Committee; justice is swift and terrible, but sure; a certain "herculean labor and divine fidelity," Mr. Carlyle, "draining the Stygian swamp, and making it a fruitful field." [1] And what came of this? A State that refused to admit slavery; a State that held loyally to the Union during the war, and gave enormous sums to the Sanitary Commission, though she might have set up an independent empire of the Pacific; a State that kept her currency and her faith under the wrenchings of war and of financial disaster; a State that pushed her railway eastward up the slopes of the mountains to link her destiny with the valley of the Mississippi and the Atlantic coast. And how came this to be? Along with the medley of that first emigration went a leaven of religious faith, — bands who went forth from the bosom of churches consecrated by prayer, and missionaries ready to "endure hardness as good soldiers of Christ." Some carried with them the framework of churches to be set up on

[1] The New Downing Street.

arriving; but at first both churches and schools were built upon the sand, so suddenly did population shift with fresh discoveries of gold. In April, 1848, a public school was opened in a tent at San Francisco. The next year, a State Constitution was formed; and, in this community of gold-hunters, provision was made by law for the proceeds of 500,000 acres of land as a perpetual school-fund. In 1850, California had 8 schools, 7 teachers, 219 pupils; in 1860, 598 schools, 816 teachers, 28,654 pupils; in 1870, 1,548 schools, 2,444 teachers, 85,507 pupils. Add to these private schools, and the number of pupils is 100,000, the yearly cost $2,500,000, the value of school-property over $4,000,000. Of incipient colleges and seminaries the State has even more than enough, and her young university may yet become the light of the Pacific coast. Her topographical survey, with the memoirs of Whitney, Clarence King, and others, is of high scientific value; and her "Lick" Observatory will rival the best of the Old World. Her literature has produced 150 volumes of native birth; and among these are the names of Bret Harte, Joaquin Miller, and Herbert H. Bancroft, whose great work on the "Native Races of the Pacific States" has accomplished for the prehistoric times of America what George Bancroft's has done for the era of Christian civilization. In 1850, California had 28 churches; in 1860, 293; and in 1870, 643 churches, with a property valued at $7,404,235, — some of them with buildings that would do credit to any city of the New World or the Old. One can by no means claim for California a social paradise corresponding with her climate: but she has elements of culture that are unsurpassed; homes of taste, literature, science, music, art; and the best musicians and lecturers of Europe find their reward in the appreciative circles of that far-off coast. Carlyle once warned us that we confounded the big with the great. We took the warning in good part, and gave heed to it; and now the philosopher who can look beneath the surface sees in this triumph of education and religion over Mammon seated on his mountains of gold one "great, noble thing" that he can "loyally admire."

There was a time when one of our own prophets[1] lifted

[1] Dr. Horace Bushnell.

up the warning, that, in the rapid roll of emigration westward, "barbarism was our first danger:" the loose and lawless elements of society drifted to the frontier; and even decent, honest men grew coarse and vulgar in the constant struggle with Nature for a bare subsistence. Besides, there is something demoralizing in a life divided between attacks of the shakes and the Sioux. That frontier-life, with its rough cabins, rough men, rough sports, rough drinks, rough fights, would have sunk to downright barbarism had it only been let alone long enough to act itself out; but it was not let alone. No garrisons were sent to check and tame it, as Russia holds her frontiers in Asia; but behind this frontier-life, pushing it forward, was a Christian civilization, to which these rough-handed men were but hewers of wood and drawers of water, preparing in the wilderness a way for its coming. Since the Pacific coast has checked the movement westward, and the extinction of slavery has suppressed the lust of conquest southward, the old land-fever has abated; pioneer-life is hemmed in between two cordons of settled communities; and though its traces linger here and there, and in some places it has left upon society an evil stain, it is steadily vanishing before the moral forces of civilization. The march of American emigration across the continent has no analogy with the old westward migration of Oriental tribes. It has ever been the advance of a civilized and Christian people to secure the continent to the highest form of society. Bryant has pictured it in his prairies:—

> "I hear
> The sound of that advancing multitude
> Which soon shall fill these deserts. From the ground
> Come up the laugh of children, the soft voice
> Of maidens, and the sweet and solemn hymn
> Of sabbath worshippers."

Every new State, as it has been organized, has made provision for the education of children at the public cost. We still have need of the obligatory school-system of Prussia,—in this feature the best in the world. But in the United States the people have voluntarily cared for education to such a degree, that over seven million children are enrolled in the public schools; and these schools have an income, from endowment, taxation, and public funds, of sixty-five million dollars. Some forty years ago, this people of "cotton-crops and Indian-corn and dollars" had a surplus of several millions in the national treasury. What did they do with it? They did not hoard it in vaults as a provision for war, nor bury it in mounds and fortifications. They did not speculate with it to win more, nor use it to purchase other lands. They put it into funds for schools, that the woodman, the fisherman, the miner, might learn to read "Sartor Resartus." This is no suggestion of fancy. Two of the prettiest episodes of American working-life are told by two of the most human of our poets. One is a scene that Lowell witnessed in a railroad-car, where a knot of working-men crowded together to listen to a comrade: —

> "He spoke of Burns: men rude and rough
>   Pressed round to hear the praise of one
> Whose heart was made of manly, simple stuff,
>   As homespun as their own.
>
> And, when he read, they forward leaned,
>   Drinking, with thirsty hearts and ears,
> His brook-like songs whom glory never weaned
>   From humble smiles and tears.
>
> Slowly there grew a tender awe,
>   Sun-like, o'er faces brown and hard,
> As if in him who read they felt and saw
>   Some presence of the bard.
>
> It was a sight for sin and wrong
>   And slavish tyranny to see, —
> A sight to make our faith more pure and strong
>   In high humanity.
>
> . . . .
>
> All that hath been majestical
>   In life or death, since time began,
> Is native in the simple heart of all, —
>   The angel heart of man.
>
> And thus among the untaught poor
>   Great deeds and feelings find a home,
> That cast in shadow all the golden lore
>   Of classic Greece and Rome."

The other is Bret Harte's picture of the story of Little Nell in the miner's camp, his own offering to the tomb of Dickens: —

> "And then, while round them shadows gathered faster,
>   And as the firelight fell,
> He read aloud the book wherein the master
>   Had writ of 'Little Nell.'
>
> Perhaps 'twas boyish fancy; for the reader
>   Was youngest of them all:
> But, as he read, from clustering pine and cedar
>   A silence seemed to fall.
>
> The fir-trees, gathering closer in the shadows,
>   Listened in every spray;
> While the whole camp with Nell on English meadows
>   Wandered and lost their way.
>
> . . . .
> Lost is that camp, and wasted all its fire,
>   And he who wrought that spell.
> Ah! towering pine and stately Kentish spire,
>   Ye have one tale to tell.
>
> Lost is that camp; but let its fragrant story
>   Blend with the breath that thrills
> With hop-vines' incense all the pensive glory
>   That fills the Kentish hills.
>
> And, on that grave where English oak and holly
>   And laurel wreaths intwine,
> Deem it not all a too presumptuous folly
>   This spray of Western pine."

That coarse, homespun civilization that Dickens held up to ridicule, true to the inborn gentlemanliness of its nature, made him the honored guest of the camp-fire, and paid to his genius the tribute of honest manly feeling, with more than critics' praise. Indeed, the United States *in re* Dickens is a faithful picture of American character and life. No doubt we made fools of ourselves in the first reception of Dickens; and he avenged himself of our gushing, boisterous, hand-shaking welcome, by caricaturing our foibles, ridiculing our manners, ignoring our finer tastes, and suppressing our virtues. But the folly was not all on one side. It is an offence against truth for a traveller, in describing a foreign people, to take a lot of incidents, each of which may be true in itself, and put these together so as to make a false story, and give that out as the whole story. It is an offence against delicacy to caricature certain peculiarities of manners in a people so as to disparage their true refinement in the arts and amenities of life. Suppose my sense of good-breeding is offended by the free use of pocket-combs and pocket-handkerchiefs, the loud clamor of voices, and the uncouth handling of knives and toothpicks, at a German *table d'hôte:* it would mark ill-breeding in me to deride the culture of a people because they do not meet my notions of table etiquette. Worst of all, it is an offence against honor to accept one's hospitality, and then publish derisive comments upon the host. All these offences Mr. Dickens was guilty of in his "American Notes" and in "Martin Chuzzlewit."[1] Since his partial revelation of himself in "David Copperfield," and the full unveiling of his life by Mr. Forster, we know better how to apologize for offences in 1842 that we so heartily condoned by the second reception in 1867. In early life, Dickens had no opportunity of mingling with gentlemen, or of observing and acquiring what belongs to the proprieties of social intercourse. And how seldom, indeed, in all his writings, does one find the true lady or the perfect gentleman! Suddenly his genius dazzled the world, and its reflection dazed his own brain. Lifted into genteel society before he was ripe for it, his head was turned with vanity; and in this mood, at thirty, he went to the United States, the guest of a nation already made wild over the "Pickwick Papers," "Oliver Twist," "Nicholas Nickleby," the "Boz Sketches," "Old Curiosity Shop," and "Barnaby Rudge." Dickens was even more widely read and more intensely popular in America than in England. His name was a household word. In my college set, every fellow was dubbed with some title out of

---

[1] Macaulay did not disguise his contempt for the American Notes. He wrote to Napier, declining to review the book in the Edinburgh. "I cannot praise it, though it contains a few lively dialogues and descriptions; for it seems to me to be, on the whole, a failure. It is written like the worst parts of Humphrey's Clock. What is meant to be easy and sprightly is vulgar and flippant, as in the first two pages. What is meant to be fine is a great deal too fine for me, as the description of the Fall of Niagara. . . . In short, I pronounce the book, in spite of some gleams of genius, at once frivolous and dull."

"Pickwick:" we even had our Mr. Winkle, who showed himself a "humbug" on the skating-pond. I received early copies of the "Papers" from England; and my room was crowded for readings and extemporized actings, that shook the college-halls with mirth. Not a student but would have run miles to see and cheer the author. Just such boyish enthusiasm seized upon the nation when it was known that Dickens was coming. Well, he came, expecting to be received like the Great Mogul; and we took him for a hale fellow, — a sort of cross between Mr. Pickwick and Sam Weller, — and showed very little respect for his privacy. We ran after him in the streets; we blocked the entrance to his hotel; we gave him balls, which, in the promiscuous jamming of all sorts of people and of toilets that one would not care to come so near to again, were like subscription-balls at the Opera House in Berlin; and, worst of all, we inflicted upon him a huge quantity of American after-dinner eloquence. All this was very naughty of us, and very silly; yet it was an honest enthusiasm for genius. But Mr. Dickens, alas! had come to America, not to enhance his praise, but to enrich his pocket. Well, we owed him much; and it was shabby of us not to have paid it. But we were not altogether guilty. There was no international copyright (which is a monstrous wrong to authors); and some American publishers had pirated Dickens's books, just as English publishers since have re-issued American books, by wholesale, without following the improved method of respectable American houses in giving a handsome *honorarium* in lieu of legal copyright.[1] Had Mr. Dickens trusted to our sense of honor, we should have sent him home with such a national testimonial as never author had received; or, better still, our leading men would have used his popularity for urging

[1] Three books of mine were reprinted in England by different publishers, neither of whom had the grace to send me even a presentation-copy. Once, in London, I went to a house that had reprinted one of my books; and, after buying half a dozen copies of this pirated edition, I introduced myself as the author to the publisher, who was standing by. With some confusion, he offered to present me with the copies I had just paid for; but I declined that sort of recognition of an author's rights, and never received any other. Still the English law of copyright is more just and liberal than the American; and some English publishers follow the example of the more honorable American publishers, in paying a royalty to a foreign author who has not secured a copyright.

a law of international copyright. But Dickens abused the hospitality of his public and private entertainers by lecturing us on our shortcomings in this matter; by babbling of his claims, even to the extent of using his welcome at Washington in urging that Congress should pass a copyright law for the protection of foreign authors. On returning to London, Mr. Dickens denied that he "had gone to America as a kind of missionary in the cause of international copyright."[1] Of course he did not go as a missionary for others, or for a cause. His philanthropy, public spirit, or sense of justice, did not take on the "missionary" type: but he did look out for number one; he did talk copyright everywhere, and make everybody understand that he wanted to be paid for his books, — as most assuredly he ought to have been. Now, though the American people have a weakness for money and the possessors of money, they thoroughly despise a man who avows that he is after money in all that he says and does. Their regard for Mammon may be coarse and vulgar, but is not apt to be mean and mercenary: so, when we found what Mr. Dickens was after, we were vexed and disgusted, and we dropped him. He went home mortified and mad, and abused us. Some things he said of us were true as well as funny, and we laughed at ourselves; some were sharp, but merited, and in Chinese fashion we thanked the corrector, while we felt the rod: but a great part of his caricature was so ludicrously libellous, that the author stood impaled in his own pillory, and there we pelted him. It had not occurred to Mr. Dickens how he depreciated himself as an author in sneering at a people who showed their literary taste by buying his books by the million; but, when he saw himself served up in his own characters, he rather wished he had let them alone. Moreover, American publishers had made him voluntary proposals of a percentage on sales; but, alas! both sales and fame had collapsed together. Mr. Forster fills his twenty-seventh chapter with "Chuzzlewit Disappointments," which he tries to explain away; but he says of the Americans, "Though an angry, they are a good-humored and a very placable people." It was not long before we began to feel, that, in

[1] Forster's Life, chap. xxvi.

pouting at Dickens, we were punishing ourselves. We wanted to laugh with him once more, and so began to laugh even at his exaggerated pictures of American society. A quarter of a century passed by: Mr. Dickens had grown more to the manners of a gentleman, and had ripened and mellowed under his experiences of life. The American people, too, had improved in manners and culture, not, however, because of Mr. Dickens's castigations, but through the upward working of those moral and spiritual forces that underlie our civilization, and which Mr. Dickens had neither the training to discover, nor the aptitude to appreciate. Ruskin has put forth an ideal society in his "Company of St. George," in which the best culture in manners, art, and nobleness, shall not only be associated with, but grow out of, the tilling of the soil and other homely manual labor; and he has even sought to induce his art-students at Oxford to take their physical exercise in trundling the barrow, and handling the spade. If, now, one should come upon a squad of such art-laborers in their working-dress, and rate their culture by the compost they were using as a fertilizer, he would be as wise as Dickens was, when, in 1842, he estimated the capacity of Americans for culture by seeing them yet in the sweat and toil of their material fight with, yes, and their most "material" conquest over, Nature. Well, in 1867 the two parties met again. Mr. Dickens had come to repair his fortunes by public readings. The American people went to greet him as a benefactor, and to enjoy the intellectual treat of hearing the master interpret his works. At first, he was a little nervous as to the reception he might meet. But the tone of the American people was faithfully expressed by a New-York journal, which said, "Even in England, Dickens is less known than here; and, of the millions here who treasure every word he has written, there are tens of thousands who would make a large sacrifice to see and hear the man who has made happy so many hours. Whatever sensitiveness there once was to adverse or sneering criticism, the lapse of a quarter of a century, and the profound significance of a great war, have modified or removed."

The tickets to his readings were at a high figure; but

the rush to hear him was unprecedented. He said of his audiences, "American people are so accustomed to take care of themselves, that one of these immense audiences will fall into their places with an ease amazing to a frequenter of St. James's Hall; and the certainty with which they are all in before I go on is a very acceptable mark of respect." He often wrote of his reception as magnificent; his audiences as fine, appreciative, swayed by every sentiment and emotion of the piece, — moved now to laughter, and now to tears. This was the people whom he had derided. They came to fill his heart with love, his ears with applause, his pockets with gold. They decked his table with the choicest flowers; they honored his birthday with costly gifts: and, after every reading, Mr. Dickens wrote home, "We had above four hundred and fifty pounds English in the house last night." "We have not yet had in it less than four hundred and thirty pounds per night." "A charming audience; no dissatisfaction whatever at the raised prices; rounds upon rounds of applause. All the foremost men and their families had taken tickets. A small place to read in: three hundred pounds in it." At Rochester he had "above two hundred pounds English;" "at Syracuse, three hundred and seventy-five pounds odd." He has "a misgiving that the great excitement about the President's impeachment will damage his receipts;" but he remits three thousand pounds, then ten thousand pounds, and winds up with a total of one hundred thousand dollars. All this Mr. Forster has seen fit to give to the world; and the world will judge on which side of these audience-rooms were the tokens of refined culture, and on which those of a mercenary and material spirit, — whether with the hearers, who thought nothing of high prices for an hour of intellectual enjoyment, who sat silent, respectful, earnest, laughing, crying, applauding, under the play of literary taste and feeling; or with the reader, who was coolly counting them at so many pounds in his pocket.

But to the credit of Mr. Dickens be it said, that, at a farewell dinner in New York, he made the *amende honorable:* he used the occasion to bear his testimony to the changes of twenty-five years, — the rise of vast new cities;

growth in the graces and amenities of life; much improvement in the press, essential to every other advance; and changes in himself, leading to opinions more deliberately formed. He promised his kindly entertainers that no copy of his "Notes" or his "Chuzzlewit" should in future be issued by him without accompanying mention of the changes to which he had referred that night; of the politeness, delicacy, sweet temper, hospitality, and consideration in all ways, for which he had to thank them; and of his gratitude for the respect shown, during all his visit, to the privacy enforced upon him by the nature of his work and the condition of his health.[1] So ends the affair of the United States *in re* Dickens. The case was dismissed from court, the parties to divide the costs.

I have dwelt thus long upon Carlyle and Dickens, because, as impugners of American society, they were entitled to respectful consideration, and because their criticisms have gone over the world, and are fixed in literature; but chiefly because, by the analysis of their criticisms in the light of facts, one sees in American society a kind of moral greatness of which Carlyle knows little, and a spiritual culture of which Dickens knew less.[2]

The source of these it is easy to unfold. I have alluded to the provision for popular education made by the State governments, in part by general funds, in part by yearly taxes levied upon school-districts. This the State does of right and of necessity, since the safety of political society in a free State hinges upon the intelligence and virtue of its citizens. As a rule, knowledge favors virtue and order. As Rousseau said, " To open the schools is to shut the prisons:" hence the State must require and provide that every citizen shall have knowledge of his duties as a

[1] Forster, chap. 60.
[2] The names of Carlyle and Dickens represent genius; and what they said of America had at least the merit of raciness and originality. But a generation afterwards, in the chair of history in a university, — where one has a right to look for accuracy of knowledge, depth of wisdom, breadth, candor, and liberality of opinion, — to encounter narrowness, ignorance, bigotry, and hear the stale phrases of Irving and Carlyle, "the almighty dollar," and "America has produced no men," repeated and repeated without the flavor of wit or the smack of originality, — this is simply pitiful. Such talk American students hear from more than one professor in Germany; but the dignity of philosophic history and the nobility of the world of letters forbid any more specific notice of a style of criticism already in its dotage.

member of civil society. But virtue and religion, lying within the domain of will and conscience, the State, by the American theory, leaves to the training of the family and the Church, with entire freedom of choice and action to the individual, except so far as his acts may be injurious to society. Now, it is in this moral sphere that the renovating, purifying, saving energy of American life has shown itself in results that are without parallel in the history of Christendom. One must master this mighty, inner, untiring force, — the progressiveness, rather the aggressiveness, of a free religion, — before he can begin to understand how American society has made the material conquest of a continent without becoming itself materialized; how it has amassed enormous wealth without being mammonized.

New England, for instance, has among ourselves, and to some extent abroad, a sort of Nazarene reputation for "Yankeeism," — a shrewd, sharp, calculating, close, perhaps overreaching, habit in money-matters; yet it would be hard to find a community more removed from the spirit of mammonism, or more happily combining with the practical and material the ideal, the spiritual, the æsthetic, the philanthropic. How many good things in theology, poetry, science, letters, patriotism, beneficence, have come out of that Nazareth! No doubt the struggle for existence on the hard soil and in the hard climate of New England, and with the competitions of trade and manufactures, gives to the average New-Englander a sort of shrewd and wary look, and a seemingly tenacious habit, until, perchance, he finds himself enrolled among "the solid men of Boston," and relaxes with the consciousness of being at "the hub of the universe." No doubt, too, the driving business-ways of New York and Chicago compel every one to be smart who would get on. Indeed, with too many of our countrymen, smartness is the standard virtue, and lack of gumption the one damning sin. An English friend told me, that, going out one evening from his hotel in an American town, he pitched headlong into a ditch that had been excavated for gas-pipes, and left without warning lights. Next morning, at breakfast, he denounced in true English style the "beastly" neglect of the authorities:

whereupon a quaint Yankee at the table gave him this counsel: "I tell you what, stranger, if you're going to travel round in this country, you must learn to use your intellects. I've been in England, and know how you do things there. When you go to the railway-station, one policeman sees that the cabman doesn't cheat you; another then takes you on his arm to the booking-office, and sees that you get the right ticket and the right change; then a porter lifts you in his arms, and puts you into the carriage; then the guard comes, and hopes you're comfortable, and locks the door so that you can't fall out. But when you go to a railroad-station here, and see six trains ready to start at once for nobody knows where, then you've got to stir round, and use your intellects; and I tell you, stranger, if you can't learn to use your intellects, then you'd better go home, where there's always somebody to keep you from tumbling into ditches." My friend told me he profited much by this advice in his further travels. This habit of self-dependence, of finding or making his own way, obtains in the American from the news-boy and boot-black to the party politician, either of whom may have hopes of the presidency, if only he can "get on." I can well fancy that this national smartness is not relished by foreigners, and not understood by them. But this activity of intellect in practical every-day life does not suppress the tastes, the affections, the humanities, in the higher, nobler life of the soul.

Père Hyacinthe, after a tour in New England, said he had remarked in every town three institutions that epitomized American society, — the bank, the school, and the church. A true picture. And you see the intellectual and the spiritual are two to one against the material, — the bank the storehouse of gains and savings, the school and the church the distributing reservoirs of what is freely taken from the bank, and given to these educating and spiritualizing forces of society.

"The Americans," says De Tocqueville, "show by their practice that they feel the high necessity of imparting morality to democratic communities by means of religion. . . . In the United States, on the first day of every week, the trading and working life of the nation seems suspended;

all noises cease; a deep tranquillity, say rather the solemn calm of meditation, succeeds the turmoil of the week; and the soul resumes possession and contemplation of itself. Upon this day the marts of traffic are deserted: every member of the community, accompanied by his children, goes to church, where he listens to strange language, which would seem unsuited to his ear." This last expression shows that even the philosophical acumen of De Tocqueville had failed to penetrate to the secret of religious life in America. That is no "strange language" to which the American banker, merchant, farmer, mechanic, listens when he goes to church on Sunday: it is the language he was accustomed in childhood to hear from his parents; the language that perhaps he himself has used in his own family every day of the week at morning prayer; the lessons that he inculcates to his children, — "of the finer pleasures which belong to virtue alone, and of the true happiness which attends it." It is not on Sunday alone, as De Tocqueville imagined, "that the American steals an hour from himself, and laying aside for a while the petty passions which agitate his life, and the ephemeral interests which engross it, strays at once into an ideal world, where all is great, eternal, and pure." Thousands upon thousands of the busiest men in America do this every day with undeviating regularity. This *is* their life, — in that ideal world; and they bring from this springs and motives to action in the world of affairs. Hence these same busy men are to be seen on Sundays teaching the poor in mission-schools, on week-days attending prayer-meetings and committees of benevolent societies: hence these same rich men are found with their check-books always open to the calls of Christian work and duty.

I have spoken of the mass of pauperism, vice, and crime, that immigration pours in upon New York. But see, now, how Christian zeal and beneficence seek to purify and renovate this. In addition to hospitals, infirmaries, reformatories, supported by taxation, and to special charities of every name endowed by private munificence, or sustained by yearly donations, the whole city is divided into mission-districts, and the several religious communions unite in sustaining missions and free churches for the poor. There are in the city a hundred and forty mission-stations, many of which have connected with them industrial schools, reading-rooms, infirmaries, and, in winter, the systematic distribution of food and fuel. In addition to these missions, there are, in New York, two hundred and forty Protestant churches, with sittings for two hundred and fifty thousand persons, while the missions will accommodate fifty thousand more; and a total of three hundred thousand church-sittings are a large provision for the non-Catholic inhabitants, which may be estimated at six hundred thousand in a population of a million. The valuation of these churches is twenty million dollars. Notwithstanding the rapid increase of population since 1830, and the enormous advance in the cost of building-sites, the churches have kept pace with the growth of the city; and to-day there is a Protestant church in New York for every 1,578 of the Protestant population. Still more striking are the results of evangelistic zeal in the country at large. From 1850 to 1870 the population of the United States increased sixty-six per cent, and in the same period the provision for the religious wants of the people increased ninety per cent; so that to-day there is one evangelical minister to every seven hundred and ninety-one persons. The evangelical church-property is valued at three hundred and fifty million dollars, and the American people pay yearly for the support of their churches about fifty million dollars. He who reflects that all this is done of free will, without taxation or compulsion, or aid in any form from the State, will see that a people who have given money for church-extension to a degree that has outstripped the growth of the population are not given to the sordid pursuit of this world, and do not count material good the chief end of life.

There are forms of religion that repress certain forms of culture. But in the United States the prevailing tone of spiritual life has always favored the highest type of mental and social development. "The word of ambition at the present day," says Emerson, "is culture."[1] This is indeed a most pretentious word, and is uttered with a

[1] Conduct of Life, Essay IV.

most pretentious air by many who would be sorely puzzled to give a definition of the term, and still more puzzled, on hearing it defined, to feel themselves wanting in the first rudiments of the thing. Mr. Emerson discourses of it as something that shall at last "absorb the chaos and gehenna, — convert the Furies into Muses, and the hells into benefit;" but he fails to tell us what this enchantment is, or how to be attained. His nearest approach to a definition is this, — which is like many another riddle from the same oracle, — "Culture is the suggestion from certain best thoughts, that a man has a range of affinities through which he can modulate the violence of any master-tones that have a droning preponderance in his scale, and succor him against himself." In plainer words, this means that culture gives balance to one's powers, and represses his excesses and conceits through wider knowledge, sympathy, diversity, experience. But these are fruits or manifestations of culture, and do not acquaint us with the art or its methods. Mr. Matthew Arnold, who preaches culture as the new gospel for humanity, defines his theme with tantalizing vagueness: it is "a pursuit of our total perfection by means of getting to know, in all the matters which most concern us, the best which has been thought and said in the world, and, through this knowledge, turning a stream of fresh and free thought upon our stock notions and habits."[1] He is a little more precise when he speaks of culture as leading us "to conceive of true human perfection as an *harmonious* perfection, developing all sides of our humanity; and as a *general* perfection, developing all parts of our society:"[2] "Perfection is an harmonious expansion of *all* the powers which make the beauty and worth of human nature, and is not consistent with the over-development of any one power at the expense of the rest."[3] Hence "culture places human perfection in an *internal* condition, in the growth and predominance of our humanity proper, as distinguished from our animality."[4] But all this is rhetorical description, not philosophical definition; and Mr. Arnold recurs continually to his favorite figure of "the play of conscious-

---

[1] Culture and Anarchy, Preface, x. [2] Ibid., xiii.
[3] Ibid., p. 13. [4] Ibid., p. 11.

ness upon stock notions and habits." The figure is good as far as it goes. But planting your garden with the best, and watering it well, is not the whole of culture: if it has been "stocked" with worthless roots and weeds, these must be exterminated by something more effective than a fresh stream. Besides, culture does not begin and end in thoughts, notions, habits: there are principles, motives, feelings, to be formed or directed aright.

Wilhelm von Humboldt marks a fine gradation in the progress of society: "*Civilization* is the humanizing of peoples in their outward institutions and customs, and in the inner disposition that has regard to these: *culture* adds to this ennobling of the social condition the pursuit of the sciences and the fine arts; but still higher is *Bildung*."[1] And Fichte says, "All *Bildung* aims at producing a stable, definitive, and permanent being (or state of being). Did it not aim at such a state, it would be not *Bildung*, but an aimless play."[2] For this *Bildung*, this formative process, the English has no exact equivalent; but the term "culture" covers the whole ground, if we keep in view its etymology and the subject-matter to which it is applied. *Cultus* is labor carefully bestowed for improvement, for developing nature, and, if need be, refining upon nature, so as to produce the best. Hence the term is applicable to any thing capable of being improved by care or training, be it the soil, a flower, a fruit, a tree, an animal, a man, a people; but, whatever skilled labor may accomplish for improvement, the thing cultivated remains as to its essential nature the same, — either land, plant, animal, man, or society. It is obvious, then, that the grade of culture is to be estimated not only by outward results produced in any given direction, but by the nature and value of the material or substance wrought upon; as, for instance, the civilization of a savage people is an achievement of a higher order than the domestication of their wild animals. The definitions or descriptions of culture given by Emerson and others are, therefore, too limited, in that they restrict culture to knowledge and manners; whereas the whole man is properly the subject of culture, and the man centres in that spiritual nature,

---

[1] Kawispr. 1, xxxvii. [2] Fichte, 7, 281.

that positive definitive being, of which thoughts, tastes, habits, are but functions, predicates, or appendages. The true culture of man must begin with this inner spiritual nature, this reasonable, conscionable soul, and proceed from this outwards, as the cultured soul, by its own higher capacities, aims, and affinities, shall appropriate to itself as a garment all worthy knowledge, graces, arts, attainments. It is true that one cannot cultivate a science or an art without, in a sense, cultivating the soul; but to spend the labor of life in cultivating the science or art as the sum and end of life is to furbish and adorn the case, but leave the diamond within uncut, unpolished, unseen, or perchance, when seen, found to be no diamond, but a mass of uncrystallized carbon. What we want of culture is, that it shall bestow its thoughtful and careful labor upon the proper subject; that the man shall be wrought out and brought out in what Mr. Arnold has fitly styled his "total perfection," and this not simply by knowing the best in all the matters which most concern him, but by having the best, doing the best, being the best, possible for himself and others. I would define culture as that condition of man and of society in which all capabilities for the noble, the beautiful, the true, the good, are brought into supreme exercise, to the exclusion of the unsightly and the evil, and in harmonious adjustment for the perfection of the individual and the whole; and the process of culture is the training of man's spiritual nature to this end.

Looking thus at man as the prime subject of all culture, we see at once that materialism would block the way to the truest and noblest culture by discarding the spiritual nature, — which is capable itself of the purest refinement, and also of refining external nature from itself, — and substituting for this a mere atomical organism, of which thought, consciousness, sentiment, are but functions, and which, so far from answering to Fichte's determinate and imperishable *Sein*, has but a frail and perishable hold upon existence, amid the flux and reflux of atoms. However far such culture may be carried, however much it may refine upon its material, it cannot change the nature of that material; and the sum total of materialistic culture is the polishing of one set of atoms by another, like grinding down the surface of a diamond by grains of emery. Such culture makes of man a statue without a soul, and of society a temple without a divinity. And, materialism aside, this is pretty much the limit of all forms of culture that rest in knowledge, in the restricted and unphilosophical sense in which some physicists use that term, making intelligence the only thing in man that is susceptible or worthy of culture.

But those three short, simple questions of Kant, touching the ideal of the highest good, unveil to us in man capacities for ethical, spiritual, and æsthetic culture far above the range of physical objects and materials. "Every interest of my reason (the speculative as well as the practical) is united in the three following questions: (1) What can I know? (2) What ought I to do? (3) What may I hope?" Of the last he says, "All *hoping* looks toward happiness, and, in regard to the practical and the law of morality, is precisely the same as are knowing and the law of nature in regard to the theoretical knowledge of things." And he clinches the point by saying, that "without a God, and a world as yet to us invisible, but hoped for, the glorious ideas of morality are indeed objects of approbation and admiration, but not springs of purpose and of action, since they do not fill out the whole end which is natural and necessary to every rational being, and is even determined *a priori* by pure reason itself."[1] It is this spiritual nature in its totality that is the subject of culture in man; and that culture is yet rude and unfinished that rests in arts and sciences which cultivate the eye, the hand, the ear, — a culture that furnishes the chambers of the cerebrum, but does not penetrate to the shrine of the soul, or rather come forth from that clothed with a divine beauty and majesty.

Were I called upon to select from the whole range of literature the man whose writings evince the highest soul-culture, I should name the apostle John as seen in his Gospel, his Epistles, and his Apocalypse. John wrote no system of philosophy; but in his Gospel there is a philosophy so transcendently high, that criticism has sought to deprive him of its authorship, and transfer this to a trained

[1] Kant, Des Kanons der reinen Vernunft, zweiter Abschnitt.

school of Platonists. John wrote no poetry; but where in Dante or Milton have we such grandeur of imagination as in the Apocalypse?[1] John seems not to have been conversant, as was Paul, with *belles-lettres;* but where in literature have we finer examples of the delicate in style, the pure and refined in feeling, than in his second and third Epistles? John held no painter's pencil; but what artist has yet rivalled his New Jerusalem, swinging there in mid-heaven, with its walls of crystal, and gates of pearl? John composed no symphony; but what music charms us from his celestial choirs! John gathered no museums of science; but where do the precious stones of earth appear so glorious as where jasper and amethyst, sapphire and sardonyx, emerald and topaz, are set as foundations in the city of God? What form of culture was not possible to this cultured soul, — and this the soul of a fisherman! No mind has yet outreached the thought of John, no heart yet fathomed his love. Art pictures him as the type of manly beauty graced with woman's tenderness; and history tells us he was "the disciple whom Jesus loved," and to whom he intrusted his mother.

Purity reflecting the image of the Divine, perfection reproducing the love of the Divine, — is there any thing nobler or richer than these? How meagre the culture that begins and ends in ignoring these! Now, it was a peculiarity of American society, and especially of New-England society, which did so much to stamp and shape the nation, that it began in this royal valuation of the soul, and set its culture above all price. Because of its intrinsic worth, and because of the freedom it should have in religion and in political action, the soul should be trained in knowledge and virtue, and, through its affinities with the spiritual and immortal, be cultivated to the highest nobleness of being. As I have before shown of liberty, that in America religion was its spring and sup-

---

[1] The genuineness of the fourth Gospel I have discussed in my Theology of Christ. Now that the Tübingen School has died out in Germany, it is not worth while to revive the question here. An amusing episode of that controversy is, however, worth recording. An English critic, who had demonstrated to his own satisfaction that the same pen could not have produced two compositions so different as John's Gospel and the Apocalypse, actually attempted to prove that the author of the Novum Organon wrote also the plays of Shakspeare!

port, so was it of learning also. Two of the oldest colleges in the United States, Harvard and Yale, now grown to be universities, were founded with the prime object of saving the churches from the evil of an uneducated clergy. Can history show a more beautiful example of religion in support of culture than was seen in the Colony of Massachusetts Bay on the twenty-eighth day of October, 1636? It was a troublous time. The Colony was but seven years old. Its spirit of freedom had roused the jealousy of England, and occasion had been sought to revoke its charter. "Provision had hardly been made for the first wants of life, — habitations, food, clothing, and churches. Walls, roads, and bridges were yet to be built. The power of England stood in attitude to strike. A desperate war with the natives had already begun."[1] Yet in these critical circumstances the legislature voted to found a college, and to this end appropriated a sum "equivalent to the Colony tax for a year." Among the leading men in that infant Colony were John Winthrop of Trinity College, Cambridge; Hugh Peter, also of Trinity, Cambridge, afterwards one of Cromwell's chaplains; Harry Vane of Oxford, son of the privy councillor, who also returned to England, became a leader in the Long Parliament, and, like Peter, was beheaded by Charles II., because, said the king, "he is too dangerous a man to let live if we can honestly put him out of the way;" John Humphrey, eminent for his gifts and learning, son-in-law of the Earl of Lincoln; Simon Bradstreet of Emanuel College, Cambridge; John Cotton, fellow of Emanuel College, Cambridge, and for twenty years rector of the splendid Church of St. Botolph's, Boston, England; Samuel Stone, also of Emmanuel College, Cambridge; and Thomas Hooker, a fellow of the same college. These are specimens of the men who at the first presided in the councils of the Massachusetts Colony, and ministered to its churches. They had brought with them all of learning and culture that England possessed in the age that followed the lustrous reign of Elizabeth; and they took the noble resolve to reproduce in the virgin forest, and beside the Indian wigwam, the dear Cambridge of their

[1] Palfrey, History of New England, i. 548.

native land. The Assembly, which in 1636 voted to tax the Colony for a college, is said to be "the first body in which the people, by their representatives, ever gave their own money to found a place of education."[1] Now, that which moved them to care for literary culture was their concern for spiritual culture. Here is their own testimony: "After God had carried us safe to New England, and we had builded our houses, provided necessaries for our livelihood, reared convenient places for God's worship, and settled the civil government, one of the first things we longed for and looked after was to advance learning, and perpetuate it to posterity, dreading to leave an illiterate ministry to the churches when our present ministers should lie in the dust."[2] In a word, what Prussia has just now provided for upon political grounds,—that all her clergy shall have a broad university training,—those settlers in the wilderness provided for upon spiritual grounds two hundred and forty years ago.

The spirit of Massachusetts for liberal education animated the other New-England Colonies. In 1643 a confederation of these Colonies was formed for their mutual welfare and defence; and among the first acts of this confederation was a recommendation that every family throughout the plantations should give yearly "the fourth part of a bushel of corn, or something equivalent thereto, to the maintenance of poor students at the college at Cambridge. How rich the harvest from those grains of corn! The wisdom and wit of Emerson, blending the Pundit with the Puritan, and Socrates with Swift; the mellifluous verse of Longfellow, touching the heart of humanity in every tongue; the fine sense and feeling of Lowell in prose and poetry; the humor of Holmes; the dignity of Dana, Nestor of American poets; the scholarly eloquence of Buckingham, Everett, Winthrop; the legal lore of Story the father, and the chaste art of the son, alike with the chisel and the pen; the scientific breadth and accuracy of Peirce, whether exploring the skies or the seas; the humane ethics of Channing and the Wares; the philanthropic statesmanship of Sumner; and

[1] Edward Everett, in Palfrey, i. 548.
[2] New England's First-Fruits, 12.

that wealth of historic research in Sparks, Eliot, Palfrey, Prescott, Hildreth, Ticknor, — whose portrait adorned the library of the late King of Saxony, — Motley, — whose portrait is the one favored picture in the private *salon* of the Queen of the Netherlands in her summer palace at the Hague, — Bancroft, who, having so enriched his country with the materials of her history, has imitated her early settlers in giving the material proceeds of his work to aid poor scholars at Cambridge, — these, and scores like these, are fruits of that pious provision for learning, in arts, sciences, and letters, two centuries and a half ago. What land of Europe has not been enriched by this New-England culture of the spiritual nature of man?

No less significant of the affinity of religion for culture was the act of a few ministers who came together in 1700, each with an armful of books culled from his own library, and — with the simple formula, " I give these books for the founding of a college " — began what has grown to be the University at New Haven. And from Yale College what treasures of culture in learning and science have enriched mankind! — Percival and Hillhouse among the poets; Webster, Gibbs, Hadley, Salisbury, Whitney, among philologists, and especially Eli Smith, whose work in translating the Bible into Arabic placed him among the foremost Semitic scholars; Dana the naturalist, honored by scientific academies throughout the world; Edwards, Taylor, and Porter, among philosophers; Calhoun, Woolsey, Evarts, among statesmen and legists; Lyman Beecher, Dwight, Bacon, Bushnell (the last more widely read by men of thought than any recent theologian). The mention of this name leads me to speak of one product of mind in New England that holds no mean place among the philosophic systems of the world: I mean the distinctive New-England theology that is represented by such names as Edwards, Hopkins, West, Bellamy, Emmons, Taylor, Park. This theology has dealt mainly with the questions of the human will, the origin of evil, the atonement, and the moral government of God; and the whole literature of theology nowhere presents a theodicy more strongly marked with deep and keen metaphysical speculation, thorough exegesis, and cogent logic.

The power of this theology in training the minds of men, when books were few, was sometimes wonderful. After the death of Dr. Bellamy, an old negro who had always attended on his preaching was asked how he liked the new minister. "H'm: he preach smart; he make God big, but no so big as Massa Bellamy. Massa Bellamy — he make God Almighty *awful big!*" There was an instrument of soul-culture — the power of making spiritual things real, great, majestic — that took hold upon the rudest minds, and lifted these into the unseen and eternal; and a mind that is not capable of realizing such things can no more judge of American culture than a blind man can judge of color.

I come back to the proposition, that all true culture must have for its basis the spiritual nature in man. Why is it that Germany has enlisted the sympathies of enlightened and cultivated men throughout the world in her conflict with Ultramontanism? It is because she would maintain for the human mind that freedom of thought and development that Luther won at the Reformation. But if there be no *mind* to be cultivated, — nothing but sciences, arts, and manners, — the strife is not worth our concern. Why is ecclesiastical tyranny the most hateful and hated of all? Because it binds its chains upon the mind. Other tyrannies can be broken by force of will, by the uprising of mind; but clerical tyranny palsies the will, and holds the soul in vassalage. The struggle with Vaticanism enlists my whole being, only because I look upon this as the emancipation of man's spiritual nature from worse than material bonds. Surely the Latin Church has not been wanting in that æsthetic and materialistic culture that some account the perfection of civilization. Who conserved the Latin tongue? Who built the cathedrals, illuminated windows and missals, gathered great libraries, founded universities, gave to Titian, Giotto, Michael Angelo, Leonardo da Vinci, Raphael, the themes and motives of their greatest works? Is it against such a Rome as this, such a culture as this, that modern society is up in arms? Nay: but Luther said, "You sha'n't build St. Peter's in Rome at the price of souls here in Germany;" and so he, in his rough way, struck for that culture of the spiritual in man which has made Germany what she is to-day. The planters of America made that spiritual nature their first care. It was because of this, that their descendants, in the huge struggle with nature that was laid upon them, did not sink toward barbarism. It was because this heavenward side of their nature was kept always open, and full of light, that, when the pressure of their material work was over, they had an aptitude for the intellectual and the æsthetic, and began to create a literature, and are now giving themselves to art, with the intensity of a nature that has mastered the material and the political, and now goes on to crave and claim all that is noble, good, beautiful, in earth or man, as the heritage, the appanage, of a cultivated soul.

This accounts for the rapid growth of American literature. Many of us can remember the sneer of " The Edinburgh Review," " Who reads an American book?" The laugh is turned, now that everywhere in England one sees the railway book-stalls, and the shelves of circulating libraries, crowded with American books in ready demand; that one can count up scores of American authors reprinted in England (in the catalogue of a single London publisher I lately saw twelve American names); that in " The International Scientific Series," published at London and Leipzig, the names of Cooke, Dana, Draper, Flint, Whitney, appear side by side with Bain, Carpenter, Huxley, Lubbock, Spencer, Tyndall, Bernstein, Liebreich, Leuckart, Steinthal, Virchow; that every leading English review now has its department of American literature. " The Athenæum " finds much to praise, and even the hypercritical " Saturday Review " now and then throws us such tid-bits as these: " Hawthorne is one of the most fascinating of novelists. Whittier's ' Mabel Martin ' is enough to make the reputation of any poet." True, we have given birth to no Shakspeare nor Byron; but with the list of contemporary English poets, from Tennyson down to Swinburne, we need not hesitate to compare our list from Bryant down to Whitman, each after his kind.

Of humorists America has spawned more than enough, and cannot but marvel that her English cousins are so taken with the " Artemus Ward " and " Mark Twain " style, in which the higher culture of America finds so little trace of genius. As yet, we have produced no Beethoven, Mozart, nor even a Wagner; but what may not be possible in this direction, when all the sound of which America is capable shall be wrought into "the music of the future" by some new master of the sensations of tone? Lowell has wittily said, "The German who plays the bass-viol has a well-founded contempt, which he is not always nice in concealing, for a country so few of whose children ever take that noble instrument between their knees."[1] Yet nowhere do the best musicians now find more appreciative and critical audiences than in the United States; and the wide sale of classical music and of the best pianos argues a musical taste among the people at large, which, even in the absence of great native composers, may be taken as evidence of culture.[2] Must one be a poet to appreciate poetry, or a musician to appreciate music? The man to whom I owe more than to any other, if not all others, is Beethoven. He it was who first opened to my inner consciousness the majesty of the soul, the height, depth, length, breadth, of the Unutterable. Plato had foreshadowed this dreamily; Paul had asserted it dogmatically: Beethoven seized upon its inner source, and made it felt and realized as consciousness itself. When I approach the master with such homage, will he demand that I shall conduct a symphony, play a sonata, or even take the bass-viol between my knees? There is a Free-Masonry in music, and even the republican can give the secret sign.

No one would suspect De Tocqueville of wit; and therefore the caption of one of his chapters is the more exquisitely droll, — "Why the Americans raise some insignificant monuments, and others that are very grand." This came to me as a conundrum; and, having pored over it in my study, I walked over to the Thier-garten, and took a look at Victory flying her brazen skirts on top of the "asparagus" pillar; walked through the Brandenburg Thor, which might be "grand," if stucco were not always "insignificant;" went up the Linden; paused before the

---

[1] My Study Windows, p. 70.
[2] A college of music has been founded in New York, which will furnish an incentive to composition as well as to execution.

really grand monument of Frederic the Great; admired the statues on the bridge, and that marvellous juxtaposition of palace, cathedral, museum, arsenal, opera-house, university, library, academy, — that groups all the symbols of civilization as nowhere else in the world, — when I found myself staring at that prodigy of ecclesiastical architecture, the Dom; and I asked myself again, " Why do the *Americans* raise some *insignificant* monuments, and others that are very grand?" Thus musing, I bethought myself of London as I saw it on a bright October day, — the majestic dome of St. Paul's, the stately Victoria Tower, the Abbey, the embankment and bridges, and then Nelson's monument with the four lions, the equestrian statues, and especially the "Iron Duke" astride his iron horse, — and again I asked myself, "Why *do* the Americans raise some insignificant monuments, and others that are very grand?" And I gave it up, seeing only it could not be because they are Americans or republicans, and having a vague notion, that, of all humbugs in this much humbugged age, on nothing has so much humbug been spoken and written as upon art as the measure of the culture of a people.

That museums, galleries, buildings, monuments, statues, are no sure criterion of the present stage of national culture, — no, not in art itself, — Greece, Spain, and even Italy, are melancholy witnesses. When I first saw Paris, many years ago, I fancied that the omnipresence of art in that brilliant and tasteful capital must have a refining influence upon even the meanest of its inhabitants, and that one could trace this influence in the very air of business and the manners of the common people. The Commune dispelled that illusion. The prostrate Vendôme column, the blackened ruins of the Tuileries and the Hôtel de Ville, the Louvre scarce saved from the torch and petroleum, are a warning to the panegyrists of æsthetics, that, through all forms of culture and of society, human nature remains the one unchanged factor of evil. Plato had already admonished us of " the lovers of sounds and sights, fond of fine tones and colors and forms, and all the artificial products that are made out of them, having a sense of beautiful things, but whose mind is incapable of seeing or loving absolute beauty."[1] Augustine, too, had said of his own devotion to the liberal arts, "I had my back to the light, and my face to the things enlightened; whence my face, with which I discerned the things enlightened, itself was not enlightened." Art-culture is not always the key to soul-culture, nor are art collections always a true index of the culture of the beautiful. The Germany of to-day may be in advance of the Italy of to-day in the æsthetic spirit, though the chief treasures of her museums are of Italian origin, and her best models, casts, or copies, of Italian masters, and though Italy is tenfold richer in the great originals. Again: the possession of a museum or a gallery of exceptional richness in this or that locality may be due to the taste and liberality of an individual prince, or line of princes, rather than to an elevated taste in the people or the race; just as the possession of a grand cathedral may be owing to the accident of an architect being born in the place, or to the wealth or vanity of the cathedral chapter. Would Dresden acknowledge itself inferior in culture to Cologne or Strasburg because it can boast no cathedral like theirs? Would Berlin confess itself behind Dresden in art-culture because the gallery at Dresden is incomparably richer in the best works of the best masters? Or would either capital rate itself below Florence or Madrid, though the galleries of these are still richer? Taste and wealth, judiciously applied, have enabled St. Petersburg to profit by the impoverishment of Italy, and to enrich her imperial gallery with the spoils of Southern art. But does this indicate that the Russians, as a people, are surpassing the Italians in art-culture? When, however, the simple American citizen buys the gallery of some bankrupt European noble, either for his private enjoyment, or to found by his munificence a museum for the public, this *is* a true indication of the growth of art in America, and points to a surer test of culture than the size and value of collections, — the diffusion of taste among the people.[2] It is the

---

[1] Republic, book v.
[2] In the private galleries of New York, in addition to the best productions of American artists, — Bierstadt, Boughton, Church, Cole, Cropsey, Gifford, Gray, Hicks, Huntington, Ingham, Eastman Johnson, Leutze, Page, and others, — may be found many choice specimens of famous

glory of Italy, as it was once the glory of Greece, that she has achieved great things in art; and this attests a special art-capacity in the race. We must honestly confess that our national taste in art has not much to boast of, either in originals or in selections; though we are beginning to have a school in landscape-painting. The proverb, "A fool and his money are soon parted," has been often illustrated in the art-purchasers of our *parvenus* abroad. But, though the taste needs to be educated, the capacity is there. We are learning to laugh at our follies and our fools. Looking beyond the factitious culture of modern Europe to the glory of Praxiteles and Phidias, of Zeuxis and Apelles, we are beginning to ask ourselves, Why should not democracy, as the nursery of man, be again true to its mission as the nursery of art? Why should the American people erect " insignificant monuments," though European powers have done the same? The growth among us of a guild of the cultivated, men of wealth and their sons, who use wealth for the adornment of life; the growth of art-criticism; the founding of schools and museums of art in New York, Philadelphia, Boston, and other cities, and at Yale and other colleges; the improvement in church architecture, and in the taste of public buildings and of suburban villas; the increase of art-students, and of journals devoted to art, — these all are healthy signs, that, our rougher work and sterner duties being so far accomplished, we shall turn the training of the inner nature to the culture of the outer.

The fashion of rich men to found libraries, lyceums, colleges; the wide demand for books of science; the popularity of scientific lectures, and of journals that reproduce these cheaply for the million; the effort of indigent students and teachers to see and learn all that the Old World has to show or teach; the creation of an International Exposition with appropriate architecture, art, and adornment, — are cheering tokens of the diffusion, among the masses, of that degree of knowledge which creates the

---

European painters, — Achenbach, Rosa Bonheur, Camphausen, Cooper, Gérôme, Girard de Haas, Jordan, Kaulbach, Knaus, Merle, Meissonier, Meyer von Bremen, Ary Scheffer, Troyon, Verboeckhoven, Horace Vernet.

desire for more, and conducts to the higher culture. The intellectual activity of the American people has shown itself largely in discoveries and inventions serviceable to mankind. Franklin had already a European reputation as a philosopher before he appeared on the stage as a statesman; and where he led, in drawing the electricity of the clouds harmless to the earth, there Morse followed, in appropriating electricity to the transmission of thought, and making this intelligible through an alphabet; and Henry, with his application of the helix, and the combination of circuits through the receiving-magnet and the relay; and Field, with his personal magnetism organizing the company for the Atlantic telegraph, and with his indomitable pluck laying the cable when everybody said he had failed. And now comes Gray, with his studies upon the electric current, and his arrangement of batteries, by which the same wire can be made to transmit two, four, and even eight messages at the same instant of time. Eli Whitney invented the cotton-gin, and the heir of his name and genius contrived machinery for making guns in convertible parts. Colt, Remington, Sharps, Maynard, Winchester, and other American names, are known throughout the world for inventions in fire-arms. Hare, the earliest American chemist, invented the oxyhydrogen blow-pipe; and the laboratories of the United States, though but inefficiently equipped, have been tireless in their researches, and productive in results for the service of humanity. Prominent among these is the twin-discovery of Jackson and Wells in anæsthetics, by which the pains of surgery are turned to pleasurable dreams. The war of the Rebellion brought prominently before Europe the skill and tact of American surgeons. The American ambulance and the American field-hospital are extensively copied by foreign armies. The Empress of Germany, who takes a lively interest in the medical service of the army, was desirous of sending to the Philadelphia Exposition a complete assortment of the German field and hospital apparatus. "It would hardly be worth while, your Majesty," said a high officer, " since so many of the best devices are borrowed from the United States." The organ of the Thuringian Medical Society lately published (from the pen of

Medicinalrath Dr. Meusel of Gotha) a highly favorable notice of the Catalogue of the United States Medical Museum at Washington. Commending this review and the catalogue, a prominent physician of Germany wrote as follows to the editor of " The Chronicle of the Continent: " —

"The various reports of celebrated American surgeons which appear from time to time concerning important operations sufficiently indicate the extent to which surgical science and skill in America have been developed, and show also the number of masters in this branch of the profession which your country has produced. The recent consultations and operations in Germany of your esteemed countryman, Dr. B——, have also contributed in no small degree to the high value which is placed upon American surgical practice. Naturally, a surgeon so celebrated as he is an isolated instance. But from this catalogue, which Dr. Meusel has reviewed, we can clearly see what a large number of skilful investigating surgeons America possesses, and what a splendid example was shown by them in the treatment and care of the American armies during the late civil war, — something which has never been properly acknowledged in Europe."

The pre-eminence of Americans in dental surgery is everywhere recognized. Indeed, it was in the United States that this department was first raised to the dignity of a science.

It was an American who discovered the process of vulcanizing caoutchouc; and the pains and privations that Goodyear underwent in making a familiar vegetable substance so widely serviceable to mankind entitle him to a name among the heroic benefactors of the race.

The invention of the cotton-gin was followed by a number of valuable American improvements upon the various English inventions for carding and spinning.

In printing, Adams, Bullock, Hoe, and other American inventors, have carried the press and its accessories to a degree of perfection widely recognized in Europe, and not yet surpassed. American industry and invention have been remarkably developed in the manufacture of iron, which had long been a monopoly of great Britain. Says "The London Times," —

"The Centennial Exhibition at Philadelphia has brought together such an assemblage of the products of American industry as to impress the visitor with a strong sense of the manufacturing activity of the

United States. In every department of manufacture, the United States are creditably represented; and the practical result seems to be, that, in the United States, we have now powerful competitors in all branches of industry, and especially in that which we considered our own,— the iron trade. Such a state of affairs deserves the attention of Englishmen. It presents to us important lessons."

Following the experiments of Fitch on the Delaware, Fulton first made the steamboat practicable upon the Hudson; and, since Stephenson invented the locomotive, what valuable improvements have been made by American genius, both in the engine, and in brakes and other appliances for the trains![1] The steam fire-engine is an American invention; as is also the extinguisher, by which a chemical antagonist to combustion is scientifically combined with water for the speedy extinction of flames. Machinery for heading pins and tacks from the body of the wire, for making boots, shoes, and regulation watches, for relieving the household of the drudgery of the needle, and the husbandman of the hard hand-labor of the plough, the spade, the scythe, the sickle, and the rake, machinery for every conceivable purpose of domestic utility and manual dexterity, witnesses for the fruitfulness and the usefulness of American invention. While millions of homes and farms are rejoicing in the sewing-machine, the mowing and reaping machines, by which America has lightened their labor, now comes the writing-machine to turn the drudgery of the composer and the copying-clerk into the pleasure of playing a well-toned piano without the tediousness of that practice. But why need I reproduce the records of the patent-office?[2] America is bristling with inventions; and, though she had much to learn, she had little to fear, from competition with other nations in her World Exposition. Nor is the inventive genius to be disparaged as belonging to a lower mechanical grade of culture. It detracts nothing from the scientific genius of Galileo that he invented or copied the telescope, nor from Helmholtz that he invented the ophthalmoscope.[3] Not all the valor and discipline of European armies could avail, were not

[1] In Russia the American locomotive takes precedence of all others.
[2] From 1800 to 1870, 120,298 patents were issued by the United States, of which 79,612 were between 1860 and 1870.
[3] See note at the close of the Lecture.

inventors continually improving the weapons of war. What were Moltke without Krupp? Germany has not hesitated to erect a monument to the genius of Gutenberg, and has grouped Theology, Poetry, Science, and Industry in an attitude of admiration around the inventor of movable type. England has reared monuments to Stephenson; and America may well rear statues of Franklin, Fulton, Morse, Field, as benefactors of mankind.

Indeed, it marks the dignity and worth of American civilization, that, from first to last, it has sought the good of diversified and collective humanity, — for mankind in its aims, to mankind in its results. I marvel, that, in his ode to Boston, Emerson should have opened on so low a key: —

> "The merchant was a man.
> The world was made for honest trade:
> To plant and eat be none afraid."

True, as he advances, he rises to a nobler key, and sings, —

> "Each honest man shall have his vote,
> Each child shall have his school;
> For what avail the plough or sail,
> Or land or life, if freedom fail?"

Yes, the merchants of Boston were men; and noble, princely men have they been. But, from the first, the glory of Boston was to provide for knowledge and religion, and open to men, of whatever grade, avenues to that self-culture that marks the man. And as of Boston, so of the proper American type of civilization, it is cosmopolitan in the spirit of elevating humanity. I know a civilization where the plough-boy and the smith's apprentice were taught to put all knowledge in their heads, and all virtue in their hearts; and from the plough came the statesmanship of Daniel Webster, and from the anvil came the philology and philanthropy of Elihu Burrit. I know a civilization that taught the factory-girls of Lowell, in the good old times when farmers' daughters went there to spin, to diversify their labor with editing a literary magazine, and learning accomplishments in music and the arts.

I know a civilization where the farmer sweats over his hard-handed toil, that his son may go to college, and his daughter may have her library and piano; feels that an education is the true patent of nobility, and the best estate for his children; and then is grateful to God, if his children, educated by his toil and theirs, shall go forth as missionaries of Christian civilization. It is because of this view of the worth of the individual and the brotherhood of humanity, that the United States, having set the example of codifying her own laws, has taken the initiative in schemes of arbitration and for the reform of international law in the interest of peace and unity, which shall one day bring in an era of culture such as Europe has not yet seen.

NOTE ON AMERICAN PROGRESS.

In a spoken lecture it was impossible to give more than an outline of the progress of the United States in the century; and no audience would have been patient of an array of statistics which the reader can study at leisure on the printed page. Even the most moderate statement of what has been done in America for learning, science, art, and general culture, is apt to be received in Europe with incredulity or disparagement. But the cultivated American cannot be surprised or annoyed at this. He will remember, that, down to a very recent period, he has had ten reasons for studying the civilization of the Old World where the European had one for studying the civilization of the New. As to England, even if he has had no personal experience of the fact, his Emerson, Lowell, and Hawthorne will have taught him how completely insular is her national spirit and ideal, even to a degree that " makes existence incompatible with all that is not English ; " but, as he listens to the tone of English criticism upon his country, the honest American will remember how " faithful are the wounds of a friend," and, pardoning much to a chronic and grotesque dogmatism, will consider, also, that family criticism more often springs from a secret pride than from real bitterness or dislike. Still less can any well-balanced American be affected by the new style of French criticism, represented by Claudio Jannet and Talleyrand-Perigord. He understands perfectly that it is the cue of clericalism in France, as of conservatism in Germany, to disparage the United States as a check to liberal aspirations at home; and he reflects, that, in France, liberty is an imperishable aspiration, and Lafayette, De Tocqueville, and Laboulaye are imperishable names.

But the cultivated American will be especially considerate of the *insouciance* of German society touching the condition and culture of the United States. He will consider how slowly new ideas penetrate the learned mind of Germany from outside the prescribed routine of its own investigations. He will consider how indifferently the German press is, for the most part, appointed and conducted. Above all, he will consider how short an interval has elapsed since Germany began to create a truly national literature, and how recent is her emancipation from the humiliating superiority of France in arts and arms, and hence will make allowance for an air of youthful assumption, which will be toned down by a broader experience of the responsibilities of national independence. Just now, the intoxication of a military success, which the sober reports of the staff-office show was more than once due to some lucky accident, leads the untravelled German to prate over-much of "Bildung," "Kunst," "Kultur," "Wissenschaft," and to assume that every American who visits Germany must look with wonder and envy upon its higher civilization. But the American, who knows too well this infirmity in his own countrymen, can afford to be indulgent toward the Teutonic braggart, who really has so much to boast of. I have had much innocent amusement, as well as some patient discipline, in the supercilious comments of this new-fledged Germany upon the United States. In Germany, breadth and solidity of *information* are by no means commensurate with depth of *learning*. A person of the highest social position, and who has always moved within the sphere of university-life, asked me, "Who is this Mr. Morse? and what has he done, that your countrymen propose to erect a monument to him?" Suppose I should ask who was Gutenberg? who was Stephenson? — what shrugging of shoulders there would be in "cultivated" circles in Germany and England!

One of the foremost monthlies, which well represents the literature and learning of Germany, in an article on railways, written by a university professor, attributed to "a speech of Pres. Lincoln in the Senate of the United States" the astounding statement, that, "in building a railway, it was better to finish the road rapidly, because, though such immature work would cost more lives, it would hasten the development of the country." I wrote to the editor, that Mr. Lincoln never was in the Senate; that, excepting in the case of the Pacific roads, the Senate had had nothing to do with railways; and though Mr. Lincoln had once urged the rapid and vigorous prosecution of the *war*, on the ground that the salvation of the Union would infinitely overbalance all present cost and loss, he was utterly incapable of thus staking human life against the gains of a railroad. The editor promised to make the correction; but just then an American newspaper at Berlin made a squib upon his article, to the effect, that, on the occasion referred to, "Alexander Hamilton, senator from Toronto, had replied to Mr. Lincoln with great eloquence and power." The bewildered German *Gelehrte* hereupon sent me this paragraph, which he took to be serious, and said, "Though I have much confidence in your knowledge, I suspect that my allusion to Mr. Lincoln was correct, since the accompanying paragraph, which gives evidence of minute accuracy, confirms my statement." I was obliged to answer,

"My dear sir, don't you see that this paragraph is making a fool of you? Don't you know that Toronto is in Canada? that Hamilton was never in the Senate? and that he was killed five years before Lincoln was born?" But the learned editor never made the correction.

Another journal that aspires to lead opinion in the capital, and whose editor is certified by a doctorate of the university, some time ago enlightened its readers with an account of the American Thanksgiving. After describing the sour New-England Puritan, who would allow no holiday nor festivity, but enforced the Jewish sabbath by stringent penalties, this journal discovered a hopeful triumph of human nature in the fact that the great national festival of Thanksgiving had won its way even into New England, and, by captivating the hearts of the rising generation there, had somewhat relaxed the Pharisaism of the elders. I dropped a respectful line to the editor, assuming that he would be interested to give the true history of the Pilgrim festival that flourished in New England a century and a half before there were any United States, and more than two centuries before it was adopted as a national institution; but an educated German, whose journal has ridiculed an English author for making an error of one year in the date of an incident of German literature, confessed that his readers did not care enough about American affairs to make it worth while to correct such an egregious blunder.

One evening, at a *salon* where were assembled only the most learned and cultivated society, I was presented first to Prof. ——, who said at once, "From America? I believe you have as yet no universities: you are too young to have any science." — "On that point," I replied, "I prefer to accept the verdict of the Berlin Academy, which crowned with its prize a work of our Sanscrit scholar, Prof. Whitney; the verdict of the various European academies that have elected Prof. Dana an associate; the verdict of" — "Ah, *so!*" And this interlocutor gave place to a second, who said, "I suppose you have no museums yet in America: you are too young for these." — "If you intend museums of science, I might remind you of the Smithsonian at Washington, the Peabody at New Haven, the Agassiz at Cambridge. In museums of art and antiquity, of course we cannot compete with nations which were in the market before we were born. Still we have some treasures from Egypt and Assyria that European museums would like to possess; and Berlin or London would be glad to get hold of the Cesnola Cyprus Collection, now at New York. This you know is genuine. But how about those Moabite antiquities in your Berlin Museum, and that other lot from Italy bought by your first Roman archæologist as a precious find? How, too, about the indorsement of the Cardiff giant by German *savans* after American scholars had promptly exposed the fraud? You see we take an interest in these matters to the extent of our opportunity." — "Ah, *so!*"

I was next honored with a presentation to an eminent musician. "In America," said he, "you are not at all musical." — "If you mean that we have not produced great composers, nor many eminent artists, you are quite correct: nevertheless, your artists seek fame and fortune in America, and wince, too, under our criticisms. As to the love of music, I may mention that two piano-manufactories in New York alone turn out each at the rate of ten pianos a day for every day of the year; and these are sold at prices from five hundred dollars up to three thousand dollars." — " So!" and " *So!*" and " So!"

"Russia has been called a despotism tempered by assassination," said my host one evening at a supper-table, "and your government is democracy tempered by the revolver. In your Senate, every man has a revolver on his table." This was said in sober earnest by a university professor; and the company, composed entirely of official and educated persons, laughed heartily at what they fancied was a fair hit at a foreign guest. In a few patient words, I pointed out that the violence of slaveholders in former times, and the roughness of frontier-life, did not represent the character and habits of the Senate of the United States. But it was of little use to talk with men who had never heard the names of Calhoun, Webster, Everett, Seward; who knew nothing at all of the Constitution of the American Government, and met every fact with that annihilating threat (in which the tax-ridden, army-burdened German finds a momentary consolation), " You'll have to come to a monarchy at last." These are not selected instances, but could be multiplied by the score. I do not adduce them either to caricature or to characterize the German people. I think it indecent in a foreigner to caricature the people among whom he lives, by exaggerating their faults, and ignoring their virtues; and a people so kindly and sincere as the Germans, a people of so many fine and noble qualities, could never form a subject for caricature. Neither would I intimate that such examples fairly characterize the higher classes of German society; for though too often the German *savant* is ignorant of general subjects in the degree that he is learned in his specialty, and vain of his opinion where he is least informed, yet there are many notable exceptions, — men of breadth as well as of accuracy, men of information as well as of learning, men of the cosmopolitan spirit of true science. The many modest, manly Germans whom it is a pleasure to know, the quiet, learned Germans, of broad and liberal training, whom it is an honor as well as a pleasure to know, are a truer type of the national culture. These have travelled far enough to learn that the world is not bounded by the Rhine, the Vistula, and the Danube; and that other countries have a civilization older, or, if newer, yet in some respects better, than their own. Nevertheless, such crude questions and comments upon the United States as one hears in the best circles of Germany do illustrate a prevailing tone, and must conduct to two inferences, — that the reputation of Germans for general knowledge has been strangely overrated; and that American culture should not seek to measure itself by any foreign standard, but should build itself up quietly upon its natural and enduring basis, assimilating from other civilizations what it may find useful for ornament or expansion, but only in subordination to its own broad plan and lofty aims.

The superiority of the United States in many inventions and manufactures, which was so apparent at the Philadelphia Exposition, was gracefully conceded by the correspondents and commissioners of several foreign countries. Most conspicuous among these was Prof.

F. Reuleaux, director of the Royal Gewerbe-Akademie at Berlin, a member of the German Commission and Jury at the Exposition; a gentleman eminently qualified by scientific and practical knowledge, by sobriety of judgment and candor of spirit, for the delicate task of comparing the products of other countries with his own. With marked emphasis Prof. Reuleaux admonishes his countrymen that they have been too much in the habit of undervaluing American industry, which they now find has outstripped that of Germany. He points out that American machinists have brought the steam-engine to its highest perfection, through the combination of beauty of form, and nicety of adaptation, with smoothness of working, and strength and endurance of materials; and that, in tool-serving machines, American ingenuity and skill have outstripped all competition, in new practical ideas, apt adjustment to special ends, precision and harmony of movement, elegance of appearance, and perfection of results. In American steel-ware, surgical instruments, glass manufacture, gas-fixtures, chandeliers, &c., and in gold and silver workmanship and ornamentation, Prof. Reuleaux finds indications of a native skill that may well incite the rivalry of European nations. It is beginning to be understood that Americans can make a watch as well as a sewing-machine, a telescope as well as a revolver. Now, the lesson from all this is, that skilful and tasteful improvements in the industries and comforts of life mark an advancement in the average culture of the people, and may even indicate a higher general culture than is marked by the existence of royal galleries and museums or the art-treasures of the privileged few. The farmer or mechanic who buys some nicer or more convenient article of household furniture, some tasteful knick-knack to adorn his home, shows the spirit of culture, the preference of the æsthetic and the enjoyable to the purely useful; and when the inventive genius of a nation is turned to the improvement of all manufactures in quality, appearance, taste, this is an evidence that the market calls for such elements, because the average culture of the people appreciates them. Germany, which has but little debt, received from France as an indemnity for the war of 1870–71 a thousand million dollars. Since then her taxes have increased, and her industry and manufactures have notoriously deteriorated; yet the conquest of France is constantly adduced as an evidence of the higher culture of the German nation. The United States has a public debt of two thousand million dollars; yet in the past six years that debt has been reduced by more than four hundred millions of dollars, the annual interest by nearly thirty millions, and the taxes by nearly three hundred millions; while, at the same time, American industry and invention have advanced to a position of recognized equality, if not of superiority, in competition with Europe. Is there no token of culture and civilization in these conquests of peace? Prof. Reuleaux discerned the connection of which I have spoken between the general improvement in technic and the spirit of culture in the people. He testifies that the æsthetic consciousness is thoroughly awake in the United States; that cottage life in America has a charm, in the combination of domesticity, comfort, taste, and refinement, which Germany might profitably take as an example. As further evidence of this, he adduces the eagerness with which the best foreign wares were bought up for the industrial museums of Philadelphia, Boston, New York, and other places. In short, the æsthetic consciousness showed itself everywhere, in life, in incitement, and in the zeal to appropriate spiritually all that is already possessed materially.[1]

But, though this inventive type of American progress is getting to be conceded, there are still those who fancy that America has contributed nothing to the scientific progress of the century. On this point, Prof. J. W. Draper, who, so long as he keeps within the domain of the physical sciences, is an unquestioned authority, gives testimony as follows: —

"We may without vanity recall some facts that may relieve us, in a measure, from the weight of this heavy accusation. We have sent out expeditions of exploration both to the Arctic and Antarctic Seas. We have submitted our own coast to a hydrographic and geodesic survey not excelled in exactness and extent by any similar works elsewhere. In the accomplishment of this we have been compelled to solve many physical problems of the greatest delicacy and highest importance, and we have done it successfully. The measuring-rods with which the three great base-lines of Maine, Long Island, Georgia, were determined, and their beautiful mechanical appliances, have exacted the publicly expressed admiration of some of the greatest European philosophers; and the conduct of that survey, their unstinted applause. We have instituted geological surveys of many of our States and much of our Territories, and have been rewarded not merely by manifold local benfits, but also by the higher honor of extending very greatly the boundaries of that noble science. At an enormous annual cost, we have maintained a meteorological signal system, which, I think, is not equalled, and certainly is not surpassed, in the world. Should it be said that selfish interests have been mixed up with some of these undertakings, we may demand whether there was any selfishness in the survey of the Dead Sea. Was there any selfishness in that mission that a citizen of New York sent to equatorial Africa for the finding and relief of Livingstone? any in the astronomical expedition to South America? any in that to the valley of the Amazon? Was there any in the sending out of parties for the observation of the total eclipses of the sun? It was by American astronomers that the true character of his corona was first determined. Was there any in the seven expeditions that were despatched for observing the transit of Venus? Was it not here that the bi-partition of Biela's comet was first detected? here that the eighth satellite of Saturn was discovered? here that the dusky ring of that planet, which had escaped the penetrating eye of Herschel and all the great European astronomers, was first seen? Was it not by an American telescope that the companion of Sirius, the brightest star in the heavens, was revealed, and the mathematical prediction of the cause of his perturbations verified? Was it not by a Yale-college professor that the showers of shooting-stars were first scientifically discussed, on the occasion of the grand American display of that meteoric phenomenon in 1833? Did we not join in the investigations respecting terrestrial magnetism instituted by European governments at the suggestion of Humboldt, and contribute our quota to the results obtained? Did not the Congress of the United States vote a money-grant to carry into effect the invention of the electric telegraph? Does not the published flora of the United States show that something has been done in botany? Have not very important investigations been made here on the induction of magnetism in iron, the effect of magnetic currents on one another, the translation of quality into intensity, and the converse? Was it not here that the radiations of incandescence were first investigated; the connection of increasing temperature

---

[1] Briefe aus Philadelphia, von F. Reuleaux, Prof. Braunschweig, 1877.

with increasing refrangibility shown; the distribution of light, heat, and chemical activity in the solar spectrum ascertained, and some of the fundamental facts in spectrum analysis developed, long before general attention was given to that subject in Europe? Here the first photograph of the moon was taken; here the first of the diffraction spectrums was produced; here the first portraits of the human face were made, — an experiment that has given rise to an important industrial art.

"Of our own special science, — chemistry, — it may truly be affirmed, that nowhere are its most advanced ideas, its new conceptions, better understood, or more eagerly received. But how useless would it be for me to attempt a description in these few moments of what Prof. Silliman, in the work to which I have already referred, found that he could not include on more than a hundred closely-printed pages, though he proposed merely to give the names of American chemists and the titles of their works! It would be equally useless, and, indeed, an invidious task, to offer a selection; but this may be said, that, among the more prominent memoirs, there are many not inferior to the foremost that the chemical literature of Europe can present. How unsatisfactory, then, is this brief statement I have made of what might be justly claimed for American science! Had it been ten times as long, and far more forcibly offered, it would still have fallen short of completeness. I still should have been open to the accusation of not having done justice to the subject."

To this enumeration must be added the repeated efforts of the United-States Government to open a ship-canal between the Atlantic and Pacific Oceans, the explorations and surveys crowned at last by the treaty with Nicaragua, securing a feasible route, and pledging this impartially to the commerce of the world. A new Arctic expedition is also in contemplation, notwithstanding the declaration of the latest English explorers that "the north pole is impracticable."

In the department of physics alone the United States has contributed no mean share to the science of the century. It is enough to mention in acoustics Henry, Leconte, Mayer, Rogers; in heat, Draper, Hare, Rumford, Wells; in optics, Draper, Gibbs, Gould, Rood, Rutherford; in electricity and magnetism, Bache, Gray, Henry, Morse, Page, Rowland.

The widespread zeal for science in America was gracefully recognized by Agassiz in the preface to his great work, "The Natural History of the United States:" "So general is the desire for knowledge, that I expect to see my book read by operatives, by fishermen, by farmers, quite as extensively as by the students in our colleges, or by the learned professions." A fine comment upon this tribute was given in the subscriptions to the Agassiz Memorial Fund, which embraced several hundred names of men, women, and youths, from all classes and occupations of life, and ranged from twenty-five thousand dollars down to fifty cents. The total sum thus given to complete the Museum of Comparative Zoölogy at Cambridge was $260,674, to which the State added a grant of $50,000. Here, too, is an illustration of the American method of endowing science, which Prof. Huxley, in his speech at the meeting of the American Association of Science at Buffalo, complimented in these words: —

"The English universities are the product of the government; yours, of private munificence. That among us is almost unknown. The general notion of an Englishman, when he gets rich, is to found an estate, and benefit his family: the general notion of an American, when fortunate, is to do something for the good of the people, and from which benefits shall continue to flow. The latter is the nobler ambition.

"It is popularly said abroad that you have no antiquities in America. If you talk about the trumpery of three or four thousand years of history, it is true. But in the large sense, as referring to times before man made his momentary appearance, America is the place to study the antiquities of the globe. The reality of the enormous amount of material here has far surpassed my anticipation. I have studied the collection gathered by Prof. Marsh at New Haven. There is none like it in Europe, not only in extent of time covered, but by reason of its bearing on the problem of evolution."

What we need in America to continue to deserve such praise is, first of all, *concentration*, the building-up of a few great universities (half a dozen would be enough for the whole country) as centres of learning; and, next, the *endowment of research*, as is contemplated, for instance, in the fellowships of the Johns Hopkins University at Baltimore.

One branch of American culture too often overlooked is that linguistic training by virtue of which American missionaries have won such renown as translators of the Bible into foreign tongues, and, in repeated instances, as the creators of a written language and literature for barbarous tribes. Not even the famous Indian service of the British Government can compare with the mission service of the leading American societies in linguistic and scientific attainments.

A striking indication of the place of the fine arts in American culture was lately given in the sale of a private picture-gallery in New York. This gallery contained works of the most famous artists of England, France, and Germany; and, in "hard times," there were buyers enough to pay over three hundred thousand dollars for its treasures. In the chief cities of the United States such galleries may now be counted by the score.

But enough. I should be sorry if this note should be perverted by any of my countrymen to a boastful use. In all reason, in the matter of culture, we have yet enough to learn and acquire. But neither self-depreciation nor foreign imitation is the lesson that we need. Our calling is to perfect that culture which is distinctively American, — the culture which springs from and tends to that which is spiritual in man, and which diffuses its refining influence over the whole body of the people.

LECTURE VI.

THE PERILS, DUTIES, AND HOPES OF THE OPENING CENTURY.

IN what I said of culture as the perfecting of society in the noble, the beautiful, the true, the good, through the training of each citizen to the highest exercise of knowledge and virtue, I was placing before you the ideal of a perfect State. If, now, from this platform you challenge me to forecast the actual of American society in the opening century, I can but repeat the answer of Socrates to Glaucon: "You must not insist on my proving that the actual State will in every respect agree with the description of the ideal. . . . But is our theory a worse theory because we are unable to prove the possibility of a city being ordered in the manner described? . . . Until philosophers are kings, or the kings and princes of this world have the spirit and power of philosophy, and political greatness and wisdom meet in one, and those commoner natures who follow either to the exclusion of the other are compelled to stand aside, cities will never cease from ill; no, nor the human race, as I believe; and then only will this our State have a possibility of life, and behold the light of day. This was what I wanted but was afraid to say, my dear Glaucon; for to see that there is no other way either of private or public happiness is indeed a hard thing."[1]

Could any thing be more sad than this lament of a great soul over the impracticability of its own ideal of private and public happiness? It is like the mysterious warning that haunted Mozart, — that the noblest, sweetest harmonies that ever issued from his soul were for the requiem of

[1] Plato, Republic, B. v., Jowett's translation.

his own genius and art. Yet as, in the requiem, there are strains of hope rising out of the very wail of sadness, so may we gather courage and patience from the wisdom of Socrates, when he further says, that having discovered the absolute justice, and set this up as the standard, — as the artist minutely paints an ideal of a perfectly beautiful man, though unable to show that any such man could ever have existed, — so in the State "we may be satisfied with an approximation to the absolute, and the attainment of a higher degree of justice than is to be found in other men."

It is worth remembering that this ideal of a State ordered by intelligence and virtue, ruled by greatness and wisdom joined in one, which Plato put into the mouth of Socrates, is essentially a republic in its constitution, — " a voluntary rule over voluntary subjects,"[1] though vested in the aristocracy of intellect, — a community of equals ruled willingly by the wisest and the best. But the resurrection of democracy in modern times has called out a class of critics who argue that the sovereignty of the people, in its very nature, makes impossible a just, wise, and virtuous State. The latest of this school, Mons. Claudio Jannet, in contrasting the United States of to-day with the United States of Washington's time, ascribes the corruption and decay of the republic to " the false principle of the sovereignty of the people."[2] But his criticism both of the corruption and its cause should be viewed in the light of the remedy that he proposes, — the supremacy of the Roman-Catholic Church, which should repress the quarrelsome sects, do away with the fatal (*funeste*) system of public schools, and put down the impious and revolutionary notions of recent times, — such as the original perfection of humanity, the sovereignty of the people, the native equality of men, and progress indefinite and necessary.[3]

A more friendly and philosophical critic, De Tocqueville, says, " Corruption is the special vice of democracies." But has the Swiss Republic been marked by corruption? Or is Turkey a democracy, the stench of whose corruption now fills all Europe with disgust? Is Austria a democracy,

[1] Jowett, Introduction to the Republic.
[2] Les États Unis Contemporains, par Claudio Jannet, chap. ii.
[3] Ibid., chap. xxv.

whose tribunals have unveiled some of the grossest frauds of modern times? Are Italy and Spain democracies?[1] Or was France a democracy under Napoleon III.? Is Russia a democracy? But, if Mr. Schuyler's revelations were undiplomatic or indiscreet, have they ever been disproved? And who will question the testimony of Koscheleff, late Russian minister of finance?—" Employees formerly purloined and perhaps robbed by the copeck: now-a-days they are too highly civilized to confine themselves to such bagatelles, but feast upon thousands and tens of thousands of roubles, joint-stock company shares, regular salaries from banking-offices, railway companies, &c." Even in Germany, once proverbially honest, has not *Gründer* become a by-word for swindler?[2] And do not Germans contribute

---

[1] In this very year (1876) an Austrian lieutenant of noble birth has been stripped of his title, and condemned to ten years' penal servitude, for having sold military papers of the Vienna war-office to Col. Molostroff, military *attaché* of the Russian embassy at Vienna.

In Italy, a nobleman who pretended to the confidence of the king has been convicted of forging his Majesty's name to the amount of several hundred thousand francs.

There have been no worse scandals than these in the United States. The London Spectator of Oct. 28, 1876, in vindicating Disraeli from the charge of venality in his Eastern policy, said, —

"The Emperor Napoleon no more regulated his policy with a view to his profits than Lord Beaconsfield does; but very great men who knew what his policy would be made very great profits out of their early knowledge. Great officials in Austria did not sell contracts; but great officials in Austria were not ashamed to make money out of their early knowledge of the way in which profitable contracts would be distributed. Great Russians are not paid for their political influence; but great Russians' dependants make, or have made, fortunes out of their knowledge of the way in which influence, often secret and personal, would ultimately be exerted. The public, always shrewd, more especially under a despotism, when 'society' acquires much of the power of observation as well as of the suppleness of a slave, perceives these facts, and, after the manner of gossips, makes every story a little worse, and therefore a little more piquant, than the reality. Because contracts for regimentals are sold, therefore defeat may be purchased from generals in command. Because early information is utilized to procure money, therefore events are arranged in order to yield gain. Because money is made out of statesmen's vacillations, therefore statesmen can be made to vacillate by promises of money."

[2] The name *Gründers* is applied to the originators of a company, who deposit the necessary pledges of money or other securities, and thus procure the legal authorization under which they organize the working corporation. Of late, many such parties have been found guilty of falsifying securities, and of repaying themselves roundly from the treasury of the company for imaginary services of organization. Since the French war, swindles and bubbles have been as abundant in Germany as in the worst times of inflation in the United States. Besides this, the most worthless American "securities" are palmed off by *German* speculators upon their innocent countrymen. Thirty years ago, the late King Frederic William IV. of Prussia felt constrained to issue an order forbidding in his army a form of bogus speculation which some would have us believe is a special vice of democracy: —

"It has come to my knowledge that even officials lately have taken part in the present all-ruling railway speculations, and by signing bonds, and buying certificates

their full quota of frauds upon the New-York custom-house?[1] Let *us* at least be honest, — honest with ourselves, honest toward one another, — and admit that corruption is not a special vice of race or institutions, but a vice common to human nature under opportunity. It is the old plaint of Socrates and Plato about the "human race;" and only when this shall be reformed "will our ideal State have a possibility of life, and behold the light of day." And, my dear Glaucon, the radical trouble is, that human nature refuses to be reformed, but is the one constant factor of evil in society, and we must do with it what best we can.

Rahel Varnhagen, who lived through the eventful experiences of Prussia in the beginning of the century, and whose observation of human nature was remarkably keen, wrote, "We must not exact too much of mankind: they are all in a bad plight; full of inbred wrong; physically distorted and maimed; inheriting a nature which they have not gifts enough to understand, and therefore to use; apart quite from the consideration of the general politico-social deficit. If they do not lie and boast, that is all that can be expected of them: they are always paining as well as misunderstanding each other, because their nature is empty, foolish, and tiresome, ourselves included in the number. We must not, however, overlook our obligation, but see to this carefully." Yet Rahel adds, "The nature of great things, countries, and peoples, is essentially right when left to itself."

Freedom of will, which is the most sublime, is at the same time the most perilous, endowment of human nature. Yet it should not, for that reason, be annihilated or suppressed, but guided by the sense of responsibility to a higher Power. John Adams had the true philosophy, when he wrote to Mrs. Adams, July 3, 1776, "The peo-

and shares in railway projects, have assumed obligations which often are far above their means. As such proceedings show a state of recklessness which is dangerous to the respect in which the rank of officials ought to be held, and which is incompatible with the interest of the state service, I hereby order that such swindling business on the part of officials shall be punished like gambling and debt-contracting according to the law of March 29 of this year. The chiefs of departments are to inform the officials of my determination in the most strictly private manner.
(Signed) "FRIEDERICH WILHELM.
"SANS SOUCI, May 14, 1844."

[1] The adulteration of seeds by mixing quartz ground and dyed is very extensively practised in Germany.

ple will have unbounded power; and the people are extremely addicted to corruption and venality, as well as the great. But I must submit all my hopes and fears to an overruling Providence, in which, unfashionable as the faith may be, I firmly believe." Even the "Positive Philosophy" teaches us that there is in the world a moral order, and that, sooner or later, society shall work out the behests of this invisible Power.

It must, however, be admitted, that a republican form of government affords, in some directions, facilities and temptations to official corruption, not common to the best ordered monarchies of Europe; and also, that in the United States, for a few years past, the revelations of such corruption have been frequent, startling, and humiliating. But, in order fairly to weigh this evil as against the republic, we should ascertain how far it is exceptional, how far exaggerated; what is its proportion to the scale of population; what is the array of popular feeling, and of legal and moral forces, for arresting and subduing it.

That corruption is not the normal state of our body politic, nor the necessary fruit of our free institutions, is shown by the history of the government and of corporations down to the period of the war. Before that, peculation and corruption were on the scale of the copeck. The social demoralization so apt to follow a long war was increased, in our case, by the fact that it was a civil war, by the gigantic and often lavish outlays of the government, and by the creation of a fictitious medium of exchange. Men became accustomed to enormous figures in expenditure and debt; prices went up; speculation was stimulated; and the handling of money that the printing-press could multiply indefinitely, no doubt obfuscated the old-fashioned notions of economy, simplicity, and honest gains. Contemporary European nations have not escaped such demoralizing effects of war; but in the United States they have had larger license, partly because of the very suddenness and novelty of the experience.

Again: this corruption, which is in no small degree an exceptional phase of political society, has been exaggerated, at least in its impression abroad. The good citizen, intent upon reform, exaggerates the evil; the partisan, eager for political change, exaggerates it; the editor, who looks to sensations for his profits, exaggerates it; the stock-jobber, who speculates upon rumors and the public credulity, exaggerates it; and the cynic exaggerates it, whose profession it is to decry every thing, and to improve nothing. Hence one must learn to discount tales of detraction, whether told of individuals or of a people. For instance, since I have lived in Berlin, its foremost preacher has publicly denounced the city as a Sodom that nothing but fire from heaven could purify; and a prominent citizen, after serving as a juryman on criminal cases, affirms that Berlin is indeed a Sodom in beastly vices and crimes. As I would not pretend to be one of the ten exceptionally righteous, had I taken this literally, I should have hasted to flee from this doomed "city of the plain." Three years ago, the foremost orator of Parliament inveighed against stock companies and speculators so roundly, that the Bourse felt called upon to send in a protest to the Reichstag. Yet, after what Prince Bismarck said lately, in the Reichstag, of the lying propensity of the press and of stock-jobbers, whom can we trust? And, to crown all, the Imperial Parliament has twice called attention to the immorality of the city, even to the details of photographs in shop-windows; as though the average country member was scandalized at the sights and doings of the capital, and Berlin was likely to become what every devout German has imagined Paris to be. Against such testimony I dare not maintain that human nature is here above its average in large mixed communities; yet, in all the outward decencies and privileges of civilization, Berlin is a fair average of great capitals, — better than some, if not so good as others. I find it only just to the great bulk of its population, that one should largely discount such sweeping denunciations, whether due to the fervor of piety, the energy of patriotism, or the zeal of reform. And if I refuse to take without qualification the testimony of pulpit, police, and parliament, against the fair fame of their own city, I may be indulged in discounting the wholesale charges of corruption in my native land, exaggerated as these are by the fears and fancies of good men, the unscrupulous detractions of parties, the sensational rumors of newspapers, the tricks of stock-jobbers, and the sneers of cynics. Much as the Senate of the United States has declined in the personal dignity and ability of its members, and the statesmanlike character of its debates and decisions, yet, if I read that the Senate as a body is corrupt, and open to sordid influences, I tell over the names of the men I know there, and say, "This is a lie."

An amusing illustration of the extent to which the cynical spirit will drive even noble minds in depreciating their country and age is found in Mr. Ruskin, in his "Fors Clavigera." Having had some sorry experiences of the tricks of mechanics and trades-people, he vents his indignation in this wise: "It is merely through the quite bestial ignorance of the moral law in which the English bishops have contentedly allowed their flocks to be brought up, that any of the modern English conditions of trade are possible; for the modern English conditions of trade are, so far as I have had any experience of them, simply dishonest." Having charged upon the bench of bishops the fraud of substituting sham ornaments glued upon his bookcases for the solid carving which he had paid for, Mr. Ruskin uses that same unlucky pot of glue to stick upon the English nation his pontifical sentence of major excommunication: "I do verily perceive and admit, in convinced sorrow, that I live in the midst of a nation of thieves and murderers; that everybody round me is trying to rob everybody else, and that not bravely and strongly, but in the most cowardly and loathsome ways of lying trade; that Englishman is now merely another word for blackleg and swindler, and English honor and courtesy changed to the sneaking and the smiles of a whipped peddler, an inarticulate Autolycus, with a steam hurdy-gurdy instead of a voice."[1]

I am not wanting in respect for Mr. Ruskin as a critic in morals as well as in art, and a master of English style; but this oracular entheasm of his in the "Fors" reminds one of Horace's *insanire certa ratione modoque*. If, however, upon the strength of Mr. Ruskin's piety and patriotism, I should take up his notion of English corruption, I

[1] Fors Clavigera, October, 1875.

should do no worse than the Englishman who mistakes the cynical severity of " The Nation "[1] for a sober representation of American society. As it happens, I know England too well to be imposed upon even by so great a name. Setting aside my own countrymen, — who are just now under arraignment, — I have found the English the most honest and straightforward, the most manly and upright, among peoples. This is saying no more, indeed, than that Englishmen were worthy to be our ancestors. The English have their foibles; but, so far as I know, they have but a single vice that can be said to be universal and incurable: this is their drawling, sing-song, slovenly way of speaking our noble mother-tongue. In this their " corruption " is, I fear, hopeless.

John Adams, like all men of vehement moods, had something of Mr. Ruskin's cynical intolerance. In 1776, in the midst of his enthusiasm for independence, some fit of indigestion moved him to write to his wife, " The spirit of venality you mention is the most dreadful and alarming enemy America has to oppose: it is as rapacious and insatiable as the grave. . . . This predominant avarice will ruin America, if she is ever ruined. If God Almighty does not interfere by his grace to control this universal idolatry to the Mammon of unrighteousness, we shall be given up to the chastisements of his judgments. I am ashamed of the age I live in." Whatever the venality was that Adams thus deplored, this could not have been due to republican independence, since that was but just thought of, and was in a deadly struggle for existence. It is more than likely that Adams had in view the venality of British colonists who were willing to sell to the British Government the liberties of America for office or gold. Such avarice might, indeed, have threatened to ruin Ameri-

[1] As a critic of art, literature, science, morals, and affairs, the Nation is a journal of which every American has reason to be proud. Yet I venture to suggest to its conductors, that the excessive use of satire weakens the effect of that instrument of reform; that the habit of treating persons and topics in a serio-comic way cheapens praise and blame alike; and that an extravagant Caudle-style of lecturing misleads foreigners, who cannot see behind the curtain. If the Nation were compelled to spend as much time as I do in explaining its burlesque and satire to the Teutonic mind, and in showing that its political sarcasms are not to be taken as Bible truths, it would either label its articles for the foreign market, or have recourse to plain, straightforward English in self-defence.

ca; but this was not "a vice of democracy." In looking back, we see how morbid and exaggerated were the fears of that incorruptible patriot; and a century hence the American people will look back with a smile upon the evil prophets of to-day, just as Englishmen will laugh at their Cassandras, from Ruskin to Carlyle.

Still the shameful fact remains, that, in American politics, corruption is rife; and one is hardly startled by any new exposure. If, however, we analyze it, we find it chiefly under three forms, and these fairly within reach of remedies: (1) The abuse of official trust for private gains; (2) Combinations to defraud the government of revenue; and (3) Agencies for bribing legislative bodies in the interest of individuals or of corporations. For the last a remedy is already found in a constitutional provision, adopted by many States, against any form of private or special legislation in this category of cases. The second both government and people are now roused to ferret out and punish; and many of the chief conspirators and criminals have already been brought to justice. The unanimity of parties, press, and public, in hunting out the guilty, is a healthy sign: it shows that the corruption festered by the fever-heat of war is sporadic, not endemic; that the disease is of the surface, not in any vital part; and though it seems, of a sudden, to have broken out all over, its area is limited as compared with the whole body politic. The people are largely to blame for the partisan blindness on the one hand, and the neglect of affairs on the other, that have given to rogues the opportunity and the temptation to cheat and steal; but *they* are not rogues and swindlers in their private affairs, nor willing to be ruled by such in public affairs, if they can help it.[1] The suspicion of

[1] A German lawyer, now of Berlin, who spent many years in professional practice in New York, has told me that no American client ever disputed his bill, or failed to pay it; that often the fee was proffered in advance: but in Germany his fees are often disputed, and payment evaded.

A German banker has expressed to me his amazement at the enormous transactions on an American Change, with nothing more binding than the word of mouth, always sacredly kept.

The late Pelatiah Perit, Esq., long president of the New-York Chamber of Commerce, and thoroughly acquainted with the mercantile community, and also with the best foreign society, was accustomed to say that the merchants of New York were among the most honorable and high-minded men in the world.

During the late war, in order to enforce the use of "greenbacks" as a

malfeasance in office is a bar to one's political future that few men of ambition are bold enough to encounter. The seeming excess of political corruption in the United States as compared with some other forms of government lies more in the greater publicity than in the higher ratio.[1] And it should not be forgotten, that, in a popular government, the exposure of evil is a part of the remedy. Ex-

legal tender, the government withdrew the protection of law from contracts made in gold. Nevertheless, the importer was obliged to meet his obligations in gold, and to make contracts upon that basis. Here was an opportunity for rogues to dispute or repudiate a specie contract as having no validity in law; but, though such contracts were made to the extent of hundreds of millions of dollars, there was no attempt to dishonor claims that could not be legally enforced. Mercantile honor was stronger than written law. My authority for this is one of the heaviest importing firms of New York.

[1] The partisan clamor of the past few years, and the notoriety of certain cases of political dishonor, have created the impression abroad, that fraud and corruption are on the increase in American official life, and that the nation is hopelessly corrupt. But the speech of Attorney-Gen. Taft, in New York, Oct. 25, 1876, puts a different face upon the matter:—

"There is a record kept in the treasury department of the United-States Government, in which are entered all the pecuniary transactions,—all the receipts and all the disbursements of the moneys of the government,—and which shows infallibly how much has been lost in the handling, whether by stealing, or corruption, or mistake, or neglect. On the call of the Senate, made in the present year, that record was produced. It shows in general the following facts: that during the administration of Gen. Jackson, which lasted for eight years, the average loss upon every thousand dollars collected and disbursed during that time was $10.55, or about one per cent; that, in the administration of Martin Van Buren, the loss was $21.00 and upward, or a little more than two per cent; that, during all the succeeding Democratic administrations, the losses were approaching $10.00, until we come down to that of James Buchanan, in which the losses upon the receipts and disbursements averaged $6.98 on every thousand dollars. That same record shows that during the first Republican administration, under Mr. Lincoln, the losses upon all the transactions of the government —all the receipts and disbursements—averaged $1.41 on the thousand dollars, in place of $6.98, which represented the losses in the time of Mr. Buchanan; and that loss has been reduced, in the administration of Gen. Grant, to forty cents on the thousand dollars in his first administration, and twenty-six cents on the thousand dollars in the second and current administration, in place of $6.98 under Mr. Buchanan. This record is indisputable, and leaves no more to be said on the subject of corruption in the receipt and disbursements of the funds of the nation. It is an effectual, everlasting refutation of the charge, that the government under Republican administration has been or is honeycombed with corruption. It is probable that the present administration of our government has reduced the losses, the defalcations, and the stealings, to their lowest terms; that the method of doing business, and of recording transactions in books, has been perfected to such a degree, that it is hardly to be expected that greater perfection will hereafter be attained. Twenty-six cents on a thousand dollars in all the transactions of the government is so small a loss, that the best governments in Europe have failed to attain to it."

I read this statement to an officer of the British Government, who himself has to do with large financial transactions. "But," said he, "ought you not to be ashamed of *any* corruption? Stealing should not be a matter of percentage." — "Quite right," my friend; "but let us beware of Pharisaism. You in England abhor official bribery, and breach of trust; but you have just told me facts concerning the social morals of men in your highest posts of judicial honor, which, if they could be told of the Chief Justice of the United States, would compel him to retire from his office within twenty-four hours. Each nation has its own way of airing its conscientiousness, and its own besetting types of depravity."

posure is a disinfectant; and like carbolic acid, though it makes the atmosphere more offensive for a time, is a sign that the sanitary police are doing their duty.

The first form of corruption — the abuse of official trust for private gains — is more difficult to deal with than either of the others: it can often be concealed for long; its success tempts to repetition; and it can sometimes use the machinery of party, and even of the law, as a screen. Far worse than individual cases of defalcation and peculation is that system of rings which has become the scandal of great cities, and, in some instances, of legislative and executive bodies. In great cities, this finds its fatal facility in the basis of suffrage and the largely irresponsible character of the constituency. Commercial, political, and manufacturing capitals attract to themselves the best and the worst elements from the whole country; and, as we have seen by the criminal statistics, the worst elements of the foreign population gravitate to the same centres. These all are voters; and, so long as the city authorities will favor the poor at the expense of the rich, the poor care little how property-holders are robbed by unjust taxation, or cheated by wasteful expenditure. The tendency of well-to-do people to make the city simply a place of business, and fix their homes in some rural suburb, is fast leaving the political control of cities to those who have the least risk in their financial prosperity or their public reputation; and the danger is, that city corruption will go on from bad to worse. Boston has found a remedy in the annexation of the rural homes of its sterling population, thus preserving their right to vote in city affairs. New York is crippled as to such a remedy by its physical conditions; and the spasmodic efforts of leading citizens to rid the city of rings, though for a time successful, do not work a radical cure of the evil. How to secure the wise and good government of great cities is a problem as yet unsolved, perhaps hopeless under democratic institutions with universal suffrage. But why permit a suffrage that enables loafers and ragamuffins to vote away property they had no hand in creating, and have no interest in preserving? What "natural and inalienable" right have the shiftless to administer upon the estates of the thrifty? To preserve their own credit, to retain the really "working-class" of citizens, — the merchants, bankers, manufacturers, mechanics, who create capital by labor of hand and brain, — our cities must provide, that while the civic administration is chosen, as now, by common suffrage, there shall be a distinct board, chosen only by those who have taxable property, whose sanction shall be necessary to any transaction affecting property, and to any levy or appropriation exceeding a given rate. Then every man of property will have a motive to look after his own interests in the election of such a board, and the board cannot hope to elude responsibility by an appeal to a miscellaneous and irresponsible constituency. The interests of property are, in their very nature, "hostages to society" for such municipal regulations in regard to streets, fire, water-supply, police, &c., as will best serve the community at large. Moreover, by this system, women who are independent property-holders can be admitted to vote upon matters in which they have an undoubted concern, without entering upon the debatable ground of woman's suffrage in the field of general politics. This is a very different thing from making property a qualification for suffrage: it simply denies to mere manhood suffrage the right of disposing of property not its own. In some States, special statutes now confine to tax-payers the right of voting money for improvements. For the country at large, as a check upon official corruption, two measures seem indispensable, — to remove the civil service from the caprices of party politics and the chances of mediocrity by making it competitive, and permanent during capability or good behavior; and to pay good salaries, and assure a retiring pension, any malfeasance to be punished with dismissal, fine, or imprisonment, and loss of civil rights; in a word, to reduce the temptations to wrong to a minimum, and raise to the highest point the motives of dignity and honor. At a moment when the diplomatic service requires to be looked after on the point of pecuniary honor, it is the meanest of party frauds to reduce its salaries below the dignity of a gentleman.[1]

[1] When I gave this lecture in London, I paid a compliment to the English nation for its freedom from official corruption and dishonor. Sir George Campbell, M.P., late governor of Bengal, who presided, rose and

Macaulay, who knew what it was to toil for the bare necessaries of life, and who resolutely banished himself from England for five years, that, by his earnings in the Indian service, he might lay up enough for future comfort, wrote frankly to Lord Lansdowne, "Without a competence, it is not very easy for a public man to be honest: it is almost impossible for him to be thought so." We are too apt in America to place public men under temptation by denying them a competence, and then to weaken the salutary fear of public opinion by creating around them an atmosphere of suspicion in advance. This pernicious habit of imputing dishonesty to public men was recently exposed by "The London Spectator" in a philosophical warning by which Americans should profit: —

"The Duc Decazes said openly from his place in the tribune, that it would have been impossible for him or any other minister in France to make such a *coup* as the purchase of the Canal shares, because he would have been suspected by his opponents of making it for his own pecuniary advantage; and his audience laughed an assent. So deeply rooted in Paris is this form of distrust, that it exercises a definite political influence, and sometimes cripples the boldest plans of otherwise resolute men. No assertion of the kind is too wild to receive some credence. There are men in Vienna in reputable positions who will tell you gravely that the defeats of the Austrian army were due to money dexterously employed; and a wild story of an archbishop whom Bismarck bought, and the Emperor ordered to be shot, was related in the writer's presence, without an idea on the speaker's part that he was in the least drawing upon the credulity of

---

said, "The courtesy of the lecturer has rendered us a compliment that we do not deserve. We *have* corruption in this country, enough of it, both political and official. I know it, and you all know it. Here we keep it rather private; but our American cousins wash their dirty linen out of doors, and that is the chief difference between us." Several members of Parliament and other public men were present; but no one dissented from this statement. Soon after, the public was startled by the revelation that an English nobleman, a member of the ministry, had accepted a hundred qualifying shares in consideration of the use of his name as director in a company that turned out to be an enormous swindle. He had done precisely the same thing that had brought such scandal on the American minister, and had precisely the same excuses to offer. A gentleman connected with the government told me that a commission was once sent out to investigate rumors against a diplomatic agent in the East. They found him guilty of almost every crime in the Decalogue; but as he was a putative son of Lord P——, and had friends in high quarters, he was quietly dropped, and the affair hushed up. Such cases furnish no cover for American delinquencies; but they do show that corruption is not special to republics. A few rogues bring great scandal on the country, but the "interviewers" far more. Punch (July 29, 1876), significantly said, "There is still one place where ill-gotten gain *has* a bad smell: that is on the hands of a minister, when once attention has been called to it."

his audience. In Pesth they will tell you stories of contracts, which, if you believed them, would make you believe the high Austrian aristocracy — who, to do them justice, never think about money even when they ought — a gang of peculators; and discontented Magyars will prove to you, if you have the patience, that every leader in Hungary, except Deak, has at some time or other been sold. Muscovites in a gossiping mood explain every thing by crime, and no more believe that an official, however highly placed, can keep his hands clear of pelf, than an Englishman can believe a Jesuit honest, or a Greek free from political guile. Political society is honeycombed with suspicion, till in every capital of Europe, except Berlin, great men are compelled to defend themselves, either by a caution which makes them alike weak and sensitive, or by a cynical callousness which ends in the first cause of tyranny, — contempt for the judgment and the motives of ordinary mankind.[1]

The indiscriminate suspicion of corruption may prove more perilous to the public honor and safety than is actual corruption detected and denounced. Many a public man in the United States might break all the commandments, and yet not be half so vile as his political opponents had pictured him during his candidacy. If "the price of liberty is eternal vigilance," universal suspicion is a premium for tyranny. When all men distrust one another, the first bold usurper will master the whole. Our civil service should be above temptation, and beyond suspicion. Prussia has such a service. The pay, indeed, is not large; but this is graduated to the economical habits of the people. The service is honorable, and brings a certain social consideration: it admits of promotion as a reward of merit, and it insures a pension for the decline of life. Above a certain grade, an official position in Prussia is evidence of a university education, or equivalent scholarly attainments.

"What in the world will you do with these thousands of law-students now in your universities?" I asked a professor. "Oh!" he replied, "very many of them have no thought of making the law their profession; but there is constant need of jurists in all departments of our public service. In the administration of schools, churches, railways, banks, post-offices, customs, consulates, everywhere there must be at hand some one who is well versed in the law; and hence this legal training is an avenue to

---

[1] Spectator, Oct. 28, 1876.

the higher civil service." Now, such a service as this, so admirably planned and so thoroughly disciplined, must be rooted in the constitution of society. We could not hope to reproduce it by a bare act of Congress, or the will of a single administration: the people must set themselves resolutely to build up a sound and stable system for the support of the national life. It is often said, that to require a competitive examination for appointments to the civil service would work injustice to the average citizen by excluding him from the right to hold office, and restricting this to the favored and educated few. Now, I do not dispute the right of any man to be eligible to office: I only maintain that he shall *make* himself eligible; that the people shall refuse to intrust their affairs to any man's ignorance or incompetence; and that no party shall have the opportunity of thrusting ignorance and incompetence into places of public trust for mere political services. Moreover, since in every State education is now so cheap and liberal, it would be no hardship to require that every candidate for the public service shall be educated up to a certain standard. The poor man would thus have before him an object of ambition in training a son for a service that would be also an elevation honorable in itself, and giving a lifelong position and support. To insure the separation of the service from political partisanship, every one accepting a place in the civil service should thenceforth cease to be a voter, and should forfeit place and pension upon taking part in politics.

If the loftiness of the Prussian system would deter us from attempting that, we may take encouragement from the English system, which is a thing of recent growth, and already yields satisfactory results. In 1853 the ministry called upon Parliament to enact " that a nomination for the civil service of India should thenceforward become the reward of industry and ability, instead of being the price of political support, or the appanage of private interest and family connection." Macaulay advocated a system of competitive examination upon the ground that he who has proved diligent and successful in prescribed studies shows the qualities needed for the public service. The proposal, that the governor-general should have the power of appointing, he met as follows: —

"There is something plausible in the proposition that you should allow him to take able men wherever he finds them; but my firm opinion is, that the day on which the civil service of India ceases to be a close service will be the beginning of an age of jobbing, — the most monstrous, the most extensive, and the most perilous system of abuse in the distribution of patronage that we have ever witnessed. Every governor-general would take out with him, or would soon be followed by, a crowd of nephews, first and second cousins, friends, sons of friends, and political hangers-on; while every steamer arriving from the Red Sea would carry to India some adventurer bearing with him testimonials from people of influence in England. The governor-general would have it in his power to distribute residences, seats at the council board, seats at the revenue board, — places of from four thousand pounds to six thousand pounds a year, — upon men without the least acquaintance with the character or habits of the natives, and with only such knowledge of the language as would enable them to call for another bottle of pale ale, or desire their attendant to pull the punka faster. In what way could you put a check on such proceedings? Would you, the House of Commons, control them? Have you been so successful in extirpating nepotism at your own door, and in excluding all abuses from Whitehall and Somerset House, that you should fancy that you could establish purity in countries the situation of which you do not know, and the names of which you cannot pronounce? I believe most fully, that, instead of purity resulting from that arrangement to India, England itself would soon be tainted; and that before long, when a son or brother of some active member of this House went out to Calcutta, carrying with him a letter of recommendation from the prime-minister to the governor-general, that letter would be really a bill of exchange drawn on the revenues of India for value received in **parliamentary support in this House.**

"We are not without experience on this point. We have only to look back to those shameful and lamentable years which followed the first establishment of our power in Bengal. If you turn to any poet, satirist, or essayist of those times, you may see in what manner that system of appointment operated. There was a tradition in Calcutta, that, during Lord Clive's second administration, a man came out with a strong letter of recommendation from one of the ministers. Lord Clive said in his peculiar way, 'Well, chap, how much do you want? Will a hundred thousand pounds do?' The person replied, that he should be delighted, if, by laborious service, he could obtain that competence. Lord Clive at once wrote out an order for the sum, and told the applicant to leave India by the ship he came in, and, once back in England, to remain there. I think that the story is very probable: and I also think that India ought to be grateful for the course which Lord Clive pursued; for, though he pillaged the people of Bengal to enrich this lucky adventurer, yet, if the man had received an appointment, they would have been pillaged and misgoverned as well. Against evils like these there is one security, and, I believe, but one; and that is, that the civil service should be kept close."

A member of the present government, who went to India in 1875 on an official tour of inspection, expressed to me his great satisfaction with the Indian service, in its punctuality, thoroughness, and efficiency, and especially in the absence of any trace of peculation in a country where the temptations are great, and the opportunities easy.

An attempt to apply the same system of competitive examination to the civil service of England was made by the ministry in 1854; but this met with the same sort of opposition in Parliament which the civil-service reform has encountered in Congress. "Very few leading politicians," says Mr. Trevelyan, "had their hearts in the matter. It was one thing for them to deprive the East-India directors of their patronage, and quite another to surrender their own. The outcry of the dispensers and expectants of public employment was loud and fierce; and the advocates of the new system were forced to admit that its hour had not come." That system, however, at last prevailed; and Mr. Trevelyan testifies, that "to this, more than to any other cause, we owe it that our political morality grows purer as our political institutions become more popular, — a system which the most far-seeing of American statesmen already regard with a generous envy."[1] The success of Great Britain in carrying through a reform which thirty years ago was as much needed in England as it now is in the United States, and which triumphed at Westminster over the same obstacles that resist it at Washington, should determine the American people to secure the same.

Meanwhile, unless official corruption is punished as fast as exposed, there is danger that the exposure will so familiarize the public with this form of iniquity, that it shall lose something of its grossness. And, indeed, there are not wanting critics who charge corruption in high places to the prevailing tone of *luxury* among the people. Now, this word "luxury" is one of the most indefinite of terms, its application being graded by circumstances of individuals and of society for which there can be no common measure. You know the story of the pietist who took her Christian sister to account for wearing

[1] Life and Letters of Lord Macaulay, chap. xiii.

feathers in her hat. "But," said the accused, "my feathers are not so costly nor so showy as the flower-garden on your hat." — "Well," retorted the first, "we must draw the line between the church and the world somewhere; and *I* draw it at feathers." Some of our domestic manufacturers denote certain imported articles luxuries, and would have these heavily taxed in order that they may produce and sell the same at a higher rate; as, for instance, Connecticut tobacco for Havana cigars. And, by the new custom-house regulations, every lady who shall take home from Europe more than six pairs of gloves, more than two new dresses (already made and worn), one hat, and one set of jewelry, shall be summarily convicted of seeking to corrupt the country with luxury, and fined accordingly. To pay a thousand dollars for a picture would for me be a bit of extravagance that would justify my friends in sending me to an insane-asylum; but it was no extravagance in my old neighbor — the richest merchant of New York, and a public benefactor — to outbid European noblemen and galleries, and pay seventy-five thousand dollars — which might represent his income for as many days — for a bit of canvas four and a half feet by two and a half, on which Meissonier had painted the battle of Eylau. And here, by the way, we must hold criticism to its proper bounds. The critic who berates us for want of culture; who tell us that the American is only a merchant, and worships the dollar; who, like the architect of the London school board, with such profundity of self-assertion issues his *dictum*, that "America is profoundly ignorant of art,"[1] — this same censor of our sordid tastes shall not be permitted to whisk about and rebuke our luxury, when the American merchant shows the best possible taste in giving his dollars over all competitors to possess the best works of art. After all, does there not lurk in much of this criticism the feeling that a republican citizen has no right to be a cultivated gentleman, and show his culture beside that of nobles and princes? If only a duke had bought the Meissonier, what a noble use of wealth in the patronage of art! For a man to live

---

[1] Mr. E. R. Robson, *Builder*, Oct. 9, 1875.

beyond his means is extravagance: for him to do this knowingly and persistently is criminal. The American people do need a caution against living too fast, — a habit encouraged by the spirit of speculation; but the peril of luxury, like that of sectionalism and party-spirit, the republic has more than once survived. In 1786 Jefferson wrote, "I consider the extravagance which has seized my countrymen as a more baneful evil than Toryism was during the war. Would a missionary appear who would make frugality the basis of his religious system, and go through the land preaching it up as the only road to salvation, I would join his school."[1] His Letters from Paris in 1787 are full of lamentation over the tales of extravagance he heard from America. "From these accounts," he writes, "I look back to the time of the war as a time of happiness and enjoyment, when, amidst the privation of many things not essential to happiness, we could not run in debt, because nobody would trust us; when we practised by necessity the maxim of buying nothing but what we had money in our pockets to pay for, — a maxim which, of all others, lays the broadest foundation for happiness. . . . The eternal and bitter strictures on our conduct which teem in every London paper, and are copied from them into others, fill me with anxiety on this subject."[2] Jefferson was at that time minister plenipotentiary of the Confederation. Franklin, who had preceded him in this capacity from the Colonial Congress, bewailed the growth of luxury even during the war of the Revolution. In 1779 he wrote to John Jay, then president of Congress, "The extravagant luxury of our country in the midst of all its distresses is to me amazing. When the difficulties are so great to find remittances to pay for the arms and ammunition necessary for our defence, I am astonished and vexed to find, upon inquiry, that much the greatest part of the Congress interest-bills came to pay for tea, and a great part of the remainder is ordered to be laid out in gew-gaws and superfluities."

I have already quoted the plaint of John Adams over the spirit of venality in 1776, and have shown that this spirit was not *then* the offspring of republican institu-

---

[1] Works, i. 550.   [2] Ibid., ii. 191, 193, 219; iii. 285.

tions. Forty years later, when Jefferson was still harping on luxury, Adams took a more sober view: "Will you tell me how to prevent riches from becoming the effects of temperance and industry? Will you tell me how to prevent riches from producing luxury?"[1]

In 1784, after peace had been declared, Franklin was again moved to write upon "the growing luxury of the States, which gave so much offence to English travellers, without exception." But his economic philosophy now came to his aid; and he met the question with his unfailing good sense and humor. "I have not yet, indeed, thought of a remedy for luxury: I am not sure, that, in a great State, it is capable of a remedy, nor that the evil is in itself always so great as it is represented. . . . Is not the hope of being one day able to purchase and enjoy luxuries a great spur to labor and industry? . . . The skipper of a shallop employed between Cape May and Philadelphia had done us some small service for which he refused to be paid. My wife, understanding that he had a daughter, sent her a present of a new-fashioned cap. Three years after, this skipper being at my house with an old farmer of Cape May, he mentioned the cap, and how much his daughter had been pleased with it. 'But,' said he, 'it proved a dear cap to our congregation. When my daughter appeared with it at meeting, it was so much admired, that all the girls resolved to get such caps from Philadelphia; and my wife and I computed that the whole could not have cost less than a hundred pounds.' — ' True,' said the farmer; 'but you do not tell all the story. I think the cap was, nevertheless, an advantage to us; for it was the first thing that put our girls upon knitting worsted mittens for sale at Philadelphia, that they might have wherewithal to buy caps and ribbons there; and you know that that industry has continued, and is likely to continue and increase to a much greater value, and answer better purposes.' Upon the whole," adds Franklin, "I was more reconciled to this little piece of luxury, since not only the girls were made happier by having fine caps, but the Philadelphians by the supply of warm mittens."[2]

[1] Letter to Jefferson, 1819; Adams's Works, x. 386.
[2] Life of Franklin, by Bigelow, iii. 274–276.

From all these reminiscences, it is plain that the press, foreign criticism, manners and customs, the principles of political economy, the love of good living, and, to cap the whole, the taste of woman for the newest and the best, or at least as good as her neighbors, are to-day just what they were a century ago; and the country is no more likely to be ruined by luxury now than then.

But there is one luxury the people of the United States cannot afford, though they have begun to indulge in it at the risk of the nation's life: that is, the luxury of a philanthropy, or a political philosophy, or a partisan and demagogic zeal, that makes every man a voter on the attainment of his majority, with no test or question as to his personal fitness for this grave responsibility. How far Jefferson, "the apostle of democracy," was from the notion of universal suffrage, or of suffrage as a natural right, I have shown in the Second Lecture. No such notion found place either in the Declaration of Independence, or in the original Constitution of the United States. The first approach toward universal suffrage was in the Act of Congress of 1790, which provided that any foreigner could be naturalized after a residence of two years. From this advanced position Congress receded in 1795 to a requirement of five years' residence, and in 1798 to fourteen years, but again, in 1802, fixed the period at five years. But, though Congress has power to prescribe the terms of citizenship for foreigners, the conditions of suffrage remain within the prerogative of the individual States; and, though the general qualifications are the same in all, there is considerable diversity upon minor points.

The emancipation of the slaves introduced a new phase into the problem of suffrage. It was foreseen that the Southern States might deny suffrage to the freedmen, and thus hold them without remedy as a subject class, and even oppress them as pariahs having no recognized place in the social system. To provide against this mischief, it was sought to clothe the former slaves with the right of suffrage, that they might defend their liberty by their political action; but, lest the Supreme Court should overrule any attempt to vest in the United States a direct power over suffrage in the States, the Fourteenth Amendment, intended to secure the suffrage to the negro, was framed with a circumlocution that has already proved mischievous. The Fifteenth Amendment is explicit enough: "The right of citizens of the United States to vote shall not be denied or abridged by the United States on account of race, color, or previous condition of servitude." But this does not touch the action of individual States. The Fourteenth Amendment, however, attempts in a back-handed way to influence that action. In the first place, it declares that "all persons born or naturalized in the United States, and subject to the jurisdiction thereof, are citizens of the United States, and of the State in which they reside." Thus far, the article simply places all citizens upon an equality of *civil* rights, with no reference to their *political* status. Then, without declaring that every citizen shall have a vote, the amendment goes on to provide, that "when the right to vote at any election for the choice of electors for President and Vice-President of the United States, representatives in Congress, the executive and judicial officers of a State, or the members of the legislature thereof, is denied to any of the male inhabitants of such State, being twenty-one years of age, and citizens of the United States, or in any way abridged, except for participation in rebellion or other crime, the basis of representation therein shall be reduced in the proportion which the number of such male citizens shall bear to the whole number of male citizens twenty-one years of age in such State." Now, nothing could be farther from a tendency to crime or rebellion than learning to read and write; yet, should a State insist upon this rudimentary education as a condition of suffrage, its representation in Congress must be reduced in the ratio of the number of male adults who cannot read and write to the whole number of male adults in the State.[1] Did ever a people so stultify themselves as did the people of the United States when they adopted the Fourteenth Amendment? For one, as a lifelong opponent of slavery, I protested against this abuse of emancipation, and, as a friend of the negro, refused to join in the

---

[1] In point of fact, Connecticut denies suffrage to those who are "unable to read an article in the Constitution, or any section of the statutes of the State;" and Massachusetts, to those "unable to read the Constitution in the English language, and write their names."

cry for "negro suffrage." *Impartial* suffrage should have been the watchword, — suffrage open to all, upon the same conditions. But if slavery had been what was charged upon it, if its tendency had been to imbrute the slave, to keep him ignorant of things that every child should know, to make him deceitful, dishonest, immoral, then it was absurd to suppose that emancipation could at once transform him into a man worthy to be intrusted with the high interests of political society. And the advocates of the ballot as an educating power overlooked the fact, that, while millions of ignorant creatures are being educated how to use it, they are all the while using it, in the actual government of society, at the greatest peril to its liberties and their own. Had the amendment been made to read, "Or in any way abridged, except for participation in rebellion or other crime, for inability to read and explain the Constitution of the United States in the English tongue, and for entering into an ecclesiastical or other combination against the sovereignty of the State," then the natural and legal rights of all men would have been secured; suffrage would have been a motive to self-improvement, a prize to be won; and we should have been forearmed against the degradation of ignorance in our politics, the attempt to establish foreign nationalities within the pale of United-States citizenship, and the intrigues of sectarians to subject the government to ecclesiastical control. But philanthropy took up the *rôle* of perpetuating the negro as a caste; and republicanism, that of using him as a make-weight in elections.

How this educating process of suffrage has worked in those Southern States where nearly one-third of the population over ten years old cannot read, the past ten years of violence and misrule, of fraud and corruption, wasting the very soil with all that grows and lives upon it, bear melancholy witness. It has been one long saturnalia of barbarism led by demagogism. In opening the polls to the freedman who did not know his A B C, we opened them equally to the European who could not read a line of English, and to the Asiatic who brought with him the castes and superstitions of the Eastern world. Now that our own egregious folly has brought this peril to the republic, the cry of political danger sharpens the appeal to religious and philanthropic zeal to counteract it by education. But this is repairing the timbers of the bridge while the foundations are being swept away by the flood. Either a limitation of suffrage by a strict educational test, or compulsory education in every State; and I see not well how to get the one without the other.

Prof. W. G. Sumner, whose studies in political science entitle his opinions to serious respect, has said, "Reform does not seem to me to lie in restricting the suffrage, or in other arbitrary measures of a revolutionary nature. They are impossible, if they were desirable. Experience is the only teacher whose authority is admitted in this school; and I look to experience to teach us all, that the power of election must be used to select competent men to deal with questions, and not to indirectly decide the questions themselves."[1] But what is there of an "arbitrary" nature in insisting that every man who would vote upon public affairs shall be able to read, so as to inform himself of the principles and aims of parties and candidates? And what could be more "revolutionary," more utterly subversive of the government as established by the fathers, than this letting in the ignorant and irresponsible masses to share in its administration? The "revolution" that would transform Jefferson's ideal government of a "natural aristocracy" chosen by "men of ripe years and sane mind, who either pay or fight for their country," into a mobocracy of ignorance, idleness, bluster, and fraud, — that "revolutionary measure" has already foisted itself into the Constitution under cover of justice to the negro, and protection against rebellion; and all the wisdom and patriotism of the nation are now required to save the Constitution, the government, society itself, from being shattered by this explosive element in the organic law. "I expect," says Prof. Sumner, "that this experience will be very painful; and I expect it very soon." Has, then, the science of politics no higher lesson than the old *laissez-faire* habit, the drifting, do-nothing policy, that waits for some painful experience to rouse us to exertion, and then runs on as listlessly as before? Shall we bring an evil

[1] North-American Review, January, 1876, p. 86.

upon ourselves, and then wait for experience to teach us how evil and bitter it is? Prof. Sumner's plank of selecting "competent men to deal with questions" is good timber to build the bridge after we shall have braced the piers against the furious flood we have let in upon them by the breach we have made in the dam. Either that huge gap of universal suffrage must be stopped, or a choice of compulsory education be built to regulate the flow. How are "competent men" to be selected, unless the voters shall know enough to realize the importance of questions to be dealt with, and the competence of candidates to deal with them? We must look first to the foundation; must raise the voter, either by raising the standard of suffrage, or by creating better material through the compulsory training of the schools.

What we really need is character; but the attempt to set up a moral test for voters, such as honesty or truth, would only lead to hypocrisy in the Church, and to Pharisaism in the State. We are no longer in the Massachusetts Colony of 1639, where, on the day of the public fast, a member of the Boston church was openly admonished by the pastor, in the name of the church, "for selling his wares at excessive rates, to the dishonor of God's name, the offence of the General Court, and the public scandal of the country."[1] Could such discipline be made international, it would cause a squirming, not only among American tradesmen, but among foreign tradesmen that Americans do wot of. But, though the State cannot set up a test of morality, it can fix a standard of knowledge. We cannot know how to read a man's heart; but we can know if *he* can read a book. And, though knowledge does not guarantee all the virtues, crime is so generally associated with ignorance, that we may look hopefully to knowledge as a corrective: hence, for its own preservation, society is bound to insist that every voter shall be in condition for the free and intelligent exercise of his suffrage. We need no further experience to teach us that: we cannot hope for "competent men" as rulers till we practise that.

Some such system as Mr. Hare has recommended for securing the rights of minorities would tend to purify the

[1] Flint's Eccles. History of New England, i. 388.

polls, and would relieve elections of the most dangerous elements of party-strife.[1]

But some one will say, "It is all very well for you, who would be likely to retain a place among voters under any system of classification, to propose a restriction of suffrage; but why should you deny this right of manhood to those who have been less favored in education and position than yourself?" I respect this appeal, and, since it is personal, beg permission to answer it with a fact of personal experience; which is, that, for years after I had attained to majority, I lived in New Haven under a legal disqualification for voting, but never felt this to be a restriction upon my manhood, nor an injustice to me as a citizen. As a public teacher of morals and religion, I had a recognized position in the community: but education and position did not avail one whit toward making me a voter; and I saw the ignorant and the vicious going to the polls to perform a function for which I had not the required fitness. The reason was, that the law of Connecticut at that time required, that, in order to vote, one must be the owner of real estate to a small amount. My salary left me no surplus to invest in such a dignity; and I could not demean myself to do what others about me were doing, — accept a deed of land the day before election, giving a quit-deed to return it the day after. Had the law continued, I should have "died without the sight" of that promised land. Yet I never felt this to be a personal grievance, nor the privation of a right. I must here insist once more, that voting is not a prerogative of anybody's manhood or womanhood; that no human being is born with a natural and inalienable right to go to the polls to vote, or be voted for. My judgment approved of *some* conditions of suffrage for the security of liberty and order, and for good government: the property qualification might not be the most judicious; but any qualification must be unequal and imperfect in its application. If the law of New York should limit the decision of measures affecting property to the owners of real estate, I should not feel myself touched in any right of manhood or of citizenship; for what right or what qualification have I for levying upon the property of

[1] The Election of Representatives, by Thomas Hare.

an Astor, a Stewart, a Vanderbilt? In what respect would my manhood be abridged if I should be required to keep to my library, and leave such men to the care of their ledgers? The merchants, manufacturers, and mechanics of New Haven, who had chosen me to be their teacher, did not rate their manhood above mine because they could vote, and I could not. Moreover, my studies in history and political philosophy had already taught me, that even political power does not reside in place, or in the polls, but in personality; that time advances in the direction of ideas, and that one good idea may have more weight than a thousand votes. A droll illustration of this occurred at that period. One day, during the fierce presidential contest between Mr. Clay and Mr. Polk, I chanced to be returning to New Haven from New York by steamboat, and, to while away time, entered into a friendly discussion of the tariff. A group gathered round; and for some three hours I maintained the cause of free trade against a dozen protectionists. It was but a free-and-easy steamboat talk; yet hardly had I reached home before the town was on fire with the report that I had been making a speech on board the boat that might damage Mr. Clay's prospects in the election. Some influential Whigs of my congregation absented themselves from the next public service, and sundry citizens favored me with remonstrances and admonitions. What a laughable commentary it was upon the power of the ballot, that a beardless youth, who had never cast a vote, could put a lot of politicians into a scare by venting a few ideas! And what donkeys "we the people of the United States" do make of ourselves by our adulation of the ballot-box as the symbol of power! He who holds converse with ideas, who grasps a principle, who states a truth so clearly that they that run may read it, lays hold upon the inner sources of power. He need not concern himself about parties or majorities. Events follow ideas, and time will take care of truth. Such a one may never have office, never be popular, but at last may approve his manhood as the friendly counsellor of statesmen, the unofficial leader of parliaments and peoples.

Bluntschli has well pointed the distinction between political equality and eligibility to office. "It is an advance in true equality, that the modern State opens to all, in like manner, the way to public office, and no longer reserves this to privileged classes. But it is a false equality to appoint by lot the officials, — for whom a thorough preparatory training is an indispensable necessity to good official service, — instead of making the bestowal of office dependent upon examination, capacity, and the selection of the fittest."[1] This wise discrimination he enforces by the vital distinction between the people as a nation, a unified moral person incorporated in a constitution, and a mere conglomerate of all the inhabitants within the boundaries of the State. Offices should exist to serve the body politic, and not to give places to persons or parties as members of the political community. This holds also of voting. Dr. Franklin threw ridicule upon a property qualification for voting by his story of the man admitted to vote as the owner of an ass. The ass dying, the man could not vote in the following year. Query, Did the man vote, or the ass? But "manhood suffrage" really brings asses to the polls in droves. A wiser condition of suffrage is education, since education once acquired becomes an inalienable possession of the man himself.

A system of compulsory education would tend to settle two other questions that now threaten the peace of the country, — that of religion in the schools, and that of race distinctions. Compulsory education should be limited to the plainer elements of knowledge, in reading, writing, arithmetic, geography, history, &c.: these every child under the age of twelve should be obliged to master, whether in the public school, a private school, or by tuition at home, — in the last two cases, the fact to be duly certified. This education the State must insist upon as obligatory upon all its citizens, without exception; and for this it is bound to make provision in schools of its own.[2] The State may add to these, at its discretion,

---

[1] Lehre von Modernen Staat, iii. 55.
[2] For a few years past, a law of compulsory education has been in force in the State of New York. This law provides that every child between the ages of eight and fourteen years shall attend school for fourteen weeks in every year, of which eight weeks must be consecutive; or shall receive equivalent instruction at home. No child can be employed in any labor

schools of a higher grade; but the law of compulsion should end with the elementary training, and leave entirely to parental or other private methods instruction in religion and in foreign tongues.

This last point brings us face to face with the latest aspect of the race-question in the United States. Singularly enough, the most formidable phase of the race-question is not the political *status* of the negroes and the Chinese, as European observers imagine, but the moral and political attitude of a portion of the German immigration. The Irish can be dangerous only through ignorance, which makes them tools of politicians, or through a religious training that makes them tools of priestcraft; and even the small measure of compulsory education that I have insisted on would help to emancipate them from both. They mingle kindly with the native stock; and though still clannish, and fond of a row, they are loyal to the country that has endowed them with manhood, liberty, and comfort.

From the negro and the Chinese society has little to fear, so long as they are let alone, provided always that education up to a certain standard be made a condition of suffrage. The negroes are a docile race, prone to indolence, good-natured, easily contented, and, though addicted to petty vices, not likely to array themselves in open hostility to the laws or to their neighbors. Their behavior

---

or business so as to conflict with this requirement, under a penalty of fifty dollars on the employer.

The trustee of every school-district, or the corresponding official, is to make a semi-annual visitation of all manufacturing establishments where children are employed, to see that the law is obeyed. Penalties are affixed for violation of the law by parents or guardians. School-books are to be provided at the public expense in case of necessity. In case of obstinate refusal of a child to attend school, he is to be regarded as a truant; and the trustees or school-board of each town are to make arrangements for the confinement and discipline of truants as may be necessary. The following cogent arguments secured the passage of this law. The report of the committee demonstrated from an analysis of the last census, *first*, that, on the average, in this country illiterate persons furnish ten times the number of paupers that they would if given such an education as our free schools offer gratis; *secondly*, that, in the State of New York, we have one hundred and eighty-nine thousand adults who cannot read and write, of whom seventy-three thousand are males, and hence are or may be voters; *thirdly*, that this State expends twelve millions of dollars a year upon free schools, thus providing a good elementary education for every one of the million and a half of school-children in the State free of cost; *fourthly*, that one-third of the children of the school-age are on the average each year kept out of school altogether.

during the war, their patience, and faith in the hope of emancipation, and their self-restraint amid temptations to plunder and massacre, should satisfy their former masters that they have nothing to fear from the negroes, if they will but let them alone in the enjoyment of their liberties and rights; or rather if outside politicians and party tricksters will leave both whites and blacks at the South alone to adjust themselves to their new relations with time and experience. Of themselves, the negroes would hardly organize a race party; and, though led into this error by bad advice and bad example, their native sagacity is teaching them to break the line of color in politics, in order that the best of the blacks may join the best of the whites in saving society from the worst of both races. Time is here the best reconciler.

How far the present apparent conflict of races in the South is due to the mistaken policy upon which the war was conducted, and peace concluded, I have shown in a preceding Lecture. The Rebellion was not a revolt of the Southern people: it was an organic attempt on the part of *States* to break up the Union by secession. The State organizations were put in motion to destroy the government to which they owed their existence: hence they forfeited all recognition as States. They were not States outside of the Union; neither were they States within the Union as integral members to be conquered back to their allegiance: the States as political entities had lapsed by their own suicidal act; and there remained only a territory *under* the Union, and a population to be made obedient to its laws. Slavery, being the mere creature of State law, perished in the self-annihilation of the State.[1] It was then open to the government of the United States to erect the pacified Southern Territories into States as one by one they should renounce the dogma of secession, establish a republican form of government, make all men equal before the law, and open suffrage to all upon the same conditions. By the salutary working of human nature seeking its own interests, some States would have been constituted and

---

[1] See my address of June 20, 1861, in the Independent of July 11; also my discourse on Abraham Lincoln, April 30, 1865 (Loyal Publication Society).

admitted to the Union sooner than others, thus forestalling the danger of "a solid South." And just as political parties in the North have bidden for the Irish vote, the German vote, the working-man's vote, so parties in the South would have courted the negro vote, thus merging the "conflict of races" in their own conflict of political interests. But the erroneous theory of dealing with seceded States having been adopted at the outbreak of the Rebellion, common sense and human nature were lost sight of in the rigmarole of "reconstruction." For one, I am not in the least disappointed in the consequences of making the negro a specialty of politics and philanthropy, instead of treating him simply as a man, to be aided and protected just as other men, neither more nor less. Having fought for twenty years for the emancipation of the slave, — when to care for the negro was to risk what most men prize in life, — the moment the slave was made a freeman before the law, I felt bound in his interest as a man, no less than in the interest of society and the State, to protest against coddling the freedman as "the ward of the nation." Directly after the war, a worthy black man applied to me for aid in starting a special theological school for black men in Ohio. I declined. With much surprise he said, "I was sent to you, sir, as a strong friend of my race." — "Exactly so; and it is as a friend of your race that I decline to aid a project, which, now that you are free, would stamp you as a separate caste. In times of obloquy I did what I could to aid Oberlin College, because there the black man was treated as the equal of the white in all opportunities for study and improvement; and now you ask me to turn my back on Oberlin, which has fought your battle, and help you start a rival *caste* college near by in Ohio. I shall do no such thing. In any community where as yet you have no opportunity for equal education, I will help your schools and churches on the ground that they are needed and are poor, but not on the plea that they are *black*. If your race would rise, you must at once begin to act as men, and not expect to be either pitied or petted as negroes." My applicant was sorely puzzled at the discovery, that though it were worth the blood and treasure of the nation to redeem the slave because he was a man, yet, on becoming a freeman, he was *only* a man, and must not look for exceptional favors " on account of race, color, or previous condition of servitude." Some time after, I was much gratified at seeing this wholesome and needed truth put forth with his accustomed manliness and vigor by that noble and eloquent champion of freedom and equality, Mr. Frederick Douglass. In a Fourth-of-July address at Hillsdale, Mr. Douglass said to and for his race, —

"All we ask is a fair field to work in, and the white man to leave us alone. We have been injured more than we have been helped by men who have professed to be our friends. Fellow-citizens, we must stop these men from begging for us. They misrepresent us, and cause the country to look upon us as a poor and helpless people. They say, 'Please give something to help to educate the poor black people; but do, I pray, pay it to me:' and, if it is a hundred dollars, it is reduced to about a hundred cents when it gets to the 'poor black people.' We do not want, we will not have, these second-rate men begging for us. We protest against it."

Smarting under the experience of the Freedman's Savings Bank, as one of the guardians of "the wards of the nation," Mr. Douglass said, "We propose to cut loose from all invidious class institutions, and to part company with all those wandering mendicants who have followed us simply for paltry gain. We now bid an affectionate farewell to all these plunderers; and in the future, if we need a Moses, we will find him in our own tribes."

These are brave words, and sensible as plucky. The whole negro problem in the South would be solved by the formula, "A fair field to work in, and the white man to leave us alone." We cannot recover in a day the ground lost by the mistaken theory of the war and of reconstruction; but the case is by no means hopeless, nor so formidable as some imagine. In a paper on "The Question of Races in the United States," read before the Association for the Promotion of Social Science at its session in Glasgow, October, 1874, I ventured to say, "If the political element of the problem could be withdrawn, the so-called conflict of races would be greatly modified, if, indeed, it would not wholly cease. The present commotion in the South, though marked by the formation of the 'white man's league,' is to be ascribed more to political misrule than to prejudice of race." Since then, the experiences of the presidential election have fully confirmed this opinion. No former slaveholder had any objection to the negro's voting on the ground that he was a *negro*. The negro who presented himself at the polls for the avowed purpose of voting the Democratic ticket encountered no prejudice of race, and needed no United-States troops to protect him in the exercise of his suffrage. Had the Southern States been re-organized upon the basis of impartial suffrage, — that is, suffrage upon local conditions fairly within the reach of all, instead of indiscriminate universal suffrage enforced from without, — the native whites of the South would have been divided into rival parties, each bidding for the negro vote, and each caring that the negro should have a vote. But the just-emancipated slaves, in all their ignorance and incompetence, were thrown upon the South *en masse* as voters and rulers. To the whites of the South, defeated in war, impoverished, and in some cases disfranchised, these black voters and rulers represented the power that had conquered them, and the party that sought again to conquer them in the field of politics. Here was a chronic cause of distrust and disturbance; and can any wonder at what has followed? Careful and candid observers, such as Mr. Charles Nordhoff and Mr. Watson (of "The London Times"), testify, that, wherever society is left to its normal conditions, industry and comfort are advancing in the South; and that whites and blacks live amicably together, unless disturbed by attempts from without to direct the political action of the negroes as a class. Through all the excitements of the late presidential election, the South attested its loyalty to the Union, and its aversion to another civil war. There can be little doubt, that, if the South is left to itself, the "conflict of races" will gradually die out; that justice and confidence will gain with time. If, unhappily, there should arise a conflict of arms between the whites and blacks in any State, is there any resource under our political system but either to localize the conflict, and leave the parties to fight it out, or, on the ground of anarchy, to declare the State dissolved, and govern it as a Territory by the military power of the nation? But such an alternative is not likely to be presented, and is sure to be averted by two simple rules:[1] —

1. Let the General Government refrain from all further legislation or interference on behalf of the negro as such. If riots arise that the State authorities cannot quell, the National Government, duly invoked, should interfere, to preserve the public peace; and also, if necessary, it should use the arm of power to sustain the courts in putting down injustice, outrage, and wrong, by the arm of the law. But all this without making a point of caring for the negro in distinction from any other man; for the best way of caring for the negro is to cease to know him as a negro, and to treat him always and only as a man. Above all should the government refrain from legislating upon social customs, instincts, or prejudices. A legal injustice can be done away by law; a moral wrong, in the form of overt action, can be dealt with by law: but a taste, a sentiment, a feeling, an instinct, a prejudice, — these pass the bounds of all legislation; and the attempt to rectify or regulate these by law serves only to irritate opposition. At these points human nature has much in common with the porcupine.

2. The black race should be taught that they are to depend upon themselves. Having freedom, schools, the rights of citizens guaranteed by the law, and the inducement to self-culture presented by opportunities of political action, they should be made to feel that their future is in their own hands; that, if they would rise to a position of respect and of responsibility as men, they must show themselves to be men. There is no other way for any race. If they cannot do this, they must go under. If they will not do this, they ought to go under. But no one who knows the negro race in America can doubt, that with time upon their side, and patience and justice toward them on the part of others, they will rise to the full measure of their opportunities, and, with their capacity for work, their docility, their kindliness, their adaptivity, their mirthfulness, their religious faith, will form as good a part as any in the social sytsem of the future. Time,

---

[1] See paper, read at Glasgow, on the Question of Races.

patience, justice, will cause the friction of races to disappear in the working of the American system of harmonized humanity.

The Chinese, as yet, show little inclination to become naturalized as American citizens. Industrious, thrifty, clannish, they use America as a mine of gold to be worked for accumulations to be spent in that Celestial Empire where gold still passes current. If let alone, they are not likely to make war upon a society that opens to them so many avenues to industry and wealth. If they bring with them vices, the vicious must be dealt with as law-breakers, not as Chinese. If they would practise immoralities in the name of religion, I will show presently how we should deal with these. But, as a race, they seem to exhibit no elements of danger that will not be overcome by education and usage.

So far as there is any race difficulty with the negroes and the Chinese, it does not originate with them, nor lie in their race qualities, but is created usually by the whites; and, leaving prejudice out of view, it has more to do with labor and politics than with color or nationality. For prejudice there is no remedy, save in the growth of Christian magnanimity over unreasoning instinct. The Jew is no longer locked up at night in his quarter in the Christian capitals of Europe, nor burnt for his gold; but who will quite trust the Turk to keep faith with his Christian subjects? What means the constant appendage to London advertisements for servants, — "No Irish need apply"? Such antipathies come and go with change of times; and there is no remedy for them in laws or in philosophy. But race antipathies are appealed to in America to create political capital among the working-classes. Working-men hate competition in wages and skill, whether this arises from their own associates or from intruding foreigners. Trades-unions attempt to monopolize labor, and to deter any from working except upon their terms. Each class treads down that next beneath it. Hence, when Chinamen began to crowd into the labor-market of California, and, by living cheaply and working skilfully, to crowd upon the Germans and Irish already there, these resented this competition of labor by antipathies of race; and the stump politician was at hand to catch "the working-man's vote" by promising to prohibit Chinese immigration. He had been ready enough to have a small game with Ah Sin, and to pluck him with a "right bower;" but, finding that "bland and childlike" party could cover him with his sleeve, he at once rose to explain: —

"Then I looked up at Nye,
 And he gazed upon me;
And he rose with a sigh,
 And said, 'Can this be?
We are ruined by Chinese cheap labor:'
 And he went for that heathen Chinee."

Bret Harte's ridicule caused a sudden collapse in the anti-Chinese fanaticism of the hour. This, however, has since been revived with greater malignity and in more formidable proportions. The motive is given in the fact that more than fifty per cent of the voters in California are of foreign birth, chiefly Irish and German laborers; and thus the lower classes of European society come into competition with the lower classes of Asiatic society for the means of subsistence. If the Chinese were voters, some political party would begin to use them as an offset to the Irish and Germans, who now intimidate politicians into the policy of proscription. Yet what friend of free institutions would recommend the admission of these raw pagans to the polls? Cheap labor is not the sole condition of even material prosperity. The sense of justice will finally prevail; and, in all cases where the prejudice of race is used for a political game with labor, it needs only that law and public sentiment should protect every man in his right to earn his living; and the laws of trade will soon settle the *status* of competing races.

Quite different, however, and far more serious, are the difficulties created by a portion of the German immigration in the United States. These bad representatives of a good race would use their very training in knowledge, and their newly-acquired experience of freedom, to pervert the nationality of the American people, and overturn the foundations of morality and order on which their freedom rests. For the first, they demand, as a right of their nationality and their numbers, that the German language be taught in the public schools, and provision made for teaching their own children all knowledge through the medium of the German tongue. If the demand were on the part of American parents that their children should be taught German as an accomplishment to the same extent that English and French are taught in public schools in Germany, this would be merely a question of expediency as to the form and extent of common-school training. But this is a demand of naturalized foreigners that the State shall assist them in bringing up their children as Germans, with all the fond associations of nationality that cluster about one's mother-tongue, with the feeling that Germany is their real fatherland, and America only their business factory; in a word, that the State shall make provision for perpetuating a distinct German nationality within the American Republic. The demand is presumptuous, disloyal, suicidal, such as no State could admit for a moment. Presumptuous; for what is Germany now doing, what must she do, in the provinces of Posen and Elsass, if she would there have loyal subjects in the next generation? She is compelling every child to learn German, and every official to speak and write German. In Strasburg she has even painted out the liquid French names of the streets, and substituted her own jaw-breaking gutturals. This is sound policy. If you would build up a nation loyal and true, you must begin at the foundation, and "out of the mouth of babes and sucklings must ordain strength, because of its enemies, and to still the enemy and the avenger." While the German nation is thus compelling all its members to be of one speech, is it not a pretty impertinence for Germans in the United States to demand that theirs shall be the language of the schools? As a specimen of this impertinence, take the following resolve of a meeting of Germans at Cooper Institute, New York: —

"*Whereas* the German language is the natural idiom of a large portion of the population of the United States of America and of this metropolis, thus offering such additional practical advantages as would best recommend that language for adoption as a regular branch of instruction in our public schools, —

"*Resolved*, That we, as citizens and tax-payers, most solemnly protest against any measures looking to the exclusion or curtailment of instruction in German in such of our schools where this study has already been established as a regular branch of instruction."

Could there be a greater peril to national unity and liberty than this scheme of fostering and perpetuating within the State a brood of children alien in tongue, in name, and in moral allegiance? This is disloyal also. In being naturalized, the foreigner swears "to renounce and abjure all allegiance and fidelity to every foreign prince, potentate, state, and sovereignty whatever," and particularly to that of which he was born a subject. He should therefore in good faith identify himself with the interests of his adopted country as his own. As a man of honor, he cannot take this oath with mental reservations, nor hold a divided allegiance. In the event of war with Germany, non-naturalized Germans residing in the United States should be protected in person and property while remaining neutral; but the naturalized German must fight for America, or quit. No other rule is admissible. Now, the children of the naturalized citizen are native-born Americans; and it is the duty of the father to train them up in allegiance to American institutions. This used to be done when Germany was a country to run away from, and America a country for a refuge and a home; but, now that Germany is a very good country to come back to with the spoils of American trade, there is a class of naturalized Germans who would bring up their children with Germany in view as their home, using their American citizenship only as a protection against military service, — a speculation in disloyalty that both nations should frown upon.

Further: the policy of using the public schools for training the children of foreigners to perpetuate a foreign speech as a symbol and bond of foreign nationality would be suicidal. If done for the Germans, this must be done by and by for the Chinese; for the Mexicans who may join us; for the Icelanders, if they shall emigrate to their newly-found paradise of Alaska: in short, Americans must cease to be an harmonious, unified people, and degenerate into such a rabble of quarrelling tongues and nationalities as one finds in Turkey.[1]

Not content with thus attempting to pervert our nationality, there are radical and fanatical Germans who seek to overturn the very foundations upon which our freedom rests. They make war upon the Sunday observances, the religious faith, the moral usages, of the people, and aim at a libertinism of thought and action, in these particulars, worthy of the days of the French Revolution. The honored professors and pastors who went over from Germany to the Evangelical Alliance in New York brought back with one accord the lament, that, while the entire American press of the city reported the conference with favor or respect, there were German newspapers that sneered at the body, and blasphemed its work; and that a class of Germans was foremost in demoralizing the nation by outraging its religious sentiment and observances. This was the testimony of German witnesses.[2]

On this point I must speak plainly, perhaps strongly; but I am sure I shall be sustained by high-minded, sober-minded Germans both in Germany and in America. You may not like some of our customs: we do not like some of yours. You think you could improve our civilization: we return the compliment most heartily, and should be glad to improve yours. But you do not wish an Americanized Germany; neither do we wish a Germanized America. When we point you, for instance, to our free church and free powers, you answer, "This may do very well for you; but we are a very different people, and our development must proceed from our historical back-ground." Very

---

[1] The Board of Education in Detroit has put this point very forcibly:—

"As a nation, we should not, for our own preservation, teach any language but the English. To do otherwise would be to establish and encourage communities, which would be no more nor less than colonial dependencies of foreign countries; which every sagacious man must see would be detrimental to our best national interests. If we do it for one nationality because of the numbers, wealth, or influence, then we must do the same for others, no difference what their origin may be. If the Chinese or Japanese should come over to this country in vast numbers (a thing not improbable), then it may be just as important for us to teach or use their respective languages. It will at once be conceded that such a policy would be national suicide."

[2] See Deutsches Leben in Nord-Amerika, von H. Krummacher; and the speech of Prof. Dr. Dorner before the Evangelical Alliance of Berlin. The National Zeitung of Berlin boasted that the German press in the United States had made an energetic protest against closing the Centennial Exhibition on Sundays.

true: and we, also, are a different people; and our development must cling to its historical root, which is morality and religion. Severed from that, we perish.

Now, there is a higher issue at stake than the inner development of Germany and of the United States; namely, that for which both nations are worth developing, the influence upon the future of mankind of two great free peoples conserving under different forms the essentials, without which no human society can endure, — religion, law, liberty, order, culture. And, for this influence on our part, it is necessary, that, in respect of religious practices and moral customs, America should not be Germanized. No people can be governed without the sense of a supreme authority vested somewhere. Where the government rests in the collective will of the people, the sense of authority is secured in the subjection of the individual will to conscience, to the feeling of moral obligation; in one word, to duty and to God. The Bible, the Church, the Sunday, and the social usages that have grown out of these, have nurtured in the American people that public conscience that gives sanctity to law, and, in the end, gives victory to right. Take away that conscience, demolish the institutions that nourish it, break down the barriers that protect it, and you leave government and society to the license of individual, irresponsible wills. That is anarchy; and the road out of anarchy is military despotism. Hence the Germans in America who are seeking to free society from all restraints of law, custom, religion, are preparing to subject it to the severest of all restraints, — that of a despot usurping the name of order. I appeal to the sober sense of Germans, I appeal to the instinct of self-preservation in Americans, against the fanaticism that would destroy the tried and proved foundations of our national freedom, and put in their stead the crude theories of the European democracy of 1848. I repeat it, the strength of a republic lies in character; but there is no character without morality, and, for the average man, no morality without responsibility to a higher Power.

Let me not be misunderstood. The doctrines and purposes imputed to the Native-American party I utterly detest. Never would I consent to make race or religion a barrier to the privileges and honors of citizenship in the American Union. What I am here insisting upon has not the remotest affinity with the demands of Nativism. Every man has the right to expatriate himself. The foreigner who prefers to retain his nationality, and his allegiance to his native land, is entitled to the protection of the laws of the country in which he lives, or of treaty stipulations between that country and his own, so long as he does nothing contrary to the laws; but if he voluntarily renounces his allegiance to his own country, and makes himself a citizen of another, then he is bound to identify himself fully with the country of his adoption, and give to this his sole and unreserved allegiance. To use his vote, his office, the political opportunities of his new citizenship, to further the interests of the nationality he had sworn to renounce, would be an act both of perjury and of treachery. The man who could be guilty of this is not deserving of citizenship in any country. The point I here insist upon is as really for the interest of Germany as of the United States, and is indispensable to the honor and respectability of Germans in the United States: it is simply that the German is perfectly free to live in the United States as a German, keeping his heart and hopes in his fatherland, and refusing to be Americanized. But if he chooses to become an American citizen, then, in every thing that concerns the State, he must cease to think, feel, act, as a German, and be simply and wholly American.

In the course of these Lectures I have felt bound to allude impartially to some of the less pleasing incidents of German character and life; but the whole tone of the Lectures testifies to my high regard for the German people, which, indeed, circumstances have made a matter of public record in Germany, England, and the United States. Intelligent and candid Germans will see that I am none the less zealous for the good name of Germany in this view of citizenship. Let Germans come to America by the thousands; let them stay as Germans if they will, keeping their language and customs, but subject to the laws: but, if they would be naturalized, they must be American, and nothing else, never planning or acting as

Germans in public affairs, nor seeking to pervert the nation from its good old ways.[1]

As to those who would use their American citizenship to cover a fraud upon both countries, I would say to them, as a shopkeeper in Berlin said to an Englishman who used his shop as a lounging-place, without buying, "I say, next time you comes inside, petter you stays outside,"— "Next time you emigrates, petter you stays at home!"

Here opens before us the wider question of the possibility of a religious conflict in the United States,— a conflict springing, from one side, out of the attempt to practise immoralities in the name of religion, and, from the other, the attempt, in the name of conscience, to subjugate civil government to ecclesiastical control. In dealing with the social and political questions raised by Mormonism, Free-Lovism, and Ultramontanism, we must take our stand upon the absolute freedom of religion and the absolute inviolability of conscience. These principles we ourselves would never part with; but they are not worth holding for ourselves, unless we are equally ready to maintain them for all others. Religious freedom for ourselves, as against others, is not a principle, but a pretence and a presumption. Freedom of conscience for ourselves, as against others, is not virtue nor faith, but bigotry and proscription. Never, under whatever provocation of danger or fear, never let the United States swerve one iota from the broad principle they were the first among nations to maintain,— that "all men are equally entitled to the free exercise of religion."[2]

---

[1] I have a great regard for Mr. Carl Schurz. Now, it was made a point in the late presidential election, that Mr. Schurz could influence the German vote; that the German vote would be so and so. But what have we to do with a *German* vote? Is the naturalized citizen a German, or an American? If he purposes to vote as a German, he should not be suffered to vote at all. The United-States consul at Frankfort very properly refused to receive from Germans an address reflecting upon their own government. Hereupon the Germans in the United States went into a paroxysm of indignation. But what business was this of theirs? What have German *voters* in the United States to do with politics in Germany?

[2] The separation of Church and State, and the absolute freedom of religion, distinguish the United States from even the most advanced nations of Europe. In England, the spirit of toleration gives a large degree of religious freedom; but the State church remains to overshadow the dissenting sects. In Prussia, the equality of confessions (that is, of the Catholic and Protestant communions) has been long maintained; and, of late, a larger liberty of dissent from the privileged churches has been allowed by law.

But we cannot allow religion to be a cover for vice, conscience a pretext for conspiracy. Religion and conscience as ruling within the soul of man are one thing: religion and conscience as acting in society are quite another thing. Many questions and actions that are assumed to lie within the domain of religion and conscience lie equally within the domain of civil society; and society has a right to decide these for itself, in view of its own security, peace, and welfare, without asking counsel of men's faith, or taking note of their consciences. Nay, in such matters, society is bound to have a conscience of its own; and that moral person called the State must ascertain and obey the law of right, even against the so-called *dicta* of religion.

The Mormon makes polygamy a part of his religion: the Christian State makes polygamy a crime. Is it, then, a violation of religious freedom, or of the rights of conscience, if the State sends a Mormon to the penitentiary for bigamy? By what right does the State interfere in a social relation which is set up in the name of an express revelation from God? The answer is plain.

The family, in some form, is the necessary unit of civil society. A community organized of individuals as separate units would be an army, not a civil society, nor properly a State. By the law of nature, no new individual can be produced as a member of society save through wedlock, — at least in its lowest form of pairing or coition; and, since civil society has a vital interest in the production of its future constituents, it has a right to concern

---

But, in the United States, religion stands on the basis of absolute freedom. One of the earliest champions of religious liberty was Roger Williams. Dr. J. Hammond Trumbull of Hartford has lately discovered a tract of Williams's, published in London in 1652, in which he contends for "soul-freedom as of mighty consequence to this nation."

The four proposals in support of which it was written are, in substance, for liberty of preaching without license from magistrates, for leaving to God the punishment of false teachers and heretics, for the denial of jurisdiction in spirituals to the civil power, and for permission to the Jews to live freely and peaceably in England. The argument is clearly and forcibly presented, and in literary merit the tract is unsurpassed by any work of its author. There was no subject on which Roger Williams so well loved to speak, or could so well, as on "soul-freedom." "Oh that it would please the Father of spirits," he says, "to affect the heart of the Parliament with such a merciful sense of the soul-bars and yokes which our fathers have laid upon the neck of this nation, and at last to proclaim a true and absolute soul-freedom to all the people of the land impartially!"

itself with the modes, conditions, and antecedents of that production, — in other words, with the family, which is at once the germ and the unitary form of its own life. This necessary supervision of the constituents of its own continuous being, modern society secures by demanding in the parental relation certainty and publicity, in order that responsibility may be fixed for the production of offspring, and for their training and support. At this primal source of its own life, the parental function, society must defend itself against such license, abuse, or irresponsibility, as might entail disorder, corruption, and even disorganization, upon the civil community or state. This obvious rule of self-protection in civil society empowers it to deal with any immorality that may be set up under the shield of religion.

The danger of ultramontane aggression we share with all Christian peoples, since the Vatican has committed itself to open warfare upon modern society. We cannot look to any European nation for a satisfactory solution of this conflict. Each nation must meet it in its own way. The German method cannot be ours; but assuredly a republic possesses every right of self-protection that belongs to any government. That is no government which cannot defend itself and society against all who conspire for its overthrow. The Vatican Council has organized the Romish hierarchy into a conspiracy against the freedom and the sovereignty of civil society. In the United States we have nothing to apprehend from the spread of Roman Catholicism as a faith, nor from the increase of the Roman-Catholic Church. As a faith, as a church, let Romanism spread and grow as it may. It shall be defended in every right of worship, of conscience, of propagandism; and it *must* be defended in these, or our religious liberty is gone. If it has errors, let truth dispute them; if it has superstitions, let light scatter them. Against these, freedom is our defence. The century shows us that Romanism has not gained relatively in its hold upon the American people. The prophecy so often heard in Europe, that we shall be swallowed up by Catholicism, is but another illustration how the sea breeds monsters to those who know it only by the story of Sindbad the sailor. There is always a sea-serpent to be seen by those who very much wish to see one, and keep a constant lookout through colored glasses. As compared with itself, the Roman-Catholic Church has increased sensibly and largely in the last two decades; but the ratio of its increase to other religious bodies and to the population is by no means so great. Here are the figures: —

		1850.	1870.
Parishes,	R. C.,	1,222.	4,127.
"	All others,	36,839.	68,332.
Sittings,	R. C.,	667,863.	1,990,514.
"	All others,	13,566,952.	19,674,548.
Church	Property, R. C.,	$9,256,758.	$60,985,566.
"	All others,	$78,072,043.	$293,498,015.

In percentage, the gain of the Roman-Catholic body upon itself runs higher than the gain of other bodies upon themselves; but percentage is of course higher where the figures are low. As to numbers, the increase of the Roman Catholics runs parallel with immigration, which has now reached its maximum; and as to property, theirs is largely in great cities, where property reached fanciful prices during the war. A map given in connection with the last census shows how narrow is the belt of Roman-Catholic influence over the whole population above ten years of age. As a church, the Roman-Catholic is not gaining upon the body of the American people; and, if it were, let it do so by all lawful means. America wants no anti-Popery crusade, no Protestant war-cry, above all, no secret organization, to counteract the Jesuits by imitating their odious practice of mining in the dark. Light, air, an open field, fair play, — this is all that should be asked or granted in a contest of faiths or religions. If Protestants should seek for more, they would be enemies of religious liberty. But on the political side the Romish *hierarchy* require to be watched, and summarily checked in any attempt to pervert the government of the country, or any of its institutions, to ecclesiastical control. The decrees of the Vatican Council, and especially the definition of Papal infallibility thenceforth made obligatory as an article of faith, have clothed the Pope with a power more absolute than any of his predecessors ever had within the church, and given him an enginery more potent than the armies and allies of his predecessors against the movements of free society. Vaticanism has practically Jesuitized the entire Romish hierarchy by subjecting its every member to the personal will of the Pope, beyond intervention of prince or council. That hierarchy is now a standing army always under drill and mobilized, and doing, in time of peace, that which modern civilization has pronounced nefarious in time of war. Such a body may become dangerous to liberty in the United States by directing voters in its own interest, and by bargaining with politicians for concessions to ecclesiastical control in civil affairs. Just now it is making a strong effort to win over the freedmen of the South. There is that in the pomps and ceremonies of the Roman-Catholic Church which appeals to the negro's fondness for display, and there is that in its mysteries which appeals to the superstitious element in his nature. Moreover, the practical equality that this church admits among worshippers, veiling its despotism over conscience through the confessional, may lure the ignorant freedman with the fancy that he is protecting his own liberties by voting for the aggrandizement of the church. It would be a new danger to liberty if the Romish hierarchy should find in the negro population of the South a constituency as pliant as the Irish immigration in the North and West.

This danger is to be met, first, by education, and especially by a voluntary religious education that shall acquaint the freedman with the bearing of Vaticanism upon his liberty of conscience and of thought, and at the same time shall satisfy the religious sensibilities and affections of his nature; and, next, it must be met by such a practical exhibition of justice and equality on the part of other confessions as shall assure him that he has no need to look to Rome for recognition as a man. It would be a lasting shame to the religious bodies that have had the negro, when a slave, in their fellowship, if, by any lack of sympathy with his elevation as a freedman, they should leave him to become the prey of priestcraft.

But the more pressing danger from the Roman hierarchy is through its alliance with political demagogues, who, as a consideration for the political support of their church, will concede to this privileges contrary to the Constitution, and perilous to freedom.[1] In many cities, and in some States, this hierarchy, with its unquestioning adherents, holds the balance of political power. It is compact, organized, unified, persistent, and always ready for action; and such a body, controlling votes, can make terms with politicians, unless public sentiment shall warn these that they are watched, and shall get their due.

That the American people will maintain their liberty and union at whatever cost of treasure and blood, they have fully shown in the war of Independence and the war for the Constitution; and not only is the patriotism of the past secure, but it secures the future also. I am sure my own feeling is the feeling of all Americans who have had like experience, — that which our grandsires fought for a hundred years ago, that which our fathers fought for sixty years ago, that which we and our sons fought for fifteen years ago, we may trust our childrens' children to defend. We need not fear to leave to posterity the country that three generations have taught them to hallow with blood. Such blood does not run out. No doubt the American people will rise up against any usurpation of their liberties and rights. But, just because they are ready to fight against any real open enemy, they are too apt to let alone an insidious and encroaching enemy until he has gained some formidable vantage. Their magnanimous confidence in liberty and light, their forbearance toward all forms of error and folly, make them unsuspecting and incredulous as to enemies working in the dark. Thus it was that the treason plotted in the Senate of the United States, where it might have been throttled, was hardly credited until the cannon belched it forth at Sumter.

Now, after this warning, we shall be inexcusable if we

[1] For instance, in the contest in Ohio, in 1875, over the perversion of the common schools to sectarian ends, a Catholic journal of Cincinnati said, "The thousands of Catholics in this city exercising their rights of suffrage have a very strong claim upon a political party, which it will not be safe for political leaders, or aspirants to political office, to ignore or despise." But the American people are now awake to the danger of priestly interference in public education, and, by strong constitutional prohibitions, are defending the public schools against sectarian control.

leave to our successors the risks of a war against the usurpations of the Vatican, when we can forestall those usurpations by timely and energetic measures of our own. That which makes Ultramontane propagandists a real danger to the State is the doctrine that the Pope may order their consciences, and of course their actions, upon questions of obedience to the civil law; and hence a power is wielded from Rome that may at any time unhinge the allegiance of its subjects to the State of which they are citizens. The remedy for this mischief is, that the citizen shall be required to make his choice between an undivided allegiance to the State, as having a complete and undivided sovereignty, or disfranchisement or expatriation. The first constitution of the State of New York contained a provision, that foreigners seeking to be naturalized must "take an oath of allegiance to the State, and abjure all allegiance and subjection to all and every foreign king, prince, potentate, and state, in all matters *ecclesiastical* as well as civil." That provision stood for forty years, and ought to stand to-day in every constitution of the Union.

It was in the spirit of this article that the Protestant-Episcopal Church in the United States absolved itself from the government and control of the Church of England. In putting forth its "Book of Common Prayer" in 1789, the convention of that church said, "When, in the course of Divine Providence, these American States became independent with respect to civil government, their ecclesiastical independence was necessarily included;" and hence the convention had set out to model the church and its forms "consistently with the constitution and laws of their country." Is there a person in the Episcopal Church of to-day who would consent that the church in New York, for instance, should again be brought under the ecclesiastical jurisdiction of the Bishop of London, as it was before the Revolution? But the Roman-Catholic Church is under the supreme jurisdiction of the Roman pontiff, — a jurisdiction which the Vatican decrees have now made immediate and final, — above all councils or appeals. The syllabus denounces the notion that "the Roman pontiff can and ought to reconcile himself to and agree with progress, liberalism, and civilization as lately introduced;" and specifically and emphatically condemns the doctrine that public schools "should be freed from all ecclesiastical authority, government, and interference, and subject only to the civil and political power." Suppose, now, a collision should arise between the Roman hierarchy and the State upon this question of ecclesiastical interference in the schools, and the hierarchy should take the ground that allegiance to their ecclesiastical superior at Rome obliged them to withstand the school-system that the State has established for its own safety and the fundamental well-being of society: could the State allow that plea of extra-territorial allegiance, compound its sovereignty for a divided allegiance, or intrust its own administration to hands sworn to obey the mandates of a foreign power? Nay, should not the *avowal* of such allegiance be made a disqualification for the rights of citizenship?

The plea that the matters in question are ecclesiastical, and the allegiance rendered is an act of conscience, has no pertinence in such a case. Any question can be made "ecclesiastical;" and obedience to the State is, or ought to be, a matter of "conscience." The ultramontanes are fond of quoting the saying of Christ, "Render unto Cæsar the things which are Cæsar's, and unto God the things that are God's." They profess allegiance to the State "within its sphere," but claim the right to limit that sphere by their higher allegiance to the church, which in the person of its head, the now infallible Pope, is above the civil power, and can define its bounds. But this admeasurement of claims between State and Church, or the civil and the ecclesiastical powers, was not in the contemplation of Christ, and is in no way implied in his memorable saying. There stood before him two parties, the Pharisees and the Herodians, which, however hostile to each other in politics and in dogma, could agree in the attempt to entangle Jesus in his talk. Though the Jews were held in vassalage by the Romans, the Pharisees clung to the proud faith in the Jewish *theocracy* as above all the governments of the earth. In their view, for a Jew voluntarily to acknowledge a foreign government, and pay tribute to a pagan prince, was treason against Jehovah. Though the royal house of David had long ceased to reign, and the Idumæan Herod had held the throne by favor of the Roman emperor, the theocracy was still visibly represented in the temple and the hierarchy. The high priest stood as the head of the nation and the vicegerent of God. The Pharisees would pay their temple dues only in the old Jewish shekel, and regarded the payment of the poll-tax to the agents of the Roman procurator as an act of impiety. In the time of Herod, however, there had sprung up among the Jews a party who favored some sort of compromise with the Roman civil power as a means of preserving their own nationality. Herod the Great was dead, and Judæa was ruled directly by a governor sent from Rome. But Herod Antipas was tetrarch of Galilee; and, while he courted the popular favor of the Jews, he sought by flattery and bribes to obtain from Cæsar the title of king. Those who favored this semi-Roman policy were known as Herodians.

These two parties set out to catch Jesus by asking, "Is it lawful to give tribute unto Cæsar, or not?" Should he say no, the Herodians would denounce him to the government as teaching sedition; should he say yes, the Pharisees would denounce him to the people as an advocate of their oppressors. He called for a piece of money. They had to confess that in every-day life they were using money stamped with the "image and superscription of Cæsar." Then Christ said to them, "Pay that which is Cæsar's to Cæsar, and that which is God's to God;" and both parties were silenced and amazed.

Just so the ultramontanes set up their high priest at Rome as the incarnation of the theocracy, the head of the Christian commonwealth, the vicegerent of God. He cannot be a subject, but gives law to princes and governments. To recognize any power as superior to him is treason against the church, and so against God. Nevertheless, the Romish hierarchy do not object to having their coffers filled with coin stamped with the image and superscription of the princes of this world. Thus far the analogy is exact: the modern ultramontane and the Pharisee of old are one.

Now, from the Pharisaic point of view, what should have been the antithesis of Christ? "Render unto Cæsar the things that are Cæsar's, and unto the *high priest* the things that are the high priest's." Against the visible temporal power he should have set off the visible hierarchy as representing the theocracy. He did no such thing. The thought of balancing a spiritual power on earth against the civil power was not present to his mind, and finds no cover in his words. He simply said, "Render your visible, manifest duty of tribute and allegiance to the civil government: but the spiritual life is of the inner nature; this is not an affair of laws and taxes. With full heart render to God all that is his." There is not a shadow of pretext here for setting up an *ecclesiastical authority* against the State. The fundamental note in Christ's teaching was, "My kingdom is not of this world;" "The kingdom of God is within you." Hence he did not set up one class of institutions to make war upon another, nor to divide with others the homage and service of mankind. He established an inner law of truth, light, and love, that should regulate the conduct of the whole life toward God and man. The Christian, therefore, should act conscientiously, and, so to speak, religiously, in all that he does. He cannot go against his conscience. But Christ never authorized the setting up of a concrete, organized spiritual power or authority on earth, to be pitted or paired against the authority of civil government. Not Cæsar and the Pope, not the State and the Church, but Cæsar and God, was his antithesis.

A simple example will clear up the confusion that is raised by the terms " conscience," " religious liberty," &c., whenever the conspiracy of Ultramontanism against the State is exposed; and the example will serve at the same time to settle certain points in the labor-question.

The proprietor of a shoe-factory in Massachusetts notified his workmen, that, in the dull state of business, he must reduce their wages. He offered to open his books to their inspection, and satisfy them that he was making no profit. He was unwilling to discharge them, or to run on half-time, and agreed to raise their wages as soon as they could get more at any like factory. The workmen consented to his terms, but, a few days after, told him they were forbidden by the Crispin Union to work for a reduction. They quit work, and he procured from another source a temporary supply of hands. By and by his workmen reported they had the consent of the Union to work on his terms, and he took them all back. Some of the substitutes had done a style of work with a better finish, and the proprietor stipulated for this quality. Again the workmen came, and said they were forbidden by the Union to do that style of work at such a price. He then said, "You have twice broken your contract at the dictation of an outside power: I will now employ you only from day to day." He sent at once to California, and procured a body of Chinese workmen, and then discharged the old. Attempts were made to burn the factory, to mob the Chinese; but the law protected both.

The moral of this is obvious. Each workman was entitled to fair wages, to the best price that his work would fetch; he had a right to fix his own terms; he had a right to combine with his fellow-workmen for a given rate of wages; and they all had a right to quit work if that rate was not given. They had a right, also, to join a Union, and surrender to this the control of their labor; to give up making bargains for themselves, and agree to obey the rules and terms of a body outside of themselves, and whose head was in another town a hundred miles away.

But what of the proprietor? He had a friendly interest in the men who had worked for him for years, and who lived as neighbors in the same town. This interest he showed by his several proposals. He addressed himself to their reason and their sense of honor, and was successful. So long as he could deal with them as individuals, or collectively as his workmen, he had no trouble: he was a man dealing with men, and they came to a good understanding. But, in committing themselves to the Union, the workmen surrendered their individual wills, and merged their personality in an outside corporation. That corporation the proprietor was not bound to know. To him it was a foreign body. It had no personality; no ties of acquaintance, of neighborhood, of sympathy, of community of interest: it was a dictator that came in between him and his men to hinder the freedom of their choice, to take away their personality, and make it impossible for him to deal with his work-people on the equal basis of man with men. They had a right to sell out their personality; but he was under no obligation to ratify the sale: and, when their corporation sought to interfere in his dealing with other persons, the law was bound to put it down. Just so every man has a right to the free exercise of his conscience. The State is bound to see that conscience — that is to say, the faculty of moral judgment, the inner sense of right and wrong — is left absolutely unhindered by law or by force. Every man has a right to decide for himself whether any law or requirement of the State is to him right or wrong; has the right to protest against any law or requirement, to refuse to obey it, and take the penalty. Any man has a right to consult with others concerning any law or requirement of the State, and to join others in protesting against it with a sort of collective conscience. The question, however, of combining in overt resistance to a law of the State, lies beyond the pale of individual conscience, and falls within the category of revolution, which, I have shown in the Second Lecture, has ethical principles of its own.

Again: any person has a right to submit the guidance of his conscience to another person or power outside of himself; to make it a matter of conscience to accept the decision of an outward authority as fixing his duty toward the State, so that, on the word of command from such authority, he shall refuse to obey the State, shall even denounce and defy the State. All this he has an abstract right to do; but, from the moment he does this, *he forfeits all claim on the State to recognize and respect his conscience.* As the workman, in bringing in a third power to dictate to his employer, merged his personality, so this recusant citizen merges his conscience in a corporation, a power, an authority, the State cannot know nor deal with. As between him and the State, his disobedience has lost the dignity and sanctity of conscience: he is no longer a distinct personality to be considered as to his views and feelings; he is on a strike, at the dictation of his managers. If then he does any thing to molest others or to disturb the public peace, if he conspires with or for his managers against the State, no plea of conscience can shield him from the penalty provided for such high crimes and misdemeanors. The machinery of conspiracy and rebellion the State is bound to break. There can be no fear of a religious war, and no footing for an ultramontane conspiracy, if the State will betimes enforce undivided allegiance as the basis of civil rights.[1] But one more phantom seems to skirt our political horizon, under the fitful names of political centralization and Cæsarism. Of the strife between labor and capital I make no account as a special danger to American institutions. This is not a product of those institutions, but an importation from the Old World. It is not in America, as in Europe, political in its origin, nor socialistic or communistic in its aims. In America the working-man uses the machinery of politics, and especially uses the pliant and tricky politician, to gain his ends; for, in the United States, the working-man is a voter; but he is also a voter in France, in Germany, and, to a growing extent, in England. In America he does not, as in Europe, threaten the foundations of society: he does not seek to change the form of government, but to use legislation more directly for what he conceives to be his own advantage. In the United States there are four checks upon socialism or communism that well-nigh neutralize its influence with the masses. The first check is in the facility with which any man can change his occupation, enter upon any thing for which he is competent, and so make his way onward and upward; and he who has taken his first step upward drops his levelling theories behind him.

The second check is in the facility with which one can procure a piece of land, or a something that he may call his own; and he who has begun to acquire property no longer believes in the community of goods.

The third check is in experience. "A burnt child dreads the fire." Now, the working-man has so often been used by the politician, and cheated by Unions, that he knows "their tricks and their manners," and is shy of new-fangled theories for his relief. To-day he is

---

[1] See Platform at end of the Lecture.

For a fuller discussion of the relations of the State to religion, see my Church and State in the United States. The laws recognize religion as under their protection, and tacitly assume the Christian religion to be that of the people as a whole; but they do not know a church as a confession, a communion, or a worship, but only as a corporation.

called upon to "vote himself a farm;" to-morrow, to vote that a day has but eight hours; next day, that the government shall "move the crops," or print money for him by the bushel. But he has seen so many of these bubbles burst, that he is chary of investments in soapsuds. Even the Grangers are finding out, that if they combine to raise wheat to an artificial price, and, in prospect of this fancy price, raise more wheat than the world can consume, the world will not buy, and they must drop their price below the old average to work the crop off their hands; and also that railways will not transport crops, unless paid for it; and, if railroads do not pay their owners, no more will be built. Thus one fallacy after another is set aside by the sure working of the laws of trade, just as the tide effaces castles and cities that children draw upon the sand. True, the element of humbug in human nature is something incalculable; and we must make large allowance for this in our estimate of a free State in which men can set up their humbugs *ad libitum*. It is with political speculation in America much as with what is called philosophical speculation in some other countries. Every new professor of the art has a patent system for a universe of his own, built of the fragments of his predecessors, or evolved from the depths of his inner consciousness. Sometimes he amazes the crowd as he lifts himself in his balloon so far above their vision, till they discover he is not in the clouds, but only in a fog; then a healthy breeze sweeps by, and both fog and philosophy are gone. It is this healthy breeze of common sense, springing from a free press and free discussion, that disperses popular illusions in the United States before they have poisoned the air with epidemic disease.

And hence the fourth check upon false theories of society and life in the United States is "the sober second thought of the people," their average good sense. A fisherman with whom I was accustomed to deal in New York used often to argue with me, that no man had a right to amass property above his neighbors, but all were entitled to an equal share, for which government should make a paternal provision. One day I purposely said, "This fish is not fresh." — "I assure you," he replied with warmth, "it is fresh. I was up at three o'clock this morning, and ahead of everybody else at the fishing-smacks: so I had the best pick, and I know there is not another such lot of fish in New York." — "Then certainly I shall not buy of you; for I should make myself an enemy of society. You had no right to get ahead of other fishmen, and to have a better lot at a higher price than theirs. You should at once send them some of yours, or government should compel you to share your profits with your neighbors." The hearty laugh with which he said, "You have me there," exploded his communism; and I never heard of it again. Depend upon it, all such humbugs in the United States will be talked down, argued down, and finally laughed down.

There is one spectre that of late has swayed before us like the fog-giant of the Alps, — Cæsarism. Yet I mention this only out of respect to Mr. Sumner, who coined the term, and rang changes on it to his dying-day. Political centralization and imperial usurpation are impossible in the United States, if the people are simply true to the practice of local self-government. We have so many local centres of government, — town, city, county, state, — that no man nor party can rule the country by orders from Washington, nor by official machinery worked from Washington as its centre. Congress has none of the omnipotence of the British Parliament over local affairs, the President none of the power of the central government at Versailles over municipal and communal appointments; and, outside the specific list of United-States officials, there is no way of getting at these local officers and administrations from Washington so as to usurp the appointment or control of them.

The military organization of the country gives no facilities for centralization or usurpation. The standing army is too small to overawe a single section of the country, if that section is resolutely organized for resistance; and it cannot be increased, except by vote of the people through their representatives. The army is not concentrated in Washington: the general holds his office for life, quite independent of the President. No man can perpetuate himself in office. He may deem himself necessary to the government; but the people have only to vote another into his place, and the machinery and materials for usurpation are utterly wanting. Fears of Cæsarism and centralization are phantoms. One marvels that a statesman should be swayed by such morbid fancies, and scare the country with such crude alarms.[1] The President can indeed manipulate the civil service to personal ends and to the public detriment; but this abuse is at most short-lived in the hands of any one person, and the remedy lies in establishing the civil service upon the permanent basis of competence and good behavior.

A party long in the ascendent may seek to monopolize power, and to concentrate the whole administration of the country in the hands of its own adherents; but any such attempt is sure to provoke re-action, and to return with interest upon the heads of its contrivers. Besides, there is a sure and practical remedy for this in a system of cumulative voting, by which party-lines shall be broken, and a just representation be secured to the minority in every election. Since the majority of to-day may become the minority of to-morrow, it is the interest of all parties alike to secure themselves from the tyranny of the majority. In view of all the evils now enumerated, there remains the cheering fact, that the government, while fixed in principles, is flexible and improvable in forms and methods. Nothing should be despaired of that can be improved, and that contains within itself provision for its own improvement. The Constitution of the United States, by its provision for amendment, invites the people to make experience their law.

And for this there is need of training for the higher statesmanship. The breed of politicians has so degenerated, that the people would have none of them. The war taught us that true generalship lay in the scientific train-

[1] This phantom of Mr. Sumner's is offset by the jubilant announcement of a member of the British Parliament in 1861, that "the great American bubble had burst." Mr. Gladstone, who rebuked that utterance at the time, has publicly confessed the error of his own opinion — "too hastily and lightly formed" — that the Union should and would be divided, and his "graver error in declaring this opinion at a time when he held public office as a minister of a friendly power." When will statesmen learn not to utter crude opinions or flippant judgments? or, rather, when shall we have men in public life, who, being statesmen, would be incapable of uttering crudities and inanities?

ing of West Point, and our political blunders and failures have taught us to look to scientific training for successful statesmen. Already the leading universities have established professorships of political science with this end in view; and in a few years more we shall have men whom the State more wants for its service than they want office of the State.

But the essence of all improvement, as the ground of all hope, lies in the people themselves. The State has need of men; for in the republic only men can make and be the State. And here there is hope, in those ethical qualities of the American people that give to national life the natural and providential elements of stability. (1.) Their generosity of spirit. America has her full share of mean and calculating men: yet, after large experience in my own country, I must testify that the meanest men I have known in church and in affairs were not of native birth; and, after wide observation in many lands, I do candidly believe that my own countrymen have least of the mercenary spirit. Quick as they are to make money, they are as quick to use and give it for worthy and noble objects. Eager as they are to get riches, theirs is not the greed of gain, nor the lust of hoarding. As a rule in life, money is a means, not an end, for enjoyment, for improvement, for beneficence, not for sordid idolatry. The richest citizen of the United States had lived a blameless and upright life; had done somewhat for charities, literature, and public improvements: but, when he died, the entire press, reflecting the spirit of the people, mourned that he had so missed the aim of life in not giving more in proportion as he had acquired. The Americans honor generosity of spirit. (2.) Theirs is also a quick sense of justice as between themselves and toward others, — the business integrity that is above fraud, the social frankness that is above deceit. (3.) The spirit of peace and goodwill toward mankind, the sentiment of universal brotherhood, marks their private intercourse and their public acts. And as, perhaps, the spring of all the rest, they have (4) a profound susceptibility to religious impressions, and sense of religious obligation. I sketch these outlines of character as the ethical ground of stability in the national life.

But the future of the nation lies in the filling out of such a character by every man for himself. However dark and threatening the evils of the present, I adopt the heroic faith and prophetic hope of the noble Queen of Prussia, the sainted Luise, in the gloomiest hour of her land: "I believe firmly in God and in the moral order of the world. . . . Assuredly a better time will come; but it can only become good in the world through the good. . . . Let us care only for this, that we with every day become riper and better." The stream cannot rise higher than the fountain; and seldom in political life does it rise so high. If we would have the republic worthily represent us, we must remember that we represent the republic; that its life and character are our own. More and more is there need of men whom no office could honor, no position elevate, and who, though ready for any service to their country, feel that the highest dignity is that of the citizen who clothes himself with all virtues, and so represents and honors his nation in his own person. The republic is the school of manhood. If it does not train men, lift up the average man above the average level, and raise the higher man to the highest dignity and worth of character, how shall it justify its claim to be? Ah! should Americans but live up to their opportunity, and fill out the ideal of manhood under freedom, there would be no longer care for the republic at home, nor criticism of the republic abroad. At home, truth, justice, honor, virtue, generosity, magnanimity, culture, would adorn every person, every house, every office; or rather cease to *adorn* the individual, as the common features of the whole. Abroad it would be said of such a one, "He is an American: I know it by his breadth of view, his liberality of opinion, his generosity of spirit, his courtesy of manner, his brotherhood of feeling; by his freedom from prejudice, bigotry, particularism, vanity; by his quiet self-possession, and his respect for others; by the gentleness of his bearing and his speech; by his taste for music and art; by his sympathy with truth and freedom; by his enthusiasm for humanity, and his reverent and loving devotion to God." Let our schools and churches produce a generation of such men, and especially such women, and the future of the republic is sure.

A PLATFORM FOR THE NEW CENTURY.

As a summary of the recommendations of the preceding Lecture, and to give them a practical shape, I here reprint an article which I furnished to "The Christian Union" of Aug. 18, 1875, as a "Platform for our Second Century:" —

In these days of political uncertainty, when parties are dissolving, and "independent voters" are floating about, seeking some new line of crystallization, it seems open to any one to offer a platform of public policy that may serve at least for a basis of speculation. The platform which I herewith volunteer has several advantages. First, not being framed as a bid for office, nor to obtain the suffrages of any party, it declares itself openly and explicitly upon the questions that are of real and present interest; secondly, since no one could hope just now to be elected to office upon this basis, the acceptance of it could not be imputed to any other motives than those of the purest patriotism; thirdly, ten years hence, no one need look for the votes of intelligent and conscientious Americans for any place of public trust who shall not plant himself squarely upon the principles of this platform.

(1.) *Trade.* — Trade of every description, domestic or foreign, commercial, agricultural, manufacturing, carrying, should be entirely free to follow its own laws, without interference from government, whether for hinderance or for guidance. If, for the ease and convenience of raising a revenue by indirect taxation, the government shall impose duties upon certain imports, these should be taxed upon precisely the same principle as articles of domestic growth or manufacture, — that is, as *articles* which, by their nature or consumption, are likely to yield the most revenue with the least inconvenience to the public, — and not at all as articles that come into competition with the products of domestic labor or skill. Any form of "protective" tariff is false in principle, unjust in its application, and ruinous in its effects.

(2.) *Finance.* — The only true and safe financial basis for government and people is specie, in such proportion that it serves as the circulating medium of commerce, or is faithfully represented by paper, which the holder knows to be, at any time, convertible into specie at par. The government of the United States in its financial policy should aim directly and constantly at a return to specie payments: indeed, as often happens at a critical turn of disease, it might be best for the patient to take the whole of the bitter potion at a single gulp. After a few convulsive contortions, he would recover the equilibrium of health.

(3.) *Education.* — The German notion, that it belongs to the State to provide for the culture and the religion of its citizens, cannot be applied to the American system of government. In matters of taste, as in matters of conscience, men must be left free for their own improvement and development, in so far as they do not trespass upon the rights of others, nor threaten the peace and order of society. But the American system does demand that every man shall be sufficiently educated for the intelligent discharge of his duties as a citizen; and this education the State must not only provide, but *require* of every man as a qualification for voting, jury-duty, and the like. As this education is indispensable to the safety of the State, every citizen must be taxed for it, whether he makes personal use of it or not, just as he is taxed for the police, firemen, militia, &c. The State must prescribe a course of preliminary education, simply and purely secular; and this course should be obligatory as to the fact and matter of it, but optional as to the place and method of it; that is to say, there should be public shools for a plain secular education, open to all. This same education, or its equivalent, should be obligatory for all; but it should be at the option of parents to send their children to the public school, or have them taught in a private school, or by tutors at home.

The State should be forbidden to provide for religious instruction under any form in the public schools, or to make a grant of money to any sectarian school, or to aid any religious institution whatsoever, either directly by grant of land, money, or credit, or indirectly by exemption from taxation.

(4.) *Suffrage.* — Suffrage should be equal and impartial; that is to say, the conditions of suffrage should be alike for all, and fairly within the reach of all. Though the Fourteenth Amendment to the Constitution of the United States aims to make each male citizen twenty-one years of age a voter, — so far as the United States could fix the terms of suffrage, — yet each State should make it a condition of voting, that the native citizen shall have received the schooling specified in Section 3, and that every citizen of foreign birth shall pass a prescribed examination in the English language. It is true, that, at first, several States would disfranchise a portion of their citizens, and thereby lose a *pro rata* representation in Congress. This, however, the plan of obligatory education would remedy in one generation. And, by the way, the disqualification rule should at once be enforced against Massachusetts, Connecticut, and other States that already have an educational test. This would satisfy the South that the Fourteenth Amendment was not an act of sectional tyranny, and would open the eyes of the nation to the egregious stupidity of the second clause of the Fourteenth Amendment, against which the writer of this platform protested at the time.

(5.) *Races.* — The government of the United States, and the several State governments, should know no races as such, but deal with all men — Negro, Indian, German, Chinese, Native American — upon the basis of equal laws. And as, on the one hand, the Fifteenth Amendment provides that the right to vote shall not be denied or abridged on account of race or color, so, on the other hand, when political organizations are formed upon the basis of race, and for the exclusive interest of a race, — white, black, German, or Chinese, — the ringleaders of the same should be punished by forfeiture of citizenship for a term of years, and the candidates of such "race" party be declared ineligible to office.

(6.) *Immigration.* — The government of the United States should do nothing to invite or facilitate emigration from foreign countries to America, but should leave this to the operation of natural laws. Least of all should it interfere with the civil or military laws of other countries touching their citizens, so as to tempt these to emigration as a relief from obligations at home. The overstocking of the labor market, the overcrowding of cities, the increase of strikes and of communistic demands, are a warning that immigration has been urged far beyond the normal condition of demand and supply.

(7.) *Capital and Labor.* — Government should in no wise seek to regulate by legislation the relations of capital and labor, but, protecting both alike from violence, should leave them to their own bargains in their own way.

(8.) *The Civil Service.* — The civil service should be settled upon a basis of competitive examination and graded promotion, offices to be held during good behavior.

(9.) *Sovereignty.* — The sovereignty of the State is supreme and indivisible. Whoever, therefore, acknowledges any other organized power as superior to the State in claiming or defining his allegiance, should be denied the rights of citizenship in the United States and in any State thereof.

The above platform is not put forth with the idea that anybody will accept it. Nevertheless, it deals with the questions of the present and the near future; and whoever has a noble ambition to serve his country in public life, will find, ten years hence, that such views as these will command the confidence and support of a great body of the American people.

CONGRATULATIONS FROM EUROPEAN SOVEREIGNS.

BERLIN, June 9, 1876.

WILLIAM, *by the grace of God Emperor of Germany, King of Prussia, &c., to the President of the United States.*

GREAT AND GOOD FRIEND,— It has been given you to celebrate the hundredth anniversary of the day when the great nation over which you preside took rank among independent States. The institutions organized by the founders of the Union, who wisely consulted the lessons of history with regard to the formation of States, have developed beyond all expectation. To be able to congratulate you and the American nation upon this occasion is all the more pleasing to me, because, since the friendly alliance which my august ancestor, now reposing in God,— Frederic II., of glorious memory,— concluded with the United States, nothing has troubled the good understanding between Germany and America. Their friendship has been increased and developed by a growing interchange in every branch of commerce and science. That the prosperity of the United States and the friendship of the two countries may continue to increase is my sincere prayer, as it is my firm belief. I beg you to receive this fresh assurance of my highest esteem.

WILLIAM.

EMS, June 5, 1876.

ALEXANDER, *by the grace of God Emperor of all the Russias.*

MR. PRESIDENT, — At a moment when the people of the United States celebrate the centennial period of their national existence, I desire to express to you the sentiments with which I take part in this celebration. The people of the United States may contemplate with pride the immense progress which their energy has achieved within the period of a century. I especially rejoice, that, during this centennial period, the friendly relations between our respective countries have never suffered interruption, but, on the contrary, have made themselves manifest by proofs of mutual good-will. I therefore cordially congratulate the American people in the person of their President ; and I pray that the friendship of the two countries may increase with their prosperity. I embrace this occasion to offer to you at the same time the assurance of my sincere esteem and of my high consideration.

ALEXANDER.

To his Excellency GEN. GRANT.

VICTOR EMANUEL II., *by the grace of God and the will of the nation King of Italy, to the President of the United States of America, greeting.*

MY DEAR AND GOOD FRIEND, — On the day upon which the great American Republic celebrates the centennial anniversary of its existence, it is our desire to address our congratulations and those of our people to you personally, and to the nation over which you preside, and which with admirable ability you have succeeded in directing to its noble destiny. Neither the distance which separates us, nor any difference of race, will ever weaken in us and in our people that firm friendship which unites us with the brave American nation with which for a hundred years Italy has had relations productive of mutual esteem. We are inclined to convey to you these sentiments so much the more readily, because, for the purpose of the more worthily celebrating the memorable day by the monster Exhibition at Philadelphia, you were pleased to invite to the festival all the nations of the earth. Accept the assurances of our highest esteem and friendship, together with the prayers which we offer to God that he may have you, my very dear friend, in his holy keeping. — Given at Rome on the 11th of June, 1876.

Your good friend,

VICTOR EMANUEL.

Countersigned, MELIGARI.

PUBLISHERS' NOTE.

THE preceding pages show the remarkable favor with which Dr. Thompson's Lectures were received, and the estimate placed upon them by the foremost men and journals in Berlin, Dresden, Florence, Paris, and London.

[From the Berlin "Kunst-Correspondenz" of March 1, 1876.]

"Dr. Joseph P. Thompson began, on the 21st of February, a course of lectures, in English, upon the origin, development, and results of that remarkable and unparalleled event in the world's history, the American Declaration of Independence. Dr. Thompson is welcomed by crowded audiences, composed of American and English residents, and an influential and learned German circle, including many members of Parliament. The lectures exhibit a fulness and depth of historical study, and are rich in philosophical reflections and intellectual comparisons of different nations and of the founders of political systems. The lecturer — a patriot of the New World in the finest sense of the word — is thoroughly penetrated with the historical spirit, and is especially fair toward the rich cycle of events in Germany."

[From the Berlin "Fremdenblatt," Feb. 25, 1876.]

"Dr. Thompson's lectures are attended by a very numerous and highly cultivated audience, including several members of the diplomatic corps, university professors, and members of Parliament. The well-known, ready, forcible, and clever orator is followed with marked attention."

[From the Berlin correspondent of the "Weser Zeitung," Bremen.]

"Sachse's Art Salon, in which these lectures are given, is scarcely able to contain the audiences, which are composed of Germans as well as of Americans sojourning here. Dr. Thompson, who has an enviable reputation as a scholar and as an expounder of the German Church polity, is an excellent speaker, a perfect master of his subject, and knows how to engage the attention of his hearers."

[From the Berlin "Staats Anzeiger," an official journal, of March 15, 1876.]

"The famous American scholar now residing here, Dr. Thompson, has just closed his course of lectures on the American nation, delivered before a large and select audience. In the style of pragmatic history, these lectures handled the institution and the philosophical development of the United States with interesting points of comparison in the history of France, England, and Germany. Dr. Thompson is known to be remarkably versed in German and Prussian affairs, which he has made a fundamental study. The style and manner in which he handled the historical development of Germany since the Reformation, the just appreciation which he awarded to the Prussian form of State life, the high tribute that he paid to the royal house that founded the State and had led it on to greatness, evoked the warmest applause of his hearers, at least half of whom were Germans. At the close of the lectures, special acknowledgments and thanks were tendered to Dr. Thompson for the highly intellectual tone and the friendly international spirit in which he had carried out his historical parallels. It is hoped these most substantial and instructive lectures will be published."

[From the "Berlin Post" of March 1, 1876.]

"Last Wednesday, at the close of a series of lectures on the history of the United States, delivered by Dr. Thompson to a numerous and applauding audience, Prof. Zumpt arose to thank the orator in the following words, which well characterize America's civilization and its relations to Germany:—

"'It seems to me both improper and ungrateful that we who have listened to these lectures should silently separate, at the close of the course, without expressing our feelings. I therefore venture to propose a vote of thanks.

"'This vote has a double signification, at least for that portion of the ladies and gentlemen here present, who, like myself, are Germans. We have been told of the origin of the United States, its development, and its hopes for future welfare. America and Germany, although taking their origin in opposite elements and having different forms of government, have still the same principles,—religious and political freedom. We may, perchance, choose different paths; but the goal is the same.

"'If, during the struggle for independence, some rulers of German principalities were base enough to sell their subjects as instruments for tyranny, on the other hand we Prussians—nay, we Germans—are proud that one of our Great Frederic's best officers fought at Washington's side. Light-hearted, like a German soldier, brave, and true to his commander, he helped to organize the army of the newly-born republic.

"'We are accustomed in Germany to celebrate birthdays; also, when a person has for a number of years held office, we assemble around him to wish him a long life and the continuation of his happiness. In the course of this year the American nation will celebrate its birthday, after having gloriously lived through the first century of its existence. A hundred years are long for human life: they are but short for that of a State. Yes, America is young, very young; but the more time has she to develop, the more can we expect from her, the more can she accomplish for the advancement of humanity and civilization. Now that we have heard these six lectures on the birth and growth of this nation, how can the purport of our vote of thanks be other than "Long live and flourish America"?

"'The second part of our thanks is personal, and refers to Dr. Thompson: it is in common to all, both Americans and Germans. Our learned and eloquent friend is a warm patriot in the noblest sense of the word; but next to his own country, which he naturally prefers to all others, Germany is probably that which is dearest to him. He lives amongst us, and knows us well: our customs, and ways of thinking, are familiar to him. He is also a glowing admirer of those who are at the head of our government, of our emperor, and of the whole illustrious family of the Hohenzollerns. Dr. Thompson fights like a veteran at our side in the war which we wage against religious oppression. Of his lectures themselves I will say nothing. They are above my praise. Words would fail me to value them according to their worth. I will only add, that, as to myself, I have listened to them with ever-increasing interest and rising admiration. I therefore consider it a duty of simple gratitude openly to express our thanks to Dr. Thompson.'"

This address was accompanied with a crown of laurel, presented by the German ladies who had attended the course. This was bound with the Prussian colors, and bore the motto, —

"Du gabst so Viel uns, aus dem Schatze Deines Geistes!
Doch nicht Verstand allein, die edle Seele sprach aus Dir;
D'rum sagen wir aus ganzer Seele, Dank dafür."

The lecturer having met all the expenses of the course (the lectures being free), at the close a handsome testimonial was presented to him by the American residents of Berlin "as a token of gratitude for the able and impartial manner in which he had brought before a German audience a fair picture of America and its institutions."

In Dresden the lectures were given in the commodious rooms of the "American Club," which were filled to their utmost capacity. At the close of the course the following address was made by George Griswold, Esq., president of the club: —

"On behalf of the club which you have so greatly honored, and of the ladies and gentlemen here assembled who have been attentive and delighted listeners, I desire to return you heartfelt thanks for your very able and eloquent lectures.

"Especially do we thank you for your disinterested kindness in having taught us so much concerning the causes which led the States to separate from the mother-country, and concerning the virtues of our forefathers who framed and organized the government which has been such a boon to mankind, and under which, in so brief a period, the United States of America have been enabled to take a foremost stand amongst the most enlightened and powerful nations of the world.

"To you, sir, we are indebted for much valuable historical and political knowledge, enlightened ideas of government, and statistical information which we could not have acquired or even collated for ourselves, but which could not have been imparted in more impressive, eloquent, and agreeable language or manner; and, although in numbers we are less than the brilliant and learned assemblies you have so recently addressed at Florence and Berlin, be assured that we have not been less attentive, less instructed, or less gratified, and that we are not less grateful, than they.

"Again thanking you for the benefit of your vast researches and of your impartial comments on the centennial history of our free institutions, we bid you God speed in your disinterested, praiseworthy, and patriotic endeavors to enlighten your countrymen and the people amongst whom they are temporarily sojourning.

"We wish you health, long life, prosperity, and happiness."

In Florence, by the generous invitation of the "Circulo Filologico," their spacious and elegant hall was placed at the disposal of the lecturer. James Jackson Jarves, Esq., the well-known art-critic, wrote to "The American Register," Paris, "Dr. Thompson's accomplishments as an orator and scholar, and his specially patriotic course in Germany as a fitting representative of the more serious side of American character, are peculiar qualifications for his opportune appearance at the present moment in Italy as a lecturer; although it is to be regretted that he could not deliver this course in Rome, where he would be certain to have an appreciative Italian audience, in part from the members of Parliament and statesmen interested in the science of politics and social problems of the period." But Italy was well represented in the brilliant and enthusiastic auditory at Florence; and, at the close of the course, Prof. P. Villari, also a member of Parliament, paid a most eloquent tribute to the United States, and moved the thanks of the assembly to the lecturer "for his appreciative recognition of Italy in her relations to the progress of liberty, learning, and art, as well as for his clear, learned, and impartial analysis of American freedom."

In Paris the following resolutions were adopted, being moved by Isaac H. Birch, Esq., and supported by Prof. A. V. Wittmeyer: —

"*Resolved*, That we, citizens of the United States sojourning in Paris, have seen with pride and satisfaction that our compatriot, Dr. Joseph P. Thompson, has, on many occasions during his residence in Europe, rendered invaluable service by his able, timely, and patriotic endeavors to teach the history, expound the principles, and defend the honor, of the institutions and government of the United States, and secure for them juster appreciation and a more legitimate influence among European nations.

"*Resolved*, That in the series of comprehensive, discriminative, interesting, and impressive addresses upon the *origin, principles, progress,* and *probable future of the nation*, with which Dr. Thompson has favored us, we have discovered fresh proofs of the purity, patriotism, wisdom, and statesmanship of the founders of our government; and, while our admiration of our country and its institutions has been heightened by the history and the vindication to which we have listened, our hearts have at the same time been warmed by renewed assurances of their perpetuity.

"*Resolved*, That with the expression of our high appreciation of his good offices, and the hope that his valuable addresses may soon be given to the world and come to us again in printed form, we hereby tender to Dr. Thompson our warmest thanks.

"PARIS, May 29, 1876."

In London the lectures were repeatedly noticed with favor by the "Times," "Daily News," "Morning Post," "Advertiser," "Hour," and other journals. The audience was almost exclusively English, and of a highly distinguished and representative character. In moving thanks, Dr. Henry Allen said of the lecture on the Declaration, "It was as strong as wise and good. He had never known more thought and information compressed into a single discourse." Henry Richard, Esq., M.P., said, "The lecture on the Constitution combined in a rare degree a profound political philosophy with a manly eloquence. He wished it might be printed, and widely read in England." Prof. Legge of Oxford said "his ideas about America had, for the first time, gained coherence through these lectures. They ought to be published for the million."

INDEX.

Abolitionists, 128.
Absolutism, 142.
Adams, C. Francis, 98, 99.
Adams, John, anecdote of, 59.
" " death of, 61.
" " on corruption, 251, 255.
" " on revolution, 17, 89.
" " on Samuel Adams, 60.
" " speech of, 55 *note*.
Adams, John Quincy, 198.
Adams, Samuel, 55.
" " on Establishment, 96.
Admiralty, British, 135.
Alabama, 136 *n*.
Amendments, constitutional, 128.
America, her defence, viii, ix, xi.
" more a society than a government, x.
Americanism, native, 287.
Americans, character of, 305.
" in Europe, vii, ix.
Anglo-Saxons, 22.
Annexation, 177.
Appeal to the South, 137.
Arbitration, 240.
Aristocracy, a guild, 80.
" Church an, 80.
" natural, 79, 141.
Army, Continental, 1, 110.
" standing, 179, 192.
Art as culture, 234.
" in Berlin, 234.
" in Dresden, 234.
" in London, 233.
" in Paris, 233.
Assassination of Lincoln, 192.
Aumale, Duc d', 5.

Bazaine, Marshal, 4.
Beccaria, 72.
Bellamy, 230.
Bell, Independence, 53.
Benefits of United States, 202.
Bentham, 72.
Berlin, character of, 253.
Bluntschli, 102, 141 *n*.
Board of Trade, 39, 40 *n*.
Books in America, 39.
Bordeaux Assembly, 5.

Border ruffianism, 180.
Boston, early culture of, 227.
" evacuation of, 53.
" merchants of, 239.
" port bill, 48.
" tea-party, 47.
Brougham on Washington, 151.
Brown, John, 190.
Bryant, 209.
Bulgaria, horrors in, 155.
Bunker Hill, 1, 4, 51.
Burke on taxation, 19, 28, 99, 100.
" quoted, 5 *n*, 6, 16, 17.
Burr, his treason, 170.
Bushnell, Horace, 208, 229.
Buxton, Sir Thomas Fowell, **xxiii**.

Cæsar and God, 298.
" his character, 159.
Cæsarism, 163, 301.
Calhoun, John C., 172, *seq*.
California, Chinese in, 282.
" the story of, 206.
Calvinism and freedom, 30.
Capital and labor, 302.
Carlyle on America, 203.
Carolina, North, 129, 130.
Carolina, South, 129, 130, 172.
Carroll of Carrollton, 56 *n*.
Caste, 278.
Catholicism, 291.
Centennial, the, viii, **ix**.
Centralization, 301.
Charta, Magna, 80.
Chinese, 282.
Christ Church, London, xxiii.
Christ, doctrine of man, 105.
Christian progress, 205, 209, 220.
Church and liberty, 29.
" Establishment, 94, 96.
" independence of, 33.
Churches in New York, 220.
Cities, evils of, 258.
Citizenship, obligations of, 288.
Civilization, effect of, 24, 180.
Civil service, 199.
" " Bluntschli on, 274.
" " in Prussia, 201, 272.
Clericalism, 230.

319

INDEX.

Colonies, confederation of, 111.
" loyalty of, 14.
" patience of, 46.
" praised by the king, 14.
" statistics of, 5.
" variety of government, 6.
" various government of, 27.
Commons, journals of, 14, *seq.*
" votes supplies, 25, *seq.*
Communism, 301.
Confederacy of New England, 7.
Confederation, 61.
" failure of, 111, 120.
" not a constitution, 137.
" of colonies, 111.
" rejected, 137.
" Swiss, 114.
Congress, contests in, 198.
" Continental, 1, 3, 109.
" weakness of, 111.
Conscience, rights of, 289, *seq.*
Constitution, adoption of, 61, 106, 139.
" and nation, 161.
" character of, 103.
" English, 106.
" glory of American, 111, 161.
" preamble of, 138.
Continental army, 109.
Convention, Constitutional, 122.
" character of, 123.
" wisdom of, 130.
Copyright, 213.
Corliss Engine, 195.
Correspondence, committees of, proposed by Mayhew, 37.
Corruption in America, 249.
" in Austria and Italy, 249.
Cotton-gin, 188.
Crime, percentage of foreign, 182.
Cuba, 177.
Cultivated, guild of the, 80 *n.*
Culture, Arnold on, 222.
" Emerson on, 221.
" in Germany, 230.
" true, 224, 230.

Dana, Richard H., jun., 48.
Debt of Revolution, 116.
Declaration of Independence, 1.
" effects of, 95, 104.
" indictment of king in, 93.
" in Philadelphia, 98.
" meaning of, xiv, 63.
" moderation of, 85.
" not a declaration of war, 1, 10, 65.
" of Rights, 3, 10, 53.
" philosophy of, 66.
" signers of, 57.
" syllogism in, 66.
De Kalb on Continental money, 186.
" on Washington, 157 *n.*
Demagogism, 142.
Devonshire, xxv.
Dickens, Bret Harte on, 211.
" his mercenary spirit, 216.
" Macaulay on, 212 *n.*
" on America, 211, 215.
Douglass, Frederick, 279.
Dred Scott decision, 189.
Duties of century, 248.

Education compulsory, 275.
" in Prussia, 201.
" in United States, 209.
Election of President, 145.
Elector, the Great, 154, 200.
Emancipation, xxiv.
Emerson on Boston, 239.
Emmons, Nathanael, sermons of, 36.
England in the Rebellion, 135 *n.*
" love for, xvii.
" perils of, 195.
" separation from, xiv.
Englishman, the, in America, 218.
" the insular, 240.
Englishmen, liberties of, 2, 101, 102.
Equality, xx, xxi, 102.
" French notion of, 68.
" of men, 66.
Establishment, 94, 96.
Ethics in government, 88, 101, 102.
Eulogy on Lincoln, 193.
Evarts, W. M., 98, 99, 103.

Federal, United States not, 138.
Fehrbellin, victory of, 200.
Filibustering, 178.
Forms of government, 101.
Forster, Life of Dickens, 214.
Fourth of July, celebration of, 105.
" " in London, xiii, xxiii.
France, a nation, 5, 202.
" New, 143 *n.*
" Revolution in, 88, 106.
Franklin and Grenville, 39.
" before Parliament, 26, 42, *seq.*
" Laboulaye on, 107.
" letter of, to Quincy, 58.
" letter of, to Strahan, 58.
" on Union, 111, 122.
" return of, from England, 57.
" wit of, 55, 64 *n.*
Fraud in Germany, 250.
Frederic, 52, 145, 148, 151.
Freedom, ethical, 91.
" inertia of, 117.
" spirit of, 118.
Freeman, Mr. E. A., 23, 106.
Free trade, 185.
French *égalité*, 68.
" war, 14, 44.
Fugitive slaves, 132.

Gasparin, Count, 2.
Generals, United-States, 192.
Geography of United States, 175.
George III., character of, 105.
" indictment of, 94.
Georgia, 129, 130.
German ignorance of America, 241.
German in public schools, 284.
Germans in America, 181, 185, 276.
" on America, 253.
Germany, liberty lost in, 24.
" unity of, 63, 230.
Gettysburg, 191.
Gladstone, 12, 304 *n.*
Goodyear, 237.
Government a science, 75.
" by people, 102.
" its object, xiv, 70.
" local, 22, 46.

INDEX. 321

Government. Teutonic, 23.
"Greatest happiness," 72.
Greeley, Horace, 125.
Grenville, 39.
Grote on Switzerland, 140 n.

Hall, Rev. Newman, xxiii, **xxv**.
Hamilton, Alexander, 108.
" " on finance, 186.
" " on national government, 118.
Hampden, John, 20.
Hancock, John, 54.
" " proscribed, 55.
Happiness an ethical right, 92.
Harrison, Gen., 187.
Harte. Bret. 211, 283.
Hartford Convention, 170.
Harvard College, great men of, 228.
" " origin of, 227.
Hayne, Senator, 171.
Heroes, true, 152.
Hohenzollern, house of, 63, 117, 152.
Holst, Von, 12.
Hooker, Thomas, 101.
Hope, grounds of, 306.
Humbugs. 302.
Hume on Puritans, 35.
Huxley on American museums, 246.
" on the United States, 194.
Hyacinthe on America, 219.

Ilfracombe, xviii.
Immigration, 180.
" its benefits and evils, 181.
Independence, Declaration of, xiv, 1, 10.
" in Philadelphia, 98.
" resolution for, 59.
Independent, The, 128.
Indian war, 14, 44.
Individual, 144 n.
Indulgences. sale of, 20.
Inertia of freedom, 117.
International, Christianity more than, xxvi.
Irish in America, 182, 185, 276.
Iroquois, treaty with, 7.

Jackson on Bank of United States, 186.
" on the Union, 172.
Jannet, C., on America, 249.
Jefferson, author of Declaration, 61.
" death of, 61.
" false views of, 89.
" on aristocracy, 79.
" on government, 77.
" on jury, 82.
" on slavery, 95.
" on suffrage, 74.
" on the Union, 171.
Johnson, Andrew, 192.
John the apostle, 225.
July 4, celebration of, 98.
" in London, xiii.
Jury, trial by, 81, 82.

Kalb, De, 52.
Kant on development, 225.
Kemper, Gov., on the Union, 174.

Labor question, 282, seq.

Laboulaye on France and America, 106, 144 n.
" on Washington, 108.
Language, unity in, 284.
League of colonies, 113.
Lexington, 1 n.
" battle of, 50.
Liberty, religious, xvii.
" " Adams on, 169.
" " English, 103.
" " Mill on, 76.
" " organized, 107.
Life-boat, 69.
Lincoln, Abraham, xxiii, 23, 110.
" " as President, 120.
" " assassination of, 192.
" " eulogy on, 193.
" " interview with, 126.
" " on slavery, 190, 199.
Lincoln Tower, xxiii.
Long Parliament, 111.
Louisiana, purchase of, 170.
Lowell on Burns, 210.
" on Frederic, 154.
Loyalty, Sherman on, 153
" spirit of, 153.
Luise of Prussia, 306.
Luther as reformer, 20.

Macaulay on decay, 160.
" on Reform Bill, 166.
" on republicanism, 166.
Madison, his papers, 123.
" on confederacy, 116.
" on slavery, 132.
Magna Charta, 80.
Majority, tyranny of, 72.
Mammonism, 218.
Manhood, xiii, 137, 306.
Man in society, 71.
Manners of early times, 124.
Mason and Dixon, 172.
Mason on slavery, 134.
Material civilization, 203, 205.
Materialism hinders culture, 22 x.
" not American, xvii, **xxiv**.
" tyranny of, 69.
Mayflower, 32.
Mayhew, Jonathan, 37, seq.
Mecklenburg Declaration, 59 n.
Men created equal, 67.
" rights of, Jefferson on, 77.
" " Mill on, 76.
Mercenaries, German, 52.
Mexico, 177, 188.
Military occupation, 179.
Mill, John Stuart, 76.
Mississippi, the, 170, 175.
Missouri Compromise, 172, 189.
Mobocracy, 142.
Mommsen on Rome, 159, 177.
Monarchy, predictions of, 62.
Money, Continental, 186.
Monroe on confederacy, 120.
Morier on government, 23 n.
Mormonism, 289.

Napoleon, xiv, 146, seq.
Napoleon. Louis, 125.
Nationalities, foreign, dangers of, 284.
Nation analyzed, 4.

322   INDEX.

Nation defined, 4, 80 *n*.
" France a, 5, 9, 12, 83, 96, 161, 202.
" the colonies a, 4.
Nations mixed in colonies, 34, *seq.*
"Nation, The," 255.
Native Americans, 180, 183.
Nativism, 287.
Negroes as "wards," 278.
" characteristics of, 276.
New England, confederacy of, 7.
" influence of, 218, 229.
" names in, xxv.
" spirit of, 143 *n*, 226.
News, The Sussex Daily, xix.
New York, churches in, 221.
North-west Territory, 134.
Nullification, 172.

Oberlin, 278.
O'Connell, 167.
Office not a right, 74, 75.
Ordinance of 1787, 134.
Otis, James, advises a congress, 8, 16, 37, 40, 55, 101.

Paine, Thomas, 60.
Palfrey, 28 *n*.
Parliament, English, rows in, 167.
" Franklin before, 26.
" subservient to George III., 26.
" the German, 127 *n*.
" the Long, 111.
Party-spirit, 162.
" in England, 165.
Patriotism, viii.
Peace, xviii, xxv.
People, a, 11 *n*.
" government by, 78, 102, 115.
Perfection not to be looked for, xv.
Perils of the century, 248.
Personality, xiv, xv.
"Person" in Constitution, 133.
Philadelphia, convention at, 122.
" Declaration in, 98.
Pilgrims, memorial of, xxv, 31.
Pius IX., 173.
Platform, 307.
Plato on Republic, 248.
Plymouth, Pilgrims in, xxv, 31.
Political rights, 75.
Population of United States, 182.
Prayer, Book of, 295.
Preachers of New England, 35, 101.
Presbyterians, Washington's reply to, 150 *n*.
President, first election of, 145.
" how elected, 142.
" making the, 125.
" powers of, 142.
" re-election of, 126.
Press in England, 168.
Priestley, 72.
Property suffrage in cities, 258.
"Protection," xvi.
Prussia, 149.
" Crown Prince of, 200.
" origin of, 200.
Puritan spirit, 189.

Qualitative, 141.
Quantitative, 141.
Quincy on Adams, 58 *n*.

Race in the United States, Chinese, 282.
" " " German, 183.
" " " Irish, 182.
" " " native, 183.
" " " negro, 282.
Rahel quoted, 251.
Ranke on the Reformation, 21.
Rebellion of 1861, 61, 197, 277.
" Shays's, 71, 121.
" true view of, 277.
Reconstruction, its blunder, 278.
Reeleaux, Prof., on German industry, 244.
" " on the United States, 244.
Religion and liberty, 29.
" in America, 220.
" in colonies, 30, *seq.*, 218.
Religious liberty, xvii, 289, *seq.*
" " abuses of, 289.
Representation, slave, 131.
Republican party, 189.
Republic, a study, 63.
Repudiation, 187.
Resistance, duty of, 86.
Revolution, American, distinguished from French, 2, 87, 111.
" American, justified, 11.
" English, 83.
" French, 145.
" John Adams on, 17.
" right of, 84, 85, 100.
" sources of, 21.
Revolutionist in Europe, 84.
Rights, Declaration of, 3, 10.
" from God, 69.
" "inalienable," 68.
" Jefferson on, 77.
" natural and political, 77.
Robinson, John, father of liberty, 29, *seq.*
Romanism in America, 291.
Rome, Mommsen on, 159, 177.
Ruskin on corruption, 254.
Russia, corruption in, 250.
" expansion of, 177, 201.

Saturday Review, 13.
Schiller on rights, 19.
Schurz, Carl, 289 *n*.
Search, right of, 188.
Secession, Calhoun on, 173.
" excluded from Constitution, 140.
" no right of, 11, 12, 115.
Sectionalism of slavery, 171.
" Washington on, 169.
"Self-evident truths," 63.
Self-government, 7, 9.
Sermons of New England, 35.
Shams, 204.
Shays's Rebellion, 71, 121.
Sherman, Gen., 153.
Sidney, Algernon, 101.
Signers of Declaration, 57.
Simon on France, 143 *n*
Slavery, 28.
" brought in by abolitionists, 128.
" cause of rebellion, 197.
" in representation, 131.
" Jefferson on, 95.
" not in Constitution, 128.
" sectional, 171.
Slaves, fugitive, 132.
Slave-trade, 131.

INDEX.   323

Slave-trade, abolished, 135.
Socialism, 301.
Society, American, 100.
" for man, 71.
" Mill on, 76.
" rights of, 79.
" sovereignty, 73.
Sonderbund, Swiss, 114 n, 140 n.
South, appeal to, 137.
" reconstruction of, 197.
Sovereignty, 72.
" Mill on, 76.
Spain, 202.
Speculations in Germany, 250.
Stamp Act, 13.
" how resisted, 42.
" of Leo X., 20, 42.
" repeal of, 46.
Standing army, 179, 192.
Statesmanship, 304.
State rights, 173.
Stephens, A. H., on slavery, 197.
" " on union, 174.
Steuben, 52.
Storrs, R. L., 98.
Suffrage, experience of, 274.
" in cities, 258.
" Jefferson on, 74.
" Mill on, 76.
" negro, 199.
" not natural right, 74.
" restriction of, 271, seq.
" woman, 259.
Sumner, Charles, 303.
Sumner, Prof., on suffrage, 271.
Sunday in America, 219.
Supreme Court, 143.
Surgery, American, 236.
Surrey Chapel, xxiii, seq.
Sussex Daily News, xix, seq.
Switzerland, government of, 114, 140 n.
" Grote on, 140 n.
Syllabus, 295.
Syllogism in Declaration, 66.

Tacitus on Germans, 22.
Taft, Attorney-General, 257 n.
Tariff, 172, 185.
Taxation and representation, 19, 40.
" Burke on, 19.
" why resisted, 13, 18.
Tea-party, Boston, 47.
Tea tax, 47.
Tecumseh, 187.
Territory, North-western, 134.
" of the United States, 177.
Tests of government, 162.
Teutonic race, 22.
Theology, New-England, 229.
Thiers on Napoleon, 157.
Thought, vitality of, 102.

Times, London, on the Centenary, xvi, 13, 50, 160.
Tocqueville, De, 12, 219, 232.
Town-meeting, 22.
" attempt to suppress, 48.
" described, 27.
Townshend, 41.
Trades-unions, 298.
Tripoli, war with, 187.
Troops quartered on colonies, 49.
Tyranny of materialism, 69.

Ultramontanism, 230, 291.
Union, geographical, 175.
" spirit of, 9, 115.
United States, area of, 203.
" benefits of, 202.
" no failure, xvi, 10.
Universal suffrage, 272.
Usurpation of George III., 18.
" of Parliament, 46.

Vaticanism, 230.
Versailles Assembly, 5.
Veto, President's, 142.
Vicissitudes of century, 159.
Virginia, 130.

Walpole, Horace, 15.
War, civil, 196.
" of Independence, 110.
Wars, how conducted, 192.
" of United States, 61, 187, seq.
Washington, xxiii, 3, 52, 53, 108.
" as general, 149.
" election of, 145.
" Farewell Address of, 150.
" greatness of, 151.
" his solitary joke, 127.
" his style, 150.
" on confederacy, 117, 121.
" on Constitution, 139.
" on independence, 109.
Webster on Adams and Jefferson, 61.
" on Hartford Convention, 171.
" on nullification, 172.
" on territory, 177, 239.
Westminster Review, mistakes of, 13, 16.
Whittier, 50.
Wilberforce, xxiii.
William, Emperor of Germany, 152.
Williams, Roger, 290 n.
Winthrop, R. C., 98.
Witherspoon, 57 n.
Woman, influence of, 207.
" suffrage, 259.
Wrangel, Marshal, 152.

Yale College, origin of, 229.
Yeomanry of New England, 36.

Other Recommended Reading on this Subject

Fighting For Liberty and Virtue, Marvin Olasky, Regnery Publishing, Washington D.C.

Just War Against Terror, Jean Bethke Elshtain, Basic Books.

Arguing About Slavery, William Lee Miller, Vintage.

Why We Fight: Moral Clarity and the War on Terrorism, William J. Bennett, Doubleday.

Clergy Dissent In The Old South, David B. Chesebrough, Southern Illinois University Press.

Our Lives, Our Fortunes, and our Sacred Honor, Charles A. Goodrich, Solid Ground Christian Books, Birmingham, AL

Other Solid Ground Titles

In addition to *Let the Cannon Blaze Away* which you hold in your hand, Solid Ground is honored to offer many other uncovered treasure, many for the first time in more than a century:

COLLECTED WORKS of James Henley Thornwell (4 vols.)
CALVINISM IN HISTORY by *Nathaniel S. McFetridge*
OPENING SCRIPTURE: *Hermeneutical Manual* by *Patrick Fairbairn*
THE ASSURANCE OF FAITH by *Louis Berkhof*
THE PASTOR IN THE SICK ROOM by *John D. Wells*
THE BUNYAN OF BROOKLYN: *Life & Sermons of I.S. Spencer*
THE NATIONAL PREACHER: *Sermons from 2nd Great Awakening*
FIRST THINGS: *First Lessons God Taught Mankind* Gardiner Spring
BIBLICAL & THEOLOGICAL STUDIES by *1912 Faculty of Princeton*
THE POWER OF GOD UNTO SALVATION by *B.B. Warfield*
THE LORD OF GLORY by *B.B. Warfield*
A GENTLEMAN & A SCHOLAR: *Memoir of J.P. Boyce* by *J. Broadus*
SERMONS TO THE NATURAL MAN by *W.G.T. Shedd*
SERMONS TO THE SPIRITUAL MAN by *W.G.T. Shedd*
HOMILETICS AND PASTORAL THEOLOGY by *W.G.T. Shedd*
A PASTOR'S SKETCHES 1 & 2 by *Ichabod S. Spencer*
THE PREACHER AND HIS MODELS by *James Stalker*
IMAGO CHRISTI by *James Stalker*
A HISTORY OF PREACHING by *Edwin C. Dargan*
LECTURES ON THE HISTORY OF PREACHING by *J. A. Broadus*
THE SCOTTISH PULPIT by *William Taylor*
THE SHORTER CATECHISM ILLUSTRATED by *John Whitecross*
THE CHURCH MEMBER'S GUIDE by *John Angell James*
THE SUNDAY SCHOOL TEACHER'S GUIDE by *John A. James*
CHRIST IN SONG: *Hymns of Immanuel from All Ages* by *Philip Schaff*
COME YE APART: *Daily Words from the Four Gospels* by *J.R. Miller*
DEVOTIONAL LIFE OF THE S.S. TEACHER by *J.R. Miller*

Call us Toll Free at 1-877-666-9469
Send us an e-mail at sgcb@charter.net
Visit us on line at solid-ground-books.com

Uncovering Buried Treasure to the Glory of God

www.ingramcontent.com/pod-product-compliance
Lightning Source LLC
Chambersburg PA
CBHW020348170426
43200CB00005B/88